ATHENS AND JERUSALEM

God, Humans, and Nature

What is the relation of philosophy and theology? This question has been a matter of perennial concern in the history of Western thought. Written by one of the premier philosophers in the areas of Jewish ethics and interfaith issues between Judaism and Christianity, *Athens and Jerusalem* contends that philosophy and theology are not mutually exclusive.

In this masterful book based on the Gifford Lectures he delivered at the University of Aberdeen in 2017, David Novak explores the commonalities between philosophy and theology on metaphysical, epistemological, and ethical questions. Where are they different and where are they the same? And, how can they speak to one another?

(The Kenneth Michael Tanenbaum Series in Jewish Studies)

DAVID NOVAK is the J. Richard and Dorothy Shiff Chair of Jewish Studies and a professor of Philosophy at the University of Toronto.

The Kenneth Michael Tanenbaum Series in Jewish Studies

The Kenneth Michael Tanenbaum Book Series features outstanding research on topics in all areas of Jewish Studies. This interdisciplinary series highlights especially research developed within the framework of the University of Toronto's Centre for Jewish Studies. The Centre is an interdisciplinary research and teaching unit with a large and diverse cohort of affiliated faculty and an impressive roster of annual conferences, symposia, and lectures. Reflecting the Centre's vibrancy, the series highlights the best new research by local and international scholars who contribute to the intellectual life of this interdisciplinary community. The series has been enabled by a generous donation from Kenneth Tanenbaum, whose family has long supported the Centre and helped make it a leader globally in Jewish Studies.

General Editor: Anna Shternshis, Director, Centre for Jewish Studies, Professor of Political Science, University of Toronto

For a list of books in the series, see page 375.

Athens and Jerusalem

God, Humans, and Nature

The Gifford Lectures 2017

DAVID NOVAK

UNIVERSITY OF TORONTO PRESS
Toronto Buffalo London

Toronto Buffalo London
utorontopress.com

ISBN 978-1-4875-0617-9 (cloth)
ISBN 978-1-4875-2415-9 (paper)

The Kenneth Michael Tanenbaum Series in Jewish Studies

Library and Archives Canada Cataloguing in Publication

Title: Athens and Jerusalem : God, humans, and nature / David Novak.
Names: Novak, David, 1941– author.
Series: Kenneth Michael Tanenbaum series in Jewish studies.
Description: Series statement: The Kenneth Michael Tanenbaum series in Jewish studies | Includes bibliographical references and index.
Identifiers: Canadiana 2019013206X | ISBN 9781487524159 (paper) | ISBN 9781487506179 (cloth)
Subjects: LCSH: Philosophy. | LCSH: Theology.
Classification: LCC BL51 .N68 2019 | DDC 261.5/1—dc23

University of Toronto Press acknowledges the financial assistance to its publishing program of the Canada Council for the Arts and the Ontario Arts Council, an agency of the Government of Ontario.

Canada Council for the Arts Conseil des Arts du Canada

Funded by the Government of Canada Financé par le gouvernement du Canada

To the memory of my beloved granddaughter
Batsheva Stadlan

She obtained favour in the eyes of all who saw her.
(Esther 2:15)

Contents

Preface

In January 2014 I received the invitation to deliver the Gifford Lectures for 2017 at the University of Aberdeen. No greater honour could be given to a philosopher or theologian. The invitation was readily accepted with pride, but also with trepidation: pride in being included among the great thinkers who preceded me in this most prestigious lectureship; trepidation in the realization that my efforts would inevitably be compared with theirs. Still having these mixed emotions, I am reminded of the famous adage of the ancient sage Hillel: "If I am not for myself, who will be for me; but if I am only for myself, who am I?"

Having three years to prepare the lectures themselves, I decided to research primary and secondary sources as fully as possible and then write a complete monograph, from which the six Gifford Lectures were to be abstracted shortly before their delivery in Aberdeen. This book is based on the original manuscript of that monograph, which was then reworked after the lectures were delivered. It incorporates some of the points raised by members of the audience in Aberdeen, whose critical questions and comments enabled me to clarify a number of key points in my argument, actually revise some of them, and even reject a few of them as well, in this final version of the book. Furthermore, let me thank my host at the University of Aberdeen (and my fellow Canadian), Professor Philip Ziegler, and his colleague Dr. Amber Shadle (and other faculty and students of that ancient Scottish university), for making me so welcome during the three weeks I spent in their midst. Thanks too to the members of the Aberdeen Hebrew Congregation and especially to Mrs. Sarah Bronzite and her family, for their hospitality to this Jewish visitor.

Whoever accepts the invitation to be a Gifford Lecturer should take seriously Lord Gifford's goals in establishing the lectureship in 1885, particularly "Promoting, Advancing, Teaching, and Diffusing the study of Natural Theology, in the widest sense of that term." Lord Gifford further stipulated that "the lecturers shall be under no restraint whatever in their treatment of their theme." So, as long as "nature" (the subject of philosophy) and "God" (the subject of theology) have been dealt with honestly and intelligently, I hope to have complied with his charge, plus thank him and the administrators of his estate for allowing me to develop my own view of "natural theology" accordingly. Moreover, my choice of this topic is consistent with the trajectory of my thought.

Ever since my undergraduate days in the College of the University of Chicago, I have been very much concerned with the relation of philosophy and theology. That is where my concern with the connection of *Athens* qua "philosophy" and *Jerusalem* qua "theology" began. Although coming from a non-traditional home, by the time my studies in the university began, I was living a traditional Jewish way of life and was already immersed in the study of the Talmud. So, I was coming there from "Jerusalem." The College, though, took a definite ideational stance, that of "Athens." Although not as disrespectful of those with "Jerusalem-like" religious commitments like mine as were other schools, the general attitude of our teachers and fellow students was mostly one of amusement that we hadn't come over to "Athens," at least not yet. We also sensed an often patronizing tolerance that the smartest of us would eventually do so. This frequently made us few feel like outsiders, even despairingly so.

What saved me from despair, however, was meeting Leo Strauss and listening to his profound lectures. This led me to appreciate that "Athens" had not vanquished "Jerusalem" insofar as the totalizing, self-sufficient claims of philosophy are always called into doubt by theology's claim (because of revelation) to have a deeper, more comprehensive take on reality. (Theology's similar claims too are always called into doubt by philosophy.) Despite the fact that many of Professor Strauss's disciples have obviously sided with "Athens" over "Jerusalem," his own view seemed to be either more neutral or more ambivalent. Nevertheless, his own explicit view of the relation of the two "cities" does not see a positive interrelationship *between* philosophy and theology. Rather, it is one where each one *limits* the pretension of the other. Their relation to each other is essentially *negative*. Therefore, wanting to be both a philosopher/theologian who thinks there is a positive relationship between the two disciplines, I couldn't become Professor Strauss's disciple (even his posthumous disciple), but only remain an ever grateful student. All that notwithstanding, Leo Strauss surely set my intellectual agenda.

Upon graduation from the University of Chicago, I returned to "Jerusalem" so to speak, beginning my studies for a rabbinical diploma at the Jewish Theological Seminary of America. Despite the fact that some of my most impressive teachers there were anti-philosophical, I was fortunate to become a student in a special program with Abraham Joshua Heschel. Professor Heschel was a theologian who very much employed philosophy in his theological work, encouraging his students to do likewise. He also urged me to get a PhD in philosophy in order to become a better Jewish theologian. That I did at Georgetown University under the mentorship of Professor Germain Grisez, a Catholic philosopher, who in his last years became a professor of theology.

All of this personal background enables the readers of this book (and those who have heard my Gifford Lectures, either in person or in videos of them) to see just why I chose to speak and write *Athens and Jerusalem: God, Humans, and Nature.*

Having now mentioned the more formal background of this book, I need to mention some colleagues and students who over the years have engaged me in informal conversations that have immensely enriched my thinking, writing, and teaching on this and related subjects. Among my colleagues, let me mention Anver Emon, Leora Batnitzky, Robert George, Lenn Goodman, Kenneth Green, George Hunsinger, Matthew Levering, Alan Mittleman, Michael Morgan, Peter Ochs, Kurt Richardson, and David Weisstub. Among my students, let me mention Tom Angier, Martin Kavka, Jonathan Milevsky, Paul Nahme, Randi Rashkover, Thomas Slabon, and Norman Tobias.

I owe a special debt to my student and research assistant, Cole Sadler. Cole accompanied me to Aberdeen in 2017, where he was most helpful in our working up the lectures from out of the larger manuscript; later, he prepared the index to this book. More importantly, though, the time of the lectureship itself was an especially trying time for my family and me. During that time, being far away from home and family in unfamiliar surroundings, Cole's attention to me was like that of a son. He has my lasting gratitude.

Thanks are due the Anne Tannenbaum Centre for Jewish Studies of the University of Toronto (where I have been happily teaching for the past twenty-three years) and its Director and my colleague and friend, Professor Anna Shternshis, for including this book in their distinguished Kenneth Michael Tanenbaum Series in Jewish Studies. Their subsidy makes the book more easily affordable to a wider readership. Thanks are also due to the staff of the Centre, especially Galina Vaisman and Natasha Richichi-Fried, for all their help and encouragement.

Finally, let me thank the University of Toronto Press for publishing this book. Working together with an editor like Len Husband, and a copy editor like Terry Teskey, plus Robin Studniberg and Breanna Muir, has made the whole publication process successful and quite enjoyable.

Toronto, Ontario
The Festival of the Giving of the Torah, 5779
May 2019

ATHENS AND JERUSALEM

God, Humans, and Nature

Chapter One

Philosophy and Theology

Athens and Jerusalem

What is the relation of philosophy and theology? That has been a matter of perennial concern in the history of Western thought. Most famously, that relation was questioned by the third-century Christian theologian Tertullian when he asked rhetorically: *Quid ergo Athenis et Hierosolymis?*, which I would translate: "So what do Athens and Jerusalem have to do with one another?"[1] That "Athens" here stands for "philosophy" and "Jerusalem" for "theology" are clearly indicated by the query Tertullian immediately poses: *Quid academiae et ecclesiae?*, which I would translate: "What does [the philosophy of] the academy have to do with [the theology of] the church?" However, we need to immediately ask: What is "philosophy," and what is "theology"? And why have philosophy and theology so often been seen to be at loggerheads?

What is *philosophy*? For Tertullian, it is the teaching of the Athenian academy, founded by Plato, where Aristotle learned and taught, and which eventually passed into the hands of the Stoics. Despite a number of specific differences among Plato, Aristotle, and the Stoics, their great commonalities constitute what is often called "classical Greek philosophy," which has certainly survived far beyond its ancient origins. That is why it is quite easy to agree with Alfred North Whitehead's observation (in his Gifford Lectures of 1927–28 at the University of Edinburgh, which became his great book *Process and Reality*) that "the European philosophical tradition [consists] of a series of footnotes to Plato."[2] This philosophical tradition consists of the ongoing discussions of the great issues that were first raised in the Academy founded by Plato. In fact, the two philosophers in addition to Plato with whom we shall be dealing (in chapters 5 and 6), Aristotle and Kant, were both admittedly following in Plato's footsteps, as we shall see.

What is *theology*? Here, too, Tertullian gives it a location: "Our teaching [*institutio*] is from Solomon's Porch [*de Portico Solomonis*]." That is, Christian doctrine comes from the place in the Jerusalem Temple where Jesus and Peter (his first and favourite disciple) spoke as Jewish authorities. Theology, then, is what the Jews had accepted as *theo-logy*,that is, it is what the Jewish people had accepted as the *logos* or "word of God [*dvar adonai*] that goes forth from Jerusalem" (Isaiah 2:3). Theology is what Moses had told them is "your wisdom and your understanding [*hokhmatkhem u-vinatkhem*] in the eyes of the [gentile] peoples." That means you (Israel) are wise enough to understand "this Torah which I put before you this day" (Deuteronomy 4:6, 8). Now what God revealed to Israel is recorded in the Hebrew Scriptures, the Sacred Writings (*kitvei ha-qodesh*), which were canonized in Jerusalem and whose authenticity had to be validated by the authority located in the same Temple precincts that contained Solomon's Porch.[3] This is the biblical theology or *Torah* first given to the Jews, which the Christians then accepted *in toto*, although they sometimes interpreted this Torah like the Jews and sometimes quite differently. Nevertheless, what the philosophers of Tertullian's time found unacceptable were the theological doctrines common to Jews and Christians alike.[4] Thus the third-century Christian theologian Origen responded to the coupled anti-Christian *and* anti-Jewish charges of the pagan philosopher Celsus (in his by now lost work, *A True Discourse*) by arguing for the "common belief" (*ek tōn koinē*) of Christians and Jews, and for what "we both agree" (*ta homoia phamen*).[5] And all that despite the fact that Jews and Christians often interpret Scripture quite differently. Origen also states that "we have to the best of our ability responded to the charges brought by Celsus against the Jews and their teaching (*tou logou autōn*)."[6]

Couldn't it be said, then, that when Christian theologians confront philosophy, they are in fact doing so as if they were Jews? Actually, at around the same time Tertullian was playing off biblical theology against pagan philosophy, some of the Rabbis were doing much the same thing, as we see in the following text:

> There were no two philosophers who arose in the world like Balaam son of Beor and Oenomaus Gadareus. All the gentile nations [*ummot ha'olam*] came to him [Oenomaus], saying to him, "tell us how we can overcome this nation [Israel]?" He said to them, "go around to their synagogues and houses-of-learning [*u-vatei midrashot*]. If you find there children chirping [Scripture], you will not be able to do so."[7]

It must be assumed here that the philosophers were proposing their teachings to be more intellectually impressive than biblical theology.[8] What is being emphasized *au contraire* is that philosophy stands no such chance when "the Lord's song" (Psalms 137:4) is sung on its own turf.[9] The theology of Jerusalem can well withstand the allure of the philosophy of Athens,that is, when it remains true to itself.[10]

Nevertheless, in playing off "academic philosophy" against "ecclesiastical theology," both Tertullian and his Jewish counterparts thought that philosophy, which is the wisdom of the gentiles without the benefit of biblical theology, poses a direct challenge to their biblically based theology. This is a challenge the theologians have had to overcome because these two sources of wisdom seem to be in perpetual and irreconcilable conflict. The challenge was mostly mounted by philosophers against theology, rather than by theologians against philosophy. For prior to Christianity's becoming the official religion of the Roman Empire early in the fourth century, pagan philosophers were closer to the centre of political authority than were either Jewish or Christian theologians. Greater political power gives one a greater rhetorical advantage in public discourse. Nevertheless, Tertullian and those like him were mounting a full-scale counter-attack against philosophy. Just as the philosophers were dismissing theology's appeal to theoretically minded pagans, so were the theologians dismissing philosophy's appeal to theoretically minded Christians (and to Jews who, in this respect, were no different from Christians).[11]

The typical enunciations of the relation of philosophy and theology, which we have just seen, characterize that relation as an adversarial confrontation of enemies. In this confrontation, either theology wins and philosophy loses or philosophy wins and theology loses. Neither side takes any prisoners. So understood, philosophy can brook no rivals, and neither can biblical theology. Both philosophy and biblical theology claim to be the highest truth, exclusively. Neither philosophy nor biblical theology is willing to be secondary,that is, to be subsequent, to anything else.[12] As it is asked rhetorically in the Talmud: "Is it possible for two kings to wear the same crown?!"[13] As for any value in the metaphysical philosophy of the gentiles, many Jewish thinkers in one way or another have said, in the words of the Talmud: "What does our perfect Torah have to do with your idle chatter [*sihah beteilah*]?!"[14] And by "idle chatter," the Rabbis clearly meant those Jews who had been badly influenced by pagan philosophy.[15]

Centuries later, the thirteenth-century Jewish theologian Rabbenu Asher (Rosh) asserted that "anybody who first enters into this wisdom is unable to depart from it and enter the wisdom of the Torah into his mind. He is unable to return [to the Torah] from natural wisdom [*hokhmah tiv'it*] in which he has become accustomed, because his mind is drawn after it."[16] In this respect, Rabbenu Asher was reiterating the view of his senior Spanish-Jewish colleague, Solomon ibn Adret (Rashba), who in 1305 led the Spanish rabbinate in banning anyone under the age of thirty from studying philosophy.[17] And even those over thirty had to be thoroughly steeped in talmudic learning to be exempted from this ban. Although Ibn Adret did not deny that philosophy as natural science had practical value for medicine, his objection and that of his rabbinical colleagues was directed against those Jews who looked to philosophy for its theoretical or metaphysical value as the prime source of truth. This inevitably leads to the abandonment of *the* core Jewish dogma: the Torah is complete divine revelation.[18] As such, it is qualitatively superior to any other wisdom, whether discovered or invented by humans.[19] Ibn Adret saw Torah and philosophy occupying two separate universes; hence philosophy has nothing to teach the adherents of the Torah. On this key point, he thought even the great Maimonides erred.[20]

Returning to Tertullian, when we look at the general historical context of his statement, it is clear he was saying that theologians and philosophers were not so much talking *to* one another as they were talking *at* one another or *against* one another. Nevertheless, both sides had to recognize that they were still thinking, speaking, and acting *within* the same world of discourse. That is, they were both speaking the same conceptual language. As such, they could not speak totally *past* one another, nor could they avoid interaction *with* one another. Neither side could imagine themselves and their adversaries to be occupying parallel universes that never intersect. Therefore, they could hardly ignore one another.

Now the common language spoken by the theologians and the philosophers is the language of philosophy, not the language of theology. It seems that the theologians could accept this linguistic priority for theological reasons. That is because the biblical revelation the theologians proclaim and explicate is not coeval with the creation of the world. The giving of the Torah at Mount Sinai did not occur on the first day of creation. Revelation does not come *along with* the world; instead, it comes *into* the world *already* there. And, the world-already-there (*Dasein*) has its own language. Indeed, if they had no language of their own in hand previously, humans would be in no position to understand any speaker who comes into their world to speak to them there. Thus the ancient Rabbis taught: "the Torah speaks according to human language [*ke-lashon bnei adam*]."[21] That is because the Torah could only be understood when spoken in a language already spoken by its hearers. Perceptive theologians surely recognize that language is most careful formulated and conceptualized by philosophers. Although there have been theologians who have attempted to speak a theological language as if philosophy were simply not there, the theologians we shall be examining here did speak a philosophically refined language, while themselves attempting to speak that language better and more profoundly than do the philosophers themselves.[22] However, not to engage philosophy seriously when philosophy claims to put forth a better, more intelligently formulated way of life is to tempt the most intelligent Jews or Christians (or Muslims) to abandon their ancestral theology for it. That temptation surely cannot be ignored by Jews (and by Christians and Muslims) if the Torah is to be "your wisdom in the eyes of the peoples" (Deuteronomy 4:6), that is, if the Torah is to function intelligently in and for the world.

Theologians and philosophers had to speak a common language, because in their first confrontation in the Hellenistic age, both theologians (Jewish and Christian) and pagan philosophers were attempting to attract to their respective versions of the truth the same intellectuals who were seeking a new version of the truth and a new way of life as its corollary in the Graeco-Roman world. In this charged proselytizing atmosphere (when Jews still had the right to proselytize gentiles), pagan philosophers were attempting to attract to their philosophy other pagans, plus Jews and Christians of a theoretical or contemplative bent. Jewish and Christian theologians were attempting the same strategy, their targets being pagans, especially philosophically inclined pagans, plus fellow Jews and Christians who were tempted to reject what seems to be parochial theology in favour of much more universalist philosophy as their *modus vivendi* in the world.[23] Each side was attempting a total conversion of the other side. At issue, then, were the most basic questions: first of metaphysics, then of epistemology, and then of ethics.[24] That is, both classical philosophy and biblical theology are concerned with being, and how we humans can know it, and why we humans should act according to that knowledge. Therefore, in the confrontation of philosophy and theology, by attempting to win converts to either a theological or philosophical way of life, each side had to argue for the theoretical and practical superiority of its own position. In this polemical atmosphere, totalizing charges and countercharges were made. Whether or not one's position has to be made at the total expense of the other position largely determines whether the confrontation of theology and philosophy is a zero-sum game or not.

The close connection between the comprehensive conceptions of theologians and philosophers and their respective ways of life, that is, the interrelation of thinking, knowing, and doing, is often *the* issue when theology and philosophy confront each other, especially when they attempt to convert one another to their respective comprehensive visions. For discussions of how persons are supposed to live, and discussions of how society is supposed to be governed, are more than academic exercises; they have a real political/moral impact on a far wider range of people than just theorists, be they theologians or philosophers. This fact seems to have been recognized by the redactors of the Talmud, who at times want to know what practical difference a theoretical distinction actually makes in the real, everyday world.[25] In fact, for most rabbinic opinion, "the deed, not the enquiry (*ha-midrash*), is essential"; and the greatness of "learning" (*talmud*) is that it "leads to action."[26] Just as intellectual conversion is only possible when the antagonists speak the same language addressing the same theoretical questions, so moral conversion is only possible when the antagonists speak the same language addressing the same practical questions. These two aspects of the same language, the theoretical and the practical, are essentially interconnected.

Nevertheless, it is only when philosophy presents an alternative way of life, which is as comprehensive as the way of life presented by theology, that philosophy poses a truly existential threat to theology. But when philosophy no longer presents a comprehensive way of life as a real alternative to the theological way of life, which is when it becomes strictly method without its own content, then philosophy is more readily open to being appropriated as a methodological tool by other disciplines, especially by theology. In fact, this is what has happened to the philosophies that emerged in the twentieth century, especially analytic philosophy and phenomenology: they became almost purely methodological and could thus be employed by various content-laden disciplines. (It is no accident that in the twentieth century, the great and highly influential phenomenological philosopher Edmund Husserl and the great and most influential analytic philosopher Ludwig Wittgenstein were both primarily logicians; and that is because logic is all form and without any matter or real content of its own.) It could even be said that theology is best able to critically appropriate philosophic method, since theology – unlike, for example, psychology – is not a derivative of philosophy, and is thus not historically beholden to philosophy (i.e., pre-twentieth-century philosophy) for any of its content.

However, what about the challenges the three monotheistic religions, Judaism, Christianity, and Islam, pose to each other? Aren't these interreligious challenges as intellectually serious as the challenge classical philosophy poses to all three religions? In fact, more has been made of the theological differences between the three religions than about the challenge philosophy poses to all three.

At least for Jewish theology, however, philosophy has posed a far greater intellectual challenge than did either Christian theology or Islamic theology. The greater threat posed by Christianity or Islam has been political rather than intellectual. That is, until the rise of secular polities in modernity, Jews had to live in polities that were either officially Christian ("Christendom") or officially Muslim ("dar al-Islam"). There Jews were at best tolerated as lower-class alien-residents and at worst persecuted as pariahs. Yet when it came to the theological justifications of their historical triumphalism that Christians and Muslims made against Jews and Judaism, Jewish theologians had rather easy answers. First, Jews could tell Christians and Muslims that Judaism (i.e., the Torah) long preceded the entrance of either Christianity or Islam into the world. Christianity and Islam could well be seen as, in effect, diluted forms of Judaism, while Judaism still remains the original, unsuperseded monotheism.[27] Moreover, Jews had a ready answer to the triumphalist messianic claims of Christians against them, that Jesus of Nazareth did fulfil the criteria of the biblical prophets for authentic messiahhood. The Jews simply said that Jesus did not fulfil these criteria.[28] Jews also had a ready answer to Muslim claims that the Mosaic Torah is an inherently flawed revelation with numerous human interpolations, thus totally displaced by the revelation of the Quran to Muhammed. The Jews simply said: "The Torah of the Lord is perfect" (Psalms 19:8). As such, perfection is diminished either by adding to it or subtracting from it.[29] The same argument was made against Christian claims that many of the positive commandments of the Torah, which pertain to the God-human relationship, have been abrogated by the coming of Christ.[30] To be sure, Christians and Muslims have had an equally easy answer to Jewish claims of original superiority, namely, Judaism is in fact proto-Christianity or proto-Islam. Thus, for them, Judaism is merely the promise of what is to be fulfilled by either Christianity or Islam.

All that notwithstanding, at least some Jewish theologians recognized and respected both Christianity and Islam as valid monotheistic religions *for gentiles* who, though bereft of the superior revelation given to the Jews, still are not bereft of authentic revelation altogether.[31] Moreover, Christianity and Islam serve the ultimate messianic goal – for Jews not yet realized – of a thoroughly monotheistic world. Philosophy, though, could not be explained as being part of the divine historical agenda. That is why philosophy, unlike Christianity and Islam, poses a perennial intellectual challenge to Judaism – and to Christianity and Islam too. Unlike Christianity or Islam, classical philosophy cannot be regarded as a historical derivative of Judaism and a dilution thereof, nor does philosophy claim to be a historical improvement of Jewish origins. For pagan philosophy was operating in the world long before Judaism, Christianity, or Islam came into the world. As such, philosophy does not have to justify its independent presence in the world by arguing against its reduction to Jewish origins by invoking something like the genetic fallacy, which, of course, Christians and Muslims have to periodically invoke against Judaism. Philosophy can directly confront theology from a truly independent, ahistorical perspective.

The general thesis put forth here is that fruitful discourse between philosophers and theologians is still possible today. In fact, it has been periodically occurring for at least the past two millennia, especially when philosophy still presents a comprehensive way of life. Though it is possible to maintain the negative position about the relation of theology and philosophy, I attempt to be more critically positive than Tertullian and those like him were, while attempting neither a "take-over" of nor a "sell-out" to philosophy. I try to do this from the perspective of the Jewish theology to which I am personally committed. The interface of theology and philosophy will be explored in the last three chapters, in the thought of three Jewish theologians and the philosophers whose thought they engaged (although not ever having had to engage these philosophers face to face). The three pairs are: Philo and Plato, Maimonides and Aristotle, and some modern Jewish thinkers and Kant. The interface of theology and philosophy will be explored in what can be seen as the four types of relationality any intelligent person ought to be concerned with: (1) the relation of God and humans; (2) the relation of God and nature; (3) interhuman relations; (4) the relation of humans and nature.

However, in order to avoid demoting the question of the fruitful interaction of theology and philosophy to the level of an antiquarian curiosity, we need to overcome a number of misunderstandings that rule out any such interaction altogether. These misunderstandings have been especially prominent in modernity. Overcoming them offers us the opportunity to argue for the contemporary significance of the interaction between theology and philosophy. Now, of course, this assumes that both theology and philosophy are live existential options today. They are live options today since they are perennial options that have only been marginalized in modernity. Yet theology and philosophy are quite ready to be reasserted at present, that is, when they are carefully thought through by theologians and philosophers rather than just repeating old formulations. Only in that painstaking way can the repeated attempts of modern ideologues to relegate theology and philosophy to the irretrievable past be successfully overcome.

Misunderstanding the Relation between Philosophy and Theology

The first such misunderstanding of the relation of philosophy and theology is the assumption, on the part of many theologians and philosophers, that the engagement of philosophy and theology is a confrontation between those who are committed to human reason and those who are committed to divine revelation. Therefore, thoughtful persons have an either/or choice: either a philosophical commitment to human reason or a theological commitment to divine revelation. One either devotes his or her life to what reason can *discover*, or one devotes his or her life to what revelation *gives* to oneself. That "giving" is verbal, that is, in revelation God *tells* the elected community *what* God does for the sake of their ongoing mutual relationship; and God thereby *asks* the elected community to do *what* God requires of them for the sake of this mutual relationship *with* God, called "the covenant" (*ha-berit* in Hebrew).[32]

So, is the inevitable choice before thoughtful persons either reason instead of revelation or revelation instead of reason?

That philosophical discovery is assumed to be within grasp of any rational person, whereas revelation is only presented to some arbitrarily selected persons or people, can be used by either side of this supposed insuperable division between philosophy and theology. Philosophers can say that what they discover is *universal* truth, hence it can be demonstrated to anybody intelligent enough to understand it. Philosophy's truth claims, therefore, can be verified. Revelation, conversely, is particular; it is only given to some at the expense of most others. Since there is no criterion of verifiability for revelation, there is no way to tell whether any revelation is true or false universally; and there is no way to decide whether any revelation is truer or better than any other competing revelation. Unlike the competing revelations of Judaism, Christianity, and Islam, many philosophers assume that human reason is univocal. For them, there are no multiple rationalities (an arguable point, however).[33] What any human reports to have individually discovered in the world must be capable of univocal (today we might say "global") public demonstration to all rational human persons in order to determine the truth or falsehood of that report. What might be called "natural experience" is what anybody *could* experience anywhere anytime. Here the experience itself is readily replicable since ordinary events are experienced as moments or instances of ordinary, predictable natural processes. But the experience of unique events, what might be called "historical experience," does not admit of any such public demonstration because it is irreplaceable, especially a historical experience of the most unique event of all, that is, *when* God directly speaks.[34] To cogently assume that any revelation took place as a unique event in the world is to believe the testimony of those whom we trust to tell us what was actually spoken to and for them and then to and for us by God.[35] So, philosophy, with its more readily available truth criteria, should be more appealing to rational persons seeking universal truth than are theologies with their very particular and thus very different historical revelations.[36] But, as we shall soon see, classical philosophers too are beholden to a revelation.

On the other hand, theologians can say that the very mysterious, transcendent character of their particular revelation is also affirmed by philosophy, whose highest rational exercise is metaphysical. For reason's ultimate object, which is the truth to be apprehended, is intended by reason as what is greater than reason itself. Reason's true object always transcends the reasoning subject seeking it. As such, reason's ultimate object is not what reason projects as its goal or ideal; instead, reason must first accept what has been given or revealed to it, that is, its *datum* (from Latin *dare*, "to give") rather than what reason gives itself. As an old scholastic formula puts it: *veritas est adaequatio intellectus ad rem*, which I would translate as "Truth is the intellect adjusting itself to its greater object."[37] That object is not accessible to ordinary, repeatable experience. It is not discoverable, passively waiting to be found whenever wherever by perceptive observers of the world. Instead, its subject – who is God – actively presents Himself. That self-presentation is normative, calling for a response from those to whom God so presents Himself. It is a unique *event* that overwhelms those who accept it, no matter how well prepared they think they are for it.[38] "Surely the Lord is in this place, which I did not recognize [*lo yad'ati*]" (Genesis 28:17). God finds them, and only then can they respond to Him, rather than being able to comprehend God by making the revelatory event a component of a regularly occurring process.[39] To do that, though, would make ordinary what is essentially extraordinary. "Seek the Lord whenever wherever He lets Himself be found [*be-himats'o*]; call Him whenever wherever he is near" (Isaiah 55:6). That, of course, means that God is often absent from us; often far away from us.

Furthermore, even though the experience of the revelatory event is esoteric, the content of revelation lends itself to rational explication and even speculation about its ultimate rationale. The event of revelation is experienced as unique and ineffable, and thus it can only be expressed in highly metaphorical language (*mashal* in Hebrew).[40] Nevertheless, its content-laden teaching message or *Torah* is still expressed straightforwardly "in human language," as we have seen.[41] It is the Torah's content that is the object given for general human reason to understand and apply. The revelatory event itself need not be re-experienced in order for that content to be treated with the reverence its Giver deserves. As the ancient Rabbis said about the Torah as the object of human enquiry to those enquiring into it, "if it seems empty [*reiq*], the emptiness is yours [*mikem*]."[42] Revelation's message or content is generally accessible by those intelligent enough to partially understand it – though never comprehend or enclose it – and who are thus able to publicly discuss it.[43] Yet revelation's content does lend itself to explication in universal propositions that apply to ordinary or natural rather than to extraordinary or supernatural situations in the world.[44] In that way, then, theology can employ reason (even acknowledge philosophy to be reason's most impressive expression) and truly respect reason's own integrity as being what humans bring to the content of revelation from the world, not what revelation itself also has to bring to the world.

Had revelation's content not been taken as having emerged from a transcendent event, however, the hearers of the message might presume to have been able to originate or invent that message themselves. Yet that means whoever did originate the message was a human or a humanoid person. And, as the Bible puts it: "My plans [*mahshevotai*] are not your plans; your ways are not My ways; says the Lord" (Isaiah 55:8).

In like manner, Socrates, the archetypal philosopher, insists that his enquiring dialogue with others is not an autonomous activity that began by his own initiative. Instead, his activity was initiated by a command from a god, presumably the same god or a god like the god who from his youth interacted with him in a way he was to imitate in his interactions with others. The revelation of this god, not unlike the revelation of the God of the Bible, is normative, issuing both a negative or restraining command ("turning me away from anything I am about to do") and a positive command or injunction ("to question those who think they are wise").[45] So, both philosophy and theology involve a total existential response to a revelation a philosopher or a theologian has received, either directly (via prophecy) or indirectly (via tradition).[46] Such a receptive response is an act of faith, which is required of both theologians and philosophers. Both philosophy and theology engage content by means of the method each brings to what it has received unambiguously and unconditionally, that is, what it has received faithfully.[47] That method does not come from revelation; it can only be brought to the content of revelation by its recipients. Both philosophy and theology have an objective dimension regarding content and a subjective dimension regarding method. When that method deals with what prepares one *for* the reception of revelation and its content therewith, it reasons *a priori*. When that method deals with what one derives *from* revelation, it reasons *a posteriori*.

As enquiring methods, both theology and philosophy are seeking truth as their ultimate object. When appreciated for its ultimacy, truth is irresistible to those who have in any way accepted it, as well as the demands it brings to those who have received it in good faith. That is why philosophically or theologically ignited souls desire to know more about what truth is (ontology), how to know it properly (epistemology), and how to live according to its message (morality). For theology, "the Lord God Himself is truth [*emet*]" (Jeremiah 10:10). As such, "other than You I desire [*hafatsti*] no one else on earth" (Psalms 73:25). For Plato, especially, philosophy is basically desire (*eros*) directed to its true, ultimate object.[48] On this point, Plato is largely followed by Aristotle and the Stoics.[49]

Just as the ratiocination of philosophers constantly presupposes their faith commitment to truth, so too does the faith commitment of theologians constantly entail ratiocination. Indeed, it could be said that both classical theology and classical philosophy are based upon their different revelations, about which theologians and philosophers have reasoned respectively.[50] If so, theologians could be said to be philosophers who reflect on the most important issues of the culture to which they are faithfully and unconditionally committed. This is where they are coming from. That enables them to say and do many radical things, but not to deny the legitimacy of the community where they live in good faith. In fact, would we take seriously a philosopher having no commitment to any pre-philosophical cultural community? For example, would we take seriously a philosopher of law who has no commitment to any particular system of positive law? So, despite his marginal status in Athens, Socrates was still committed to the authority of Athens and its law.[51] Similarly, despite his outsider status in Israel, and his severe condemnation of King Ahab's violation of the law of God, Elijah still does not deny the royal authority of the king and his dynasty.[52] Neither Socrates nor Elijah (nor any of their epigones) was a revolutionary attempting to overthrow their own traditional societies in order to replace them with something altogether new. Instead, they were reformers, radical in the way they challenged the status quo of their societies, but conservative in the way they tried to bring their societies back to their founding revelations.[53]

The second misunderstanding about the relation of philosophy and theology follows closely after the first misunderstanding we have just examined. It is the presumption that *universal* questions of truth and falsehood, of right and wrong, can only be properly discussed among philosophers themselves. But, surely, questions of truth and falsehood, of right and wrong, can be discussed by all rational persons in a setting of civil discourse, without any credentials being required for admission to the conversation. To confine discussion of these questions to philosophers alone presumes that adherents of historical revelations or theologies like Jews and Christians (and now Muslims as well) are irrational sectarians who are, therefore, incapable of engaging in such civil discourse. For it is presumed that "those people" simply make dogmatic assertions based on their faith commitments when dealing with these universal questions instead of making reasoned arguments.

In fact, many modern philosophers have often proposed that discourse about ideas of truth and falsehood, of right and wrong, are only to be conducted in a strictly inter-philosophical context, and that theologians be precluded therefrom or be admitted thereto only when they are willing to leave their faith commitments at the door before being allowed to dine at philosophy's table. In effect, that means theologians must be converted into philosophers before they can participate in what becomes a philosophical monologue. To be sure, there are theologians who have surrendered to this entrance requirement just for the privilege of dining at what they believe is a richer, more attractive table than their own. Nevertheless, this kind of imperial conquest or obsequious surrender also presumes that philosophers themselves are without faith commitments, that is, they are without pre-philosophical assumptions, and that they alone are the true, legitimate rational interlocutors. But that presumption, as we have seen, is erroneous.

Lest one think, however, that such intellectual triumphalism is only the prejudice of philosophers, especially modern philosophers, we need to remember that many mediaeval theologians (Jewish, Christian, and Muslim) made the same kind of imperial demand on philosophers. And there were philosophers who duly surrendered to that entrance requirement in order to gain the political privilege that surrender gained for them. In fact, who can make this public demand more powerfully depends on which side is closer to the seat of political power at the time. In modern times, it is the universities (with their "doctors of philosophy") who hold that place of public privilege, being closest to the secular state (and who are frequently supported by it). In mediaeval

Christendom, the church was closest to the Crown. As for mediaeval Jewry, the rabbinical theologians and jurists were closest to the non-clerical communal leadership, who themselves received political authority in the Jewish community from the Crown whose subjects the Jews were. The closer the theologians and jurists were to this seat of power, the more likely their voice would be heard and have influence. Often at the instigation of theologians, philosophers were branded as heretics, thus putting them outside the official realm of public discourse.[54]

However, the contemporary political situation has changed for both theologians and philosophers, and that thereby changes their interactions with each other. Just as Jews and Christians have recently learned that they can engage in unmediated, direct discourse among themselves because they are both distant from the seats of power in their increasingly secularized societies, so are philosophers learning of late how distant they too are from the seats of political power whose occupants are as suspicious of authentic philosophy as they are of authentic theology. The fact is, theologians (Christian and Jewish) and philosophers are now all marginalized in a political order that rejects both classical philosophy and classical theology as being too "metaphysical" or transcendently oriented. Yet that makes for a new, exciting, more even playing field for philosophers and theologians to engage one another, and engage those holding political power in their society. Philosophers and theologians might be better able to do that when they are like Socrates in Athens or Amos in Beth-El, that is, when they are political outsiders rather than would-be political ideologues.[55]

The most fruitful discourse between Jewish and Christian theologians on one side and philosophers on the other side can only take place in a context where neither side requires the other side to give up (even temporarily) their faith commitment as the price of admission to the public conversation of universal questions of truth and falsehood, of right and wrong.

Such a faith commitment is not the exclusive preserve of theology, though many philosophers still like to think so. Philosophy as science or systematic methodology (i.e., *scientia* or *Wissenschaft* in the broadest and deepest sense) has its own faith commitment, its own pre-philosophical commitments.[56] For classical philosophers have believed that nature *in toto* is supremely intelligible, the very repository of truth. And that must be affirmed even before we humans can show anything therein to be true because of it. That faith commitment continually accompanies all subsequent efforts of rational confirmation of truth in any particular case. More obviously, theology as science has its own faith commitment, which continually accompanies all its efforts of rational explication too.

That is, the revealed Torah is taken to be supremely intelligible qua truth, even before its human recipients can show anything therein to be true because of it. Furthermore, that faith commitment and its attendant method of knowing, be it philosophical or theological, is humble: it recognizes it is never fully adequate to its object. For that object can never be fully grasped or conceptualized (*begreifen* in German) by any finite, fallible intelligence (a point philosophers and theologians need to regularly confess). "It measures longer than the earth and wider than the sea" (Job 11:9). "But where is wisdom [*hokhmah*] to be found, and where is understanding to be located? ... It is hidden from the eyes of all living beings ... only God understands its way; only He knows its place" (Job 28:20, 23–24). Socrates's humility is that he recognizes he can never know what the gods know.[57] And when Wittgenstein stressed that one must be silent about what cannot be spoken, he clearly implied that no speech can comprehend or even apprehend reality fully.[58] Human speech can only grasp external reality partially.

That is why "faith" (*emunah* in Hebrew; *pistis* in Greek; *fides* in Latin) should not be confused with "belief" (*doxa* in Greek; *de'ah* in Hebrew; *opinio* in Latin), even though this is often the case in ordinary parlance. A "belief" is an unsubstantiated opinion, which can lead to actual, substantiated knowledge, especially when it seems to be coherent and is held by evidently rational persons.[59] Conversely, a belief diverts one from attaining true knowledge when it seems to be incoherent and is held by evidently irrational persons.[60] The difference between belief and knowledge is that knowledge coherently corresponds to external reality as its object, while belief only assumes such a correspondence. As such, belief's object could just as easily be the product of one's imagination as it could be a good clue of an actual correspondence to external reality. Whether that belief deserves to be verified or not largely depends on who has enunciated that belief, and how it has been enunciated. Moreover, unlike belief that can be forgotten once knowledge of its object is attained, faith as acceptance of external-reality-to-be-known ever accompanies the knowledge of that external reality as the continuing, necessary acceptance of its true object. Knowledge of that object, if authentic, must correspond to the way the object gave itself to be accepted or received in faith. That continuing acceptance prevents the object of belief-into-knowledge from being taken as the mere project of one's own imagination. Thus the biblical assertion that "the righteous one lives by his faith [*b'emunato*]" (Habakkuk 2:4) is seen in the Talmud to be the most succinct summary of the whole Torah.[61] So, one can only correctly speak *about* that revealed datum when one regularly acknowledges the way it has been given to one, not invented by one.[62]

Just as the ratiocination of philosophers constantly presupposes their faith commitment to truth, so does the faith commitment of theologians constantly entail ratiocination. As one version of a biblical text reads: "If you will not be faithful [*ta'aminu*], you won't understand [*tavinu*]" (Isaiah 7:9).[63] Or, as the eleventh-century Christian theologian Anselm of Canterbury taught, "faith is seeking understanding" (*fides quaerens intellectum*).[64] One can also see Maimonides's designation of faith that God exists to be a commandment to the truly intelligent faithful who are obliged to know for themselves what they have already accepted by faith.[65] Hence theology is no more blindly obedient than is philosophy arrogantly all-knowing. Both philosophy and theology have a transcendent or objective dimension and an immanent or subjective dimension. Knowledge is the coherent, comprehending correspondence with the desired transcendent object. Faith is the subjective, immanent acceptance of the object and the way that object presents itself to those who are to receive it and then know it. This coherent connection of subject and object is immediate when what has been given is what has been spoken to the subject, then what a subject says *about* it, plus what a subject does *because* of it. This speaking and doing *intend* (in Hebrew *kavvanah*) what has been said and the way it has been said.[66]

The third misunderstanding of the interrelation of philosophy and theology is uniquely modern. It comes from a common modern notion that in an essentially secular society, no metaphysical commitments may be brought into public political discourse. In this view of a secular society, all sides in matters of public policy must give up their prior metaphysical commitments in principle or privatize them in fact. To be sure, emphasizing the *secularity* of a secular society is important inasmuch as philosophy and theology could only interact today in a secular society, which is a society that has no official ideology – whether religious (as in many officially Islamic polities) or irreligious (as in officially communist societies) – and where all belief systems – whether they be philosophical or theological – have the right to be heard in all discussions of public policy. Only here is there the even playing field genuine public dialogue needs. But the ideology of *secularism*, which turns *secularity* from a desirable political situation into an ideal to be fully realized, refuses to acknowledge the limits of the secularity it so idealizes. It thus becomes quite undemocratic, even anti-democratic, when it attempts to shut out of public discourse anyone who is committed to any criterion that transcends the secular state.

Indeed, the very secularity of our Western democracies is threatened when, as the most influential contemporary political philosopher qua democratic theorist, the late John Rawls, insisted, all these matters of public policy are approached from behind what he called a "veil of ignorance."[67] (Others, though, have called this the "view from nowhere," and still others have called it "the naked public square.")[68] As such, whatever agreements are reached by the various sides engaging in what Rawls called "public reason" are not based on anything the parties have brought with them through the veil of ignorance. That means that all those who have what Rawls calls "comprehensive conceptions of the good," who seem to be both philosophers and theologians who have their own prior, pre-political metaphysical commitments, must keep their metaphysical commitments out of public discourse altogether. If not, they themselves must be kept out of public discourse because of their refusal to do so.[69] This reminds me of how we Jews have often been told by those who wield political power over us that we should give up or hide our particular faith commitments, because these commitments keep the Jews separate from the larger general society, thus making us suspicious foreigners. In effect, this is a "might-makes-right" argument. Happily, most thoughtful Jews have resisted this threat, as it is not intellectually but only politically intimidating.

This anti-metaphysical point of view is as anti-philosophical as it is anti-theological. But, as history has shown, without what might be called a "transcendent dimension," the public position that usually prevails is the position of those having the most power rather than those who can make the most reasonable argument. In order to make a sound argument that could be accepted by seriously rational people, one has to show an existential commitment to a prior ontological foundation. Is a given public position being advocated consistent with a standard the advocates themselves did not make up, or not? If not, to what standard could we hold them? To what or to whom are they answerable for what they are advocating publicly? In other words, by what criterion can we hold them to their promises to practise what they preach?[70] Moreover, this point of view is also anti-historical in its refusal to recognize the cultural context in which philosophers, like theologians, are initially situated, though not wholly constrained by.

Public Faith Commitments

How do theologians and philosophers engage in fruitful public discourse without each side having to give up what they hold nearest and dearest in the world? In other words, can either theologians or philosophers engage in fruitful public discourse with their respective faith commitments still intact, yet without attempting to deny the legitimacy of the other side? That is a very important question to raise today, because authentic public discourse in a truly secular society – which, recall, is a society that doesn't have or impose an official public ideology – ought to be very different from the mediaeval disputations in which Jews had to justify their self-chosen exclusion from that ideology and thus their exclusion from full membership in that society. Back then it was assumed that if Jews could not do that, they had no good reason to refuse conversion or accept expulsion from the society where that ideology had dogmatic authority.[71] Indeed, much the same is occurring today when, for many in positions of political and cultural power in our Western societies, *secularism* has become the official ideology that requires the conversion of non-secularists – like Jews, Christians, Muslims, and classical philosophers qua metaphysicians – or their exclusion from public discourse altogether. So, how does public discourse between philosophers and theologians avoid the extremes of precluding the questions of truth and justice on the one hand, or engaging in a zero-sum game on the other hand?

What is required is that each side *not* represent its position on any public question as having been *deduced* from the ontological foundation it accepts in faith. For when that happens, when one's position on a public question is deduced from one's ontological foundation as a conclusion deduced from a premise, we then have an all-or-nothing situation: either we agree on everything theoretically and therefore conclude we must agree on everything practically, or we agree on nothing theoretically and therefore conclude we can agree on nothing practically. That is, if you agree with me on a practical question, you must have accepted my ontological foundation that functions like a premise in a logical deduction, and that it functions as the only premise from which a position on this public question could possibly be deduced. When that happens, we are then left with either a monologue or silence: either you become just like me, or I will have nothing more to say to you or hear from you. However, if one's position on public questions is not deduced from an ontological foundation formulated as a premise, what then is the better connection between theory and practice?

The answer, it seems to me, is that each side must show how its position on a question of public importance is *informed by* the ontological foundation to which they are committed rather than being necessarily *deduced from* it. What is the difference, though? How is a publicly reasoned position's being informed by an ontological foundation different from its being deduced from such a foundation? Let me cite an example that will be discussed at greater length in chapter 5.

The philosopher Aristotle and the theologian Maimonides both agreed that public morality (what some have called "social ethics") deals with what are *right* and what are *wrong* acts; what are *good* and *bad* deeds. Now, both thinkers inherited certain traditional moral norms already in place in their respective communities, which were considered to be venerable traditions long before each thinker came upon the scene to offer better reasons for them than had been offered by his predecessors. In the Jewish tradition, this is called finding "reasons of the commandments" (*ta'amei ha-mitsvot*).[72] Nevertheless, these reasons are not theoretical principles functioning as premises from which one could deduce the practical norms as conclusions. So, thinkers in the traditions in which these moral norms have been transmitted and upheld should only try to argue for the greater rationality of their theoretical justifications, that is, *why* it is inherently just and not unjust for humans to do what they have been previously commanded to do or not do.[73] Nevertheless, neither Aristotle nor Maimonides proposed any radical new norms for their respective communities. The principles each of them formulated theoretically had a heuristic, interpretive function, not a radically innovative one. That is how theoretical principles inform the practical norms, rather than entailing them. The norms are not deduced from the principles that inform or explain them. Moreover, the principles or reasons have to affirm rather than deny the normative data, by explaining them rather than explaining them away, thus negating their original normativity.[74]

Even Kant, who is more radical in theory than are his predecessors, insisting that there must be autonomous intention for an act to be morally valid, still claimed he was only providing a new formulation of old moral principles (and precepts).[75] Therefore, Aristotle, Maimonides, and Kant could still engage in sustained rational discourse with members of their own historical communities and with members of other historical communities, because they were not demanding that those with whom they disagreed should radically change their practices. That is, they were not demanding some sort of practical conversion. Nevertheless, there must be some theoretical agreement too, lest practical agreement be nothing more than agreeing to agree conclusively so as not to be bothered with seemingly unending disagreement, which is usually a pragmatic stop-gap measure that rarely withstands a real political crisis.[76] There needs to be more than the "overlapping consensus" John Rawls thought sufficient for public reason.[77]

Neither philosophers nor theologians could say their ontology provides the *only* reason for acting well in the world and still expect somebody unwilling to agree with them to remain in the conversation. Philosophers and theologians can only show that their ontology informs, in the sense of providing a better reason for, an ethically significant act like not harming another person, which is something we can assume is very hard to argue against. Neither of them can rule out the reason offered by their counterpart altogether. At most, each side can only argue they offer a more plausible reason than does the other side. Authentic discourse is possible and actually fruitful when thinkers explain their position on a public issue by showing how their metaphysical faith commitment strengthens it, yet without thereby trying to argue somebody out of their own faith commitment (or lack thereof). In fact, I have yet to know (either first hand or second hand) anybody, whether a theologian or a philosopher, who was actually argued into a true faith commitment or out of one as some sort of conclusion logically deduced from a prior premise. Instead, such persons who have undergone either theological or philosophical conversions have, in fact, experienced some sort of epiphany, to which their faith is their own existential response.

All that notwithstanding, each faith can still be a challenge to the other, not by actively challenging the other faith to justify itself (which it cannot and should not do), but rather by just being present in the same world of discourse with the other faith, and thus being concerned with the same unavoidable theoretical and practical issues that the other faith also has to be concerned with. That is why that very presence in the same world must be taken seriously by thinkers in the other faith's traditional community, but with neither conquest nor surrender in mind. If nothing else, that challenge can cause those so challenged to more profoundly rethink their own metaphysical commitment.

The Challenge of Philosophy

Both Jewish and Christian theologians have to deal with philosophy's challenge to theology similarly, since philosophy challenges biblically based theology on the points Jews and Christians still hold together in common. Yet some have thought that the mutual challenge of philosophy and theology can be overcome by one side capturing the other. Thus there have been theologians who tried to turn philosophy into theology's "handmaiden" (*ancilla theologiae*).[78] And there have been philosophers who tried to turn theology into philosophy's handmaiden. But once philosophy *serves* theology, doesn't theology eventually become philosophy? And once theology *serves* philosophy, doesn't philosophy eventually become theology? Doesn't the increasing need of the mistress for her handmaiden turn the handmaiden into somebody whom the mistress needs more than her handmaiden needs her? (The logic of this inverted relationship was brilliantly explicated by Hegel in what came to be called the "master-slave dialectic.")[79] Theology can only confront philosophy and vice versa when there is an even playing field between them, where one is not subordinate to the other. But once theology's formulation is largely determined by philosophy, or philosophy's formulation is largely determined by theology, there is no even playing field and the truly discursive game is effectively over.

Along these lines, "Jewish" philosophy or "Christian" philosophy is as problematic as "Aristotelian" or "Kantian" theology.[80] To be sure, there are some Jewish philosophers who draw upon the Jewish tradition for illustrations of points they have arrived at as secular philosophers only. And although there are some Jewish theologians and some Christian theologians who employ philosophical methods in their respective theologies to warrant the name "philosophical theologian," their use of whatever philosophical method still does not make their theology "Aristotelian" or "Kantian" (or whatever). It is still *Jewish* theology or *Christian* theology, only with the methodological help of philosophy. So as not to confuse their univocal devotion to their own revelation-based theology with their use of someone else's philosophy, philosophical theologians should be more eclectic, more pluralistic, even more syncretistic in their philosophy than they could be in their theology.[81]

To be as univocal in philosophy as one has to be in theology is to commit a major category error. It is to treat merely human wisdom as one should treat divine revelation. Biblical revelation is taken to be "given from one Shepherd" (Ecclesiastes 12:11), whereas the sages and their pupils are a plurality who argue *among* themselves from a variety of positions. The sages argue with one another, either agreeing or disagreeing, but one cannot agree or disagree with revelation. God's word can only be accepted in theory and obeyed in practice, though with considerable interpretive leeway.[82] In other words, in order for a revelation to retain its normativity, its overall truth must be unconditionally accepted in faith. Only its meanings can be open to ongoing debate. To question revelation's overall truth value can only be done on the basis of another revelation, one that either precedes or supersedes the revelation being so questioned or doubted, and whose normativity is thereby destroyed.[83]

Now, there have been Jewish and Christian theologians obsequious enough to want to turn their theology into the "handmaiden of philosophy," even though she is a servant fewer and fewer philosophers have been willing to use altogether.[84] Very few philosophers have been willing to see theology as providing answers to the questions posed by philosophy, which is a highly arguable point about the correlation of philosophy and theology made by the twentieth-century Protestant theologian Paul Tillich.[85] Even fewer modern theologians have been willing to accept this correlation, which seems to require theology to speak only after the philosophers have posed their questions, that is, after the philosophers have set the entire agenda. Here again, the handmaiden would have in effect become the mistress.

The characterization of theology and philosophy as two different, comprehensive, substantial doctrines occupying totally different worlds assumes that philosophy is one body of teaching, having one content, while theology has an altogether different content. And, as we have seen, some have assumed that different content means opposing content, an either/or standoff, while others have assumed that there is both commonality and difference between theology and philosophy. Yet there have been others who have assumed that theology and philosophy have the same content or subject matter, which is human talk about God. This is the meaning of Aristotle's neologism *theologikē*, which could be translated as "God-talk."[86] This term denotes what we now call "ontology," which for Aristotle and those who followed him is the science of natural *Being*: God being within nature, albeit at its zenith. This equation of God and Being entered into Jewish discourse when the Septuagint, the translation of the Torah into Greek done in the third century BCE, translated Exodus 3:14, "I shall be who I shall be" (*ehyeh asher ehyeh*), as "I am Being" (*egō eimi ho ōn*). Thus many have called this ontology "natural theology," which is in fact "philosophy of nature" or "natural philosophy."

Taking natural theology to be the zenith of philosophy, that is, as the "queen of the sciences" (*regina scientiarum*), however, would make any distinction between theology and philosophy meaningless. Philosophical theology and theological philosophy become two sides of the same coin. Along the same lines, one could even say that the ancient Athenian philosophers were the theologians of Athens. In fact, in such non-Western systems of belief and praxis like Buddhism, there doesn't seem to be any real difference between theology and philosophy, because there do not seem to be competing revelations requiring people to choose between them at the level of ultimate commitment. However, after the encounter of Athens and Jerusalem in the Hellenistic Age, philosophy of nature could no longer claim to be the only way for metaphysical speculation about God to be conducted. Biblical revelation now provided an independent ontological foundation for that ultimate speculation. Philosophers and theologians were now truly distinct from one another. Yet at the dawn of modernity, in the seventeenth century, Baruch Spinoza thought he had eliminated biblical revelation from metaphysical speculation altogether, relegating its role to popular moral teaching.[87] Ontology, in his view anyway, now became once again the exclusive domain of natural philosophy. It took the efforts of such twentieth-century Jewish theologians as Franz Rosenzweig and Abraham Joshua Heschel, and Christians theologians like Karl Barth, to retrieve metaphysical speculation for theology proper. This was done at a time when most twentieth-century philosophers (i.e., most phenomenologists and most analytic philosophers) had abandoned metaphysical speculation, thus making its retrieval by theologians largely irrelevant to philosophers. (The exceptions have been philosophers like Karl Jaspers, Martin Heidegger, and Paul Ricoeur.) The achievement of these theologians and philosophers is to have provided a level playing field for them to engage each other on the same issues of existential importance differently.

Content and Method

To be sure, some modern Jews are uncomfortable with the term "theology," but that is due more to the connotation of the term than to its actual denotation.[88] True to the etymology of the word itself, "theology" as content denotes "the word" (*logos*) of "God" (*theos*).[89] As the "Word of God," *theology* means a body of teachings that can be the object of sustained ratiocination. It is a *datum* literally, that is, it is what has been *given* by God *to* His covenanted people. In the Jewish tradition, revelation is called "the gift [*mattan*] of the Torah."[90] That is *what* theology qua revealed data, qua *Torah*, is. *How* this content is then taken intelligently – *how it* is to be understood after it is experienced – is through exegesis or hermeneutics (*parshanut* in Hebrew). That is its *method*, its "enquiring way" (*odos* in Greek means a "road," and roads have destinations), its "seeking" (as in the Hebrew *derash)* the truth its object shows to those prepared to accept it and explicate it. Indeed, it is asserted that biblical revelation, the Torah, actually calls for its recipients to explicate its message: "Hearken Israel to the laws and statutes that I speak into your ears today, that you shall learn them, and that you shall keep them to do them" (Deuteronomy 5:1). This hermeneutics is what enables the Torah "not to be in heaven [but on earth]."[91] And that could only be the case because "the Torah speaks according to human language."

Only when speaking of theology as subsequent to primary revealed content can we then speak of theology as being a method. The content – "theology" qua "Word of God" – is the object of the investigation enquiring subjects employ as their method or way to reach it and understand it. As in any methodical enquiry that assumes its object is a datum given to enquiry rather than a projection of the enquirer, God's

Word (*dvar adonai*) is the content-laden object that calls for methodological enquiry, not vice versa. Therefore, when using the word "theology," one should carefully indicate in which sense it is being used: either to denote content or to denote method.

Whereas the word "theology" denotes both the content and the method of enquiry into biblical revelation, the word "philosophy" denotes only a method of enquiry. The content-laden object given to philosophical enquiry, however, is not philosophy. That content-laden object is *Nature*.[92] And Nature is the repository of wisdom itself insofar as Nature is the supreme intelligibility of the cosmos, its ultimate form.[93] We see this sense of "philosophy" used by Socrates, the archetypal philosopher. He speaks of himself (and by implication all those who would follow him) as "living the life of a philosopher, examining [*exetazonta*] myself and others."[94] However, that examination is not itself "self-knowledge" in the current sense; instead, it is the examination of each other's opinions (*doxa*) about ultimate wisdom, and whether or not their opinions cohere and adequately intend this higher reality standing above those seeking to know it.[95] The philosopher, then, is one who lovingly (the *philo* in "philosophy") seeks "wisdom" (*sophia*), that is, the wisdom that is inherent in the natural, cosmic order. Philosophy is unlike theology in its primary sense of being objective content, for the content philosophy desirously seeks (what Plato saw as philosophical *eros*) is wisdom. Philosophy does not claim to be wisdom, but only the best way wisdom is to be sought. What philosophers seek is something other than, greater than, themselves, which can never be fully comprehended.[96]

Similarly, when theology is a method of enquiry into revealed wisdom, there is also no guarantee that it will understand all or even most of what has been given to it and which it receives by faith. Moreover, if the body of wisdom seems to be unintelligible, that is because we are not intelligent enough to understand it at all, let alone fully comprehend it. "As for wisdom [*hokhmah*] where may it be found; and where is understanding [*binah*]? No human knows its value [*erkkah*]. It is not to be discovered [*timmats'e*] in the land of the living" (Job 28:12–13).[97] Nevertheless, the fact that we cannot know ultimate wisdom does not imply that we may not try to know any of it. Only those who attempt to know all of ultimate wisdom, and who think their goal is attainable, sooner or later despair of knowing any of it. On the other hand, those who try to know as much of it as they can know, and who accept their noetic limitations, do learn that knowing some of it is better than knowing none.[98] That is because "it [ultimate wisdom] is longer than the earth's measure, and broader than the sea" (Job 28:12–13) and, as such, it does not lend itself to anything but partial knowledge.[99] Of course, worst of all are those whose despair at not knowing ultimate wisdom leads them to conclude that there is no ultimate wisdom to be known at all. Epistemological scepticism stems from metaphysical scepticism.

Accordingly, it would seem that the Athens-Jerusalem divide is not in fact a specific divide between reason and revelation. *There is both revelation and reason in both Athens and Jerusalem.* That is why each tradition poses such a challenge to the other. There is no simple division of labour between rational Athens and pious Jerusalem.

Philosophy should be thought of as method; in fact, it can even be thought of as exegetical method. The content it attempts to explicate or understand is *Nature*: the intelligible whole that can alone elicit the most intelligent explication. In fact, philosophy can even be designated as the "hermeneutics of Nature." That was Galileo's point when he spoke of his epistemology as the way of "reading the book of Nature."[100] His mathematical method was clearly a scientific epistemology directed to an existing object that had shown itself to him (and, in principle, to all other enlightened observers). So, the fundamental confrontation is not one of reason *or* revelation, since there is both reason *and* revelation on both sides of the Athens-Jerusalem divide. Instead, the fundamental confrontation is either Nature versus the Word of God, or vice versa. Nevertheless, there is an interrelation between the two because they both reveal themselves and are reasoned about in the same human world. Furthermore, since revelation comes into a world already there, methods for understanding nature – of which philosophy is the most profound – are applicable to the investigation of revelation's content: the Torah. That is because the Torah presupposes the natural world, even though the natural world neither presupposes nor entails the Torah. All theologians need ask of philosophers in order for there to be discourse between them is that philosophers not constitute nature in such a way that it is impossible for revelation to occur therein.

Faith and Reason

A great Jewish philosopher, Leo Strauss, insisted that "the discovery of nature is the work of philosophy."[101] He is right about the close correlation of nature and philosophy; but I would question whether nature is simply waiting there for philosophical discovery. Rather than nature being taken as the sum total of all phenomena that could appear to us, *Nature* in this classic philosophic view is the immanent order *implicit* in all that can be seen. Perhaps nature, as it were, has to present itself as a *Gestalt* (i.e., what must be shown before being comprehended), being there (*Dasein*) for philosophical acceptance and appropriation. In that way, it is like biblical revelation, which has to present itself for theological acceptance and appropriation. Here, both philosophy and theology are methods of enquiry. However, as Strauss himself admits, the acceptance of what has been given to understand for both theology and philosophy is "based on faith ... on an unevident premise."[102] (I assume he means by "unevident premise" what is not evident in the usual experience of ordinary people.)

"Faith" is not just "opinion," which usually means a second-hand kind of knowledge. (So, saying "in my opinion *X* is true" is like saying "I believe *X* is true"; yet that is quite different from saying "I have faith in *Y* as truth.")[103] Instead, as we have seen, faith is the acceptance of the most sublime truth as a gift from someone whom the accepter completely trusts. This gift is not what anybody could discover by their own efforts, no matter how intelligent and how diligent they are, and no matter how well prepared they might be for the revelation given to them. Being prepared is a necessary precondition for the intelligent reception of revelation; it is not, however, what will necessarily cause revelation to occur. Thus Plato thinks that a person growing up in a less than perfect, philosophically oriented society could not attain knowledge of the absolute Good unless "some god come to its rescue."[104] And Maimonides saw prophecy as being only a possibility, not a necessity, even for those best prepared for it.[105] Moreover, the faith of both theologians and philosophers is certainly based on much more than a "premise."

The gift is always what is presented to one. Faith is the full acceptance of what is claiming the recipient of the gift in that event. And its first claim on the trusting or faithful recipient is to understand it, that is, to represent the content of the event and to designate its significance in and for the world honestly and accurately. But if that is the case for both theology and philosophy, why is philosophy but not theology (in Strauss's words) "rational orientation in the world"?[106] Whether for philosophy or for theology, a sublime event shows to those privileged to experience it what the ordinary world is grounded in. That is because the ordinary world cannot explain why it exists at all. The ordinary world cannot show *from whom* or *for whom* it has come to be. Existence itself is wonderous inasmuch as it didn't have to be. That is why both philosophical and theological reflection begin in wonder or amazement.[107] The extraordinary event is accepted; one then reasons about its ordinary, intelligible effects in the world.

Along these lines, I cannot agree with Catholic philosopher Étienne Gilson when he said: "To have faith is to assent to something because it is revealed by God ... to have science [of which philosophy is its rational summit] is to assent to something which we perceive as true in the natural light of reason."[108] I also cannot agree with the late Pope John Paul II, who saw faith and reason (*fides et ratio*) as two ways of knowing truth, and theologians as having the advantage of faith plus reason, whereas philosophers only have reason.[109] The fact is, both philosophers and theologians have prior reason that prepares the way for revelation, and they have subsequent reason that responds to what has been revealed to them by explicating it. And both of them have faith that accepts their respective revelations *in toto* as truth per se (*alētheia*, which is "uncovering" or "revealing" in Greek, a point most famously explicated in modernity by Heidegger).[110]

I do, however, agree with John Paul II when he insightfully notes that this faith is "grounded ... on trust between persons."[111] In other words, the truth shown forth in the revelatory event is accepted by faith, because the faithful trust the source of that event to be the trustworthy reality (*ne'eman* in Hebrew) who is the Giver of the gift; and they trust the wisdom of the Giver's choice to give this gift to them. Finally, there are those (who are most of us) who do not experience the revelation directly, but only have the revelation transmitted to them by a chain of tradition that is founded in revelation. In the words of John Paul II, they have "knowledge through belief ... [They] entrust themselves to the truth which the other declares to them."[112] Both the direct experience of revelation and the indirect experience of revelation via tradition are "a search for the truth and a search for a person to whom they might entrust themselves."[113] Nevertheless, this "knowledge through belief," or what I would call "faith-initiated ratiocination," is the method of knowing (*modus cognescendi*) employed by both biblical theologians and classical philosophers. But before that initiation of ratiocination, faith intends the existence of the revealed object itself (*modus essendi*).

Faith ever accompanies the rational enquiry it initiates by continually giving reason a transcendent intention (*kavvanah* in Hebrew). It is not that reason carries us so far in our metaphysical quest and that faith picks up where reason has run its course, or vice versa. Instead, faith continually hands over to reason what it has accepted to be reason's primary and ultimate object to work on, as it were. As such, faith anchors reason to its proper object by never letting reason overcome or transcend (*aufheben* in German) its proper object, the object to which reason, like faith, ever intends. This faithful apprehension entails rational comprehension; and rational comprehension presupposes faithful apprehension. Faith is both personal acceptance of what has been revealed, and also one's personal conviction or certitude (*emunah* in Hebrew) that what has been given to one unconditionally (either first hand or second hand) is the truth (*emet* in Hebrew).[114] Affirming or intending (as when one says "amen" to either a liturgical or theological proposition) the revelation as truth then leads to the task of unpacking the meaning of that received datum for one's particular situation *in* the world.[115] Paul Tillich rightly called that personal commitment "our ultimate concern," which is the convergence of truth and meaning.[116] But we need to remember that because truth is ultimate we are to be concerned with it, which is essentially different from presuming that truth is ultimate because of our concern for it.

Such personally committed metaphysical knowledge is found in both Athens and Jerusalem. It is as much philosophical as it is theological. In both cases, whether that of philosophers or that of theologians, faith is the personal-existential commitment to the sublime datum as the highest revelation of truth (*torat emet* in Hebrew). However, were any primary revelation only taken to be "true" rather than *the truth*, that would presume there is something greater by which that revelation could be verified or falsified (i.e., judged to be true or false). That revelation, then, would be measured by something above it to which it is supposed to correspond, that is, it must comport with that which measures it. That is what Plato emphasized when he said that God, not man, is "the measure (*metron*) of all things."[117]

Asserting that the revelation is *of truth itself* leads to the task of unpacking the meaning of that revealed truth for one's particular situation in the world. Applying *truth* to a situation in the world where an intellectually and morally serious person cannot be indifferent but must act, that enables one to actively assert something here is *true*. Thus in the Jewish tradition, an act is true or right when it corresponds to God's commands, which are "truthful [*emet*] and consistently self-justifying [*tsadqu yahddav*]" (Psalms 19:10). This is when "justice [*tsedeq*] is looking down from heaven" (Psalms 85:12). And so is righteous King Hezekiah praised for "doing what is good, and right, and the truth [*ha'emet*] ... in the Torah and its commandments [*ha-mitsvah*]" (II Chronicles 31:20–1). Accordingly, explanations of revelation are corrected by the revelation itself; the revelation corrects, but it itself is not to be corrected. Indeed, a revelation loses it essential authority if any other revelation claims to have superseded it and is thereby able to correct it accordingly.

A particular aspect of revealed truth is itself *true*, maximally, if it corresponds to the revealed truth, and minimally, if it does not contradict that truth. Here reason functions as exegesis or hermeneutics. That unpacking also involves the task of clarifying the internal sense or meaning of what is given in the revelation, that is, making sure that its intended message is uttered coherently. This involves the use of logic, which is reason's most basic function in the world. But reason has a prior function, which is to clear away any worldly impediments that would prevent the recipients of revelation from being able to receive it when it does come into their world. It is similar to what Heidegger (who was certainly neither a Christian nor a Jew) called *seinlassen* ("letting be"), that is, our letting the datum present itself *to* the world, rather than claiming it is introduced by us *into* the world.[118] That is reason's critical function. Theologically speaking, that means the negation of idolatry as falsehood (*sheqer* in Hebrew) precedes the affirmation of God, an affirmation that could only come as a response to God's revelation.

Reasoning as the quest for truth has four tasks. First, reason must prepare the world for the entrance of transcendent truth into the world. That is reason's metaphysical task. Second, reason must understand the truthful object's evident meaning per se, that is, its immediate intelligibility in its own context. That is truth as inner coherence *within* its proper object. That is reason's logical task. Third, reason must show how its theory of the object adequately bespeaks the reality of that object, that is, it must explicate it instead of explaining it away. That is truth as correspondence *with* its proper object, which is reason's epistemological task. Fourth, reason must show how its interpretation of the object is relevant to the practical situation of the subjects who are reasoning about the object. Here truth is the object's applicability to the practical situation of the reasoning subjects. That is reason's ethical task.

It would seem that just as theology as revealed content presents itself but cannot be conjured up by human effort, so Nature presented itself to Plato, Aristotle, the Stoics, and all those philosophers who have followed them. They too did not conjure it up by their own devices. To them, their visions of ultimate reality were epiphanies. Surely, Nature appeared to them in some sort of sublime vision; it was neither their ideal construction nor their proposal of a scientific hypothesis. Like any overwhelming presentation, it is (in the words of the Talmud) "given to be interpreted" (*nittnah le-hidaresh*), that is, to be re-presented in and for the world.[119] Thus Socrates speaks of "having been commanded [*prostetaktai*] to engage [in enquiry] by God from out of oracles [*ek manteiōn*] and dreams."[120] In other words, what he has been shown and accepted calls for explication. That which Socrates saw or experienced lends itself to a rational program of interpretation. That is what distinguishes his vision from the mania of those who have had visions that do not lend themselves to rational interpretation at all.

Rejections of Revelation

Revelation consists of the narration of the unique events through which God speaks to those who have accepted these events as a gift, whether they have experienced these events first hand (as did the generation of those who were brought out of Egypt) or experienced them second hand by accepting the narration of them given thereafter in Scripture. God's speech through these events and their subsequent narration are not primarily meant to inform those experiencing these events either first hand or second hand; rather, they are meant to be the context of the imperatives that are given within these unique events as a task to be done. The task to be done involves the retelling of these events in a communal context; and it also involves prescribing how this very retelling brings those to whom the revelation has been given together into one community. This is epitomized by the celebration of Passover. "It shall be when your children say to you 'what is this service [*avodah*] of yours?' you shall say to them 'it is the Passover sacrifice for the Lord, who passed over the houses of the children of Israel in Egypt,' etc." (Exodus 12:26–7). And: "when a sojourner [*ger*] dwells among you, he shall make Passover for the Lord ... and he shall be like one who is native-born [*k'ezrah*] of the land, etc." (Exodus 12:48).[121]

Conversely, most rejections of revelation attempt to force such unfamiliar, unpredictable, irregular events (whether experienced in Athens or in Jerusalem) into the Procrustean bed of ready-made processes that only await familiar, predictable, regular events to be subsumed under them. These reductions of the unfamiliar to the familiar tend to be convincing when there is nobody present to argue against them, that is, nobody who has actually experienced these events, or nobody who has experienced these events who could make a counterargument. However, when those who have experienced these events (by now second hand) are present, even if they are not conceptually articulate, their initial reaction to the rejecters of their revelatory experience might very well be something like this: "We don't recognize ourselves in what you are explaining about experiences that are ours, not yours." It is, then, imperative that the philosophically articulate faithful pick up the task of responding with philosophical acumen to whatever rejection of revelation happens to be made at the time.[122] That is the task of dialectics, whether done by philosophers or by theologians.

Those who deny the revealed narratives in Scripture often designate them as "myths," that is, either conscious lies or unconscious delusions. Despite this frequently invoked pejorative connotation of "myth," it is still best to designate such all-encompassing narratives as myths. For in its original denotation, a *mythos* is what we would today call a "master narrative." The veracity of these myths cannot be tested experimentally because experiments repeat or replicate an event, whereas myths give voice to events that are unique and are therefore not repeatable. In fact, the myths, whether of Athens or Jerusalem, stimulate or excite their most perceptive hearers to record them. Thereafter the most thoughtful hearers of the myth's message attempt to theorize about what is permanent in them, on which the community of the faithful (*ma'aminim* in Hebrew) can intelligently base (*epistēmē* in Greek; literally "standing upon") the norms that regulate their praxis.

That is why it is incorrect to look upon myths, especially myths still accepted as foundational by a live community of the faithful, as prescientific or proto-scientific hypotheses that modern science subsequently overcomes, however much it recognizes that mythical thinking prepared the way for it.[123] Myths, however, are not overcome and then replaced by scientific theory any more than myths deny and then displace scientific theory. Myths deal with what is extraordinary; scientific theory deals with what is ordinary. It is only when scientific theory presumes that it can explain everything that it becomes preposterous by making extraordinary claims for itself. That is when science becomes "scientism." Indeed, the very ordinariness of usual experience is better appreciated when it is taken to be limited by what is extraordinary. And the very extraordinariness of the extraordinary is better appreciated when it is taken to be limited by the ordinary. In fact, we might say that the essential difference between the ordinary and the extraordinary is confused by scientism on one side and magic on the other. For magic is the presumption of the believers of a mythical narration that they can make anything thought to be ordinary into an extraordinary event, while believers in scientism presume they can make anything thought to be extraordinary into an ordinary event.

We should see the value of myths as their enabling thinkers within a tradition that accepts the truth of its myth to see their various judgments, both theoretical and practical, in the cosmic-historical setting the myth provides.[124] That gives the myth's interpreters considerable leeway in accessing just those aspects of the myth that are helpful for giving their theories cosmic-historical significance.[125] And a myth loses its value only when it no longer explains a consistently structured way of life that is still being lived in the world. A myth's truth value is appreciated by how coherent its rendering is, and how it illuminates the situation of those to whom it is addressed and who are still living according to it. Repeating the myth gives meaning to the deeds its recipients are doing in the present in accordance with it and why they ought to continue doing them.[126] The myth is not a representation of events in the world that can be described by a spectator who is not a participant in them, whether directly or even subsequently. Myths necessarily involve in their very narration the participation of those to whom the myth is addressed and whom it claims. Spectators, conversely, do not participate in the facts they describe in the way those for whom the extraordinary events are performed do. Thus those to whom these events are told and who accept them as true are themselves essential components of those events and their subsequent narration. That is because they are participating in the telling and retelling of the story of their own community. On the other hand, ordinary repeatable events represented as facts would be whatever they are irrespective of *who* is observing them.

Indeed, these extraordinary events and their narration would not be what they are without this essential participation. A myth is not like a scientific hypothesis that can be validated or invalidated by demonstrating counterfacts, for myths are not about facts at all; instead, they bespeak primal, irrepeatable events. It is only when a myth is stated as if it were a scientific hypothesis (like, for example, "creationism") that it deserves to be refuted by philosophically astute theologians invoking solid scientific evidence against it.

Furthermore, a myth only becomes socially inoperative in the world when there is no longer anyone left in the world who accepts its truth and thus lives by it. However, it is irrefutable that there are millions of Jews, Christians, and Muslims in the world who are still very much consciously and willingly living according to their respective primal myths or master narratives. Their active faith commitments cannot be either verified or falsified by any external criterion, because their commitment is not to a hypothesis they have devised to explain a phenomenon. Rather, their commitment is to a primal revelation, which itself is *the phenomenon*, that is, what has been shown (*phainomai* in Greek) or given to them *ab intio* before any attempt to explain it *post factum*.

Both Athens and Jerusalem have their foundational myths. Our task here is to show how those who reasoned about them interacted with one another.

In the biblical tradition, the foundational myth is constantly being told, interpreted, reinterpreted, and used to inform major practical judgments. "Remember the olden days; consider the years of past generations. Ask your father and he will tell you [*ve-yagedekha*]; your elders will speak to you" (Deuteronomy 32:7). Now this "telling" is called *haggadah* (or in Aramaic, *aggadah*), meaning "narration." The narration itself is the rabbinic way of doing metaphysics. Thus "the interpreters of the narratives [*haggadot*] say that if you want to recognize Who-spoke-and-the cosmos-came-to-be [i.e., God], learn *haggadah*, for from out of it you will recognize God and cleave to his ways."[127]

Plato, too, does his most profound metaphysical-cosmological speculation when he represents and elaborates on – but does not claim to have invented – an ancient creation myth.[128] And note how Plato reports how Socrates himself relates to myth. "One who is really a poet makes [*poiein*] myths, not discourses [*logous*]. But not even being a myth-speaker [*mythologikos*], I have [only] taken the myths of Aesop and have made them knowable [*ēpistamēn*]."[129] As such, there are myth-makers – who might be compared to biblical prophets (*nevi'im*); there are myth-speakers – who might be compared to rabbinic preachers (*darshanim*); and there are philosophers of myth (like Socrates) – who might be compared to Jewish and Christian theologians. The heuristic value of a myth depends on how well or how badly it informs ordinary human action in the world, whether that action be theoretical/scientific enquiry or practical/ethical deeds.[130]

The first lingering question is whether the philosophers or the theologians are allowed by their respective traditions only to interpret their traditionally transmitted myths and apply their interpretations to particular cases (whether practical or theoretical), or whether they may invoke the myths as illustrations of higher principles that ultimately transcend the myths themselves. To be sure, the classical Greek philosophers could be more selective in their invocation of myths (plural) since those came from a variety of sources, mostly oral, while the classical Jewish and Christian theologians were beholden to one canonical book: the Bible, which is believed to be one thoroughly consistent, seamless text.[131] Nevertheless, Jewish theologians at times did take considerable liberties in deciding which biblical texts to explicate and which to be silent about, even though they do not have the authority to reject the myth either totally or even partially.[132] The second lingering (and closely related) question is whether the philosophers or the theologians may only interpret their tradition's foundational myths, or whether they may ultimately take the myths to be more easily understood illustrations of higher principles that transcend the myths themselves. In other words, are the myths hypotheses or not?

Now, there are two kinds of hypothesis. The first kind is a tentative assumption or convention (*doxa* in Greek) that is useful for explaining data that would lack intelligibility without it, and over which it therefore has noetic power.[133] Nevertheless, the hypothesis can and should be replaced by another hypothesis having greater explanatory power.[134] The second kind of hypothesis is also a tentative assumption that functions as a springboard from which a philosopher can reason *up towards* ultimate, unsurpassable knowledge of the truth. The first kind of hypothesis functions as a premise from which one reasons deductively *down to* a conclusion.[135] Both kinds of hypothesis, though, are teleological in the sense they are means to an end. And, as is well known, means are always secondary to the ends they serve. Indeed, their very tentativeness and dispensability must be emphasized lest they be mistaken for ends themselves. However, foundational myths are not hypotheses, neither of the first kind nor of the second kind. Myths can only correct; they can never be corrected without losing their authority altogether. They are much more than hypotheses, even the second, more exalted kind of hypothesis.

Attempts to explain away myths themselves, however, often generate counter-myths to replace them, which are less believable, and have far less explanatory power, than the myths they are consciously designed to replace.[136] Perhaps attempts to explain away these revelatory events (whether Hellenic or Hebraic), though, are motivated by moral rather than epistemological concerns. By making a new counter-myth, myth-makers inevitably have their new myth make new, very different moral demands upon those who would accept the new myth. And the moral demands of the new myth are usually far less threatening to the myth-makers and their followers than the moral demands of the old myth from the cultural matrix they are displacing with a new one. It could be said that the new myth-makers are engaged in a radical attempt to break out of what they think are the stifling norms of their native culture, which is their own attempt to disown what was formerly their own.[137] Moreover, this is more effective than simple denial, since culture, like nature, abhors a vacuum. When something significant has been emptied out of a culture, something new inevitably comes in to replace it.

A made-up myth, however, is almost an oxymoron. That is because a made-up myth is a lie (*sheqer* in Hebrew), intended by its maker to deceive those gullible enough to believe it.[138] Since the old myths present themselves as revelations that are then recounted or transmitted through history by a tradition, it would seem that anybody who wants to present or represent an acceptable myth would have to claim either to have had a revelation, or to have fully accepted an ancestral revelation one has accepted, being convinced of its truth. Any myth that is presented (rather than re-presented) as *fiction* can hardly claim anybody's existential commitment. That is why myth-makers have to lie to their hearers, claiming to re-present what they have in fact made up.[139] Even the ancient idolaters, whom the Bible ridicules, did not themselves believe their idols to be "the work of human hands" (Psalms 115:4). Instead, they believed those idols to be ciphers of a higher divine reality, which they were copying, rather than being their own autonomous projections.[140]

Since these revelations are given to human persons who have the capacity for free choice, they can be either accepted or rejected (though not with impunity). Their being given does not necessarily entail their acceptance, because what is given is given in the form of a claim that is made upon its hearers, that is, in the form of a commandment. That acceptance or rejection is an existential choice, having immediate moral significance.[141] So, if I accept God's right to command me, I thereby have to reject anyone else's right to command me that in any way contradicts my prior existential choice to obey God unconditionally. Conversely, Pharaoh says to Moses, after God's commanding presence has been revealed in Egypt and represented by Moses to him: "Who is the Lord that I should heed [*eshm'a*] his voice ... I do not recognize [*lo yad'ati*] the Lord" (Exodus 5:2). In other words, Pharaoh does not deny the existence/presence of God in his own land. Considering the unusual events occurring there at that time, such denial would make little sense epistemologically when the situation there is hardly one of "business as usual." Pharaoh only denies God's moral authority in his land, which is God's right to make claims upon him (to let Israel go), in the land where Pharaoh, not the Lord (God of Israel), is the supreme authority. In this sense, Pharaoh's "atheism" is not epistemological; it is ethical. He can deny God's authority in his land, which Moses cannot refute with an argument. Instead, God has to reassert His presence there. Indeed, there is a modern ring to Pharaoh's denial. For in modernity, the most cogent denials of revelation have been made on ethical, not epistemological, grounds. What offends many moderns most about revelation is its inherent rejection of the moral autonomy of human persons, something consistently celebrated in modernity.[142]

The tactic of many modern atheists is to still make the dubious epistemological move of denying the very existence of these events of divine revelation, which are the stuff of myth. But can anybody assert that an event didn't occur in the world?[143] Some modern atheists, even more preposterously, presume that the existence/presence of an event is impossible. But "impossibility" is a logical category. It means that a self-contradictory assertion cannot be made about a real event, or as Wittgenstein pointed out, an illogical world could not be described, because description is only intelligible when it depicts its object logically.[144] And the most basic rule of logic is the principle of non-contradiction: *A* doesn't equal not-*A*. Nonsensical description is no description at all.

Since the assertion of revelatory events does not violate this most basic principle of logic, it cannot be said to be *impossible*; what can be said is only that these unusual events are extremely unlikely to have occurred; perhaps they are only accidents, or only highly improbable, a point that those who accept a revelation would readily agree with.

It is their very improbability that makes these events excellent occasions for revelation. That is because revelation can only break through to human recipients when they are overwhelmed, that is, when their ordinary world is so destabilized that they do not have categories under which to subsume the revelatory event and thus explain away its uniqueness as ordinary after all. Indeed, revelatory events overwhelm their recipients.[145] Conversely, if they were ordinary and familiar, they couldn't be revelatory. Even God had to catch Moses's full attention through the quite improbable event of "the burning bush that was not consumed" (Exodus 3:2) in order to reveal to him what was new and unanticipated: that God would redeem Israel from Egyptian slavery and bring them to Mount Sinai to receive the Torah, which was then still only in heaven.

These sublime revelations teach us that what is to be explained (*explicandum*) sometimes overcomes that which attempts to explain it (*explicans*) by anticipation. These sublime revelations transcend all our usual attempts to contain them in our usual categories, for these categories are only good for grasping ordinary, predictable experiences. Yet the content of these extraordinary experiences – their *what* or their *who* – is not permanently hidden or mute. Those who have ordinary experiences grasp or conceptualize its content, whereas those who have extraordinary, revelatory experiences are grasped by the content of the experience itself. That means that the content of revelatory experiences bespeaks a transcendent source that lies beyond the power of human language to grasp it and contain it. Human reason can only re-present it, and only partially at best.

Humans at best can only represent the content revealed to them (which is a good deal more than merely repeating it).[146] And that necessarily requires one to interpret the context (different from the original context) in which it is now being simultaneously proclaimed and applied. This is especially so when a new case or situation calls for a new interpretation and application of an old law or doctrine.[147] As such, in these normatively significant situations, revealed content speaks again as it were for the first time.[148]

Our usual categories only function as a priori conditions, which are the *sine qua non* of our acceptance of revelation. That is, they prevent us from accepting as divine revelation what is blatantly absurd or blatantly unjust. But these a priori categories do not explain the content of revelation; they only prepare us for it negatively (*via negativa*). On the other hand, the categories that are employed in the attempt to understand the positive content of revelation only come into play after, not before, the revelatory event itself, that is, they are a posteriori. This is especially so in the explication of the content of divine revelation that pertains to the direct God-human relationship.[149] What God wants from humans for Himself is something that could only come from revelation, hence the categories for understanding that aspect of revelation must come from the tradition that subsequently transmits it, even though that tradition is still formulated in ordinary human language.[150] However, that aspect of revelation that deals with what humans want from each other does not require new categories to understand it, since we are already familiar with these claims from our ordinary interhuman experience, hence the old categories suffice here.

Philosophical Hermeneutics

The impasse between theology and philosophy is not an impasse between "reason and revelation," as we have seen. Instead, the impasse seems to be between two substantial revelations about which their recipients (and their heirs) reasoned. There is the revelation of Nature, on the one hand, and the revelation of the Word of God, on the other hand. Both being epiphanies, these two revelations do not seem to be able to coexist one with the other. Sinai and Olympus cannot be considered parts of the same mountain range. That seems to be the impasse Tertullian and those like him were unable or unwilling to overcome.

Each of the two substantial revelations, that of Athens or that of Jerusalem, comes with its own method of explication. The question is whether these methods of explication are only analogous to one another, or whether they are essentially one method applied to two different types of data. Can one determine any commonality between these two types of data: the data of manifest nature that philosophy attempts to explain and the data of biblical revelation that theology attempts to explain? The answer to that question depends on how one sees the relation between Nature and the Word of God. Do they comprise two parallel worlds or do they comprise two aspects of the same world?

In more modern times, the philosopher who came to the Athens-Jerusalem impasse from the opposite side of a theologian like Tertullian was Baruch Spinoza. He assumed that anything like philosophy as a method of enquiry can only come from an affirmation of Nature. But, whereas Tertullian and those like him thought that the Word of God requires understanding as methodological enquiry, Spinoza thought that only Nature requires this kind of rigorous understanding.[151] The Word of God, for Spinoza, only requires obedience and the political *savoir-faire* to use it for the moral governance of a polity.[152] Politics is something philosophers cannot do, or when they do it they do it quite badly, with bad results for both themselves and their society.

Now, for Tertullian and those like him, there seems to be a hard choice between philosophical method and its object, Nature, and theological method and its object, the Word of God. But for Spinoza theology has no philosophical import, for its view of Nature is too unscientific to have any true epistemological value. Metaphysics and epistemology are the correlated methods of rigorous enquiry whose only worthy object is Nature. Accordingly, Spinoza attempted to end the dialectic between Athens and Jerusalem once and for all. Theology is now only needed to govern the obedient masses. It is concerned with what works well in the ephemeral world of politics. But theology is not to be concerned with what is true about infinite and eternal Nature; that is the proper concern of philosophy alone.

Many modern philosophers, however, soon decided that they could formulate a public morality that doesn't need theology at all. Some theologians, accepting their elimination from metaphysics and now from ethics/politics by philosophers, eventually decided that they could do an end run around issues of metaphysics and political morality altogether by simply concentrating on religious phenomena as inner experience (*Erlebnis* in German). They could thus avoid the question of what is actually being experienced (ontology), how it is known (epistemology), and even what ought to be done according to it (morality). These theologians were concerned only with how the subject of the experience that is assumed to have religious significance actually feels about it.[153]

Conversely, though, there has to be some substantive commonality between the philosophy of nature and a theology of the Word of God so that philosophers and theologians might truly take each other seriously because of their common concern with truth. And they can only do that when both are addressing metaphysical, epistemological, and ethical-political questions. That means neither philosophers nor theologians should presume to have a monopoly on these questions. For when that happens, when the others are not taken seriously when thinking of these ultimate questions, these others are then often relegated to a subservient position they cannot in good faith accept for themselves. Or the others are simply denied any place at all, even in intellectual discussions of more mundane moral and political questions (where Spinoza, especially, seemed to be willing to give theology a place, however small, at the table). In modernity, this is what philosophers have often done to theologians. Sadly enough, theologians have often been willing to let theology be demoted to the kind of psychological subjectivism that only speaks of feelings that needn't be thought of as intending any external reality, let alone any higher reality, to which truth is adequate. Yet not only does this approach have much too little correspondence with Jewish and Christian traditions to be considered authentic Jewish or Christian theology, it also opens up theology to the judgment of the psychologists. For if the practices and doctrines the religions rooted in biblical revelation are represented and argued for as being "healthy," that is, of psychological value, what happens when more and more psychologists argue they are "unhealthy"? For example, what retort do theologians have when feelings of "self-worth" rather than feelings of "guilt" are taken to be more appropriate in a culture where persons are only answerable to themselves for what they have or have not done with their lives?

The same thing has happened when theologians tried to justify their metaphysical, epistemological, and ethical-political positions by the criteria of somebody else's ontology, epistemology, or ethics. When this happens, it is now more likely to be the theologians' obsequiousness before the philosophers than that of the philosophers before the theologians. So, the philosophers have often said that the theologians' talk of *what* is real (ontology) is too imaginative when compared to theirs, and theologians' talk of knowledge is too speculative when compared to the epistemology of the philosophers. And philosophers, especially since the Enlightenment, have often said that theologians' talk of *what is to be done* (morality) is basically hierarchical, whereas an ethic of egalitarian autonomy is more appropriate in a democratic society. Needless to say, self-respecting theologians need to counter these charges, yet they need not and ought not engage in the same type of elimination of the philosophers that many of the philosophers have done to them.

Therefore, we need to locate common concerns of philosophy and theology on metaphysical, epistemological, and ethical questions. Where are they different and where are they the same? And how can they speak to one another? If all their positions are the same, then the one who expresses a position most persuasively will prevail, and the other will sink further and further into obscurity. And if all their positions are totally different, then it could be concluded that the two worldviews occupy two totally different worlds. But the fact is that both philosophy and theology, even when most isolated from one another, still occupy the same discursive world in their respective dealings with basic metaphysical, epistemological, and ethical questions. Hence they cannot ignore one another. This is especially so today when, in secular democracies, neither philosophers nor theologians control public discourse. Both being intellectual "outsiders," they have more in common than ever before.

Here the interrelation of philosophy and theology will be examined from the perspective of theology, specifically Jewish theology, since that is the only place in the world from which I can see other places in the world with my own eyes. In subsequent chapters, we shall explore how some Jewish theologians have engaged philosophy in a way that has tried to be neither obsequious nor triumphal. Instead, this effort is for the sake of truth, which is to be accepted from whoever has spoken it intelligently and in good faith.[154]

Chapter Two

God, Humans, and Nature

The Engagement of Philosophy and Theology

In the last chapter, we discussed what is actually involved in the original engagement of philosophy and theology. To a large extent, that meant identifying "classical philosophy," that is, the general thinking of Plato, Aristotle, and the Stoics (despite their many specific differences), as "Athens." And it meant, to a large extent, identifying "classical theology," that is, the general thinking of the ancient Rabbis (despite their many specific differences) and of the Church Fathers (despite their many specific differences) as "Jerusalem." It is important to know who the parties are in the ongoing engagement of philosophy and theology and what their basic concerns have been. It is also important to locate the identical issues that have continually engaged both philosophers and theologians. What do philosophers and theologians hold in common on these key issues and what divides them from each other? Without this clarity about *who* the related parties are and *what* they have been engaged with, we become confused in our understanding of the history of this engagement. The absence of this clarity also complicates our attempts to enter into their conversation, to deal here and now with the issues that originally engaged theologians and philosophers, thus impeding our carrying the conversation forward into the future.

Let us now see how the commonalities and the differences between theology and philosophy play out in the four different relational spheres of perennial human concern, about which both philosophers and theologians have thought deeply. That is so when both philosophers and theologians take these spheres of relationality to be worthy of their serious and sustained attention. Within each of these spheres, metaphysical, epistemological, and ethical questions are ubiquitous. So, we need to see the ancient matrix of these theological and philosophical concerns in order to better understand what some mediaeval and modern theologians have done with what preceded them in history.

These spheres of relationality are: (1) the relation of God and humans; (2) the relation of God and nature; (3) interhuman relations; and (4) the relation of humans and nature. In this chapter, we shall examine the first two spheres: how God is related to humans, and how God is related to nature. In the next chapter, we shall examine the last two spheres: how humans are interrelated, and how humans are related to nature.

The Relation of God and Humans

God's relation to us is the only one of God's relations that we humans directly experience; hence we should look at it first.

In both Athens and Jerusalem, the relation of God and humans is essentially hierarchal: God is greater than humans. God is therefore to be obeyed or followed by humans. And, in the case of especially insightful humans, God commands imitation of what God does. In no way, though, is God ever the equal of humans or are humans ever the equal of God. In fact, humans are basically equal to one another only because all humans are altogether unequal before God. As the prophet Isaiah reported God saying: "To whom could you compare Me; with whom could you equate [*ve-tashvu*] Me; to whom could you liken Me so that we would be comparable [*ve-nidmeh*]?!" (Isaiah 46:5). That most fundamental inequality could be called "vertical." Equality among humans themselves could be called "horizontal." As the prophet Malachi put it: "Have we not all one father; has not one God created us all?!" (Malachi 2:10). This was what Spinoza viewed as the chief political virtue of the ancient Hebrew state: God is infinitely greater than humans,

> and that inequality is shared by all humans equally. Also, in that optimal society no human member has any more access to the divine Sovereign than has any other human member.[1]

Similarly, Socrates tells the Athenians, "I shall obey [*peisomai*] the god rather than you ... I shall not stop philosophizing ... this is what the god commands [*keleuei*] me to do ... no greater good can there be in the city than my service [*hypēresian*] to the god."[2] Now, what the god orders Socrates to do is to interrogate pretentious fellow humans who think they have the positive wisdom only the gods have. By so doing, Socrates imitates what the god does with him, which is "turning me away from something I am about to do."[3] The political significance of Socrates's *imitatio Dei* comes out when he insists that his discursive activity is "fighting for justice."[4] That is, "examining myself and others" is what Socrates's god as his philosophical model does, and it is what Socrates has to imitate in his dealings with his fellow Athenians, thus stimulating them to do likewise.[5] Now "fighting [*machoumenon*] for justice" is very much like the kind of interrogative back and forth one sees in trials. It is what Socrates himself practised both before and after his own trial.[6] In fact, it could be said that philosophical dialectic is what is being done in the dialogue, that is, "the word [*logos*] between [*dia*]" philosophers themselves seeking wisdom in trial-like engagements.

Regarding the divine-human relationship, the difference between Athens and Jerusalem is about the character of the deity who is commanding humans, and who is eliciting their imitation. The difference here is ontological, ethical, and epistemological. By "ontological" I mean the way God exists as conceived in the two respective traditions. By "ethical" I mean the acts God so conceived elicits from humans. By "epistemological" I mean the way God so conceived is known by humans.

In Athens, the command of the gods is for the sake of human contemplation of ultimate divine reality, or it is for the sake of the stable order of the polis that recognizes the authority of the commanding god. Humans are to imitate the gods in their contemplation of the Divine or "godliness" (*to theion*) in this world. That is what the gods themselves have been doing from all eternity. However, the gods who do command concrete human action in the polis are different from and inferior to the gods of the heavens whom philosophers are supposed to imitate. Now, for ordinary citizens of the polis, these lower gods prescribe or authorize the prescription of political order as an end in itself. For these ordinary people, that is the extent of the divine-human relationship. But philosophers, for whom membership in the polis is not an end in itself, only need this public order insofar as they need the leisure (both physical and emotional) it gives them to pursue true divine wisdom privately.[7] Philosophers need this leisure to engage in pure contemplation of the Divine, although for prudential political reasons, they might have to engage in traditional forms of devotion to these civic gods, which they do in good faith.[8] But their souls are truly engaged with very different gods.

In Jerusalem, conversely, there is only one God, and this God is concerned with both the celestial realm beyond the human world and the terrestrial world where humankind dwells.[9] Nevertheless, the human relationship with God cannot be achieved by humans ascending into heaven away from the earth. Instead, that relationship with God occurs because of God's descent into the human world, yet without

God's abandonment of the heavenly world beyond the earthly reach of humans. Only because God has come down from His heights to meet us humans on earth could Moses ascend to heaven thereafter to receive from God the rest of God's Torah meant for earthly humans. "The Lord descended on Mount Sinai at the top of the mountain, then the Lord called Moses to the top of the mountain, and Moses ascended [thereto]" (Exodus 19:20).[10]

In Jerusalem, God is not the inert, unchanging object of contemplation. Instead, He is the God who actively created the universe, who is actively involved with His creation, and whose transitive activity is to be the model for the activity of the humans to whom it has been revealed.[11] Even contemplation of God can only be thought of as what God *does* in relation to humans in the world, which humans can experience and imitate in their own actions in the world. "You can only see My back [*et ahaorai*]; but My face [*u-fanai*] cannot be seen" (Exodus 33:23). Outside of that Creator-creature relationship in this world as experienced by humans, "no human [*adam*] can see Me and live" (Exodus 33:20). As Maimonides taught, humans can only positively speak of what God does.[12] That is, we can only know what God does in relation to us when we are shown by God how God does it for us. Being shown *how* God does this enables us to do likewise in our relations with fellow humans. Nevertheless, humans cannot know what God is, that is, what God does by Himself. Humans cannot know what God does in His own inner life, what God does totally apart from God's external relations with creation.

So far, we have been analysing the ontological difference between God in Athens and God in Jerusalem. The difference is between the God who engages in mutual relations with non-divine humans and the Divine Being (*to theion*) with whom all relations are one way, that is, from inferior subjects seeking *the* superior Object. We now need to consider the different modes of *actively* relating to God in Athens and to God in Jerusalem. That is the ethical difference between them.

In Athens, the ethic of conscious relation to God as Divine Being is essentially aesthetic. God is to be related to as "the Good-and-the-Beautiful" (*kaloskagathos*).[13] Though spectators of any beautiful object should be prepared to properly appreciate the beauty they are looking at and enjoy its light, they should not expect that beautiful object to look back at them, much less talk to them, let alone talk with them.[14] Nevertheless, these spectators are not emotionally indifferent to what they are viewing, as they are attracted to the beauty of that object, which thus becomes the object of their desire, even though it does not desire them.

In Jerusalem, conversely, the ethic of consciously relating to God is essentially practical. God is especially *responsible* for the humans God has created in His image. That responsibility is expressed in commandments to His human creatures by which humans can properly interact with God and with each other, and can relate to those who are neither human nor divine (i.e., to nature). Because of this exercise of divine responsibility, humans are *answerable* to God for how well or badly they have responded to what God has commanded them to do in the world.[15] Indeed, responsibility and answerability lie at the heart of practical ethics. Moreover, here humans desire the God who first desires them. That desire is practically expressed in God's requesting His people to engage in acts of covenantal intimacy with God, that is, "to walk humbly with [*im*] your God" (Micah 6:5). In response, that desire is expressed by humans wanting to practise these acts of covenantal intimacy with God. "Act according to Your kindness with Your servant by teaching me your statutes ... therefore, do I love [*ahavti*] Your commandments" (Psalms 119:124, 127).

In Athens, however, the celestial gods are not *the* Creator, hence they cannot be held responsible for a world these gods did not make; and humans, not being the creatures of these gods, are not answerable to them either. These gods wouldn't pose any question to us as to how we have acted in the world, as they are surely uninterested in anything we humans might have to say about what we have done in the world, even if done for their sake. So, for Plato, humans are answerable to the terrestrial gods, especially to the gods of Athens, who have made them in the sense of enabling their parents to marry, conceive, and bear them, as well as nurturing them as citizens having definite civic rights and duties. This comes out when Plato reports that his beloved teacher Socrates refused to commit suicide, even though Socrates seems to believe that his soul will be better off in the eternal divine realm. Why? It is because "a man ought not [*mē ... dein*] kill himself until the god sends some necessity [*anangkēn tina*] like the necessity that now overtakes [*parousan*] us."[16] And though Socrates may not actively flee the earthly city of Athens by killing himself, he may still passively accept the death sentence decreed by the Athenian court by not escaping (as he could easily have done). Thus Socrates accepts the Athenian court's inevitable (i.e., "necessary") death sentence as being what the Athenian god had intended all along. After all, Socrates was convicted under a legal system that, according to Athenian tradition, was itself founded by gods, and is thus answerable to these gods.[17] So it seems, these are the gods whom Socrates obeys by not flouting the death sentence delivered by the court so authorized by these terrestrial gods.[18]

It might even be said that Socrates is handed over by a lower god to higher gods. Yet Socrates is not answerable to the higher gods because, unlike the lower gods, they did not make him, hence they are not responsible for him or for anybody else like him. Whatever obligation Socrates thinks he has in relation to these higher gods is not an obligation that came from them, but rather he himself is obliged to prepare himself in this embodied life for his everlasting association with these celestial gods after his bodily death. This is not because Socrates is beholden to those higher gods for anything they have done for him, because they have done nothing for him other than, perhaps, not hiding their attractiveness from him and thus beckoning him and philosophers like him to imitate them, and to join them once those individuals finally depart this world. Yet there is no indication that these gods are at all attracted to Socrates or to any other mortal.

Aristotle goes further, working out a theory that God/Divinity as Nature's zenith is interested in no one but himself. This Highest Being is supremely attractive to all metaphysically attuned intellects, but is not attracted to anyone or anything outside himself.[19] This God is the highest good, the *summum bonum*.[20] As such, justice, as the standard for all interpersonal relationships, does not pertain at all to this God, who has no interest in any realm in which justice would be a concern. Here the key principle in philosophic ethics is *goodness*. Humans are to *do* what is *good* per se in imitation of God who *is good* per se. At the highest level here, ethics is the practical corollary in our world of the aesthetic experience of the goodness or beauty of the heavenly God, that is, *what* God *is* apart from our world.

Conversely, justice (*mishpat*) is the key principle in biblical ethics. It is the ultimate standard for all interpersonal relationships, among humans themselves and even between humans and God. And at the heart of practical ethics are the issues of responsibility and answerability. Now, first and foremost, responsibility is the exercise of justice by the Creator for His creatures, while answerability is the obligation of intelligent and volitional creatures to submit themselves to God's judgment. All this is of cosmic significance. "Listen to me you pursuers of justice [*tsedeq*], you seekers of the Lord ... for the Torah goes forth from Me, and with My judgment [*u-mishpati*] I enlighten the peoples" (Isaiah 51:4). Here the prime consideration is justice. Ethics is the practical corollary of the human experience of God's cosmic justice revealed to humans, that is, *how* God *acts* in our world and beyond it.

Now, the essentially aesthetic term "good" (*tov*), when stated in a moral context in the Bible, is used metaphorically. We are not commanded to do what we have been commanded to do because it is good or beautiful (*kaloskagathos* in Greek). We are not answerable to Plato's *Goodness* or to *Beauty* since "they do" nothing for us. They are not responsible for us. Instead, we are to do what we have been commanded to do because it comports with the justice by which God coherently and responsibly created humans. That is how and why God gives us the commandments to live by, and by which God judges us. When we do what we have been commanded to do *correctly* (i.e., "rightly"), our act comports with God's justice (*Recht* in German). It is *correct*. That is the reason we are commanded to "rightly [*be-tsedeq*] judge your neighbour" (Leviticus 19:15). To say that some activity is "good" doesn't mean that it ought to be done because it commands itself to be done, as it were.[21] Instead, we declare some act or some thing to be "good" because it pleases the person *who* did it or who made it, and because it pleases the person for *whom* the act was done or for *whom* the thing was made. Hence, what is "good" is what is *beneficial*, to the object as well as the subject of the act. Thus we are commanded to "do [*aseh*] good" (Psalms 37:27). And *beneficence* is to be done for the sake of its effects, not that "*the* good" or "goods" (seemingly self-justified acts) are to be done irrespective of their effects or consequences.[22]

Indeed, creation itself is not good per se. It is good because God declared it (Genesis 1:31) to be "very good" (*tov me'od*), that is, creation is pleasing to God who made it the way He did; and it is also pleasing to the persons who enjoy the world's goodness (*tov*) or pleasantness (*na'im*) as a gift from its Maker.[23] As such, when enjoying this gift, one is first obligated to thank God for it.[24] This pleasure, then, is like that of artists taking pleasure in their own work, plus it is like spectators being pleased with what seems to have been made for them. Yet this aesthetic pleasure only accompanies one's deeper appreciation of what has been correctly made or done.

As for God, what *is* correct conforms to what God has *made* to be correct. As for humans, what they *do* correctly is what conforms to what God has made to be correct. For God, the creation of justice as correctness or rectitude is autonomous; but for humans, their implementation of divine justice is heteronomous. Hence humans only have the free choice to act correctly or incorrectly (i.e., justly or unjustly), but not the freedom of will to create or not create justice altogether.

One might say that the pleasure, designated as *good,* is what motivates an artist. Could or would anyone engage in sustained work if he or she didn't get pleasure from it and what it produces? Artists are surely motivated to please those who appreciate their work; and spectators are also motivated to enjoy the art they partake of. Nevertheless, the reason authentic artists make and show their work is to reveal its truth artistically. (That is what distinguishes authentic artists from entertainers or decorators.) Surely, these true artists are saying to those who partake of their art much more than: "Enjoy yourself!" What they are truly saying is: "See or listen to what is being revealed through my work to you, and thus be enlightened by it!" Moreover, the reason the true aesthete partakes of authentic art (as distinguished from mere entertainment or decoration) is to accept this truth aesthetically. In fact, justice can be considered to be truth in action, as when Scripture says: "Judge true judgment" (*mishpat emet*) (Zechariah 7:9). And truth can be considered to be justice in what has been made, as in God's "just ordinances" (*mishpatim tsaddiqim*) (Deuteronomy 4:8), which are those commandments of God whose true reasons are more immediately evident.[25] To be sure, concern (*Sorge* in German) with the enjoyment of goodness/beauty is important and not to be neglected.[26] Yet it is still secondary to concern with justice as practical truth.[27] So, for example, if a person vowed not to have any pleasure from somebody else, that person is still obligated to benefit the other person if the latter has a right to that person's beneficence. That is because it is that person's duty to do what is justly commanded in the Torah.[28]

It seems God made a world that humans can appreciate as good and pleasant because God takes responsibility for His creation, especially for the welfare of the human creatures whom God has created in His image, that is, those creatures with whom God can be related mutually and reciprocally. As such, humans are entitled to be treated well by God in the world, not because of their own deserts, but rather because God has chosen to be responsible for us. Enabling beneficence for us in the world is God's exercise of His self-chosen responsibility. We humans, in turn, are thus answerable or obliged to thank God directly for God's exercise of His responsibility for us, that is, when we experience what is good or beneficial for ourselves in the world.

Nevertheless, that thanksgiving cannot be asked of us when we experience or suffer what is bad (*ra*) in the world.[29] Under these circumstances, we are only required to acknowledge what appears to us to be God's judgment or condemnation.[30] To be sure, that judgment must be regarded as ultimately beneficial, even if not immediately so.[31] After all, we are commanded to "love the Lord your God with all your heart" (Deuteronomy 6:5). But how could we love a God who is either indifferent to our suffering or malevolently makes us suffer what is bad as an end in itself? Wouldn't such a view of God's indifference or malevolence lead us to turn our love into hate?[32] Wouldn't such malevolent irresponsibility ultimately be injustice? So, in the face of considerable worldly evidence to the contrary, we still cannot lose our ability to love and trust God nonetheless. "Though He slay me, yet will I trust [*ayahel*] Him" (Job 13:15). For those already in a relationship with God, the only alternative to that difficult trust is, as Job's wife advised, "to curse God and die" (Job 2:8).[33] Blasphemy or cursing God is anger at God that turns into murderous hate.[34] One can only hate whom he or she has previously loved, and whose love was experienced as good or benevolent.[35] As the Psalmist said: "The nearness of God is good for me [*tov li*]" (Psalms 73:28). But a person cannot be indifferent to or assume indifference on the part of a God whom that person once loved or at least desired. Thus the anger of so many atheists cannot be hate of one who never existed, for a non-existent person – as distinct from a dead person – cannot be the object of either love or hate. Rather, this hate is directed against a God who many if not most atheists feel hates them and who has forever abandoned them.

God's Mutability in Relation to Humans

Now, if God is engaged in a mutual, practical relationship with humans who have enough freedom to change their actions in relation to God, then it would seem that the God in whose image humans are created has the freedom to change His actions in relation to us all the more so. An unchanging God, though, could not engage in any such *mutual* relationship with beings who have been given the capacity for free choice. Such an unchanging God is the God of the classical philosophers. For them, a God who changes would be a "moving target" rather than the eternal object who is always there. A God who was constantly changing would also be a God with whom no one could engage in a sustained mutual relationship. For persons (and God in the Bible is the subject of personal pronouns) with whom one is related today might well insist they are not the persons with whom one was related yesterday, nor are they the persons with whom one will be related tomorrow. Yet how could we be answerable to such a chameleon for anything we have done? And how could one expect such a chameleon to be questioned about His responsibility for anything He has done?

Nevertheless, sometimes the Bible teaches that God does not change and at other times it teaches that God does change. Since our theology requires us to look upon all contradictions in the divinely revealed Word as apparent, not real, we need to explain why in one situation God does not change, while in another situation God does change. We must discern the difference between these two modes of divine relationality, immutability and mutability, and how they do not function at cross purposes. (There will be more discussion of divine mutability in the next section, "The Relation of God and Nature.")

God does not change the rules by which the life of His human creatures is to be lived any more than God changes the basic structures of the universe wherein that life is to be lived. "As long as the earth is there, there will be planting-time and harvest-time, cold and heat, summer and winter; they shall not cease" (Genesis 9:1–7). About these divine commandments it is said: "Everlasting paths [*halikhot olam*] are His" (Habakkuk 2:6). A rabbinic source interprets that to mean God's laws (*halakhot*) are forever valid.[36] That is not because these laws themselves are eternal and thus unchangeable in principle. Indeed, how could a law as a freely chosen prescription be eternal? Aren't laws, whether divinely or humanly made, created by the free choice the lawgiver made at a certain time? Lawgiving is an inherently temporal activity, and time is the arena of change. Time is always moving. But if God Himself changed at a particular time from being a potential lawgiver to become an actual lawgiver, why then can't God change His mind after the law has been given by changing it, just as God changed His mind in order to then make the law initially?

However, it is not that God can't change His law; rather, God chooses not to change His law, because God has promised not to do so. "He remembers forever His covenant ... which He made with Abraham, and His promise [*u-shevu'ato*] to Isaac. He made it a law [*hoq*] for Jacob; to Israel an everlasting covenant [*brit olam*]" (Psalms 105:8–10). Indeed, were God to break that promise, God would thereby lose His moral authority over the very humans to whom He made the promise.[37] If God is a liar who contradicts His own freely chosen commitments, how could God be imitated by any morally responsible person? How could one be answerable to a God who is not answerable to Himself, that is, who doesn't keep His own promises? Furthermore, it is not that God's action must correspond to some greater criterion than Godself, for that would make God less than God Almighty. Instead, God's action – here God's lawgiving action – needs to be coherent, that is, forever consistent, in order to be intelligible, let alone morally inspiring, to those whom God wants to intelligently and willingly keep His commandments.

God does change, however, insofar as He retains the freedom to spontaneously react to human observance or violation of these commandments, and in ways humans couldn't possibly understand. In the human administration of these laws, to be sure, whether that be enforcing the commandment or responding to violations of the commandment, strict proportionate judgment is called for. So, when it comes to human enforcement of the law, "we are not to be merciful in law [*ein merahamim ba-din*]," as one of the ancient Rabbis put it.[38] Or, "let justice [*ha-din*] pierce the mountain," that is, justice must be done without any detours, without compromise.[39] So, also, when it comes to a proper human response to violation of the law: "Those who shed human blood, by humans shall their blood be shed" (Genesis 9:6). In both cases, this is what the ancient Rabbis called "measure for measure" (*middah ke-neged middah*).[40] That is the very criterion of justice in this world, and it is supposed to reflect God's cosmic justice.

Nevertheless, even here the exercise of judicial discretion is at times considered to be a judicial right, perhaps in imitation of the divine Lawgiver, with whom the true human judge is, as the Talmud puts it, "God's partner."[41] But because of His ability to know what humans cannot possibly know, God's discretion in judgment is much greater than that of fallible human judges. Inasmuch as the full results of human acts are only known by God, only God can change those results.[42] This is why King David, after acknowledging his sin, is reported to have said: "Let us fall in the hand of the Lord, for his mercies are manifold, but into the hand of humans [*adam*] let me not fall" (II Samuel 24:14). God says, "I shall be gracious with whom I shall be gracious; and I shall have compassion [*ve-rihamti*] with whom I shall have compassion" (Exodus 33:19).[43]

The apparent antinomy between divine mutability and divine immutability can be seen when we compare two different treatments of divine promises (*shevu'ot*) in the Talmud. In one place it is stated that God changed His mind: first promising to totally punish Israel because of their sinful violation of the covenant, and then deciding not to do so.[44] Elsewhere it is stated that God does not change His mind about the perpetual, promised covenant with His people Israel by annulling it (*bitul*).[45] Already in the Bible, God's covenant with Israel is even less mutable than God's covenant made with the earth and all its inhabitants after the Flood, never to destroy it again.[46] Nevertheless, both God's change of mind and God's non-change of mind are for the sake of the covenant itself. In fact, the covenant can only survive perpetually if neither it nor its human members are destroyed. That is why, for the sake of the covenant, God should not carry through with His voluntary promise to totally punish His people, which thus becomes more of a threat of what might happen, but not what will necessarily happen.[47]

Furthermore, although the covenant and the Torah as its constitution do not change, that does not mean that the covenantal Torah is not itself the product of an ontological change. After all, it is the product of God's chosen transition from primordial, transitive inactivity to post-mordial creative activity in the temporally constituted world. And God's enabling Israel to remain in the covenant, despite their continued defiance of its norms, is God's changing from the execution of strict justice [*middat ha-din*], commensurate with the unchanging commandments of the Torah, to mercifully [*middat rahamim*] waiving the deadly consequences of Israel's violation of the covenantal norms for the sake of covenantal reconciliation.[48] All of this is God's temporal response to acts performed by humans in time. This distinction between changeability and unchangeability, or mutability and immutability, has profound implications ontologically, epistemologically, and ethically.

The Relation of God and Nature

In both classical philosophy and biblical theology, God's relation to nature is only of interest to humans insofar as that relation somehow or other pertains to how humans are to be related to God, to nature, or to themselves. But "nature" has a different ontological status in classical philosophy than it does in biblical theology.

In the classical philosophical conception, Nature itself has its own hierarchy of ends (*telē*), whose superlative point, that is, its Supreme Good, stands on the insurmountable top of the cosmos. This End is divine; there is nothing greater or that could be greater.[49] Cogent affirmation of such a terminal cosmic hierarchy presupposes an essentially finite universe.[50] An infinite or unlimited universe couldn't have a *telos*, because even before the term *telos* was taken to denote a purpose or goal, it denoted a limit (*peras*).[51] Moreover, it is important to bear in mind that, for the classical philosophers, a finite universe is not an inferior universe (as in the pejorative connotation of "finite" today). For that would be the case only if the finite universe or cosmos were limited by something greater and more intelligent than itself. But the finite cosmos envisioned by the classical philosophers is taken to be inherently limited rather than being limited by something greater and more intelligent than it standing outside of it.[52] For the classical philosophers, what is outside of the finite, inherently limited cosmos is formless, unintelligible, infinite chaos.[53]

Now, in the philosophical conception of Nature, especially as explicated by Aristotle, even the terrestrial realm of plants and animals is teleologically oriented.[54] Anything living, that is, plants and especially animals, strives to improve and not just survive. As a biologist, Aristotle wrote a number of works dealing with the biosphere and its inherent teleology. Nevertheless, although humans are teleologically oriented terrestrial beings, unlike plants and animals humans do know the ends they seek, ends that they strive to instantiate in the world consciously and willingly. As such, humans are to look to the celestial bodies above them as models. Unlike the terrestrial bodies beneath them on earth, these bodies are not only intelligible, they are intelligent; in fact, they are divine.[55] Human origins (*archē*) might be terrestrial, but the truly human goal is to be celestial. These human origins are in terrestrial nature or the biosphere even if their end is in the summit of the heavens.

Being superior intelligences, and thus closer to the supremely intelligent God than humans are, these gods indicate by their intelligent activity itself that human teleological striving is not just a human projection onto the cosmos of something that was not there beforehand. Instead, it is assumed that the activity of the celestial beings is *the* cosmic precedent for human teleological striving. The divine *telos*, to whom the higher celestial intelligences are so close, is eternal reality itself, not a humanly projected ideal to be realized in the future. The essential task of humans is to discover how they can properly fit into this natural teleological hierarchy. Therefore, the God humans seek to draw close to is more closely related to intelligences higher than humans in this cosmic hierarchy. As such, the human relation to God is mediated by God's relation to those closest to God in Nature.

In the classical philosophical conception of Nature, an end (*telos*) is already there in the world *beforehand*, and is now present *before* the subjects seeking it. It is at the apex of their horizon. Being greater than the subject in its attractive wisdom makes the end the object to whom the subject's intellect (when properly educated) is irresistibly attracted. Such an object/end can only get its due attention if it is more intelligible and more intelligent than the subject seeking to know it and imitate it. Imitation is the highest form of such adulation. The Stoics designated this action to be "according to Nature" (*kata physin*).[56] For humans, living according to nature is living according to their intellectual nature that seeks the Divine, and which attempts to imitate those higher beings who have always been in close contact with the Divine. Therefore, how Nature is related to God is the medium through which humans are related to God. But God is not responsible for Nature any more than God is responsible for humans; and Nature is not answerable to God any more than humans are answerable to God (as we have seen in the previous section).

The cosmos itself is not answerable to anyone and no one is responsible for it. The cosmos (certainly for Aristotle) is neither made nor is it a maker. Not being a person, *it* couldn't be answerable to some other person above it, nor could it be responsible for anything beneath it. Even Plato's divine Artificer (*dēmiourgos*), who does form the cosmos, does not seem to be responsible for his creation. For responsibility is the exercise or care *for* what one has made. And care means personally responding to or changing for the needs of what one has made. It is not delegating or turning over to a custodian care for what one has made, which could be taken to be abandonment (however well intentioned). Thus Plato has his god turn the cosmos he has made over to subordinate gods or causes.[57] The Artificer's concern with his creation is only *ab initio;* but he has no concern with it *post factum.* The only concern of the Artificer is how well his creation conforms to the primordial paradigm he himself is subordinate to. So, it would seem, Plato's Artificer-god is answerable to himself in the sense of asking himself just how well his formation of the cosmos comported with the eternal paradigm he looked to as his creative model.[58] Yet this Artificer-god is not responsible any longer for what he has made.

The ontological difference between Athens and Jerusalem on the question of nature is that in the Hebraic tradition, God's superiority to both the human and the non-human world is pure transcendence. God is the Creator of the universe "out of nothing" (*ex nihilo*), which among other things means that the creation of everything and everybody, that is, the universe (comprising the human world and the non-human world) is the result or product of God's totally free, truly autonomous will.[59] For God, there are no preconditions. God is beholden to nothing outside Himself, because prior to the event of creation there was nothing but God. God could have chosen not to create a universe and still remain in His total self-sufficiency.[60] The universe itself, though, had no such choice. The universe is necessarily dependent upon God for its being, while God is not necessarily dependent on the created universe for anything. The universe's contingency upon God is not like a conclusion in a logical proposition that is contingent on its premise. A premise had no choice to be anything other than what it is. The conclusion necessarily emerges from what the premise *asserts* rather than from what the author of the premise *wills.* Therefore, God's relation to nature is ontological rather than logical.[61] God doesn't have to be the ground of the universe, because the universe's very existence is itself not necessary. Hence the ontological contingency of the universe is more radical than the logical dependence of a conclusion on its premise. God is not correlated with the universe. God is still God even had His autonomously initiated creation never occurred.

God truly transcends the universe insofar as God has a life of His own totally apart from the created universe. Yet God is continually concerned with universal creation and promises not to be indifferent to what happens here or to what is done here. God does not irresponsibly let the universe, as it were, slip out of His hand, that is, to have a life of its own apart from God. Indeed, were God indifferent to the created universe, it would be perfectly rational to view the universe as independent and self-sufficient. However, humans can only appreciate that divine concern for the universe when they experience God's concern for them on earth. "For the eyes of the Lord roam throughout the earth, to strengthen those who are with Him in their heart" (II Chronicles 16:9). That divine concern for the created universe in general, and for the human world particularly, is not inferred from ordinary experience; instead, humans have learned it through an extraordinary or miraculous experience narrated by God Himself (as at Mount Sinai), or by a prophet speaking in God's name.

Nature and Its Miraculous Exceptions

In the biblical view of reality, God and humans can manipulate the natural background of their relationship so that nature does not interfere in the directness of that relationship by making it subject to some predetermined, immutable order. The "natural order" (called *sidrei ber'esheet* or "orders of creation" in rabbinic parlance) is, as Hume (closer to the biblical view of nature than he was likely aware of) said, "customary" (*minhago shel olam* in rabbinic parlance) rather than "necessary."[62] That is, external nature is not ordered so tightly by a causation so invariable that we can eliminate as illusory any radical, unexpected event altogether. This customary order we call "nature" is the finite realm of predictable probabilities, best formulated by statistical ratios rather than by unilateral causal propositions.[63] Nevertheless, there is still an infinite range of possibilities beyond the ability of any mere mortal to predict before they occur and are experienced as ordinary events by humans. As such, there is more to reality than what can be framed by the parameters of our human experience and the categories we devise to describe it. These remote ontological possibilities are what God realizes in miracles (*nissim*).

How does nature, though, "allow" (as it were) miracles to occur in its midst, within its overall parameters? And how is the extraordinary character of miracles only recognizable against a backdrop of nature? Answering these questions requires a theological understanding of nature, what could even be called "natural theology" in the sense that theology includes nature within an ultimate ontological context, which is altogether different from theology dictating what our scientific understanding of nature ought to be.[64]

The term for "nature" in Hebrew, *tev'a*, did not come into Jewish nomenclature until early mediaeval Jewish thinkers began to engage Greek science and philosophy through Arabic translations of some of the works of Plato and Aristotle (plus the work of some of the

Neoplatonists). The Greek word for "nature," *physis*, became the Arabic word *al-tabi'a*, of which the Hebrew *tev'a* is a literal translation. Because of this borrowing, some scholars have questioned whether "nature" can name an authentic Hebraic concept.[65] However, the meaning of this term would resonate with Jews nurtured by the rabbinic texts inasmuch as the verb *hitbi'a*, from which the noun *tev'a* is derived, means to "impress" or "stamp" as, for example, one "mints" or "stamps" a coin (*matbe'a* or "what is stamped" in Hebrew).[66] Nature's structure or order is not so permanently inherent in it that it could not be changed. Instead, that structure has been stamped on to it by its Creator at the time of creation, but with enough flexibility in it to allow for alterations to be subsequently made, especially in the interest of the divine-human relationship. This original order, rather than subsequent ad hoc alterations, is what humans can generally describe as "nature." (*Cosmos* is the name the Greeks gave this natural, structured, intelligible universe.)[67] It alone is usually predictable in advance. Nevertheless, there is more to this universal reality than the human conceptualization of nature could ever explain. In biblical theology, cosmic reality contains nature that is manifest to our human minds and, as such, the created universe has a considerable surplus over humanly conceived nature. That larger created reality is not locked into the order we can perceive or even conceive, that is, conceptually grasp.[68]

Not only are there regular events that are part of processes already operating in the cosmos that our finite minds cannot predict and comprehend, but there are also events in the cosmos created *de novo* (and thus not part of processes already there) that couldn't be known before they actually occurred. These events are the stuff of miracles. Thus the ninth-century Jewish theologian Saadia Gaon (one of the first Jewish thinkers to employ the Greek-Arabic term *al-tabi'a*) writes about "these extraordinary miracles," which occur "only through the creation of what does not correspond to nature [*al-tabi'a*] or to the habitual course of things." He then goes on to criticize those thinkers who cannot accept the reality of anything that "contradicts the natural and habitual."[69] The possibilities God builds into the created cosmos, and which only God can realize in history, are true events nonetheless. They are not points in a spatially conceived continuum or process. Unlike points in a process, such events do not follow any predictable order. Colloquially speaking, they are "out of the box."[70]

This idea of nature as God's usual but not necessary creative *modus operandi* is developed in Kabbalah. Thus the sixteenth-century Sephardic kabbalistic theologian Moses Cordevero (Remaq) sees "the nature" (*ha-tev'a*) as corresponding to the biblical *Elohim* or "God."[71] This is what the Rabbis took as denoting God's attribute of "strict justice" (*middat ha-din*), by which God created the world with its order coequally.[72] It is the order that God "stamps" (*hitbi'ah*) on the world, which could also be termed "cosmic justice." Nevertheless, this divine strictness (called *gevurah* or "power") is not coequal with God's infinite Being, but rather is balanced by God's attribute of "grace" (*hesed*), which the Rabbis called God's attribute of "mercy" (*middat rahamim*) as expressed by the Tetragrammaton (YHWH).[73] (This rabbinic idea is already developed in early Kabbalah.)[74] As such, God's exercise of mercy shows that God is not "locked into" cosmic justice any more than artists are reducible to or bound by their own artistic products. Since God infinitely (*ein sof*) transcends His finite attributes, all the more so does God not only transcend His creation but also retain the freedom to intervene in His justly created world to save its human creatures from the death sentence that would be theirs if God let the world be governed and judged according to strict justice alone.

Furthermore, the sixteenth-century Ashkenazic kabbalistic theologian Judah Loewe of Prague (Maharal) speaks of "natural functionality" (*po'al tiv'i*) as "temporal continuity" (*hemshekh zeman*) that is "material" (*gashmi*) and "perpetual" (*tamid*). That is quite like what Einstein more recently called "space-time." This is the natural order (*ha-seder*) that all scientific endeavour assumes. And Maharal differentiates this natural order with its regular moments from an "event" (*reg'a*) that is spontaneously realized by God *in time,* but that is not "contingent on time" (*talui bi-zeman*).[75] These events are ad hoc, one-time, unrepeatable "occurrences" (*le-sha'ah*), hence they are unpredictable by ordinary scientific or even empirical criteria. Furthermore, just as human free choice presupposes that rational human action in the world is possible (*efshar*) but not necessary, all the more so God's free choice (which human freedom is meant to imitate) to intervene in the natural, worldly order presupposes such possibility within the world.[76]

What is still missing from this account of human freedom to act unnecessarily and divine freedom to act miraculously is an answer to the question: *How* does the natural order "admit" (as it were) of such free, intrusive action? The answer is that nature is not one invariable causal process. Nevertheless, though the realization of one possibility rather than another when speaking of what is neither divine nor human action seems to be random *behaviour,* when one speaks of either God or humans the realization of one possibility rather than another is a rationally intended, freely chosen *act*. Even though the realization of every possibility in the world (let alone in the whole universe that is beyond human experience) does not seem to be a rationally intended freely chosen act, still every rationally intended freely chosen act couldn't be realized in the world unless nature admitted it *could possibly* happen here. In other words, freedom of choice presupposes natural possibility, even though natural possibility does not necessarily entail freedom of choice. In fact, because of this metaphysical recognition of nature's having a range of open possibilities instead of being an immutably determined and closed system, it is much easier for biblically based theologians today to engage more recent natural science (such as evolutionary biology and quantum physics) than could earlier theologians in their confrontations with the determinism assumed by ancient and even earlier modern natural science.

Now, things in the universe are either made by God or they are made by humans.[77] Nothing is there necessarily, that is, nothing is uncaused and therefore thoroughly predictable, because whatever has been made can be unmade. Moreover, there is nothing in the universe that is accidental, that is, self-caused and therefore thoroughly unpredictable, because it can make and unmake itself willy-nilly. This is expressed by the rabbinic phrase "made by God's hands" (*be-ydei shamayim*), which refers to everything not made by human hands.[78] In fact, "made by God's hands" in rabbinic parlance means what is "natural," or what regularly and thus predictably occurs in the world.[79] Conversely, in rabbinic parlance the phrase "made by human hands" (*bi-ydei adam*) refers to what is "artificial," or the product of human technology (which, working on natural, created materials already there beforehand, is essentially inferior to God's creation of these materials *ex nihilo*).[80] Nevertheless, the difference between what is regular and irregular in created nature is one of degree rather than one of kind, for neither the regular nor the irregular is necessary or accidental as God determines both their beginning and their end in time. Nothing just happens, even though we humans do not know why most events in our world occur the way they do.[81] That is because God is continually concerned with all His creation, for which God freely assumes responsibility, even for intervening in nature when needed. Thus Rabbi Yohanan bar Nappaha imagines God chiding the angels who want to sing praises to God for drowning the Egyptians pursuing the fleeing Israelites in the Sea of Reeds: "The product of My hands [*ma'asei yedai*] are drowning in the sea, and you are singing a song!"[82] Of course, the Egyptians drowned in the sea because God intervened in nature in order to rescue the fleeing Israelites.[83] It seems that Rabbi Yohanan imagined God would have preferred a more usual or natural exodus, in which there didn't have to be so many human casualties.

God is always free to act *miraculously*, that is, to radically interfere with the usual natural order. But we humans are not to assume that such radically unusual situations will be there, ready at hand, for us to take for granted when we make practical decisions in the world. "The world is to run its usual course [*olam ke-minhago noheg*]."[84] In this world anyway, as the Talmud puts it, "we do not rely on a miracle [*a-nisa la samkhinan*]."[85] That means that while God can change the usual order of nature for His own purposes, humans are still to pursue their own purposes supposing the usual order of nature is operating. For God, anything is possible; for humans, though, there are nothing but practically significant probabilities that we know from our ordinary experience of nature. Our action is only rational when we assume "what has been will be again; and what has been done will be done again [for] ... there is nothing new [*v'ein kol hadash*] under the sun ... it has already [*kvar*] been before us since ages past" (Ecclesiastes 1:9–10). In fact, the celebration of God's miraculous interventions into the historical experience of the people Israel has become part of our regular routine. Our task, then, is to commemorate these extraordinary events, but not to recreate them. Humans need not and ought not to require new miracles to occur in order for us to experience God's being with us. Regular commemoration or celebration of these archetypal miracles enables humans to re-experience now what occurred in the world then. The observance of the commandments does not require their human subjects to perform unnatural or supernatural acts here and now.[86] Indeed, humans' effecting what seem to be supernatural events, but without a specific divine warrant (as was the case with biblical prophets), seems to be frowned upon in the rabbinic tradition (although there appear to be many concessions made to popular superstition).[87]

The purpose of the miraculous event is not to be found within the natural reality, the time and place where and when it happened. Instead, this miracle gives that natural time and place its ultimate purpose, which is to be the location of a unique divine-human encounter. However, contrary to the view of classical philosophy, nature's purpose is not inferred from nature itself. Though worldly in the sense that it occurs or takes place in the ordinary world, this event, as a divine-human encounter, is not the result of any natural process. The event is a covenantal occasion insofar as it is the opportune moment for a divine-human encounter. While the covenant does presuppose nature, nature does not entail the covenant. The covenant transforms nature, but nature is not transubstantiated by the covenant. The miraculous event transforms the humans it is intended for, but it does not transpose them into a different world altogether. That is why one can speak of a biblical "theology of nature," while one cannot speak of a biblical "natural theology." Theology as the revealed word of God explains nature, but nature does not explain the word of God.

Even the prophetic power to effect miracles is limited by the Rabbis to the authority of prophets to issue an ad hoc commandment, or temporarily dispense people from either a positive or a negative commandment, both without having to present argumentation for the ad hoc dispensation.[88] Thus the Talmud reports one Rabbi stating that "a rabbinic sage [*hakham*] is better [*adif*] than a prophet."[89] This dictum has been interpreted to mean that a rabbinic sage is one who makes a reasoned argument (based on the perpetually binding norms of the Torah), whereas a prophet only reports what has been given in an ephemeral experience.[90] And, in that same context, the Talmud reports another Rabbi as saying: "since the [Second] Temple was destroyed, prophecy [*nevu'ah*] has been taken from the prophets and given over to lunatics and babies."[91] In fact, the normative Jewish system no longer needs prophets, even though they once did have some normative authority. Perhaps because of what were deemed the misuses of charismatic authority by various heterodox sects, the Talmud privileges ordinary human reasoning about the normative data of the Torah already revealed over any new normative data brought by charismatic prophets.[92]

Now, there are times when it looks like God's miraculous interventions in the usual natural order are simply for the sake of reminding humans that their options are very much limited by the natural order. For that order comprises the limits of the world into which humans have been placed by God, but God as the Creator of both humans and their world is not so limited. "Is anything too wondrous [*ha-yipal'e*] for the Lord?!" (Genesis 18:14) The One "who measures [*va-yimoded*] the earth" (Habakkuk 3:6), who "looks to the ends of the earth [*li-qetsot ha'arets*]" (Job 28.24), this God is beyond that which He has so limited. That is God's unlimited freedom. Only the Creator who transcends His creation could possibly look at it as a whole. Only the One who created the universe and its inherent structure could possibly measure or order it properly. As God reminded Job, when God finally responded to him: "Where were you when I founded [*be-yosdi*] the earth? Tell me if you have any understanding, who set its measure [*memaddeha*]?" (Job 38:4–5). Humans are offered no Archimedean fulcrum, no position outside the world whereby they could move or change the whole world. Only God has that option.

Miracles are "wondrous" events (*nifla'ot* in Hebrew) insofar as they are very rare exceptions to the usual order of nature. As exceptions, they are neither a substitute for nor a subordination to that ordinary natural order. In fact, their exceptionality is lost when the ordinary worldly nature is not affirmed as what is normal.[93] Even thanking God for having realized in history any one of these rare possibilities requires one to use ordinary third-person language to describe the miraculous event as a phenomenon in the world. Only in thanking God for having directly caused the exceptional event to happen is there a second-person address *to* God, but this is followed by a third-person description of *what* God has done. In fact, this thankful address (*hoda'ah*) enables one to confidently address his or her request (*baqashah*) to God to act for us in the future as exceptionally as God has acted for us in the past.[94] "Be thankful [*hodu*] to the Lord; call upon His name ... recount [*sihu*] all of His wondrous deeds [*nifla'otav*] ... let the heart of those who seek [*mevaqshei*] the Lord be glad" (Psalms 105:1–3). A miracle, then, is both an objective event and a subjective experience.

The Bible frequently tells of God freely and significantly breaking *through* nature (*nes*) for the sake of directly relating Godself to those persons whom God has elected for this relationship.[95] Indeed, God's breaking into the human world miraculously to command humans to do some definite act is God's basic reason for performing a miracle.[96] Moreover, God takes direct responsibility for the event. "I am the Lord your God who has taken you out of the land of Egypt, out of bondage. You shall have no other gods before Me" (Exodus 20:2–3). Humans are directly answerable to God for whether or not they have kept the commandments God has so responsibly given to them. The active human acceptance of God's commandments is what makes the ontological reality of the miracle an actual divine-human, covenantal event. "All that the Lord has spoken we shall do" (Exodus 19:8). The event is almost as much the doing of humans as it is the doing of God. Without God's doing it *for* them, there would be nothing for humans to respond *to*. Without positive human response, though, God's action would have no recipients capable of celebrating the event *with* God. Accordingly, neither God nor humans need to look to nature as the medium of their mutual, covenantal relationship or as an impediment to this relationship. The miracle happens *in* nature, but it is not *of* nature, which means that *where* the miracle occurred does not explain *why* it occurred. Nevertheless, a miracle is not performed to be *against* nature, inasmuch as it does not come to permanently destroy nature. After all, nature is what made it possible for the miracle to occur in the world. It is only that a miracle is not ultimately explained by such "natural" categories as sequential causation.

That nature is not the medium of God's covenantal relationship with the people Israel, because that relationship is direct and thus unmediated, comes out in the rabbinic dictum "Israel has no fate [*ein mazal*]."[97] Now, the term *mazal*, usually translated as "fate" or even as "luck," literally refers to the heavenly constellations, which were considered to directly and consistently control and order earthly beings, even peoples.[98] Thus *mazal* functions as a natural cause. In fact, all creatures are considered to have their own specific *mazal* or nature, given to them by God.[99] In Hellenistic and rabbinic theology, each of the seventy nations of the world (i.e., the non-Jewish peoples) is thought to have its own *mazal*, often thought of as its "guardian angel."[100] Only the people Israel have no *mazal*, or no nature mediating their direct covenantal relationship with God. Nevertheless, as ordinary individuals they are subject to natural forces like anybody else.[101]

This notion of *mazal* assumes that the heavenly constellations, that is, the planets visible in our solar system as the zodiac, are efficient causes that determine to a large extent human life on earth. That assumption is held by those who think astrology is a science, which had long been the subject of debate. The question should be resolved by scientific criteria.[102] However, more arguable theologically is the more general assumption that humans are parts of the totally enclosing natural order, which prevents their being able to ever transcend that order so as to engage in a direct relationship with the transcendent God. The counter-assumption of biblical theology seems to be that for those whom God has elected for a direct covenantal relationship with God, such transcendence of this natural enclosure is possible, and that they are so enabled by the fact that God elicits a response from them in God's direct revelation to them. Therefore, "Do not learn the way of the gentile nations [*ha-goyyim*], and from the heavenly signs do not be dismayed, for it is the gentile nations who are dismayed by them" (Jeremiah 10:2).

Miracles and Laws of Nature

Miracles, as Hume correctly pointed out, do not "violate" the laws of nature. There is no antinomy between personal freedom and natural necessity.[103] For the so-called laws of nature are nothing more than the more or less predictable patterns of natural occurrences that we can *usually* expect to happen in the future the way we have experienced them in the past if the same conditions reoccur.[104] However, this is not a necessity inasmuch as the "laws" of nature are not universal prescriptions that cannot admit of any exceptions. The laws of nature are only generalizations that do admit of exceptions. Only the Creator God could make absolute universal prescriptions for how *His* universe is to operate. In fact, it would seem that at the time of creation, God could prescribe only what He thought *ought* to happen in the universe, since predicting what *will* happen is done by inferring from what *has* already happened; but at the time of creation there was no "already" beforehand from which to predict anything. That is why, if the universe is created in time rather than being eternally uncreated, and if it was not created out of any pre-existent material (i.e., without any preconditions for God), it could only have come into existence by a divine prescription, the result of a decision made by at a certain point in time.[105] "By the word of the Lord the heavens were made ... He spoke and it [the universe] came to be; He commanded [*hu tsivah*] and it endured" (Psalms 33:6, 9).[106]

Such universal prescriptions from God have been revealed in prescriptive language to state how they are analogous to what humans have been commanded to do. The difference, though, between the two types of divine prescription is that human creatures have the choice whether or not to obey what God has commanded them to do or not to do, whereas non-human creatures "obey" automatically since they have no such choice at all.[107] But what the two types of divine prescription have in common is that the commanding God is not in any way reacting to what is already there beforehand, as is the case in any description, as there is nothing prior to God to which God would have to respond descriptively.

That is why the "laws of nature" are not really *laws* at all. The term is, in fact, a metaphor.[108] For "law" denotes a prescription: an order or command given by a free person to another free person to do. Instead, a law of nature (*lex naturae*) is a descriptive generalization of what *will likely* occur in our experience, barring some unforeseeable possibility that is not realized in the past being realized now.[109] But these "laws" are not moral prescriptions that a person *shall* do, nor are they logical conclusions that *must* follow from their premises apodictically.[110]

Moral prescriptions, conversely, are the subject matter of "natural law" (*lex naturalis*); and natural law is essentially different from laws of nature. In the case of natural law, it is not that "nature" prescribes or commands anything; rather, it is the human condition or nature to be commanded and to command each other. When these commands are reasonable, that is, when they are consistent with our *human nature* as moral/political beings, then these commands are *natural*. By their common use of the term "nature," both "laws of nature" and "natural law" are referring to something endemic or essential in any being of which or of whom the term "nature" is predicated. (Hence, "nature" is not a homonym.) The difference between them is that laws of nature describe what *is*, while natural law prescribes what *ought to be*. And natural law is prior to laws of nature in human experience, because we humans experience being commanded to do something in the world before we learn about the objects in the world we are commanded to include in our relations with other persons here. In our practical interaction with other persons, we include these objects by our use *of* them; and in our theoretical interaction with other persons – artistic or scientific – we include these objects by our mutual discourse *about* them. But, unlike God, we humans do not command these objects into existence.

The ordinary world is the context for the regular observance of the Torah, and ordinary objects are the things employed in that observance. The ordinary world is the necessary condition for humans to perform the commandments of the Torah, though God alone is their sufficient cause, who has given the Torah miraculously in a non-repeatable event.[111] This is evidenced by the regular celebration of the miraculous exodus from Egypt at Passover-time. The regular observance of Passover includes such ordinary objects in the world as unleavened bread (*matsah*) and wine, both of which are readily available in the natural world.[112] The fact that these things are made by humans from natural ingredients imitates the active human participation in the original miracle now being remembered in a celebratory way.[113] That is why the perpetual remembrance of the event is not a scientific demonstration showing how this event could be viewed as a natural occurrence (even though this could be done), let alone an attempt to literally re-enact the miraculous event itself (which couldn't be done). To attempt either a scientific demonstration or a re-enactment would make the natural world the medium of the God-human relationship, rather than it's being only that relationship's locale. Therefore, this commemoration of the miraculous event is celebrated as a regular practice according to the liturgical calendar of the descendants of the direct beneficiaries of the miracle, which is structured according to the ordinary cycle of solar seasons and lunar months.[114]

Miracles are among such unforeseen possibilities that have been realized in the world for humans to experience, even though we need to determine what distinguishes a miracle from what appears to be a natural accident, that is, from what happens in the world without a predictable cause.

Now, the miracles recorded in the Bible do seem to have natural explanations after the fact. They do not seem to "violate" the few such cosmic "laws" we do know, such as the law of gravity. For example, the splitting of the Red Sea (*qeri'at yam suf*), regarded by many Jews as the greatest of the biblical miracles, is explained after the fact as follows: "Moses stretched out his hand over the sea and the Lord moved the sea with a strong east wind [*be-ruah qadim azah*] all night, making the sea dry land, and the waters were split" (Exodus 14:21). By stating that the "strong east wind" was the immediate cause of the sea's being split, the Bible is invoking a fact of ordinary experience. Surely those who first heard this account knew from their ordinary, that is, repeatable and even predictable experience, *what* such a wind is and what it can do. *How* this event occurred in space-time could be experienced by the people for whom it occurred. Nevertheless, what God did realize miraculously is a remote possibility that couldn't be predicted in advance by ordinary reasoning about the usual or "natural" world. Ordinary reasoning about the usual world doesn't explain extraordinary events experienced in the world. The miracle, then, is not *what* happened or *how* it happened, but *that* it happened at all, *when* it did happen, *who* made it happen, *why* it happened, *for whom* it happened, and *who* told the people for whom it happened that God changed the usual course of nature for them in a way ordinary humans could not predict. In other words, as an event in the world, the miracle admits of a "natural" explanation, at least after the fact. But as a unique, extraordinary event experienced by the people Israel, the miracle does not admit of any such natural or usual explanation.

What was truly unusual or miraculous here is *that* this happened when Moses said it would happen, and *that* it happened in order to make the people directly aware of God's saving power. They did not have to infer God's saving power from a causal chain. The fact of *what* happened is not radically extraordinary. What is most extraordinary is *that* this event happened at all, and that it happened at a uniquely opportune time in the people's history. And what is most extraordinary is *why*, that is, the purpose for which this event took place at all. That purpose or reason is to bring the people to accept God's law for them. That requires a prophet to inform the people that God directly intended that event, albeit by means of ordinary causal processes; and it requires that the prophet inform the people what God wants them to learn from this miracle. Indeed, the prophet's proclamation of the miracle and its purpose for humans is as important as the occurrence of the miraculous event itself. Thus after God appears to Moses miraculously in the event of "the burning bush that was not consumed" (Exodus 3:2), God says to him: "I am sending you that you might take the people out of Egypt so that you [plural] will serve [*t'avdun*] God on this mountain" (3:12). "This mountain" is Mount Sinai, the place where God will give

His Torah to the people Israel for them to accept it, learn it, and practise it.[115] Sinai is not only the geographic destination of the people; it is their normative destination that gives the people their true rationale or purpose for leaving Egypt altogether.

Miracles are public events (*nissim mefursamim*) originally experienced by a community. They are then subsequently incorporated into the community's historical discourse by persons who include their own comparable experience of salvation in the community's story. "You shall tell your child on that day saying that this is what the Lord did for me when I exited Egypt" (Exodus 13:8).[116] Miracles that are private or only experienced by specially privileged individuals, though, are hidden matters between these individuals and God. Hence they do not lend themselves to public discourse inasmuch as they did not occur in publicly accessible space-time, at least in this world, nor do they lend themselves to public celebration and perpetual commemoration.[117] In fact, the thirteenth-century theologian Moses Nahmanides sees "secret miracles" (*nissim nistarim*) as God's method of hidden supernatural judgment that God performs for the sake of righteous. It is certainly beyond the normal process of correlated causes and effects.[118]

That public prophetic revelation is not for the sake of the personal enlightenment of the prophet; instead, it is done by God in order to send a particularly appropriate normative message to those whom the prophet is sent to address. Thus when Moses asks God, "show me Your glory" (Exodus 33:18), which seems to be a request for some sort of private beatific vision, instead God reveals to him God's merciful, compassionate characteristics (i.e., "all My goodness" – 33:19). The Rabbis interpret that to mean God presents Godself as the merciful, compassionate exemplar to be copied by humans, and the merciful and compassionate One from whom humans are to seek mercy and compassion in prayer.[119] Humans are able to imitate that divine beneficence when they reflect on what God has miraculously done for His people.

Now, there have been those who have long argued that the orderly regularity of nature itself bespeaks a Creator standing behind it, so to speak. In this view, often called the "argument from design," the cosmic order suggests an Orderer who has imprinted that order on otherwise chaotic matter. So, for this view, there is no religious need for miracles. Affirming "nature's God" is sufficient. However, philosophers as otherwise divergent as Aristotelians and Kantians have long argued that no such transcendent Orderer (let alone a Creator *ex nihilo*) is required to explain either the order inherent in the natural world itself or the order inherent in our experiencing the natural world. It is simpler (à la "Ockham's razor") to just accept that natural order as immanent and uncaused, that is, it is just there (*il y'a* in French). In other words, nature explains itself or we can explain nature, but without either explanation requiring us to refer to an external, higher cause of nature and its intelligibility.

In fact, it could be said that the rejection of the argument from design has precedence in the Bible's seeming insistence that we cannot infer God's standing *behind* nature, but rather we only encounter God breaking *into* nature to speak to us directly and immediately. This direct encounter with the God who speaks to us in revelation is the essence of the miracle. The radical changes in the usual order of nature, which immediately precede God's speaking to the people Israel at the prime revelation at Sinai, seem to have occurred in order to destabilize humans' reliance on their natural, orderly environment so that they might directly confront God who is now addressing them and respond accordingly.[120] Without this destabilization of their natural environment, humans would most likely subsume this event into the categories they have devised to describe and predict natural processes. What happens to the people experiencing this miraculous destabilization of nature is that nature, as it were, has receded from them so that God might speak to them directly and they might respond to God directly.[121] At this point, nature no longer mediates the covenantal relationship, nor is nature a barrier to that direct "mouth-to-mouth" (Numbers 12:8) confrontation, that is, God speaking and the recipient of God's speech responding verbally.[122] "There was thunder, and lightening, and a thick cloud on the mountain, and a strong shofar blast. Then Moses brought the people out [*va-yots'e*] from the camp to greet [*li-qr'at*] God; and they stood up at the base of the mountain" (Exodus 19:16–17).[123]

This point also comes out in a rabbinic parable that speculates on the conditions that enabled the patriarch, Abraham, to be addressed by God initially. The parable speaks of a traveller wandering from place to place who happens upon a burning or illuminated palace (*birah doleqet*), wondering "could it be that this palace is without someone in charge [*manhig*]?!" At that point the master of the palace (*ba'al ha-birah*) peeps forth and says, "I am the master of the palace!"[124] Here *doleqet* is a *double entendre*: it could mean a fire that *enlightens*, or it could mean a fire that *destroys*. In the rabbinic writings, both meanings of *doleqet* can be found.[125]

Now, in terms of the first meaning of *doleqet*: if this fire is experienced as light, the parable then seems to be an imaginative rendering of the argument from design. That is, from the experience of an orderly world we infer an Orderer standing behind it.[126] In this interpretation of the parable, the existence of "the master of the palace" seems to be a necessary conclusion drawn from the traveller's experience of an orderly, intelligible world. The master of the palace doesn't have to announce his existence; the traveller can simply infer it from the worldly evidence before him. However, the parable seems to emphasize that the traveller's question is a cry for an answer that is a response from someone whose existence cannot be inferred from the dangerous disorder the traveller is experiencing. For he is a wanderer who, it seems, is looking for shelter; yet the palace seems to be on fire and is thus dangerous rather than welcoming. Indeed, the very anguish the question expresses indicates that the traveller worries there might be no master of the palace, and hence no answer to his question, or maybe there is a master of the palace who has decided to burn it down. The destabilized situation the man is in prevents him from making any inference concerning the existence of a master of the palace, and thus he cannot enjoy the certainty drawing such an inference gives one. The wanderer is not a spectator, who is standing apart from an interesting object that attracts his curiosity. In fact, the wanderer seems frightened, even repelled, by the burning palace.

God's announcing Himself as "the master of the palace," therefore, seems to assure Abraham, who is the wanderer (Deuteronomy 26:5), of three points. One, Abraham had to have this destabilizing experience so he could be directly addressed by God. Two, God now has the opportunity to give Abraham his first commandment directly: "Go forth from your land, from your native home, from your father's house, to the land I will show you" (Genesis 12:1). (God's address to humans is always normative: it tells humans what God wants us to do, rather than showing us what we want to see.) Three, it seems to be assumed that God will return Abraham's world to its normal condition so Abraham can function in a restabilized world. This comes out when the text now quotes Scripture: "The king desired your beauty" (Psalms 45:12). Where? It is "in the world" (*ba'olam*). That seems to mean that Abraham's God given beauty can be appreciated throughout the world, which wouldn't be the case if the world were too destabilized for anyone like Abraham to be appreciated for what God enabled him to bring to the world. In other words, a radically destabilized world would not be a place where anything enduring, like the Torah, could be the normal way things are done.

God's judgment of creation is an essential aspect of God's care of creation, which is something that created nature itself does not teach us. God's judgment of creation ultimately means God's bringing all created nature to its appointed temporal end or conclusion (*eschaton*).[127]

Since God's final judgment of creation is as mysterious as is God's original creation, it is understandable why the ancient Rabbis taught that God's full judgment will only take place in a world that "no eye but God's has seen" (Isaiah 64:3).[128] The existence of that "new heaven and new earth" (Isaiah 66:22) is not something that could be inferred from the natural world in which we now necessarily live. It is almost as transcendent as the God who promises to bring it into existence in the most radical future. That is why God's *care-ful* governance of nature is only understood by analogy to God's governance of His people through the Torah; it is not inferred from looking at nature apart from that historical situation, even when that "looking at nature" is according to the precise standards of natural sciences like physics and biology. (I hesitate to call this governance "providential," since *providential* means "foreknowledge," and that takes away from the idea of care as an immediate temporal response, while *providence* suggests a primordial, atemporal decree to be applied indiscriminately.) Nevertheless, divine transcendence of the limits of nature is so much better appreciated when we know how much and how rich what is so contained within these natural limits really is.

God's Mutability in Relation to Nature

At this point in our enquiry we need to deal with the ontological difference between theology and philosophy on the question: Does God change? In the previous section, we dealt with this question in the context of God's relation to humans. Here we shall deal with it in terms of God's relation to nature.

The philosophical answer, best thought out by Aristotle, is that change implies imperfection. Whatever changes *becomes* something else. That becoming could be progress towards Being (which is better) or regress away from Being (which is worse). But if God is perfect Being per se (*ontos ōn*), any change would mean that God is regressing into imperfect Becoming.[129] The God of Aristotle does not engage in any transitive activity, because this God has no interest in anything outside his own perfect self. And, if God does not engage in any transitive activity, then God certainly does not engage in any transactions in which God is not only the subject of an externally directed act, but is also the object of such an act done by another subject. Any such external interest, whether transitive or transactional, would be an ontological come-down. Hence any change could only be a detrimental transformation of God's own perfect being into something imperfect. Indeed, if God is, as Aristotle put it, "thought [*nous*] thinking itself," then self-identity is all God has, that is, all God has to do is continually self-identify.[130]

Conversely, the theological answer to this metaphysical question seems to be that change does not imply a lack in God. On the contrary, necessary immutability or immutable necessity predicated of God would imply God is not free to do whatever God chooses to do, whenever and wherever God chooses to do so. Indeed, if God cannot do something today differently from what God did yesterday, wouldn't that place a limit on the freedom of the infinite God, who transcends all limits, the God who limits the world rather than being limited by the world? "Could you examine God? Could you find the limit [*takhlit*] of the Almighty ... for such measure [*middah*] would be longer than the earth and wider than the sea" (Job 11:7, 9). Indeed, God wouldn't be God if He were to be so limited, that is, if God were limited by nature as creatures are limited by nature. God limits creation, thereby making it finite. "Everything complete I see is limited [*qets*], but Your commandment is endlessly broad [*rehavah ... m'od*]" (Psalms 119:96).

Now, freedom presupposes mutability, even though mutability does not entail freedom. For, while all those who are free to choose are only free to do so because they have the power to change their actions, all those who change are not necessarily free to change their behaviour at will. This is especially important to emphasize, as it is clear from the Bible that God has not only chosen to act in relation to His creatures, but has also chosen to *react to* His human creatures, as well as to act *with* His creatures. So, for example, God says to Israel: "Return to Me, then I shall return [*ve'ashuvah*] to you" (Malachi 3:7). God reacts to humans who are free enough to choose either obedience to or disobedience of God.[131] If so, then God's reaction to the choices they have made will be *different* when their choice has been to obey God's commandments rather than to disobey them. To act differently now from how one previously did, that is to actively change. In the Bible, God's mutability is presupposed by God's transitive action in relation to *external* creation. Then there are God's trans-actions *with* God's human creatures, when there is freely chosen change on the part of both God and humans.

When God is reported to have said: "I the Lord do not change [*lo shaniti*]" (Malachi 3:6), that might well mean: "I do not become something else" (literally "a second," i.e., *sheni*). Or to slightly paraphrase this verse: "I shall not become later someone *other* than who I am now and who I have always been." In other words, God's self-conscious identity remains the same throughout God's manifold actions in the created universe. That consistent self-identity is manifest to us when God keeps His promises that He has chosen to be irrevocable. As such, we humans have the right, indeed the duty, to remind God of His perpetual responsibility to abide in the present and the future by what God has freely committed Godself to in the past.[132] Divine mutability, then, is confined to the right God has reserved for Himself to react *differently* or spontaneously in different human situations that call for God's *response.*

Along these lines, the famous verse usually translated "I am what I am" (Exodus 3:14) has been better translated (in my opinion) by Martin Buber and Franz Rosenzweig as *Ich werde dasein als der ich dasein werde,* "I shall be there as the I who shall be there."[133] That means God reserves for Himself the right to change from being absent to being present *or* vice versa. Though it is true that God promises Israel via Moses: "I shall be with you [*ehyeh imakh*]" (Exodus 3:12), it is also clear that God will be with His people when He chooses to do so and how He chooses to do so. God's choice is a free response, not a necessary reaction. As such, the people cannot conjure up God's presence at will.[134] God, not humans, can change God's actions in the world. Thus when it is said that "God is the world's place, but the world is not God's place," that might well mean that while God can always locate (a "place" is a "location") us, that is, frame us and thereby control us, we can never locate God, that is, frame God and thereby control Him.[135] The only divine immutability we have been assured of is that God will not annul His covenant with the people Israel nor will God change the Torah He has given this people to live by in this world. This is not something God *must* do because of some natural necessity; rather, it is something God has promised He *shall* do, that is, what God *wills* to do. And the promise is believed to be true by those to whom God's faithfulness (*emunah*) has been shown.[136]

In the words of the Psalmist, "I shall not violate [*ahallel*] My covenant; the utterance of My lips I shall not change [*ashanneh*]" (Psalms 89:35). Commenting on this verse, the twelfth-century exegete Abraham ibn Ezra notes that even if God's people violate the covenant, God will not do so. In other words, even if the people Israel violate the covenant by pretending to be another, non-covenanted people altogether, God *shall* not do so.[137] Thus the covenant is not a bilateral contract that either party can get out of. Israel cannot nullify it because God will not let them do so, by always reiterating the covenant again and again. That is consistent with God's promise (*shevu'ah*) to remain faithfully involved with His people.[138] Moreover, even though God can do whatever God wants to do, whatever He pleases (and without any external restraints), nevertheless God autonomously restrains Godself not to change by virtue of the covenantal promise He has made to Israel *and to Himself*, that is, commanding them *and Himself* to remain steadfastly faithful to one another. As for the people, they cannot nullify the covenant because it is imposed upon them by God heteronomously; it is not autonomously entered into by themselves.[139] Unlike any earthly contract, there is no escape clause in the covenant. Thus, when humans freely choose to accept the covenant and live according to it, they are not initiating or even co-initiating their relationship with God, they are confirming it by not changing it. But, when the people do choose to change their covenantal relationship with God, they end up with "broken wells that hold no water" (Jeremiah 2:13). Their choice, then, is either to expire of thirst or to return to "the source of living water" who, it is clearly implied, does not change His fundamental relationship with the people.

Human observance of God's laws, and God's response to human obedience or disobedience of these laws, are considered to be of cosmic significance; hence God's relation to nature (i.e., the universal context of human observance of God's law) is also involved here. When God judges humans, that involves somehow or other the whole cosmos being judged along with humans. "Let the heavens rejoice and the earth be glad ... before the Lord, for He comes to judge [*li-shpot*] the earth. He shall judge the world with justice [*be-tsedeq*] and the peoples consistently [*b'emunato*]" (Psalms 96:11, 13). Therefore, God's judgment of humans directly involves God's relation to non-human creation, that is, God's relation to nature. As the Talmud puts it: "Had not the Torah [been given and accepted], heaven and earth would not endure."[140] In other words, just as human actions have universal significance, so all that is done in the universe ultimately has human significance. And that is because both humankind and the universe are directly related to God. Both of them are ruled by God; both of them are judged by God. All creatures are subject to God's justice and God's mercy. As such, God's concern is not solely confined to Israel or even to all humankind. Indeed, when humans think they are the sole objects of God's attention, we are reminded, as Job was reminded: "Where were you when I established earth?" (Job 38:4). One might say that a certain sibling rivalry between humankind and the rest of the universe is also a limitation on both human and non-human pretensions.

There is both structure and spontaneity in God's governance of the natural universe. It is both static and dynamic. It is static when what is probable regularly occurs; it is dynamic when what is possible rarely occurs. A probable occurrence can be predicted by humans with some accuracy, but a possible event is unpredictable. Thus when such a possible but normally unpredictable event is realized by God, humans are surprised and caught unawares. But all of this is of theological interest only to the extent that it pertains to God's relationship with humankind.

So, even when the prophets predicted unusual events happening in nature, their predictions were actually warnings of how God *might* respond to the way humans have either kept or not kept God's commandments. Nevertheless, that relationship presupposes God's static governance of the universe when it comes to what humans need to expect in order to regularly observe God's commandments. In fact, just before God gives Noah and his descendants law for them to observe upon their exiting the Ark, the Torah states God's promise that "all the seasons [*kol yemei*] of the earth [i.e., its regular cycles] shall not cease anymore [*od*]: planting time and harvest time, cold and heat, summer and winter, day and night" (Genesis 8:22). That is why the law commanded to the Noahides (i.e., post-Deluge humankind) can be called "natural law." For this law justly orders humans as *naturally* political beings, plus it presupposes the regularity of external *nature* as its regular environment.

For the classical philosophers, however, God is not free enough to transcend the universe. God is part, albeit the zenith, of the orderly world of Nature. Thus God and Nature are coequal. God and Nature are totally necessary; they could not choose to do anything other than what they have been doing for all eternity. So, what is an accident or a chance occurrence is either an insignificant exception to the natural order we already know, that is, it is a surd, or it is an event whose causes we do not know as yet.[141] Chance does not bespeak God's freedom to do what is possible but improbable, though, since the classical philosophers did not consider such natural exceptions to be due to God's free choice. For free choice presupposes an open range of possibilities, but God's active being is wholly necessary. And whatever free choice humans can exercise has no cosmic significance at all.

This difference between the classical philosophical view of nature on one side, and the biblical theological view of nature on the other side, comes out when we consider the different views of freedom in Athens and Jerusalem. In Jerusalem, human freedom is valued because humans as the "image of God" are seen to reflect divine freedom, even though the two are not identical but only analogous (as an image is analogous to the source it reflects). Unlike anything else in creation, humans have the choice to either cooperate with God's governance of the universe by obeying His commandments or to resist God's invitation to humans to become God's partner (*shuttaf* in Hebrew) in the ongoing process of creation.[142] But by resisting, humans are nonetheless unwillingly co-opted by God's cosmic plan. As the Rabbis put it: "God's beneficence [*zekhut*] is effected through those who are worthy [*zakka'in*]; God's [immediate] malevolence [*hovah*] is effected by those who are guilty [*hayyavin*]."[143]

In other words, the righteous work with God, whereas the wicked are used by God. In the end, God's purposes are fulfilled regardless.

In biblical theology, the exercise of human freedom is a positive, endemic attribute of created human nature. That is why humans are considered to be superior to angels, who are personifications of cosmic forces who are under the total control of God. Humans are penultimate beings, "little less than God" (Psalms 8:5).[144] By virtue of their freedom, though confined to the practical probabilities already in their world, humans are closest to God, who is, however, without any necessity whatsoever. In rabbinic theology, angels are often considered to be more intelligent than humans, yet the fact that humans have some freedom makes them closer to God, because absolute freedom is inherent in God's most unique attribute: creativity (*bri'ah* in Hebrew). The Creator God doesn't have to do anything He doesn't want to do. "He does whatever He wants [*hafets*] to do" (Psalms 115:3).

The capacity for free choice is thus a special privilege (*reshut* in Hebrew), which makes humans different from the rest of creation.[145] And the capacity for freedom of choice involves both answerability and responsibility. Non-human creatures, however, are without freedom of choice according to moral criteria (at least as far as we know, and they don't communicate it to us even if they do have it). Therefore, these creatures are essentially beneath humans in the order of creation. Yet humans, as God's junior partners in creation, are to be concerned *with* and responsible *for* all the rest of creation, especially when it co-exists with humans in the same domesticated world. But these creatures cannot be held responsible for humans since they cannot exercise moral authority to which anyone would be answerable. That responsibility and answerability are not reciprocal between humans and the rest of creation because their respective roles are never interchangeable. Only those who have the capacity for freedom of choice thereby have the right to exercise authority and the duty to exercise it responsibly and benevolently.

In the Hellenic revelation, however, though the gods are higher than humans in the chain of being, they still are less than God or Nature as the Absolute. The chief sign that humans are inferior to the gods is that humans have freedom of choice. That means that humans live for the most part in a world of possibilities with all its uncertainties, whereas the gods, like Divinity itself, live in a world of pure, necessary perfection. Possibilities, of course, are temporal: they could occur or could not occur. All sublunar beings live in this world of temporal possibilities. (That is why "impossibility" is a logical, not an ontological, term, since logic deals with atemporal necessities.) Humans are superior to the animals inasmuch as they seem to be aware of the most immediate of these possibilities, what we would call "practical probabilities" or "opportunities at hand." And humans are able to choose among them. Humans also share with the gods the fact that they are both "souls" (*psychai*), that is, they are both essentially intelligent beings, even though humans are at present embodied souls (*somatos*).[146] Humans are therefore inferior to the gods (of whom Aristotle reiterates the Hellenic tradition that they fill the heavens), who are beyond such temporally limited uncertainties.[147] That is because of the gods' direct participation in natural divinity or divine Nature, who is eternal Being per se.[148] As such, in this view, human freedom of choice is more of a burden than it is a blessing. Being superior to the animals does not compensate for humans being inferior to the gods. Humans, in effect, are third-class citizens in the cosmic-natural realm: they are beneath both the gods and God or the Divine; and they only overcome this third-class cosmic status when they engage in pure contemplation of the Divine. Yet in this world anyway, that state of pure contemplation is episodic, because bodily nature still makes its regular demands.

Getting back to Jerusalem, the issue of freedom there lies at the heart of interhuman relations. Just as humans are related to God *in* the natural world but not *through* it, so are humans related to each other *in* the natural world but not *through* it. The natural world in its regularity is the way we describe the phenomenal world we regularly experience. But when nature is viewed as all-encompassing reality, freedom of choice can only be regarded as tangential. It is only when interhuman relations, the divine-human relationship, and the relation of humans to nature are seen as transcending natural necessity that freedom of choice, whether by God or by humans, becomes essential.

We have just seen how in Hebraic tradition God is related to nature freely and not necessarily. The free interhuman relationship and the free human relation to nature are the issues dealt with in the next chapter.

Chapter Three

Humans and Nature

Humans Related to Each Other and to God: Jerusalem

In a profound essay on the relation of theology and philosophy, the Jewish philosopher Leo Strauss speaks of "a broad agreement between the Bible and Greek philosophy regarding morality and the insufficiency of morality. The disagreement concerns what completes morality. According to Greek philosophy, that 'x' is *theōria*, contemplation, and the biblical completion we may call ... piety ... obedient love."[1] Strauss's assertion that the two traditions require something beyond interhuman morality (though not annulling it in the process) for a truly complete human life is astute. However, his differentiation of "contemplative" Athens and "obedient" Jerusalem is questionable since, as we have seen, there is contemplation of God in theological Jerusalem as well as obedience to God in philosophical Athens.

Morality (Strauss prefers to call it "justice") is the standard by which interhuman relations are to be governed in order for human political needs to be met. While these needs and their fulfilment are an indispensable feature of human life, they do not comprise all that humans need and rightly desire. That is why morality is necessary but not sufficient for a complete human life. Now, in the Jewish tradition, the commandments that pertain to human life in its entirety are divided into those commandments that pertain to what is "between humans themselves" (*bein adam le-havero*) – what we would call "morality" – and those commandments that pertain to what is "between humans and God" (*bein adam le-maqom*) – what we would call "religion" or "piety."[2] And, while there are some big differences between theological morality and philosophic morality (ultimately concerning who the human person truly is, and the ultimate reasons for humans to act with one another justly), theology and philosophy do have enough in common for one to agree with Strauss that the deepest difference between them lies in the different way each correlates the interhuman realm and the divine-human realm.

In biblical theology, humans have a twofold nature or essential character. Each relationship deals with a different human need, even though these needs and the commanded fulfilment of them constantly overlap.[3] Both relationships, moreover, are meant to be mutual and reciprocal, though the interhuman relationship is symmetrical or even egalitarian, whereas the divine-human relationship is asymmetrical or hierarchal.

In the first creation narrative in Genesis we read: "God created humans [*ha'adam*], male and female, in his image [*be-tsalmo*]" (Genesis 1:26). That means, in my view, humans are created with the need for a mutual relationship with God, and the need for a mutual relationship with each other. This begins with the mutual need of a woman for a man and a man for a woman. "It is not good for humans [*ha'adam*] to be alone [*levado*]" (Genesis 2:18).[4] Or, as one ancient sage put it: "Either companionship [*haveruta*] or death."[5] The need for a mutual relationship with God is first activated by humans when they begin to worship God. "Cain brought an offering [*minhah*] to the Lord from the fruit of the ground; and Abel he too brought [an offering]" (Genesis 4:3–4). This is the first example in the Bible of a human person doing something *for* God and, therefore, establishing a relationship *with* God.[6] So, too, when Noah leaves the Ark to revive human life on earth, the first thing he does is "build an altar to the Lord ... and sacrifice burnt-offerings on the altar" (Genesis 8:20). The reciprocity in this divine-human relationship is evidenced when God accepts Noah's sincere sacrifice as God accepted Abel's sincere sacrifice. This mutual relationship is reciprocal, albeit asymmetrical. Moreover, the relationship is free (*reshut*) on both sides: a sacrifice can be offered or not, and the response can be either acceptance or rejection.[7] Thus there is nothing in the narrative that indicates that Cain and Abel (the first brothers) were forced to bring an offering to God; and God is free to either accept the offering (as God did with Abel's) or reject the offering (as God did with Cain's). The same is true of Noah's relationship with God.

Nevertheless, before that mutual relationship with God is opened up by humans, they are the subjects of God's commandments. These commandments, though, do not constitute anything positive *between* God and humans; they are basically negative, that is, they are proscriptions. "The Lord God commanded [*va-yitsav*] humankind [*al ha'adam*] saying ... from the tree of the knowledge of good and bad you shall *not* eat" (Genesis 2:16–17).[8] So, the initial divine-human contact is one where humans are to restrain themselves *because* God has closed off to them many possible opportunities in the world. But it is humans themselves who open up certain opportunities in the world to do something *for* God.

Even when God turned the sacrificial system initiated by humans into a system of divinely given commandments (*ma'aseh ha-qorbanot*), humans are frequently reminded by the prophets that their sacrifices (both of things and words: their offerings and their prayers) are not acceptable to God if they have been done at the expense of what God has proscribed, especially what God has proscribed in their relations with one another. Thus one of the earliest biblical prophets, Samuel, warns the people Israel: "Does the Lord desire [*ha-hafets*] offerings and sacrifices as much as listening to the Lord's voice?! Surely, obedience [*shemo'a*] is better [*tov*] than sacrifice; to hearken [is better than] offering the fat of rams" (I Samuel 15:22). Moreover, Isaiah questions the people Israel in God's name: "Why do you bring Me your many sacrifices says the Lord?! ... Stop doing evil ... learn well how to seek justice [*mishpat*]; relieve oppression" (Isaiah 1:11, 16–17).[9] Maimonides even considers the whole sacrificial system of the Torah to be a divine concession to human weakness, because humans want something visible and tangible in their relationship with God.[10] And that is due to the inherent human propensity for idolatry, stemming from the innate human desire to be able to control God like humans control things in the world. So, since the primary human desire for a positive relationship with God is correct, and only the secondary human desire for an idolatrous relationship is incorrect, from Maimonides's perspective one can see the Torah's institution of the sacrificial system to be a sublimation of this secondary desire into at least an imageless form of worship. Thus the sacrificial system turns humans away from what would otherwise be a violation of what in Maimonides's view is God's first negative commandment to humans: the prohibition of idolatry (*avodah zarah*).[11] Perhaps that is why Maimonides assumes that even in the optimal human regime of the Messiah, the Temple will be rebuilt in Jerusalem and the sacrifices will be offered there once again.[12] Yet here again, the inter-human relationship is very much present insofar as the sacrificial cult brings the whole people together before the Lord.[13]

It is not that the prophets wanted a purely moral religion devoid of any ritual that might compete with morality, or even a religion in which ritual was peripheral enough to be either taken or left. In fact, that would be absurd since a number of the prophets functioned as priests in the Temple. And there is no biblical evidence that they found their priestly and prophetic roles to be in essential conflict. So, what the prophets were saying is that the covenantal relationship with God can survive (however deficient) without the sacrificial system, as indeed it has survived during the exile after the destruction of the First Temple in 586 BCE, and the exile after the destruction of the Second Temple in 70 CE. What the covenantal relationship cannot survive, however, is when the commandments, especially those pertaining to the interhuman relationship, are in any way marginalized or trivialized. For the covenant is between God and a people. But where there is rampant injustice, especially when that injustice is institutionalized, the people are no longer a true community, hence the covenant has no place in the world to operate. The covenant's legitimacy or validity is not contingent on public morality, yet its effectiveness depends on that public morality, the ethos of an authentic human community. Without it, the Torah as the constitution of the covenant might as well have remained in heaven or in a museum.[14]

Indeed, one might well say that in biblical theology morality is the necessary condition for a complete relationship with God, but it is still insufficient without atonement (*kapparah*) coming from God, which is completed through the atonement rituals of the Temple. Thus in God's name, Jeremiah warns the people that "only when you effect justice [*mishpat*] between a man and his neighbour, ... only then shall I cause you to dwell in this place" (Jeremiah 7:5, 7). "This place" is the "Temple of the Lord" (7:4), which the people still need in order to receive full atonement for their sins against both God and other humans. And in the Jewish tradition, the Yom Kippur atonement rites are considered to be ineffective for anybody unless they are first reconciled with their neighbour.[15] Nevertheless, however necessary this prior interhuman reconciliation is, it is still insufficient to effect full reconciliation with God, who has also been offended by the injustice done by one human to another.[16] That full reconciliation is only accomplished by God's purification of Israel through the Yom Kippur rite, which is subsequent but by no means secondary or peripheral to interhuman moral reconciliation. And lest it be thought that without the sacrificial cult itself being operative no reconciliation with God can be effected, it is taught that the observance of the Day of Atonement (*yom ha-kippurim*) itself suffices to atone (*mekhapper*) by itself.[17] In other words, the sacrificial cult is optimal but not indispensable for this reconciliation of humans with God to be accomplished. Moral reconciliation among humans themselves, though, is an absolutely necessary precondition for this divine-human reconciliation to become a reality.

The fulfilment of the need for a relationship with God is what is desirable for humans. "It is good [*tov*] to praise the Lord, to sing to

Your name O' most exalted One" (Psalms 92:2). And the frustration of that need is bad. "Cast me not away from Your presence, and Your holy spirit [*ruah qodshekha*] do not take away from me; return to me Your joyous salvation" (Psalms 51:13–14). And, as in any mutual relationship, what is good or desirable for one partner should be so for the other partner. Therefore, it is noted in the Talmud that proper worship of God by humans gives "spiritual pleasure" (*nahat ruah*) to God, that is, doing what God desires from humans.[18] Proper worship is when human worshippers do not attempt to bribe God as it were into approving injustices they have committed against other humans. That is what is bad for God; it is what God says "I hate ... because your hands [lifted in sacrificial prayer] are filled with blood" (Isaiah 1:14–15).

The prophets were not advocating that morality replace religious piety; instead, they were advocating that piety must include morality. But just as piety is not to be seen as a replacement for morality, so morality is not to be a replacement for piety. Here we see how the divine-human and the interhuman relationships must always be correlated, not only in theory, but even more so in practice. Moreover, just as a bad interhuman relationship leads to a distorted relationship with God, so does a bad relationship with God lead to a distorted interhuman relationship. We see this in the relationship between Cain and his brother Abel. It is important to note that right after "God turns away [*lo sha'ah*] from Cain and his offering" (Genesis 4:5) while at the same turning towards Abel and his offering, Cain reacts to his rejection by God and God's simultaneous acceptance of his brother by "rising up to kill Abel his brother" (Genesis 4:8). When Cain says to God: "my punishment [*avoni*] is too great to bear" (Genesis 4:13), he seems to finally realize that his crime has been committed against both God and his fellow human being. For death came into the world because his father Adam didn't hearken to God's commandment, and murder came into the world because Cain didn't hearken to the Abel's plea not to kill him, as one of the ancient Rabbis taught.[19]

No one relationship suffices for the needs of the other. Humans, for their most basic orientation in the world, need to look to God who creates us specially ("in the image of God"), placing us in the world to be uniquely related to God and to bring the rest of creation into that relationship along with us. Humans do not get this basic world-orientation from other humans, even from their own human society (however just it is). For how could any human creature give this orientation to any other human creature or to themselves when we all have to say to God: "I am but a sojourner [*ger*] on earth, do not hide Your commandments from me" (Psalms 119:19)? Nevertheless, we humans need to look for our regular personal relationships among those most like ourselves ("bone of my bones and flesh of my flesh" – Genesis 2:23), to those with whom we are in regular contact (beginning with our spouses, then with our families, then with our community). Neither relationship can be well cultivated at the expense of the other. When there is a conflict between duties owed to God and duties owed to other humans, sometimes one set of duties trumps the other and sometimes vice versa.[20]

Even the most exalted human relationship with God, that relationship enjoyed by Moses with God, is still enjoyed by Moses as the representative of *the people* God has chosen for the covenantal relationship. So, when God offers Moses an individual relationship with God, which is a tempting offer to replace the public covenant with a private religion, Moses says that if that is so, "now wipe me from the book You have written" (Exodus 32:32). That book is the Torah, which commands the justice needed to hold the covenanted community together. Thus Jewish prayer is almost always situated in a "we-Thou" relationship rather than in an "I-Thou" relationship.[21]

Furthermore, even the most exalted interhuman relationship, which is the marriage of a woman and a man, is only so exalted because it reflects the more perfect marriage of God and His people, which explains the inclusion, indeed the exalted status, of *Song of Songs* in the biblical cannon.[22] No human community, whether marital, familial, or societal, is sufficient by itself to fulfil the basic human need for a relationship with God. And no religion can be lived by humans as the essentially social beings we are, let alone be sustained throughout history, without a coherent human community to house it and transmit it.

Neither relationship by itself, neither the divine-human relationship nor the interhuman relationship, is sufficient for a full or complete human life. Even when the two relationships are well correlated, a truly complete human life still requires redemption by God – redemption (*ge'ulah*) for which there is no potential but only a possibility for it to occur in this world. This final and complete redemption lies beyond the horizon of our experience in a truly radical future (*l'atid la vo*), which is the "end of days" (*aharit ha-yamim*) or the *eschaton*.[23] To presume that we ourselves, whether morally or religiously or both together, can bring about the kingdom of God on earth is to presume that while God began the creative process, we humans can succeed God by accelerating it, let alone by finishing it ourselves.[24] But as the prophet Isaiah said in God's name: "For I am He; before Me no god [*el*] existed and after Me none will ever be" (Isaiah 43:10).

There is a constant overlapping of the two kinds of essential human relationships, that with each other and that with God. Nonetheless, whereas morality can be taken up into piety with its integrity intact, piety cannot be taken down into morality without its integrity being violated. That is because piety is superior to morality. Piety involves a direct relationship with God. In morality, the relationship with God is much more indirect; it is mediated by the interhuman relationship, that is, the relationship with other humans, who are essentially inferior to the God who has made us. As the Talmud puts it: "We are to rise [*ma'alin*] in sanctity, not descend [*moridin*] in sanctity."[25]

Since revelation is essentially between God and a community, a justly governed community provides the necessary context wherein revelation could occur and be accepted. But the event of revelation transforms the community from a mundane society, a human association at best only able to look to God as the original source of its norms, into a people immediately and permanently covenanted by God. The covenant gives a heretofore mundane human community its cosmic status. (That is what all historical sustained cultures seek, which is why they are all theological-ontological to the core.) Now, in a natural human community, God as it were stands behind the law as its original and perpetual authority. But in a covenanted community, humans stand directly before God, because "the Lord has come down from the mountain to the people" (Exodus 19:14). It is only in a covenantal context that we humans can confidently say: "God is *with* us" (*immanu' el* – Isaiah 7:14; 8:10). This is quite different from the "God is with us" (*Gott mit uns*) ideology of both ancient and modern tyrannies. There God is brought down to the level of the tyrants (whether individual or collective) to automatically endorse their human-made rule. But in the covenant, the community is brought up to stand before God and become subject to God's fullest law for humans as well as to God's direct judgment of His people. In fact, "God is with us" means *we are with God*. That is, we are with God on God's terms that are revealed to us as the commandments of the Torah. It is not for us to presume that since God is with us, in the midst of our community, we can conclude from that fact what the law is to be on our terms, that is, what we want it to be.[26]

The basic moral norms of the community, its political content, nonetheless remain intact. These norms are transformed, that is, recontextualized, but they are not dissembled substantially. Conversely, to presume that God, at best, is only the original source of the law is to make God less than what the Lord God already does in the covenant. Once revelation has occurred and has been accepted, those who have accepted God's revelation should not regress to their pre-revelational, natural condition, nor should they think their natural condition has been overcome. Instead, pre-Sinaitic morality ever accompanies the fuller law of

God revealed at Sinai, though it is always in the background rather than the foreground of the life of the covenanted people.[27] Adherence to the law of that pre-revelational condition is all the covenanted people Israel have the right to expect from the nations of the world, and that is all the nations of the world (who are not full participants in God's covenant with Israel) have a right to expect from the people Israel. But God demands much more from His people, and they should demand much more from God and from themselves.[28] Just as God elevates ordinary worldly nature into the covenant intact, so does God elevate ordinary human communal nature intact into the covenant.That is why natural law (*lex naturalis*), that is, universally valid norms, are the ever-present *conditio sine qua non* of the covenantal norms of the Torah. Natural law is the "bottom line" that is to be supplemented but never to be abrogated by the full Torah.

There is also a distinction made in biblical theology between theory and praxis. That distinction is constituted quite differently than it is in classical philosophy (as we shall see in the next section). One could say, along with the great German-Jewish philosopher Hermann Cohen, that "theory is practical" (*Theorie der Praxis,* as he put it in German).[29] That is, intellectual reflection is not *contemplation* of an inert divine reality. Theorizing here is not about One who does not engage in any *praxis* or transitive action that is related *to* an external object, let alone One who doesn't engage in any *reciprocal transactions with* other persons. Instead, in biblical theology, all theory or intellection is about what active persons *do* in the world *for* and *with* other persons there. In this sense, God is a *person*; indeed, God is *the archetypal person*, because God reveals the fact that He does make deliberate choices and acts upon them in the world. These deliberate acts are what humans are often commanded to celebrate (like the Exodus from Egypt), and what they are sometimes commanded to imitate (*imitatio Dei* is the Latin term most often used). (This is quite different from saying that there is a class of beings called "persons" that we infer from ordinary experience in the world, and that God seems to be *like* them.) Thus human choices are of cosmic significance when human actors (or "agents," as philosophers like to say, due to the theatrical connotation of the word "actor") make choices after having deliberated or thought about God's revealed actions and the reasons (either stated or inferred) for these divine actions. All theory, then, is about what active persons *do* in the world in relation to and with other such persons. As metaphysics, this is reflection on what God does. As ethics, this is reflection on what humans are to do thereafter.

At times, there is more theoretical speculation (*Aggadah)* by the Rabbis; and at times, there is more practical legislation (*Halakhah)*. Yet they are interrelated in Jewish tradition, since theory and praxis are only formally distinct but not substantially different, as both involve the same God.[30] Here philosophy as ethical reflection is about the universal meaning or rationale of human actions in the political world, especially those human actions that are interactions with other persons. And here theology as metaphysical reflection is about the particular meaning or rationale of divine actions in Israel's history (what some have called *Heilsgeschichte*), especially those divine actions that are celebrated in the commandments that pertain to the relationship between God and the Jewish people.[31] Both philosophical and theological reflection are seeking what in rabbinic thought is called *ta'amei ha-mitsvot*, that is, "reasons of the commandments."[32] The reasons of the commandments pertaining to the interhuman domain are *philosophical* insofar as they are derived from reflection on universal human nature (i.e., humans as essentially social beings). And the reasons of the commandments pertaining to God-human domain are *theological* insofar as they are derived from reflection on God's actions for and with His people in history (i.e., as persons who are essentially God-oriented) as narrated in Scripture.[33] There is theory in both domains as there is praxis in both domains insofar as the two domains overlap, and they are never totally separate from each other.

Furthermore, the two types of theory are most profoundly coordinated when human action is seen to be imitation of divine action.[34] In that case, human action participates in God's action as "Master of the universe" (*ribbono shel olam* in Hebrew), because the reasons of divine action (either revealed or inferred from revelation) are what humans identify with as the reasons for their own actions. As one ancient Rabbi put it: "Make your will [*retsonekha*] like God's will and God will make your will His will."[35] And, surely, "will" here means "reasoned choice," since an irrational God could hardly be imitated by rational beings.[36]

Humans Related to Each Other and to God: Athens

In classical philosophy, interhuman relationships are a matter of much concern, and the divine-human relationship is a matter of even greater concern. In that way, as we have seen, the two traditions, that of Athens and that of Jerusalem, have much in common. In the interhuman realm, both traditions are very much concerned with justice. But whereas in biblical theology "righteousness and justice are done on earth" (Jeremiah 9:23), and there is no real difference between justice done in heaven and justice done on earth, in classical philosophy true justice is to be sought in heaven, not on earth. Thus Plato writes in Socrates's name:

"Evils [*ta kaka*] ... necessarily hover over mortal nature [*thnētēn physin*] and this [earthly] place; hence we need to escape [*pheugein*] quite rapidly ... escaping [the earth] is to be God-like [*homoiōsis*] as much as we can; it is to become just [*dikaion*] and pious [*hosion*] wisely [*meta phronēseōs*]."[37] In other words, humans become most like god-like when they despair of finding (and doing) justice in this temporal world, and thus leave it behind to find an altogether superior justice in the eternal realm occupied by the gods. Indeed, Plato and the Stoics think that mundane justice can only approximate cosmic or natural justice.[38] However, since this cosmic justice cannot be described in ordinary language, it is difficult to see how it can be the measure of the mundane justice that can be described.

Aristotle, on the other hand, seems to avoid discussion of cosmic justice.[39] For him, what philosophers seek in the eternal realm is not justice but something unrelated to mundane justice. Indeed, it seems that is why, for Aristotle, heaven and earth in no way interact. That also explains why he keeps his political philosophy quite separate from his ontology. Thus when Aristotle says that those who do not need interhuman society are either gods or beasts, surely philosophers function above that human dividing line; philosophers qua philosophers transcend the ordinary human need for society.[40] Therefore, it would seem that philosophers should not aspire to be leaders in a realm that is essentially beneath them. They don't need the honours or approval that ordinary leaders seek. Their society, though, needs leaders who do seek the approval of those being led.[41]

The reason for this great difference between the two traditions is that in biblical theology the God who creates humans for a relationship with Himself is the same God who creates humans for a relationship with each other, and the same God who enables both of these intertwined relationships to be lived and continued in this world.

In classical philosophy, the gods who are concerned with human justice and injustice are the superhuman powers who have placed humans on earth to serve them. But these are not the same gods or God whom philosophically charged humans seek to be with in heaven or the world-above-and-beyond, as we have seen. Therefore, for philosophers, the gods on earth are only to be worshipped and emulated when they enforce a standard of human action that can be considered just. Justice here means two things. At the most evident level, that of ordinary people in society, justice is (in the thought of Roman jurists influenced by Stoic philosophy) enabling people to live with integrity, that is, honestly and not deceitfully (*honeste vivere*); preventing violence being done to one another (*alterum non laedere*); and giving everybody what they need and deserve (*suum cuique tribuere*).[42] But at the more exalted level, justice is enjoying eternal contemplative bliss with the gods, "being at home [*oikēsei*] with the gods," away from the earthly place with which these gods are not concerned because these gods are not responsible for it, not having placed its inhabitants therein.[43]

In terms of his bodily interactions with other humans, which when private are domestic and when public are political, Socrates considers himself obligated to obey the gods of Athens, his city. They are his masters who have placed embodied human beings in the temporal world, and who then guard them and care for them. One of the chief ways the gods do that is to prescribe good laws by which the earthly city or *polis* is to be well governed, and these are laws whose authority Socrates, like all good Athenians, has freely accepted for himself, albeit retroactively.[44] However, there are "other gods [*theous allous*] who are wise [*sophous*] and good" whom Socrates after his bodily death in this world hopes to join.[45] By living a rational, sober life while embodied in this world, which is a life prescribed by the *civic* gods at their best, philosophers ("lovers of wisdom and the wise") will be prepared to be full members of the eternal realm of immortal disembodied souls (*psychai).* But because Socrates at present is still the possession of a civic (Athenian) god, he may not emancipate himself by a premature departure from this world via suicide. This is like the talmudic dictum "Nobody can free himself from prison."[46] In the meantime, like all humans Socrates must wait "until the god himself lets us go," which seems to be when the god decides he is ready to ascend to that higher world.[47]

That waiting is not passive inaction; instead, it is "cleansing ourselves" (*kathareuōmen*) by living a life free from the immorality that comes with the irrational indulgence of bodily appetites and desires, all of which constitute the three kinds of injustice (dishonesty, violence, and greed) that the justice mentioned above is meant to curb.[48] The difference between philosophers and ordinary people is that for ordinary people, mundane justice is something they hope will protect them from their dangerous excesses and those of others. This is a kind of moral balancing act needed for both individual and collective survival in this world, but it is not a means to some higher end. For ordinary humans, this mundane justice is accepted not because it is valuable per se, but because of its perceived good effects. That is something our political experience is supposed to have taught us.

Philosophers, too, do not seem to regard mundane civic justice as valuable per se. They view this civic justice as only a necessary instrument for maintaining public order, but not as what is desirable for itself. For philosophers, this justice is not primarily an instrument for controlling what is beneath the rational soul. Instead, the practice of this kind of justiceseems to be what is needed to prepare the rational soul for the eternal life that is mostly beyond it here and now, but which, nonetheless, beckons the rational soul to enjoy at least a bit of its bliss while living the superior contemplative life (*bios theōretikos*) in this world.[49] For philosophers, the practice of mundane justice, then, is encouraged because it is *a* means to the highest end. Nevertheless, the practice of justice is not *the* means to that end, for that would strongly imply that the practice of justice will automatically lead one to the contemplative life. It is only a precondition of the contemplative life; it does not guarantee it. Thus it is very difficult to think of a true contemplative philosopher who lives an unjust, disordered, impulsive life.[50] (*Au contraire,* think of Alcibiades in Plato's *Symposium,* whose volatile temperament prevents him from being a real philosopher in Socrates's circle.)[51] But it is quite easy to think of many people who do live just, ordered, and sober lives, who are not philosophers, who do not desire to be philosophers, who cannot be made into philosophers, and who should not be expected to be philosophers. This might well be saying that mundane justice is *a* necessary (*conditio sine qua non*) but not *the* sufficient condition or *the* true cause (*conditio per quam*) of the philosophical, contemplative life.

Furthermore, especially as imagined by Aristotle, there is no interpenetration of the lower world governed by mundane justice and the upper world where one's total attention is to God as the *summum bonum*. The practical significance of that refusal is that unlike Plato (and the Stoics to a certain extent), philosophers who have glimpsed ultimate *Goodness* ought not be obliged to descend again into the mundane world to apply what they have seen above to their just rule down below. In fact, they are well advised not to do so. (*Au contraire,* think of Plato's disastrous attempts to become the official philosopher of Syracuse, which should be contrasted with his teacher Socrates's great political reticence.)[52] For Aristotle, the most one could say is that political teleology is analogous to cosmic teleology. (That is why a number of contemporary neo-Aristotelians try to totally separate Aristotelian ethics from Aristotelian ontology.)[53] But there is a great difference between the two realms. God, not mundane justice, is the ultimate object of true contemplative desire, because God alone is loved for Godself. God is not loved because of any politically beneficial effects like mundane justice's being valued by ordinary people. God is not loved as a means to a higher end like mundane justice is valued by philosophers. God alone is the highest end.

Since Aristotelian morality is not as intertwined with Aristotelian ontology as is the case with Platonic morality and ontology, it has been easier for Jewish and Christian thinkers to correlate Aristotelian morality with their theological ontology than to correlate Plato's morality with their theological ontology. In fact, the more radical view of human nature in Plato's ontology leads to a more radical view of human action in Plato's morality.[54] That is why some mediaeval Jewish and Christian thinkers could more easily incorporate many aspects of Aristotle's more sober morality into their basically theological morality.

Humans Related to Nature: Jerusalem

As we have seen, in biblical theology the term "nature" (in Hebrew, *tev'a*) can be used to designate the whole created universe (*shamayim ve'arets* or "heaven and earth"). One can call this created universe "nature" or "natural" because it has an intelligible order (*sidrei bre'sheet* or "orders of creation" in rabbinic parlance) or "cosmic justice," though understood only imperfectly by humans.[55] The metaphysical question to ask at this beginning point of our enquiry into the human relation to nature is: Are humans related to nature, or is nature related to humans? That is, is the purpose of humane existence to be found in nature, or is the purpose of nature to be found in humane existence? This metaphysical question of *what is* the human-nature relationship leads directly to the ethical question: *why are* humans *to be* related to nature, and *how are* humans to so relate themselves to nature? Are humans answerable to nature insofar as they are to ask themselves whether or not they are living according to their natural ends? Or, are humans *to be* responsible for nature *because* nature's resources are created to be used as the means for human existence, which is nature's transnatural end? These questions are necessarily teleological inasmuch as they essentially involve decisive human action. Thus the human relation to nature is an ethical task. And in order for it to be an intelligent task, one must have some understanding of why it is to be undertaken.

This overall question seems to have been resolved by a famous rabbinic dictum: "Every human ought to say: for my sake [*bi-shevili*] is the world [*ha'olam*] created."[56] That is the metaphysical answer to the question. The ethical answer is that every human is to act accordingly in his or her relation to the surrounding world, that is, his or her *environment*. Indeed, our primary and unsurpassable contact with nature is always with this surrounding world, and that contact seems to be pragmatic: What do we do with the surrounding world so that it contributes to our survival and does not destroy us? That requires our effort. "By the sweat of your brow you will eat bread" (Genesis 3:19).[57]

Now, on the surface, this rabbinic dictum sounds like anthropocentric grandiosity. To be sure, that would be true if one interprets the dictum to mean: "Nature is created for me to do with it whatever I want to do with it!"[58] That would presume, though, that we humans are the *telos* of creation (ends-in-themselves) rather than correctly assuming that we humans have a *telos*, a purpose given to us by God rather than one that is simply innate, or one given to ourselves by ourselves. And what is that *telos* God has assigned *to* humans? It is: "Finally and definitively [*sof davar*], insofar as it has all been understood, to revere God and to keep His commandments is all [what it means to be] human [*kol ha'adam*]" (Ecclesiastes 12:13).

That purpose, though, can only be fulfilled in our own environment, that corner of the universe that surrounds us, which we have to share with the beings that God has placed here with us. Since we both occupy the same world, there is no way we humans could fulfil our divinely assigned *telos* in the world without using our fellow beings for that same purpose. That is why we are responsible for these beings. We need them in the fulfilment of our *telos*, which is our obedience to the commandments God has given us, some of which require us to imitate God's responsible concern for His creation. Hence we are judged by God, to whom we humans are answerable as to how responsibly or irresponsibly we have used the surrounding environment and the beings it contains in our fulfilment of the *telos* assigned to us by God. The difference between human responsibility for the world and God's responsibility for the world is that human responsibility is heteronmous: it is a charge given to humans. God's responsibility is self-chosen. It is truly autonomous. (In fact, autonomy is uniquely divine.) That is why humans are answerable to God, but God is not answerable to humans. God is only answerable to Godself.[59] That is why God can rightfully try His human creatures, whereas no creature may try God.[60]

Surely, this understanding of human purposefulness dispels the notion that it is human arrogance and irresponsibility to regard the universe as having been created for humans' sake, because the surrounding world has not been given to humankind's own self-invented projects. It is not arrogant, for it assumes that we humans are answerable *to* God rather than to our own worldly ideals or plans; and it is not irresponsible inasmuch as it assumes that humans are to be concerned with (*Sorge* in German) what God has commanded us to care for. Thus humans are responsible for their environment because some of God's responsibility *for* His creation has been delegated to humans created in God's image, who are God's "partners" (*shuttafim*) – albeit junior partners – in the "working of creation" (*be-ma'aseh bere'sheet*).[61] "The heavens, the heavens are God's, but the earth He has given [*natan*] to humankind" (Psalms 115:16). Moreover, lest one think that this gift may be used capriciously, the great mediaeval commentator Rashi argues against "those devoid of intelligence, who think that human rule [*memshelet ha'adam*] is the equivalent of God's rule in heaven ... for humans are only God's appointee [*paqid*] on earth."[62] This is to be constrasted with the arrogance of Pharaoh, who claims himself to "be just like God" (Genesis 3:15) when he boasts: "The Nile is mine; I made it by myself [*asitini*]!" (Ezekiel 29:3).

In the first creation narrative in the Bible, the human relation to their natural environment is stated to be "conquest" (*ve-kivshuhah* – Genesis 1:28). But in the second creation narrative, humans are placed in the world (originally, the Garden of Eden) in order "to work it and to watch it" (*l'ovdah u-le-shomrah* – Genesis 2:15). When viewing the whole biblical narrative as a seamless garment, one can see the second narrative to be qualifying the first. That is, "conquering" or "subduing" is to be done for a purpose, which is what "work" is. Work is meant to produce something, that is, its product. That purpose is not the workers' exercise of their own power. Instead, the making of the product (*Werk* in German) is the penultimate purpose of the work, which then must be justified as to its usefulness *for* human interaction with God and fellow humans. This is the final purpose of the work. On the other hand, "watching" means guarding or protecting what one is working *on* for a purpose.[63] However, that protective guarding can only be done well when a worker has respectful knowledge of what he or she is working with. Thus "working" means what we are *allowed to do* with nature. "Watching" means what we are *not allowed to do* with nature. Respectful knowledge means not tampering with the data before us to simply make it whatever we want it to become. That is why we are not allowed to totally deplete any part of nature we are allowed to use. Thus the land of Israel that is given to the people Israel to develop is also not to be worked during the seventh year, which like the seventh day is called a "Sabbath" (Leviticus 25:6). Just as the temporal Sabbath prevents our work from consuming all of our time, so does this spatial Sabbath prevent our work from depleting our place on earth.

Humans are not responsible for all of nature as is God, who has created all of nature. Humans have not been made to rule over all of nature any more than all of nature has been made solely for human appropriation. When we humans presume to have what might be called "omni-responsibility" for all of nature, that is as arrogant as our presuming we are responsible for nothing natural. Not being the creators of nature, but rather being the responsible stewards of our portion in the natural world, we humans are neither gods nor demons. We have neither made nature nor can we destroy it. We can only live side by side nature: using nature when its things are needed for our communal life with God and our fellow humans in the world; letting it be when nature's things are not needed for our communal life. We cannot avoid subduing nature lest we be subdued by nature; yet we must do this only when necessary, that is, when we have to protect ourselves from nature. But when this is not necessary, we should be nature's respectful, non-intrusive spectators.

Human interest in nature is limited by the question: How does what we know of nature, even as much of nature we do know by scientific enquiry that greatly enhances our technological power over nature, how does that empowering knowledge ultimately contribute to the enhancement of our relationship with God and the overlapping relationship with our fellow humans in the world? This is not the question of the type of pragmatic technology that only asks about the immediate "cash value" of any human endeavour. For our "use" of the knowledge of nature, gained either aesthetically or scientifically, can often be for no other purpose than admiring God's creation and thanking God for allowing us to enjoy it, and to know some of its inner processes.[64] Moreover, that thankful admiration becomes the content of what we can say among ourselves to God about God's creativity. As such, it becomes an integral part of our covenantal relationship with God.

Is and Ought

This view of nature does not get us into the philosophical conundrum of deriving an "ought" from an "is."[65] Instead, an "is" needs to be known so it might be used *for the sake of* an "ought." For, in our experience as acting beings, we are first addressed by those making claims on us, that is, they ask us or tell us or command us to do something for them.[66] For example, a mother tells her daughter, "bring me an apple; I need it to bake a pie." Now if that mother is not actually pointing to a particular apple directly in front of her daughter, the child has to know enough (whether by instruction or by her own discovery) of what an apple *is* and how it *is* distinguished from an orange because it has different properties than an orange has. Thus the daughter needs to know what an apple is *in order* to be able to fulfil her mother's request correctly. That is what motivates her to discover the distinguishing properties of apples. And the more complex the request, the more "scientific" the knowledge of the person being so requested has to be. So, too, we need to be acquainted with what is in our world so that we might know how to properly employ these things when fulfilling our duties to other persons, whether to God or to fellow humans, who make rightful or just claims on us.[67] When that "ought" or commanding claim is voiced in order to include desirable worldly things within an interpersonal, working relationship, there is mutual responsibility: I am asking you to do this *with* me for the sake of *our* common good. It is their usefulness for this commonality that makes ordinary things desirable.[68]

Even scientific knowledge, which is supposed to be factual knowledge for its own sake rather than knowledge for its technological value, is still expressed in words spoken in the human life-world (*Lebenswelt* in German), however many mathematical symbols are used in that discourse. These words that name things are uttered because someone else *wants* to hear them. As Wittgenstein pointed out, a "private language" is an oxymoron.[69] Language by definition is the medium of verbal communication between hearers and speakers (and the respective roles are interchangeable). Thus even scientists speak and write in the words used in a community of enquirers, whose members (whether explicitly or implicitly) are *asking for* information about something in the world, even if that information is not being sought for its pragmatic usefulness, but simply for its value as a means of human communication.[70]

Nevertheless, that does not mean that *what* is being communicated is *whatever* the speaker or the hearer wants it to be. Even though the natural-objective world of things lends itself to our human employment of it, its facticity must still be worked-with in order for our employment of it to be effective in the world we ourselves did not create, but in which we find ourselves already situated. These things are already creatures of God before and after they are employed by us humans. As such, that honest employment prevents us from acting as if we ourselves created them *ex nihilo*. In other words, we are still required to acknowledge the integrity of natural entities or things by speaking truthfully about them and not spoiling them, that is, not simply reducing their facticity to what they mean *for* us. That is why our natural science is not to be deduced from our ethics. A worldly thing is not just what we think it ought to be for our use of it. The natural world is not our tool, as we did not create it. It is only partially lent to us by God who has created it, which is why we can never take full possession of anything. We are to be interested in worldly things only insofar as we can include them in our normatively charged interpersonal relationships. The popular image of the "mad scientist" is one where a gifted individual attempts to use his or her knowledge of nature to escape the interpersonal world, or attempts to control nature rather than sharing his or her knowledge of nature with other persons. That is why natural science, like art, needs to justify its social value, not only because of the material products it can produce, but much more because of the subject matter it can provide for intelligent human interaction.

The is/ought conundrum assumes that human knowing is essentially that of a disinterested spectator looking *at* the world from somewhere outside of it. As such, authentically human interests, which necessarily motivate humans to do anything *to* the world from *within* the world, are totally disconnected from humans as spectators looking at the world from *without*. But can anybody really be so uninterested *in* the world where they live and want to live? Indeed, in order to sustain interest in anything, one's interest must be due to his or her desire. One must love what he or she is interested in in order for the interest to remain sufficiently motivated. Even being a spectator can only be sustained if one is looking *at* the world ultimately in order to discover *in* it or *through* it what is truly worthy of one's total devotion.[71] So, for example, the righteous king Uzziah developed the Judean wilderness "because he loves the earth" (II Chronicles 26:10).[72]

In most modern views of nature, humans as interested toolmakers (*homo faber*) have developed the technology that enables them to exercise ever-increasing control *over* nature. However, in biblical theology, humans are interested in the world because of the divine mandate to them to care *for* nature, which is for us to be concerned *with* the world. I use the term "interest" in its original sense in Latin, *inter-esse*, meaning "to be among" or "to be in the midst of the world" (what Heidegger called *in-der Welt-sein*).[73] Even Archimedes never received an answer to his request: "give me a place to stand [outside the earth] and I will move the earth."[74]

Human Appreciation of God's Creation

In the Jewish tradition, humans like the rest of the universe are *creatures* of God.[75] Yet humans seem to be unique creatures insofar as we have been enabled (via revelation) to recognize *that* the natural world all around us and beyond us is graciously created by God, and *what* God has done by creating it so intelligently. Because God has built into this universe an intelligible order, humans are obliged to appreciatively understand it as much as it is possible for us to do. That is part of the commandment to worship God.[76] Declaring that creaturely awareness of the divinely instituted natural order is a form of the worship of God (what is called *hoda'ah* in Hebrew, meaning "thankful acknowledgment").[77] "How manifold are Your works O' Lord; all of them You have so wisely [*be-hokhmah*] made. The earth is replete with Your creations!" (Psalms 104:24). In fact, according to one of the ancient Rabbis, whoever does not engage in that appreciative understanding of the natural created order is castigated by Scripture as somebody "who has not looked into the Lord's working [*po'al*], and who has not looked with favour on what His hands make [*u-ma'aseh*]" (Isaiah 5:12).[78] This clearly teaches that humans have a moral obligation to scientifically enquire into the workings of God's creation. So, before one partakes of something of nature for his or her use or enjoyment (whether sensuous or intellectual), that person is to acknowledge God's ownership of all creation.[79] And that person is also to acknowledge that his or her use or enjoyment of created nature is a divine entitlement.[80]

Since we all begin with our own situation in the world, humans ought to begin to thankfully acknowledge God here. We must be clear as to whom our thanks are being given, for confusion here could lead to idolatry: the worship of "alien gods" (*elohim aherim* – Exodus 20:3). And that intelligent thanksgiving is required, if for no other reason than the fact that God has enabled wondrously created nature to be seen with appreciative intelligence by humans. Thus humans are privileged to echo God by declaring all of creation we can experience to be "very good" (Genesis 1:31), irrespective of how nature happens to be affecting any particular individual here and now. In one rabbinic view, acknowledging God's mighty beneficence is the primary form of the worship of God. Yet even here this acknowledgment is to directly lead a person into making his or her personal requests to God who has been so acknowledged.[81] Hence such acknowledgment is not unworldly contemplation. It must always have a connection to a person's active situation in the world.

There is more to this intelligent appreciation of created nature than admiring wonder or thankful acknowledgment. Inasmuch as God is not only the Creator of the natural world, but also its guardian and protector (which seems to be known only via revelation), humans are therefore able to call upon God to exercise responsibility for what He has made by not abandoning His creation. (In Hebrew, this is called *baqashah*, meaning "beseeching" or "requesting.")[82] And when do humans have that right to call upon God to exercise His responsibility for creation? They have that right, indeed the duty, to do so when it seems from their own bad experience of earthly nature (which is their natural environment in the created universe) that God has not exercised His proper responsibility for them in their earthly habitat. "My

God, my God, why have You forsaken me [*azavtani*]; why are You so far from delivering me [*me-yeshu'ati*] and from the words of my howling?! ... Save me from a lion's mouth; from the horns of wild oxen save me!" (Psalms 22:2, 22).

Interestingly enough, in situations when somebody experiences great personal loss, Jewish tradition does not require that person to still affirm God's goodness in nature, but only to affirm God's more mysterious "justice" (*tsidduq ha-din*, literally "justification of the judgment" in Hebrew). Here the obligation is only to acknowledge God's justice, not to thank God for His goodness or beneficence, because blessing (*berakhah*) has not been experienced on such an occasion.[83] One has to wait indefinitely to see how God's justice is ultimately beneficent.[84] To require thanksgiving at this time would cruelly require a person to utter a belief that for him or her could only be a lie.[85] On the other hand, though, humans have the right, indeed the duty, to thank God when their experience of their environment is good. (In Hebrew, such prayers are called *birkhot nehenin*, meaning "benedictions for the experience of worldly pleasure.") Thus Psalm 22 continues by thanking God: "For He did not revile or despise the affliction of the poor; He did not hide His presence from him; when he cried to Him, He did hear. Because of what came from Him, I praise Him in the great assembly; facing His worshippers [*neged yerei'av*] do I pay my vows" (Psalms 22:25–6). Indeed, we would be ungrateful if we did not thank God for His beneficence, which we have experienced. This experience provides the occasion for uttering thanksgiving in the prescribed formula of a benediction, even if that is only an occasion of aesthetic enjoyment of nature.[86]

In another rabbinic view, beseeching God is the primary form of the worship of God.[87] Here it seems that praising God for His beneficence in nature is done first so that worshippers might subsequently recognize to whom they are addressing their requests. Moreover, since God's beneficence in nature is learned from God's historical beneficence to His people *through* nature, the recognition of God's beneficence in nature is to remind God of His own precedent, that is, we want God to do for us in the present and the future what God has done for us in the past. In other words, our interest in nature is motivated by self-interest. It cannot be a disinterested view from nowhere. However, what prevents that self-interest from becoming selfish desire is that worshippers are not supposed to request from God a response *through* nature that would be detrimental to other humans or to the natural world.[88] Indeed, the selfish attitude of "what is mine is mine; what is yours is yours" is castigated as being the character trait of the evil people of Sodom.[89]

Contemporary Environmentalism

Some contemporary environmentalists see in the words of Genesis, chapter 1, a biblical justification for humans looking upon themselves as the unquestioned rulers of the earth, therefore allowing themselves to do with the earth and its inhabitants whatever they please.[90] (Here we return more fully to the environmental question we discussed in the previous chapter.) But these environmentalists seem to ignore Genesis, chapter 2. There human responsibility for the care of nature is commanded by the Creator God, who is the sole proprietor of the earth. Thus when God commands his people to refrain from working the land of Israel during the sabbatical year, they are reminded that "because the earth is Mine, you are but transitory tenants [*gerim ver-toshavim*] with Me" (Leviticus 25:23).[91] Yet because we humans are God's possessions who can know that we are God's possessions, we therefore have the right to call upon God to exercise responsibility for His creation (as we saw a little earlier). The only right we do not have in this context is to indict God for not satisfying our needs here and now. But as Job reminded his wife, who was tempting him to blaspheme: "Shall we only accept what is good for us from God, but not what is bad [*ha-r'a*]?!" (Job 2:10). Or, as it is said elsewhere: "Do not the bad [*ha-ra'ot*] and the good come from the mouth of the Most High?!" (Lamentations 3:37).[92]

Nevertheless, those environmentalists who usually only seize upon Genesis, chapter 1, and ignore Genesis, chapter 2, cannot explain why if humans are simply part of nature, being no different from all other natural beings, they alone should be required to exercise responsibility for all of nature over which they have more and more control. Could this be cogently required of any other merely natural being? As Maimonides pointed out, only those whose freedom is evident enough to be commanded to exercise responsibility, only such beings can be answerable as to whether they have exercised that responsibility or not, or have exercised it properly or not.[93] It seems, then, we can exercise responsibility only for those beings who are essentially weaker than ourselves, and which are dependent on our care. Therefore, when these others are not seriously threatening us but do come into our domain in a non-threatening way, that is, we can domesticate or tame them, we humans are obligated to care for them responsibly, in a way that is responsive to their needs.[94] That responsibility is to be exercised with whatever fellow creatures we humans find ourselves together with. And that responsibility is to be exercised even though those *other* creatures cannot reciprocate our responsibility for them.

Without the acceptance of our human presence in the natural world as our appointment by God to be responsible for one another (reciprocally) and for the natural world (non-reciprocally), it seems human responsibility can only be advocated in one of two ways.

One way in which human responsibility for nature has been advocated, the way that has the most secular appeal, is a utilitarian argument. It goes something like this: Our human survival, let alone our flourishing, in the world requires that we *use* our environment prudently, that is, to our best overall advantage, even though the natural world that is our environment has no independent claim upon us; it has no "rights." But the problem with this view is that most people believe (note, especially, more economically desperate people in "developing" countries like India and China) that *their* own economic needs *now* should determine their *use* of *their* environmental resources, even if their use of them is in fact abusive and seems to be detrimental to their long-term interests. And lying behind this practical approach is the metaphysical assumption that the earth *belongs* to those who are able to most efficiently use it for whatever purposes suit them. That also explains the environmentalism of some more affluent people, whose economic needs are less pressing, who want as much of the earth as possible to remain intact in its "unspoiled" naturalness so that they can enjoy it more fully. For them, the earth is their playground. They too are basically utilitarians, though less abusive of the earth than are their poorer human cousins (who themselves frequently tend the lawns and empty the garbage bins of their more affluent human cousins).

The second way this human freedom from divine authority is advocated might be called the "naturist" way. Those who advocate this are the more principled "environmentalists." Their argument goes something like this: We humans are only parts of the larger and greater earthly environment. Parts are subordinate to the whole; accordingly, every part ought to act in the best interest of that whole. (How, though, do they get around the philosophical axiom that an "ought" cannot be logically derived from an "is," which we have examined earlier in this chapter? Only from a view of *Nature* as the cosmic teleological hierarchy can any "oughts" be inferred.)

The more practical problem with this view is that most people do not think of themselves as subordinate to their environment. Most of us want to either be answerable to ourselves for our own authorization as to how to act in the world (autonomy), or be answerable to others most like us with whom we share social mutuality (heteronomy), or be answerable to God who is above us and who has placed us in the world for God's own purposes (theonomy). In other words, most humans want to be answerable to a person or persons greater than themselves and their environment. (This poses the biggest problem to "autonomists" who, in order to overcome the problem of self-reference, would have to posit a lower self and a higher self, following Plato.)[95] Indeed, we are only responsible for the care of anybody or anything beneath us (i.e., under our authority) when we are answerable to someone above us (i.e., under whose authority we are), who has appointed us to exercise this responsible care. And in the cosmic context, that higher "someone" who so appoints us to be responsible could only be God the Creator.[96]

Responding to this human desire to be answerable to a person or persons might explain why more and more environmentalists are sensitive to the fact that utilitarians, who do not acknowledge the inherent integrity of the earthly environment, can easily co-opt environmentalism with their less radical philosophical approach to the environmental agenda. This causes the more "orthodox" environmentalists to worry. So, some more radical environmentalists are beginning to enunciate a point of view that seems to be almost theological, that is, a teaching that sees us being answerable to a person who transcends our immediate environment. Such a person becomes "the Earth," which seems to be taken as a god *who* is to be praised.[97] That is, *the Earth* (the Greek word for "the earth," *Gaia,* is more and more being used) is taken to be a transcendent person to whom we humans are answerable for how responsible or irresponsible we have been with *her* resources. (I say "her" since *Gaia* is a feminine noun in Greek: another reason for an alliance between many environmentalists and many feminists, with their easy use of the term "rape" to denote both violence done to women and violence done to the earth.)[98]

Now, what seems to be a quest for transcendence of tangible self-interest does evoke more reverence than does the self-serving domination of the environment, which seems to be a hallmark of capitalism. After all, capitalism with its seeming acquisitiveness is for many the quintessential manifestation of modern autonomy, which explains why many environmentalists are so critical of it.[99] For it is capitalism's frequent disregard of and disrespect for the integrity of earthly nature that angers many contemporary environmentalists. Capitalism seems to lack reverence for anything sacred, and it is the sacred or transcendent that these environmentalists seek. (The Hebrew word for "sacred," *qadosh,* also means what is ontologically separate from the ordinary world and, therefore, may not be used for mundane purpose.)[100] But, of course, communism has proven to be just as acquisitive as capitalism and even more contemptuous of any transcendent sanctity beyond its own technological control of nature (and much worse in its attempt to control human life).[101] Let us not forget that probably the greatest technological assault on our earthly environment was the 1986 nuclear disaster at Chernobyl in the Soviet Union.

Since most environmentalists eschew the God of the Bible (often blaming *Him* and *His* followers for offering the original justification for the abusive exploitation of the earth in Western culture), some of them seem to be looking for an "other god." For Jews and Christians (and Muslims too) this god is definitely a "strange god" (Psalms 81:10). In fact, the more environmentalists' reverence for *the Earth* takes on a religious tone, the more it looks like idolatry. (In rabbinic parlance, "idolatry" is called *avodah zarah*, meaning "strange worship.")[102] That is why, it seems, cultural celebration of a "festival" like "Earth Day" is exhibiting a more and more idolatrous character. Fortunately, most people know enough about "culture" to know that it is not something we invent but something we inherit through history, indeed through sacred history, which is the history of the divine-human relationship. Thus there is no leap-frogging over centuries of history to "return" to a romanticized past, a more "natural" past, which is a place where we have never really been anyway. No culture that has lost its historical continuity, stemming from its religious origins, is ever likely to return. So, Earth Day and similar invented "festivals" have had little impact on the broader society, and they certainly haven't replaced the older "historical" festivals, despite the fact that the older festivals no longer seem to be celebrated as widely as they were in the not-so-distant past.

Our non-subordination to the earthly environment is evidenced by the fact that we do not simply accept our place in the environment, but have to work to make the environment our home *in* the world. That is because we are not *of* the world. We have to work the earthly environment in order to survive here, let alone flourish here. So, even though the first humans were commanded to "work" the Garden of Eden (Genesis 2:15), our work, nonetheless, did not really begin until we were expelled from paradise (where our food and shelter seems to have been already there for us). As such, humans are told by God: "Painfully [*b'itsavon*] you shall eat from it [the earth] all the days of your life" (Genesis 3:17), In other words, no longer being of the earth, humans often need to act *against* the earth insofar as the earth often *resists* their efforts to be nurtured by it.

Human responsibility for the natural environment becomes most pertinent in the case of animals. That is because animals are most like us, especially in the experience of pain, which we can recognize in them and they can recognize in us. As such, there can be sympathy between humans and animals, because it is clear we can be aware of each other's pain. In Jewish tradition, even though humans are permitted to use certain animals, either by domesticating them to work for us or by killing them for food or clothing, all that is to be done while preventing them as much as possible from suffering pain (in rabbinic parlance, *tsa'ar ba'alei hayyim* or the "pain of living beings").[103] That is why, it seems, Jewish tradition prohibits killing an animal for our amusement, or even using an animal for our amusement in a way that causes that animal needless pain.[104] The model for this kind of ecological responsibility is the shepherd who cares for his flock, acting in imitation of God whom the psalmist famously called "my Shepherd" (Psalms 23:1).[105]

Because there is inevitably some pain caused to animals when they are being killed (even by the most humane methods possible), some Jews and Christians have become vegetarians. Nevertheless, it is unlikely that very many people would accept such a restriction as that proposed by vegetarians. This could explain why Jewish tradition made being a vegetarian a permitted option for some rather than an obligation for everybody. As the Talmud puts it: "A rule should not be made unless a large majority is willing and able to abide by it."[106] Or perhaps, as the Talmud states elsewhere, some practices are permitted "because of bad human inclination" (*yester ha-ra*), that is, they are concessions to human weakness.[107] In other words, most humans would violate a prohibition against eating meat, so it is better to try to limit this permission (*reshut*) as much as is pragmatically possible.[108] Furthermore, the sacrificial system (*ma'aseh ha-qorbanot*), for whose restoration traditional Jews regularly pray, requires sacrificing animals for the altar, which are most often also eaten by those who brought them to the altar. That means that Jewish vegetarians might well regard their way of life as spiritually superior, but they still cannot condemn meat-eating per se on theological grounds. Vegetarianism at best can only be regarded as the personal option to go beyond the letter of the law. However, one can opt to be a carnivore with impunity.[109]

Even though we humans cannot recognize if plants suffer pain or not (nor can we know whether they are conscious of others in any way at all), they are still not to be destroyed willy-nilly, but only when one has to do so in order to fulfil legitimate human needs such as the need for food or clothing or shelter. Thus from the biblical prohibition of destroying fruit trees, which is "because you eat from it" (Deuteronomy 20:19), the ancient Rabbis inferred a general prohibition of "wanton destruction" (*bal tashheet* in Hebrew) of any created entity.[110] The prohibition applies whether that entity was directly created by God through a natural process or made by humans artificially, though ultimately made out of natural materials and thus indirectly being a divine creation.[111]

Directly or indirectly everything belongs to God, hence humans have no right to destroy anything, unless there is a positive outcome from doing so, that is, an outcome that satisfies a tangible human need, not unnecessary human desires.[112] Since humans are but transient tenants in God's world, we have no right to destroy any of the landlord's property, whether it is of use to us or not. So, for example, even though mourners are required to tear their clothes as an expression of their sorrow (which could be because of ancient custom or because tearing one's clothes at a time of such distress is therapeutic), an ancient Rabbi warned that overdoing tearing one's clothes, even on such an occasion, violates the prohibition of wanton destruction.[113] In fact, destruction motivated by irrational anger (rather than being for the sake of a true reason) is considered to be akin to idolatry, perhaps because idolatry is considered to be the ultimate absurdity: serving the wrong master or serving the right master wrongly.[114]

Tampering with Created Nature

The reason for the prohibitions on causing pain to animals and wanton destruction of plants (and, by extension, of any entity over which humans have some control) seems to be that all God's creatures have a stipulated integrity that is not to be violated. And that is because all creation is God's property about which God is concerned, and about which humans as God's partners ought to imitate God's universal concern.[115] But does this general prohibition extend to tampering with the divinely instituted created order?[116] Does it extend to the specific differentiation in the biosphere that seems to be so natural? Is this tampering a disruption of the order made by God? Is it an intrusion into a domain where human tampering is the inappropriate arrogance of creatures (albeit the most exalted creatures) against their Creator?[117]

This question is raised in the rabbinic writings in connection with the question: Do the biblical prohibitions of "mixing species" (*kel'ayim*) only pertain to Jews, or do they also pertain to gentiles (being included in the "Noahide commandments" that are assumed to be universal norms pertaining to all humankind)?[118] Now, the majority opinion of the Rabbis is that these prohibitions only apply to Jews insofar as they are not one of the seven Noahide commandments.[119] Moreover, these prohibitions are considered to be divine statutes (*huqqim*), having no discernable reason (being akin to the prohibition of eating pork). In fact, it is stated that gentiles ridicule these prohibitions as being irrational superstitions, and hence they are unnatural.[120] There is, however, the minority opinion of Rabbi Eleazar, holding that gentiles are culpable for violating at least some of the prohibition of cross-breeding.[121] According to another Rabbi, this opinion is based on the verse "My statutes [*huqqotai*] you shall keep" (Leviticus 19:19), which is interpreted to mean "the statutes I already [*qvar*] decreed," that is, already decreed to all humankind ("the Noahides") long before the revelation of the Torah at Sinai.[122] In fact, there are even some rabbinic prohibitions of gentiles (obviously, those gentiles over whom Jews have some political control) from violating at least some of these prohibitions of "mixing species."[123] Now, it is suggested that this might be due to Scripture's description of the creation of the various kinds of living beings as "each according to its kind [*le-minehu*]" (Genesis 1:11–12, 21, 24–5).[124] One Rabbi suggested that the earth was "cursed (Genesis 3:17) because of the violation of the decrees [*gezerotav*] of God."[125] So, what seems to be a description could have some prescriptive force. Thus the sixteenth-century theologian and exegete Obadiah Sforno speaks of this general prohibition as being "contrary to the intention of nature [*le-kavanat ha-tev'a*] coming from God its Orderer [*ha-mesadro*]."[126]

Humans Related to Nature: Athens

There is no greater difference between biblical theology and classical philosophy than in their different approaches to how humans are related to nature. That can be seen in a key text from Aristotle: "From our most ancient ancestors [*tōn archaiōn*] the myth has been transmitted to their descendants that the heavens are gods [*theoi*], and that the divine [*to theion*] encompasses [*periechei*] all nature [*physin*]."[127] That difference between the two traditions will become more apparent when we unpack this noteworthy statement about the relation of humans and nature.

What underlies the essential difference between Hebraic and Hellenic myths of God's relation to nature is that in the Hebraic view the One God is the Creator of the whole universe, and that humans are God's chief creation in that universe. As such, humans have unique responsibility for caring for their earthly environment, which is the part of the universe where God has placed them to live and work. On these two key points, Hellenic revelation is essentially different.

Greek philosophers (and the poets and dramatists before them) do speak of the gods as having placed embodied humans on earth, and thus they have proprietary rights over humans and proprietary duties to them during their earthly sojourn. Nevertheless, these gods are not considered to be the creators of the temporal earthly world. Moreover, they are certainly not the creators of the eternal heavenly world, which being eternal could not be created *ipso facto*. Therefore, their responsibility to nature only extends to the natural human bodies they have placed in the world. These gods are not responsible for what they have not created, and humans are only answerable to them for what they have done with their natural bodies and to other natural bodies in the world (as we saw earlier). Therefore, human interest in the natural, earthly world is not a matter of *imitatio Dei*. But if not, and if philosophy is a god-like activity, how then is human interest in this natural world philosophically justified? At this point, we should look to Aristotle, who was the greatest philosopher-scientist, the greatest naturalist.

More than Plato and the Stoics, Aristotle was interested in earthly nature, even though there was more to be learned for human improvement from heavenly nature, that is, from astrophysics. Whereas humans by virtue of their intelligence are above the rest of earthly nature, they are still very much beneath heavenly Nature due to their incomplete intelligence. Though Aristotle's primary scientific interest was in biology (and in fact, the Greek term for "nature," *physis*, is based in the verb *phyein*, meaning "to grow"), yet his metaphysical interest was primarily in natural *teleology*, which is the theory that all beings are striving in one way or another to comport with a form that everywhere defines, has defined, and will define the species.[128]

Teleology, the theory of purposes (*telē* in Greek), is what links the Nature of heaven and the nature of the earth. In fact, Aristotle's most concentrated thoughts about teleology are found in his ethical reflection that, following Plato, is the concern of humans who exist midpoint between heaven and earth.[129] Perhaps that is because conscious purposefulness is what distinguishes genuine human action from mere animal behaviour. Other living beings on earth simply do what they have always been doing, seemingly unaware of why they are striving to do more than just survive. Heavenly beings, though far more aware of what they are doing (being "intelligent souls") than are humans, are not striving for any purpose beyond themselves. Their end or purpose has already been theirs. They have always been what they are, and they always will be what they are. Like heavenly beings, humans know what they are doing and why they are doing it; yet like the other earthly beings, humans have not fully attained perfection. That is why heavenly motion is circular, without beginning and without end, temporally speaking. Earthly motion, though is linear, having a *terminus a quo* and a *terminus ad quem* in both time and space.[130] As such, humans act upon what they find in their terrestrial world. But they are unable to act upon the celestial world, whose circular motion attracts them, though they cannot use it as they can use what moves on earth. Like the higher celestial beings, philosophers can (at least periodically) orbit around God the Unmoved Mover.

Perhaps Aristotle could justify his interest in biology on philosophical grounds inasmuch as he looks upon Nature as a hierarchal unity ("the great chain of being," in A.O. Lovejoy's words), beginning with the lowest beings on earth and culminating in the highest divine Being in the heavens.[131] Also, being the son of a physician and perhaps a physician himself, Aristotle was interested in medicine as the art that applies scientific knowledge of earthly, biological nature to the great human need for healing from natural disease. He frequently uses medical analogies when making philosophical points.[132] For Aristotle, medicine is the most scientific art and the most practical applied natural science. And since medicine is considered to be the intelligent care of the body (*therapeia*), for Aristotle ethics is about the care of the embodied human soul. Since the embodied human soul is an acting being in the world, human action is the concern of ethics, which for Aristotle is actually philosophical psychology. And because humans as seeking beings cannot avoid seeking to attain certain ends, the task of philosophy is not to find a source of imperatives for humans outside of nature. Teleology is endemic in Nature generically, and it is endemic in human nature specifically. The task of philosophy, then, is to help intelligent humans discover what are their true ends, and to help them discover what are the best means to attain those ends. But seeking ends need not be explicitly commanded, since humans are naturally end-seeking beings. So, the task humans need to assign themselves as an imperative is to discover their true ends and to then choose the best means thereto.[133]

From all of these differences one can conclude that the name "nature," when invoked by either biblical theology or classical philosophy, has a very different referent. In classical philosophy, "Nature" means the cosmic order in which both humans and God are hierarchically contained. It is essentially not-made. In biblical theology, however, "nature" is both the substance and the order of the cosmos that is different from either God or humans.[134] "Nature" is what God has made, whereas "nature" is what humans can make something out of. In the next chapter, we shall be looking at Philo, the first theologian to persistently engage the classical philosophy of nature.

Chapter Four

Philo and Plato

The First Challenge of Philosophy to Theology

Philo was born a Jew and lived as a Jew during the first century CE in the highly developed Hellenistic culture of Ptolemaic Egypt. Coming from a variety of schools, the philosophy that was so central to the surrounding culture posed a tremendous challenge to Jews, who were theologically formed by the Bible (albeit in the Greek translation of the Septuagint). The challenge to these Greek-speaking Jews was that philosophy offered all Greek speakers, irrespective of their ethnic origins, a culture that seemed to be more elevated theoretically and more coherent practically. The combination of theory and praxis into an overall way of life, historically situated, is "culture."

For Jews, philosophy posed a direct cultural challenge to their biblical theology. This challenge was quite different from the challenges posed by the polytheistic cultures of the gentiles with whom Jews had mingled in earlier antiquity. The earlier challenge was more political (the gentiles were often more numerous and more powerful than the Jews), or more aesthetic insofar as the ritual practices of the gentiles seemed to be so much more sensual than the more austere biblical religion. The sexual licence that was such a big part of polytheistic rituals appealed to what the ancient Rabbis called "the base inclination" (*yetser ha-r'a*).[1] Even the challenge of the Hellenizing gentiles and their Jewish cohorts at the time of the Maccabees (second century BCE) was more political and aesthetic than it was intellectual. It appealed to the desire of the Jewish upper classes to be just like the descendants of Alexander the Great and his generals, not only in the way they were governed but even in their cultic practices. Accordingly, there was even a program to totally Hellenize the sacrificial cult of the Temple in Jerusalem.[2] Nevertheless, Hellenization did not seem to extend to the way these Jews actually thought. At the intellectual level, Jewish monotheism or "Judaism" was considered to be inherently superior to gentile polytheism, which thus posed no challenge at all.[3]

Alexandria, where Philo was a leader of the Jewish community, was the political and cultural centre of Ptolemaic Egypt. There, especially, the old Egyptian polytheistic cults were dying or already dead because they seemed culturally inferior to what the various philosophical schools (like Platonists, Stoics, and Cynics) were offering intellectuals looking for a new, alternative way of life, something religions always offer their adherents. (Philosophy in those days was a good deal more than "academic" in the modern sense of that term.) Moreover, these philosophical schools were looking for converts to what they were proposing to be the best way of life for any rational person. They sought those persons having philosophical *eros*, that is, the spiritual desire to be related to the Absolute.

Intellectually inclined Jews, troubled by what seemed to them to be their more primitive biblical theology, were prime targets for what were undoubtedly the proselytizing efforts of the philosophical schools. Just as their gentile fellow intellectuals believed that philosophy could overtake the polytheistic religious traditions they had inherited, so did many Jewish intellectuals of Philo's time and place believe that what philosophy could do to the polytheistic theologies of the gentiles, philosophy could do even to the monotheistic theology of the Jews. That is, philosophy could and should displace all of the ancient, historically and geographically bound theologies whether gentile or Jewish. This was quite different from the earlier attempts of Jews in Seleucid Syria-Palestine at the time of the Maccabees to assimilate into Hellenistic culture. In that time and place, there seems to have been little or no philosophy as part of the attraction, let alone the chief attraction. So, I think it can be said that the intellectual Jews with whom Philo lived and was engaged in Alexandria were not using philosophy as a means to their political assimilation; instead, their attraction to philosophy justified their political assimilation. The triumph of philosophy showed that Hellenistic culture was a better means to a truly metaphysical-ethical end than was the less philosophical culture provided by biblical theology.

Now, this great concession to philosophy had both practical and theoretical consequences. Practically, it meant that Jewish intellectuals were abandoning the practices that according to the Bible were commanded by God to Jews alone, so that God could thereby "separate you from the [other] peoples" (Leviticus 20:26). Why should Jews be separate from the gentiles (i.e., the "other peoples") when (and here the theoretical component comes in) philosophy seems to speak of God in a much more exalted way than does the Bible? Philosophy thus offers not only a more exalted God, it also offers a simpler and more rationally appealing way of life oriented to this more exalted God.

As a Jew who wasn't at all convinced that philosophy had trumped biblical theology, either theoretically or practically, Philo's task was to counter philosophy's great challenge. For this challenge was making Jewish intellectuals act like gentiles and think like gentiles, which was certainly leading to their disappearance as Jews altogether. Unlike many modern Jewish thinkers for whom Judaism is the means to the ethnic survival of the Jewish people, for Philo, like almost all pre-modern Jewish thinkers, the ethnic survival of the Jewish people is the means to the survival of God's Torah in the world. That is why Philo couldn't simply say that Judaism is different, but had to argue for the superiority of the truth taught by the Torah. It was only for the sake of that truth that the Jews deserved not only to survive but to flourish. First and foremost, the theoretical superiority of the Torah had to be demonstrated.[4]

As for biblically ordained praxis, the most that assimilated Jewish intellectuals were willing to admit was that this praxis did seem to have some theoretical value, that is, it seems to suggest some philosophically cogent ideas. But once these ideas were properly understood, there was no need to maintain the practices any longer; they had become arbitrary or even dispensable symbols. At best, these cultural practices might still be necessary for the discipline of those Jews who aren't intelligent enough to appreciate the ideas these acts symbolize. But for philosophically minded Jews, to still adhere to these practices would be cultural regression. Therefore, Philo had to also show the practical or ethical superiority, that is, the goodness, of the Torah, whose observance is cultural advancement.

Philo's strategy was to deny this separation of praxis from theory and theory from praxis. For even the most exalted ideas with which theory deals are still the concern of *embodied* theorists, who not only think with their souls but also act with their bodies. As such, they cannot keep their theoretical life totally separate from their practical life; they both think and act as one person.[5] So, for example, the Sabbath teaches us the value of leisure for the contemplative life, which is more than just acknowledging that bodies need to rest regularly. Even a body simply abstaining from physical work is still prevented from enjoying the true leisure (*scholē*) politics, let alone contemplation, requires.[6] Since no embodied person can only engage in contemplation, but everybody must fulfil his or her bodily needs and that requires work, it is best that there be times for the kind of leisure as abstention from work in regular rotation with bodily work in the world. Too little bodily work more than likely leads to sloth rather than to uninterrupted contemplation. Furthermore, that regular opportunity for contemplation is available to everybody inasmuch as the Sabbath is to be observed by everybody, rich and poor alike. Thus Philo speaks of the Sabbath as "the archetype of the two best ways of life: the practical and the theoretical or contemplative [*theōretikou*]."[7]

If the ideas that properly underlie praxis are those ideas enunciated and developed by the philosophers, doesn't biblical theology, no matter how much it has been "demythologized" (to use an important term put forth by the twentieth-century Protestant theologian Rudolf Bultmann), become the "handmaiden of philosophy" (*ancilla philosophiae*)? If so, is there anything unique or ultimately significant about biblical theology, either theoretically or practically? If philosophical ideas are taken to be more universal than any particular type of theology, wouldn't *any* cultural tradition be able to take on philosophical significance? If so, wouldn't that leave the Jews, being a minority in what still seemed to be the culturally vibrant Hellenistic culture, quite vulnerable? After all, why couldn't the theoretical knowledge of God become embodied anywhere in the world? Why, therefore, shouldn't Jews become part of philosophy's most powerful embodiment in the world, which was the vibrant Hellenistic culture of Alexandria? Furthermore, as we have just seen, by the aesthetic standards of the Hellenistic world, the Torah's narrative seems rather primitive.[8]

That is why Philo had to do more than simply show that theory needs praxis like the soul needs the body, since theory doesn't seem to necessarily need Jewish praxis. So, what Philo did was to argue that the Torah provides more, not less, of what the philosophers have been looking for all along.[9] And that is because Moses's revelation is so much more impressive than any revelation the philosophers may have experienced. Moreover, theory and praxis are better correlated in Mosaic revelation. That, as we shall see, is because the God who gives the Torah is more than the God of the philosophers; more but not less. The God of the Torah is greater, and one indication of His greatness is that theory and praxis function in tandem in the lives of those humans who are in a sustainable relationship with this God. So, Philo is quite critical of those Jews who think the Torah, at best, has some philosophically valid ideas, but who disdain its particular practices. However, if a choice has to be made between those who have theory but no praxis, as distinct from those who have praxis but no theory, Philo prefers the latter. Thus he speaks of these "practical" Jews with a certain amount of respect.[10] For these Jews alone still uphold the Torah's uniqueness, while the "theoretical" Jews will sooner or later blend into a philosophical way of life that could be based on anyone's philosophy. The optimal course for Jewish theologians, then, is to develop theory on the back of indispensable Jewish praxis. This Jewish praxis should always accompany theory, so that theoretically attuned theologians can never leave it behind in their intellectual quest for God.[11] And that quest begins with one's philosophical quest for transcendence.[12] Nevertheless, that quest for transcendence goes beyond, that is, it transcends, its philosophical starting point.

Because of this basically theological attempt to go beyond philosophy without leaving philosophy behind in its wake, Philo was able to deal with two cultural-political challenges facing him.

The first challenge was to stem the tide of the assimilation of intellectually inclined Jews into what more and more of them thought to be a philosophically superior culture. Philo's message to them was to stop looking to pagan philosophers for guidance as to the best relationship with God. That guidance is already provided in the Torah first revealed to Israel, but which is finally meant for all humankind. That notwithstanding, infatuation with philosophy has provided the means to better appreciate the true universality of the Torah. Without that philosophical prelude, one would at best regard the Torah as an exception to universal truth, as something that couldn't be assimilated into philosophical culture, but could only be maintained as a historical relic that mere ethnic pride in one's historical origins won't allow one to throw away altogether. Therefore, the philosophical detour enables intellectually inclined Jews (and possible converts to Judaism) to see the Torah as going beyond philosophy by carrying philosophical *eros* beyond the point where the philosophers, bereft of Mosaic revelation, could possibly lead it. Without the philosophical detour, however, biblical theology could at best only be maintained alongside philosophy as a kind of sideshow. Indeed, Philo refers to the Jewish tradition as the "ancestral [*patron*] philosophy" of the Jews.[13]

The second challenge facing Philo was that by presenting such a universal message to his fellow Greek-speaking Jews, he was simultaneously speaking to disaffected Greek-speaking gentiles. The only difference between the two kinds of hearers of his discourses was that the Jews were being persuaded to come *back* to a philosophically reformulated Judaism, whereas the gentiles were being persuaded to be *initiated* into that philosophically formulated Judaism (even if only intellectually, even if not yet officially).[14]

As far as we know, Philo was the first Jewish thinker to engage philosophy explicitly. And though we can see him engaging a number of different philosophical positions in his discourses, it is Plato whom he engages most often and most explicitly. Plato is his greatest influence, and it is Plato whom Philo's philosophical theology must either surpass or be undone by. We see this in the four spheres of relationship that we are examining throughout this book: (1) the relation of God and humans; (2) the relation of God and nature; (3) interhuman relations; and (4) the relation of humans and nature.

The Relation of God and Nature

In the original order of the four spheres of relationality put forth in the previous chapters, the relation of God and humans is in first place. For in biblical theology, God's relationship with humans is direct and immediate; and it is from the perspective of biblical theology that the interaction of theology and philosophy is constituted here. Thus in biblical theology, "nature" means the rest of the created universe that is neither divine nor human. To be sure, the direct covenantal relationship with God always takes place *in* that environment. Nevertheless, the divine-human covenant is not *within* nature as a part thereof. That is why we need to look at this biblical "theology of nature" as being different from the "natural theology" proposed (in fact, originally proposed) by Philo.[15] As we shall see, for Philo, God's relationship with humans, which is the leitmotif of the entire Bible, seems to be very much determined by God's relationship with nature. It is only by going up *through* nature that humans can be directly related to God thereafter. We shall see how Philo does try to develop a natural theology rather than just accepting a philosophy of nature from the Greek philosophers, especially Plato.

As we have seen in the previous two chapters, in biblical theology, especially as it was developed in the rabbinic tradition, the natural order regularly experienced by humans is not the medium *through* which humans must ascend in order to meet God, nor is it the barrier that prevents humans from ever reaching God. The natural order is not impermeable. Indeed, when nature seems to be an impermeable barrier between God and humans, it is breached by God miraculously for the sake of making immediate contact with God's covenanted people.

Philo's view of nature is very much different from that of biblical-rabbinic theology; hence his theological constitution of nature is very much different too.[16] Philo's theology makes its case building on the back of philosophy; and philosophy's prime concern is Nature. Philosophy seeks Nature's ultimate intelligibility. Therefore, for Philo, how God is related to Nature is where his philosophical theology must begin. But what cannot be overemphasized is that humans rise up through nature in their search for God. Their ascent up to God originates in themselves;

it is not a response to God's original descent down to them.[17] The most God does for humans, in Philo's view, is to allow humans to rise through-and-beyond nature to finally apprehend God. Commenting on the verse "the Lord God breathed into his nostrils the breath of life" (Genesis 2:7), Philo notes this is what we could call mind-to-mind communication, or even "mental telepathy." From this he infers that the human mind (*nous*) could only ascend (*anadramein*) to the level of the Divine "if God Himself had not drawn it up [*anespasen*] to Himself."[18] So, at the beginning of his treatise on creation, Philo writes:

> There are some people who admire [*thaumasantes*] the world more than the Maker of the world [*kosmopoion*], pronouncing it to be without beginning [*anagenēton*] and everlasting [*aidion*] ... they presume God is a vast inactivity [*apraxian*]. We, on the contrary, ought to be astonished at His power as Maker and Father, and not over extol the world [*mē pleon*].[19]

Later on in this treatise, Philo insists that "Moses teaches us ... that the world came into being [*genētos*] ... because of those who think that it is without beginning and eternal ... assigning to God no superiority [*pleon*] at all."[20] Even the immaterial intelligibility that seems to be more God-like (*theoeides*) than what is materially embodied (*sōmatikos*), even what Plato thought was truly divine, is for Philo what has also been created by God.[21] We now need to examine the views of those philosophers Philo is arguing against in order to appreciate what he is offering as the Torah's philosophically superior alternative.

Plato on God and Nature

Those philosophers whom Philo was arguing against were the followers of Plato's cosmology, who ascribe to the heavens atemporality, that is, the heavenly bodies are neither born nor do they die. They are eternal. That is why they are deemed to be gods. The gods are not-made.[22] Matter, too, is not-made; yet matter can be made into something new by either divine or human makers who in-form it. The immortal gods, though, cannot be made into something new, as there is no greater maker than themselves. So, what is made is distinguished from what is not-made by the fact of both its natality and its mortality. Indeed, at his trial on charges of atheism, Socrates insists that he like "everybody else" (i.e., every good Athenian) accepts the belief that the sun and the moon are "gods" (*theous*).[23] And he explicitly differentiates himself from the physicist Anaxagoras, who held that the heavenly bodies are not gods but simply lifeless, unintelligent aggregates of atoms.[24] (This view, by the way, is quite close to the view of post-Galilean physics.) However, these atoms appear to be surds or accidents (*tychē* in Greek), which do not evince any purpose nor do they themselves seem to cause any human action; therefore, they are not divine, even though they seem to be without birth or death.

For Socrates, the souls of humans, due to their non-natal and immortal intelligence, are thereby capable of contemplation of the divine realm in which the heavenly gods are the prime participants, and in which human souls are secondary participants. Human selves and divine selves, both being souls (*psychai*), have something essential in common: their inherent intelligence.[25] Nevertheless, human souls can never be the equals of these gods because of their having to dwell on earth: being born into and dying out of essentially natal and mortal bodies. These bodies are made by the lesser terrestrial gods who are involved in earthly matters. That is why humans are not allowed to take their bodily life into their own hands by ridding themselves of it in order to rejoin the heavenly divine realm, where they dwelled before their earthly birth.[26] Mortal human bodies, unlike their souls, are neither self-made nor are they not-made. Human souls can only be released from their sojourn in earthly bodies by the lower god who put them there and who, like slave owners, has the sole authority to emancipate them.[27] This emancipation occurs unless the human soul has been so morally and intellectually sullied during its earthly sojourn that it has become hopelessly mortal. The death of the body, which Plato called its "prison" (*sēma*), is the occasion for the transfer of the immortal soul from its imprisonment *to* a lower god to its true liberty along *with* the heavenly gods, that is, with those higher gods with whom the human soul shares immortal intelligence or intelligent immortality.[28] Furthermore, human souls are like the heavenly gods insofar as their true intelligence is directed upward toward Divinity itself, yet they are like the earthly gods insofar as they have the authority to govern what is beneath them and for which they are responsible.[29]

Accordingly, there seem to be four levels of being in ascending order: (1) What is both not-made and unintelligent and, therefore, without volition (which presupposes intelligence). This is inert "matter" (*hylē*), which could be made into *something* by a being who is not-made, being intelligent and having volition. Matter cannot in-form anything, but it can be in-formed only by something else. It has no causal power, that is, it does not function as an efficient cause (*poion*) nor as a formal cause (*eidos*), hence it cannot be imitated. (2) All souls, whether divine or human, are uncreated intelligences, who continually aspire towards apprehension of Divinity itself. Divine souls apprehend Divinity directly; human souls apprehend Divinity indirectly, mediated by their engagement with divine souls whom they intelligently imitate. (3) All human souls, and some lesser divine souls, are uncreated intelligences who are capable of making things by virtue of their intelligent volition. (4) Finally, there is what is uncreated and intelligent but without volition. For volition intends an object outside itself that, after its being made, is of concern to its maker. That seems to imply that having volition is due to some lack in its subject, that is, the subject needs an other to be the object of its intended action. Hence having volition (*boulēsis*) is not a personal strength for the classical Greek philosophers, but rather a personal weakness.[30] That is how the gods are models for human imitation. Their authority is more by example than by precept, even though their exemplary heavenly action should induce human philosophers to imitate it on earth in their own interactions with others who are at least philosophically inclined.

We now need to ask: What led the Greek philosophers to accept the view of the ancient, pre-philosophical thinkers that the heavenly bodies are divine, that is, they are superior to humans and thus worthy of human worship?[31] One could say that worship is the concern (*Sorge* in German) of the lower for the higher. But this concern is of two kinds. In pre-philosophical Greek theology (which continued in non-philosophical theology), the gods were to be worshipped as the efficient causes of human life and bodily well-being. However, the philosophers assumed that there is more to human existence than simply life and bodily well-being. Although they did not advocate abolishing the cult of earthly gods, who are the makers of human life and earthly well-being, nonetheless it is clear that the philosophers did not consider this divine worship (even though they themselves still practised it, at least publicly) to be of ultimate human significance.

The crowning pinnacle of human nature, for the philosophers, is the human capacity for contemplation (*theōria* in Greek) of the eternal verities, the pinnacle of which is "the Divine" or "Divinity" (*to theion*). Now, the heavenly bodies do not show themselves to be bipolar entities of mortal body and immortal soul like humans. Unlike linear earthly motion, which for humans is the finite line running from birth to death, the circular motion of the heavenly bodies seems to be infinite: it has neither beginning nor end. Insofar as their circular motion seems to be endless, these heavenly bodies were assumed to be of ultimate significance to intelligent humans. And their significance is not due to their being efficient causes *of* the bodily human condition on earth, but rather to their being formal causes or archetypes *for* the soulful human ascent from earth up to the Divine. That is what Plato seems to have meant by his famous assertion that "the god is the measure [*metron*] of all things ... being greater than any man," which means that "all humans must think through how to follow [*xynakolouthēsontōn*] the god."[32] Indeed, the heavenly bodies (whose very matter is taken to be fundamentally different from earthly matter) seem to move themselves rather than being moved *by* an external efficient cause. So, if they are taken to be intelligently superior to humans, their motion must have an end *towards* which they move. However, inasmuch as their motion is eternal, they do not move in a linear trajectory (i.e., locomotion) that would conclude its motion by attaining its end as a spatial limit. Instead, they move circularly in orbit, centred *around* their end (*telos*) as their ultimate point of attraction. As such, they never conclude their perpetual motion, having neither a *terminus a quo* nor a *terminus ad quem*. It is this kind of intelligent, self-moved motion *with* which human intellection can seek to identity. For thought (*nous)* at this contemplative level is not moved by an external efficient cause. Furthermore, at this contemplative level, thought looks up, not down. Thought is not interested in ordering what lies beneath it. It is not like the earthly rulers, whether human or divine, who look downward rather than upward. Instead, human thought at this level only aspires to know the Divine as it is known by the penultimate deities.

Now, Socrates does speak of one god who has commanded him to philosophize, and that god is not one of the officially recognized Athenian gods who placed Socrates as an embodied man in Athens to serve the city during his embodied assignment there. This god, with whom Socrates hopes to converse after he departs this world, commands Socrates to "examine [*exetazonta*] myself and others" as he himself exhorts Socrates, that is, by restraining him from doing anything other than examining himself and others.[33] As such, Socrates fulfils the god's command by following the god's example. What this god shows Socrates is how to clear away or refute erroneous opinions so that truth might show itself in the clearing. Plato, it seems, picks up on this theme by arguing for a dialectical method that leads those who master it up to the threshold of seeing with the soul's eye the ultimate form of the Good (i.e., Goodness per se), which though it is not a thinking person like Aristotle's God, seems nonetheless to be indistinguishable from Plato's Divinity. Those who educate the budding young philosophers of Plato's republic (*politeia)* for this possible journey, precisely by making the epitome of their education dialectics, seem to function much like Socrates's examining god.[34] Indeed, they are to do with their young charges what Socrates himself did with his students, which is something Plato knew from his own experience of being Socrates's student.

Thus the philosopher-guardians of the republic are to emulate what Socrates did with his students, which is what the god did with Socrates.

Conversely, as makers, the earthly gods are concerned with the humans they have made, and humans are concerned with them in return. Socrates even sees this to be like a commercial give-and-take relationship (*emporikē*).[35] This is epitomized by Socrates's contractual relationship with the laws of Athens, where he is seen to have agreed to obey the laws of Athens in return for their parent-like protection and nurture of him as an Athenian citizen. As in any contract, each party needs the other party. That is what impels them to formalize the fulfilment of their mutual needs in a contract (written or even only oral). However, unlike some modern social contract theories, where the law is made by the same humans who made the contractual agreement among themselves, Socrates's contract (*homologēma*) is with the law itself, which is a system that neither he nor any other Athenian has himself made. Through democratic procedures, Athenian citizens can only apply the laws already given to them; and they can make new laws that add to the system without displacing it. The law itself, however, is to be followed (*keleuē*), even when one disagrees with some of its specific, humanly enacted statutes (as did Socrates), because the law itself is the object of worshipful obedience (*sebesthai*). It is to be honoured (*timiōteron*) by both intelligent humans and the gods.[36] But would the gods, let alone intelligent humans, honour and worship anything that was not itself divine? That is why the law is called "holy" (*hagiōteron*), which Socrates himself does not dispute.[37]

The divine law of Athens has every claim on Socrates's body, which he readily turns over to its authorities. And he is even more eager to turn over his soul to the divine realm above. As such, he has simultaneously pleased both sets of gods. To be sure, Socrates says at his trial: "Athenian gentlemen, I respect and love [*philō*] you, but I shall obey [*peisomai*] the god rather than you."[38] Nevertheless, he is not contrasting obedience to what is divine and obedience to what is human. In fact, the Athenian authorities consider Socrates's disobedience of the ban on philosophizing to be an unlawful denial of the rightful authority of the gods of Athens, prompted by what seems to be a non-Athenian god.[39] Socrates is then caught in a contest, as it were, between one deity (or deities) and another deity. However, the divine law of Athens only has a claim on Socrates's body, which Socrates, as noted, readily turns over to that law's authorities, who are those who interpret that law and who judge violations of their official interpretations of it. Socrates obeys these authorities by not escaping his execution that they have decreed. Even though he disobeys their law by philosophizing in their public sphere, he does not disobey their death sentence of him by escaping from the Athenian prison (which, to use current parlance, had become "death row" for him). By so doing, he is now ready to willingly turn over his soul to the divine realm above with impunity.[40] That is how he is able, in the end, to satisfy the demands of both gods.

This relationship between the Athenians and the divine law of Athens implies mutual need on the part of the gods and their human servants. Athens needs its citizens and its citizens need Athens. But needy beings are not perfect beings. This imperfection is what differentiates both earthly gods and earthly humans from the perfect heavenly gods. By not taking the heavenly gods to be makers, or at least we humans do not relate to them as their creatures, Plato and those who followed his philosophical path were able to portray the heavenly gods as being the objects of human concern rather than as subjects who are concerned with humans. Accordingly, human worship of the heavenly gods is not grateful, obedient acknowledgment of what they have actually done *for* humans; instead, this kind of worship is human emulation of what these gods do *by* themselves *for* the sake of knowing Divinity itself. Human concern *for* the heavenly gods is not a thankful response to actual divine beneficence, nor is it the human attempt to elicit divine beneficence *for* themselves. It is a one-way relation from the lower to the higher towards the highest; it is not a two-way relationship going in both directions, both up and down.

Philo on God and Nature

Philo's monotheism, his total Jewish commitment to the one and only God, precludes Socrates's polytheistic option of relating to the gods above differently from the way he relates to the gods below. For Philo as a Jew, there is and could only be one God.

What Philo does is to insist that acknowledging God to be the Prime Maker/Creator does not diminish God's greatness; instead, it enhances it. Only this kind of God could satisfy the human desire to be consciously related or to be able to intentionally apprehend *that than which nothing greater could possibly be thought*.[41] If I understand him, Philo's logic is as follows: What is made retains its being-made/having-become finite status when it is transcended by its maker: before its beginning or birth and after its demise or death. "I am the first and I am the last, and other than Me there is no god" (Isaiah 44:6). Although he doesn't actually quote this verse from Isaiah, Philo paraphrases it when he asks rhetorically: "Could there be anyone else [*tis ... heteros*]?!"[42] Moreover, only a maker who retains interest in his or her product transcends it, whereas the product cannot transcend the one who made it. That would only be possible if the maker lost interest in his or her product, abandoning it by leaving it totally independent of its maker's concern for it. Their relation is clearly asymmetrical.

For this reason, then, Philo seems to be saying that the inherent human desire to transcend the ordinary world intends the biblical Creator who, by virtue of His creativity, transcends His creation without ever being transcended by His creation. To be sure, the creation narrative in Genesis could be interpreted to mean that "the unformed mass" (*tohu va-vohu*) of Genesis 1:2 was what God found to be already there as prime matter ready to be formed by Him. Nevertheless, already in a Hellenistic Jewish text written two centuries before Philo, we find it stated: "Looking at the heavens and the earth and what is seen in them, know that God made them out of nothing [*ouk ex ontōn*]; likewise [*kai*] the human species did not just come into being itself [*ou ginetai*]."[43] This seems to be the first explicit assertion that God created the universe "out of nothing" (*ex nihilo* in Latin).[44] Now, "creation out of nothing" does not mean that there is *some* thing called "*no* thing" (itself an oxymoron) out of which God made everything. "Nothing" (*ayin* in Hebrew) has no real referent; it only denies or negates a specific referent (for example, saying "there is nothing there" means there is no identifiable object in a particular place). "Nothing" does not designate a material cause *from* which something is made. *Creatio ex nihilo* means that God is not subject to any kind of necessity (*anangkē*), to any kind of precondition. God is totally free. *Mutatis mutandis*, Philo asserts that the human mind (*nous*) is also voluntary (*hekousia*): free to rise above cosmic necessity to apprehend God as God is free to make Himself apprehensible to human minds.[45]

Creatio ex nihilo means that God needed nothing for His creating.[46] That is why the verb "create" (*bar'o* in Hebrew) has but one possible subject: God. That would not be the case, however, if God's creation of the cosmos had to employ some kind of pre-existent matter or comply with some kind of pre-existent form. God's unlimited or infinite transcendence of creation would be compromised if His creation had any sort of precondition that, at the point of creation, would be coequal with God. Hence to assert that God created the universe out of nothing is to say something significant about the Creator God, but nothing about the created universe that couldn't be said just as easily if one assumed it is not created. For the universe taken by itself could be assumed to be "just there." Saying that the universe is created by God doesn't tell us any more about the universe than saying it is uncreated, that is, it is "just there," and all we can do is map out relations among objects therein (which is a point powerfully made by Kant).[47]

When God is apprehended as the One than whom "nothing greater can be thought," which is the greatest transcendence we could imagine, then nothing less than God's creation of everything else all by Himself without any preconditions suffices to speak of God's relation to everything that is not-God. Thus Philo criticizes those who hold that "God and what has come-to-be [*theon kai genesin*] are coequal cosmic causes [*aitia*]" instead of properly affirming God to be the "sole cause" (*henos ontos aitiou*).[48] As such, they deny God's full plenitude.[49] Monotheism, then, does not come from what humans infer from the cosmic satisfaction of their desire for ultimate order; instead, it comes out of humans' disappointment with the world's inability to satisfy the human desire to apprehend what is truly transcendent. That is the goal (*terma*) of the soul's journey upward to the certain knowledge (*epistēmē*) of God.[50] This is what philosophy truly is: the desire (*spudazein*) to see clearly with the soul's eye the One who is Being itself.[51] Nevertheless, this intellectual vision is only possible when its object, God, illuminates the soul's insight.[52]

Philo is convinced that asking the question of whether the nature of the heavenly bodies is to have a created beginning (*geneseōs ... archēn*) or to be uncreated (*agenētoi*) is the summit of the philosophical quest. That is the highest, most noble human pursuit.[53] Indeed, philosophy arises when contemplation (*theōria)* of the heavens excites a "love and longing" (*erōta kai pothon*) for true knowledge (*epistēmēs*) of them. This is the way a human being though mortal becomes immortal (*apathanatizetai*).[54] Clearly, this "love and longing" on the part of humans is for immortality, which is experienced even when human souls are embodied in mortal flesh, and which becomes their total reality once humans are released from their embodied earthly state upon their death in this world. It also seems that Philo is taking human fascination with the heavenly bodies to be fascination with their immortality. But, if so, why are the heavenly bodies not taken to be divine as they are for the Greek philosophers? What is it about the heavenly bodies that still disqualifies them from being the proper objects of human worship, that is, worship as adoring contemplation, not self-serving petition?[55]

Philo would probably answer that although the heavenly bodies are immortal, that is, they have no *terminus ad quem*, they are still not eternal inasmuch as they have be-come (*genēsis*) into the world having a *terminus a quo*. They are without end, but not without beginning. They too are creatures. Thus he writes: "Such are the heavenly bodies [*asteres*] who are said to be living beings, intelligent [*noera*] ... a mind [*nous*] that is excellent [*spoudaios*]."[56] However, are they not in effect eternal insofar as their immortality is experienced by humans, whereas their natality, their "coming-to-be," lies at a time before anyone but God could experience it? And if humans believe their souls to be equally immortal, do not humans become divine when their souls apprehend what the heavenly bodies apprehend? So, for Philo, it would seem that as seers experience themselves in what is seen, so do seers who "see" God with the eye of the soul become one with God. To be sure, this identification is intermittent when the human soul is still embodied, but it becomes permanent after the body's death as it was permanent before the body's birth. Nevertheless, isn't God's absolute transcendence compromised thereby? Isn't the Creator/creature divide severely compromised thereby?

For Philo, God doesn't descend down through nature to confront humans as ensouled bodies on earth. Instead, human souls ascend up through earthly nature, transcending their bodily interests as much as possible in this world, rising up to the level of the heavenly intelligences to directly confront God as they seem to be able to do. By creating souls capable (however individually rare) of so confronting God, God has thereby created what is most akin to Godself. In fact, the only difference between God and souls (*psychai*), whether forever in heaven or temporarily embodied on earth, is that God alone can create everything and anything *ex nihilo* inasmuch as God alone is not-made. Conversely, even ensouled creatures are not divine precisely because they cannot do what God alone can do. After creation has taken place, though, that difference between human souls and God seems to have been narrowed considerably in the relationship that humans now enjoy with God. God's creation of human souls is the creation of that intelligent commonality. Just as humans leave the ordinary world in order to confront God directly and exclusively, so does God create human souls (and whatever other souls there are in the universe) directly and exclusively. This is the fundamental, intelligent commonality humans share with God. It seems to function almost as a divine-human symbiosis.

Philo is convinced that in the case of anything less than an immortal soul, whether permanently embodied in heaven or temporarily embodied on earth, it is beneath God's dignity to be directly, let alone exclusively, interested and involved with them. "God is the cause of good things [*agathōn*] only, but nothing bad [*kakou*] ... it is most akin [*oikeia*] to His nature that what is best [*arista*] be made [*dēmiourgein*] by what is best."[57] As such, God's relation to earthly, material existence is mediated through, that is, delegated to, subordinate powers. They do what seems to be the "dirty work," interest in which would compromise God's transcendence. Nevertheless, because these intermediate powers are under God's ultimate, active control, they are not to be worshipped by humans. They too are made by God, and nothing that is made deserves to be worshipped. Only God is to be worshipped precisely due to God alone being the One who is not-made and who cannot, therefore, ever be unmade.

Even though these powers (often called "angels") are delegated by God, the messengers are essentially different from the One who sent them. Thus, as agents of God's providence, that is, God's continuing interest in and concern with all of God's creation, God delegates to these subordinate causes the ability to effect in the world what humans are unable to effect here.[58] As such, they reflect God's greater beneficence and greater effectiveness more than any of God's other creatures, even God's human creatures. For God's inherent beneficence (*agathotēta*) is what seems to motivate God to create the cosmos at all, and God's inherent majesty (*exousia*) is what motivates God to rule the cosmos thereafter. Both of these creative attributes of God function rationally (*logō*) in tandem: God's beneficence is effective and God's majesty is beneficent.[59] It is the heavenly powers who extend God's beneficence and majesty throughout the cosmos, and it is rational humans who extend God's beneficence and majesty throughout the earthly world. For Plato, conversely, that the god is willing to extend his beneficence by creating the cosmos does not mean this creative god cares to rule the cosmos he has created.[60] This god, then, is good and has been beneficent, but he does not providently rule the cosmos, since he is no longer related to it.[61]

This point comes out most vividly in Philo's treatment of Genesis 1:27, where God's creation of humans is expressed in both the first-person plural ("let us make humans") and the third-person singular ("God made humans"). "Let us make [*poiēsōmen*]" means that God "took others as co-workers [*synergōn*]," whereas "God made" [*epoiēsen*] designates God's creation of "the real man who is pure mind [*nous*], whom God alone is the maker [*dēmiourgos*]." On the other hand, "there are a plurality of makers of man, so-called, having mixed into him sense perception [*aisthēseōs*]."[62] The creation of humans as intelligent or mindful beings is a direct one-to-one mutuality of divine initiation and immediate human response. The creation of everything else does not entail any such mutual relationship, as it proceeds from God through some heavenly intermediaries down to many passive earthly recipients. "To act [*poiein*] is uniquely God's; it is not to be ascribed to any creature. What is unique [*idion*] to a creature [*genēton*] is to suffer [*paschein*]."[63] That is, God is purely effective, which follows from God's not being made. All creatures, though, are affected, which follows from their having been made. Of course, some creatures are effective too, especially humans who spontaneously choose to act effectively. Philo seems to mean by this distinction that what basically differentiates creatures from their Creator is their affectivity, which is a property of anything that has been made. Unlike God, all creatures can be worked on in one way or another.

To be sure, Philo cannot say God is totally disinterested in what is material, as that would imply its existence is essentially independent of God's creative concern with everything and anything created by God. After all, God judged all of His creation to be "very good" (Genesis 1:31), which seems to mean God approved of everything He made. Perhaps, though, the Bible's insistence that God's direct concern with humans is not at the expense of God's direct concern with all creation is to emphasize to humans that God's attention is not exclusively directed to us. All creation is essentially different from God, and no creature has God's exclusive attention. As such, the difference between humans and the rest of creation is one of degree rather than of kind. Only the difference between God and all creation is a difference of kind. Even humans are not designated to be "the image of God," but rather as having been created "*in* God's image to be like Him" (*be-tselem elohim* – Genesis 1:27). That seems to be saying that humans enjoy a special relationship *with* God, not that humans and God share some common property. God directly makes everything, and everything includes much more than intelligent, speaking beings (*zō'on logikon* in Greek). Insisting that God's creativity is pluralistic rather than univocal, the Bible thereby denies that humans are an emanation *out of* God. Divine-human commonality is not substantial but relational. Whatever commonality there is *between* God and humans is not an extension of God's being. Instead, that commonality is one that God freely chose to project towards humans, and *for* which God gives humans the free choice to respond *to* or run *away from*. Yet Philo is still beholden to Plato's denigration of material existence, which Plato took to be what has been informed by an inferior god.[64] As such, Philo seems to have compromised God's transcendence in two ways. One, he sees material existence to be too far removed from God's concern; and, two, he sees ensouled beings like humans to be too much like God.

The Relation of God and Humans

As we have seen, for the Greek philosophers, there is no mutual relationship between God and humans. Instead, it is a one-way relation: humans ascend up to the level of the divine heavenly bodies, and thus they are able (however intermittently in this world) to contemplate

Divinity itself (which in its ultimacy seems to be identical with the highest form: *the* Good or *Goodness*).[65] Moreover, the attractiveness of Divinity (*to theion*) or *the Divine* that attracts lesser intellects is involuntary. This is not something Divinity willingly or even just consciously shows to any outsider. For Plato, the forms are supremely intelligible, especially the form of the Good; yet they are not seen to be acting persons, they cannot be taken as being intelligent. After all, intelligence is exercised by a person, *who* is a subject consciously intending an object. But doesn't that imply that the knowing subject intends a known object external to itself? Nevertheless, Aristotle asserts that Divinity – for him, *the God* – is both the subject and object of intellection, that is, God is simultaneously intelligent and intelligible. As such, those who do reach the highest level of intellection, which is contemplation of the Divine, know God as God knows Godself by, in effect, becoming divine themselves: thought (*nous*) thinking itself.[66] This contemplation is as intransitive as is Godself. Divinity needs nothing outside itself. Philosophers can know God, but God does not know them. Indeed, there is no incentive whatsoever for God to know them or anyone else outside of Godself.

Having accepted the biblical teaching of the Creator God, which means that God does engage in transitive action, Philo teaches – cautiously to be sure – that just as God willed the cosmos into being, so does God will that prophets be shown God's creative governance of the cosmos. That knowledge is not the product of what prophets have seen by their own efforts, but rather it is knowledge that God has extended or revealed to them. Only the Creator God could do that, that is, the God who transcends His creation and doesn't allow His creation to transcend Himself due to indifference to creation on God's part. In this way, God relates Godself to those humans who are able to rise above their natural limitations to relate themselves to God. God's extending Godself to relate to the cosmos as its concerned Creator and Ruler is the ontological basis of God's extending knowledge of Godself epistemologically to those who are able to rise up to meet God at the highest cosmic horizon. Surely, God is not an inert object simply there to be discovered. Instead, God can either hide Godself or willingly reveal Godself to souls, just as God can create or not create the cosmos at will.

Speaking of Abraham, who is the first person the Bible calls a "prophet," Philo asserts:

> But when he had departed and changed his habitation, he had to know that the cosmos does not govern itself [*ouk autokratora*], not ruling but ruled [*prutaneuomenon*] by the Cause who made it ... because of His love

> for humankind, when the soul came to meet Him, He did not turn away, but came forward to meet him and showed [*edeixe*] His nature ... For it is impossible that anyone could by himself apprehend [*katalabein*] the true Being if He did not reveal [*paraphēnantos*] and show Himself.[67]

Indeed, Abraham is the archetype of all those Philo calls "God-born" (*theou gegonasin*) who, unlike ordinary scholars and artists, are not primarily interested in what is within the world. Instead, they are interested in what or who transcends the world, to such an extent that they no longer consider themselves worldly (*kosmopolitai*) at all.[68] In fact, these prophetic souls want their knowledge of God to come from God Himself.[69] Nevertheless, as long as the human soul is embodied on earth, it is pulled in opposite directions: upward towards God (*pros theon*) or downward towards the created world (*pros genesin*).[70]

Plato on Interhuman Relations

Like the Greek philosophers whose language he spoke so expertly and whose concepts he so adroitly employed for his theological purposes, Philo was convinced that the highest fulfilment humans could achieve as essentially rational beings is to be found in the contemplative life (*bios theōretikos*), which is the life directed to God alone. However, neither Philo nor Plato could ignore the fact that humans have needs other than their intellectual need to know God. Now let us see how similarly and differently Plato and Philo envision the optimal human society, one that is truly worthy of intelligent human nature.

As embodied beings living with other embodied beings *in* this world, humans have physical needs. And as embodied beings living *with* other *intelligent* bodies in this world, humans have political needs as well. Rational humans need to be governed in a way that is not only necessary but also desirable. The governance of intelligent beings, in order to be worthy of their more than animal nature, requires the rational consent of the members of what came to be called the "body politic."[71] Rational governance is conducted by means of persuasion that is freely accepted rather than coerced, that is, governance that is generally accepted willingly rather than grudgingly out of fear of bad consequences. Coercion should only be employed when individuals act in a way that harms other members of the body politic. Minimally, humans need their society to protect them from harm from other humans; maximally, they need their society to guide them in living a practical life (*bios praktikos*) that seeks more than merely physical satisfaction, but what might be called moral satisfaction. Moreover, a society needs to protect itself from its own members who would deny its authority by publicly advocating its overthrow. Such denial usually leads to open revolt against that society's laws and the overall purposes of the law itself. If such contempt is left unchecked, other members of that society will wonder whether their society has any authority over them. They will inevitably act accordingly, thus violently bringing about in fact what began as mere verbal suggestion.

The political needs of rational humans differentiate them from the animals, who are less intelligent, as well as from the divine (or, for Philo, quasi-divine) beings, who are more intelligent than are humans. As Aristotle famously pointed out, anybody who is not in need of society (and he means more than a herd or a hive) is "either a beast or a god."[72] Humans, because of their uniquely political needs, are somewhere in between. Thus Philo speaks of Adam, the progenitor of humankind, as being of a "middling mind" (*mesos nous*), who can do bad in his vicious pursuit of what is beneath him on earth, or who can do good in his virtuous (*aretē*) pursuit of what is above him in the heavens.[73] To a large extent, this middling human person is the personification of the middle part of the human soul as imagined by Plato, that is, the "spirited part" (*thumos*), which operates midpoint between the higher part of the human soul, "reason" (*logistikon*), and the lower part, "appetite" (*epithumētikon*).[74] Unlike the higher part that is irresistibly attracted to the ultimately intelligible forms that lie above it, and unlike the lower part that is necessarily attracted to the physical objects that lie beneath it, only the middle part seems to have the choice either to serve the higher part in its attraction to what is highest, or to serve the lower part in its attraction to what is lowest.[75] Thus Philo says, "we can choose [*boulometha*] to listen to what virtue counsels [*parainei*]"; and we can make this choice properly when "virtue is our law [*nomos hēmōn*]."[76] Clearly, virtue like law is not innate in the human soul, but it is the higher criterion whereby the spirited faculty (what we might call the "ego") makes the proper choice to serve the reasoning faculty in its transcendent trajectory rather than serving the immanent passions of the appetitive faculty.[77] Virtue here seems to have the same counselling function as what the Rabbis called "the good impulse" (*yetser ha-tov*).[78] And whom does virtue, which is ultimately intellectual excellence, so counsel (rather than coerce)? Surely, the one so counselled is the "middling mind" of whom Philo speaks immediately thereafter.[79]

It is clear that for both Plato and Philo the "spirited part" or "middling mind" is meant to rule what lies beneath it. That governance is political insofar as it is the exercise of rational public authority over the non-rational private (even if not individual, but collective) appetites or drives of the members of the society, and whose members recognize this authority by their sustained (often intergenerational), obedient presence in that society. Taken in and of itself, though, this kind of political authority only represses those non-rational forces that, if left unchecked, might lead to irrational (often violent) social dissolution. A society inevitably dissolves when enough of its members do not feel their society is protecting them as individuals from violence from each other, or when enough of its members feel that their society is not protecting itself from violent enemies whether they be foreign or domestic groups. However, this is only a society's negative function. And when this seems to be its sole function, the repression tends to become more and more severe. As such, more and more do the ruling authorities in that society look upon more and more of its members as actual and even potential enemies; and more and more of the members in turn look upon society, functioning through its authorities, as their persecutor.

Even when the authorities in a society recognize the political animosity they are fostering by their repressive rule, and even when they attempt to pander to the private passions of their constituents as a solution, the result is often gradual anarchy. Or it is what the French social theorist Émile Durkheim famously called *anomie*, the feeling of interpersonal alienation in an impersonal society.[80] Here is where the rulers of the society have become the servants of its many members.

Furthermore, diminished political involvement in the private or even domestic affairs of the members of a society does not present a real alternative to the kind of political repression one finds in a society where the leaders are too involved in the private affairs of its members. That is because by letting the members of the society alone, by less and less involvement in the lives of their members, the authorized leaders of such a society send a message that they don't care about those for whom they are expected to be responsible. This kind of impasse comes about because neither political repression nor political pandering gives a society a truly positive, rational purpose or *raison d'être*. In other words, rational governance of a society requires an overriding goal or *telos*, so that the rule of the lower part of society by the middle part is to serve the upper part, which itself is to be devoted to that which nothing greater could be. Without an overriding, transcendent goal, a society becomes rudderless in the cosmos, and in the end it has no reason to live or die. In fact, without this kind of purpose, a society wastes its best minds by requiring them to attend to basically ephemeral, even trivial, concerns.

Both Plato and Philo seem to agree on how human society is to be governed because of why it exists. However, no society whose members have been taught to look upon themselves as free rational persons is going to be satisfied with being told that their essential function is to serve the interests of an elite class, irrespective of how exalted the interests of that class seem to be. So, what has to be shown is what this elite class is doing to benefit those below them in the political hierarchy. That is, how can this elite class come down from its metaphysical heights to effectively, rationally, and beneficently govern those below them? Indeed, why should the members of this elite class exercise their political responsibility at all for their society, even one that has nurtured them and enabled them to rise to spiritual heights? Here is where Plato and Philo seriously diverge; and they diverge because of fundamentally different ontologies as regards God's relation to the world, especially God's relation to the human political world. That public world of interrelated human activity is constituted very differently by Plato and by Philo, and that is due to the different ontologies that underlie their politics. Let us first look at Plato, since Philo must overcome Plato's solution to this great question, whereas Plato couldn't have the same problem with Philo, who lived long after Plato had died.

In the *Republic*, where Plato imagines what the optimal human society could be, he sets down the program of education that is to enable (though not guarantee) the "philosophical guardians" (*phylakēs*) who are the "best and the brightest," selected and then bred for the sake of the polity as a whole, to rise to the level of intellectual vision of the eternal forms, to finally apprehend Goodness itself.[81] However, why would the polity as a whole invest in this rigorous program of education of its intellectual elite if these "superstars" were only to remain at this exalted level of cognition, thereby losing any interest in performing mundane political service for the very society that enabled them to rise to this level to begin with? That notwithstanding, certainly from the point view of the elite, the society is founded to serve them rather than vice versa. Surely, the intellectual elite, having achieved what cannot even be explained to their less philosophical fellow citizens, will be tempted to look upon any requirement that they come back down to earth with disgust, even dread. Moreover, the Goodness they have apprehended as the object of their ultimate quest is surely not interested in them; only they are interested in it, because the higher is not interested in the lower; only the lower should be interested in the higher. (Interest of the higher in the lower is considered by Plato to be giving oneself over to irrational passion rather than making a rational choice.) So, if a philosopher who has apprehended the *summum bonum* participates in it and thus imitates it somehow, won't this philosopher also want to imitate Goodness's indifference to anything beneath it?[82]

Why, then, is Plato so keen on the duty of enlightened philosophers to descend to the polity where the vast majority of the citizens are not themselves philosophers? Well, one might say that Plato was probably worried that the type of political indifference of his great teacher, Socrates, was one of the main causes of Socrates's inability to escape Athens's condemnation of him and, in fact, the condemnation of philosophy itself along with him. Political indifference on the part of philosophers does more than make their society indifferent to them; it makes their society dangerously hostile to them. Philosophy only thrives in an atmosphere of open discussion among actual and potential philosophers, that is, it is an essentially public enterprise. And even though Socrates thought he was performing a service to Athens by engaging in this kind of public discussion with its back-and-forth questioning of traditionally held opinions, the Athenian authorities thought otherwise.[83] They judged him to be a public enemy rather than a patriot. They certainly judged Socrates to be more than just a public nuisance. He was, in their eyes, corrupting the best and brightest of the young by showing them how to question opinions that had become Athenian dogmas, even though he did not advocate any kind of practical rejection of the laws of Athens. In fact, Socrates was a model of political obedience all of his life right up until his acceptance of his death sentence decreed by the Athenian court.[84]

So, it seems, to avoid that kind of horrible political fate, Plato had to think of reasons to persuade these philosophical superstars to want to come back down to earth and exercise political responsibility, that is, to govern the polity that, after all, they have been taught to love all their lives. And this persuasion must be rational rather than coercive, since anyone who is coerced to rule is in fact ruled by whoever has so coerced them and is, therefore, not a ruler at all. Furthermore, coercion is not only physical. The kind of psychological coercion employed by skilled rhetoricians is much more subtle, but no less coercive with its often subliminal appeals to emotions such as fear and envy. These emotions are often not under reason's control, thus humans are often unwillingly controlled by them. Rational persuasion is quite different from emotional coercion, and even more different from coercive threats of physical violence.

Plato presents two reasons he thinks could be employed to persuade these fulfilled philosophers to govern their society not because they have to do so, but because they want to do so.[85]

The first reason is that the fulfilled philosopher will have pity (*eleos*) on his or her (Plato includes women among the philosophical elite) fellow citizens, who cannot ascend out of the unenlightened cave as he imagines the enlightened philosophers will have done.[86] (The cave is Plato's metaphor for any society less than the enlightened one he imagines to be possible, though not yet real.) These lesser souls have not seen the sun (Plato's simile for Goodness) as the truly fulfilled philosophers have. And just as the sun nurtures what is beneath it with its light, so should the philosophers who have seen the sun want to nurture their native society with the light that emanates from the Goodness they have apprehended. Just as the sun does not keep its light to itself, so truly enlightened philosophers should not keep the light they have seen (with the eye of the soul) to themselves. The philosopher's pity, then, is not the kind of condescension we usually understand as pity; instead, it seems to be genuine empathy. The philosopher seems to be very much like the creative god [*dēmiourgos*] Plato imagines in the *Timaeus* who, "being good [*agathos*] doesn't enviously resent [*phthonos*] anyone else, and who wants all things to resemble him [*paraplēsia heautō*]."[87] Pity as compassionate, beneficent, empathetic concern seems to be the opposite of envious resentment. Nevertheless, this creative god, as we have seen, does not govern the cosmos he has brought into being from chaos; he only launches it. We could say, to use a contemporary expression, that this god has put the cosmos he has created "on automatic pilot." In fact, this god seems to lose interest in the cosmos immediately thereafter, returning to his true metaphysical concern whose object lies beyond the cosmos, transcending cosmic immanence, yet being transcended by the cosmos as well because of the cosmos's subsequent independence.

Now the Goodness that the philosophers are to apprehend, like the sun to which Plato compares it, only inadvertently acts on what is beneath it.[88] Whatever good it effects in the world is unintentional inasmuch as it is not a person, and only a person can intend anything. So, Plato can tell us how rational persons can willingly participate in Goodness by their increasing identification with it, but he cannot tell us how Goodness itself actually emanates towards what instantiates it below. (This, by the way, is unlike how the sun, to which Plato compares Goodness, operates in the world, as we know how its rays nurture what grows on earth as well as how what grows on earth is attracted to it.) Accordingly, won't whatever good is accomplished in the world by philosophers who imitate Goodness be unintentional too? How effective will such unintended good actually be for the masses below? Won't any beneficence the philosophical guardians effect in their polity be seen by their fellow citizens as being haphazard at best?

Furthermore, won't these philosophers quickly become impatient with their non-philosophical fellow citizens, who most likely cannot see how this philosophical governance could be anything more than the attempt of the philosophical elite to perpetuate their own exalted political status? In fact, the plan Plato imagines for his new polity is very likely his proposed political application of the vision of Goodness he himself has experienced. Yet isn't his plan to be instituted so that the new polity might effectively serve the philosophical elite Plato wants to publicly cultivate and empower (in a way Socrates couldn't cultivate and empower them)?[89] How are the masses benefitted by this plan any more than slaves are benefitted by serving their masters? Since when are masters concerned with actually benefitting their slaves? Only slaves who have freely sold themselves into slavery could be happy to settle for such a subservient role in their society. Yet Plato never seems to grant the citizens of his polity the right to freely choose to live there or not, although he did recognize the right of Athenian citizens to freely choose either to remain in Athens, and thus obligate themselves to obey its laws, or emigrate to some other polity with impunity.[90] Indeed, Plato sees his polity as becoming a political reality in the world only by some sort of *coup d'êtat* by philosophers seizing power in a particular society, or by the rulers of a particular society being turned into philosopher-kings. (The latter was always more likely than the former.) But this is not because the rulers have persuaded their subjects to be ruled by them, but rather because the rulers have been persuaded by philosophers (as Plato unsuccessfully attempted to do to the king of Syracuse) to follow their instruction and thus politically instantiate the philosophers' view of what an optimal human polity should be.[91] Nevertheless, the masses ruled by kings under the influence of philosophers have no choice but to either accept or reject their political servitude.

The second reason Plato gives for why philosophers should come back down to govern their society is that they have a civic duty to do so. For the polity has educated them to exercise enlightened rule below once they have been enlightened above. That is the gratitude they owe (*opheilon*) their society. "Down you go [*katabateon*], each in turn, to dwell together [*xynoikēsin*] with those others; accustom yourselves to see the darker things there."[92] The hidden premise here is that this civic duty is self-chosen, like Socrates's choice to live according to the laws of Athens. Could anyone be persuaded (as opposed to being compelled) to obey a law, the authority of whose lawgiver one has not chosen to obey (whether explicitly or only tacitly)?[93] After all, being persuaded to do one's duty is still less than being inspired to exercise one's right, in this case one's politically justified claim to apprehend Goodness itself (and to do so at the polity's expense, as it were). For the former is what one has to do; the latter is what one wants to do. Duty is always done more grudgingly than the exercise of a right.

Now, Plato does warn that those politicians eager to rule are usually power hungry, really intending to benefit their own private passions rather than the needs of the public.[94] Nevertheless, aren't most people more likely to follow leaders who govern them enthusiastically than leaders who govern them only reluctantly? No matter how short the philosophers' terms of office, won't their boredom with their political duties, which will inevitably become apparent, convince the people that these philosophers really don't care for them after all?[95] Won't their inner ambivalence, which will soon become evident to the people, make them unpopular and thus politically ineffective?

Philo on Interhuman Relations

Coming from a very different ontology (as we have already seen in the previous sections), Philo constitutes the political ordering of interhuman relations he envisions in the Torah quite differently. In fact, it seems that Plato had not adequately constituted a cogent relation between the ontological order he knows above and the political order to be instituted below. Although Plato can show how the political order can be instituted to ultimately function as the necessary preparation for its elite to rise up to the level of the ontological order, he still doesn't seem to be able to show how the ontological order can actually provide the type of grounding of the political order that will benefit anybody other than the philosophical elite themselves.

Now, the Jewish political order set forth in the Bible is one that actually existed in history. Even in Hellenized Alexandria, biblically based Jewish law seems to have been at least partially normative for the governance of the Jewish community there.[96] The political order Plato imagines (even in his more conservative imagination in the *Laws*), though, has never existed in history. But to better appreciate what Philo is advocating, we have had to carefully examine the Platonic political alternative no doubt quite familiar to his Hellenized audience, both Jewish and gentile. And we have to do this just as we had to show the metaphysical differences between Plato and Philo in the previous sections, because we cannot appreciate Philo's theological position unless we first work through Plato's philosophical position.

For Plato, praxis is for the sake of theory. The ordering of the interhuman realm, where praxis operates, is for the sake of the ordering of the divine-human realm. That is, those persons whose interhuman interactions are disordered will be too distracted by their inordinate desires to have the mental equilibrium to be able to sustain a contemplative relationship to the Divine. The interhuman, practical realm, however, has no value in and of itself. Its purpose is to either prepare the philosophically capable for the contemplative life, or to prepare non-philosophers to serve the needs of the philosophers so the latter might have the leisure to engage in contemplation. The relation of theory and praxis is that one moves up from praxis into theory, not that one moves down from theory into praxis. For Philo, though, the relation of theory and praxis is very different, and that is because the God of the Bible is very different from Plato's Goodness or the Divine (the two seem interchangeable), as we have already seen.

The Creator God of the Bible is concerned with what is not-God, which is the created cosmos. The fact of creation itself indicates God's initial concern with the cosmos He has brought into being. The fact of divine consistent governance of the cosmos (according to the nature built into it) indicates God's ongoing concern with what He has created. And what is central here is that divine creation itself is praxis. In fact, it is the most radical praxis possible. The God of the Bible is much more than the type of maker (*to poion*) who, as Aristotle described it, needs what is unmade in order to make something out of it and to make something that is formed according to it (*to telos*). The form (*to eidos*) is what the maker looks up in order to in-form the matter (*hē hylē*) that lies below him.[97] Both the form and the matter are themselves not-made and are non-makers. Moreover, since the guiding form is intelligible, theoretical appreciation of it precedes what the maker is going to do according to it. Whereas matter is the *conditio sine qua non* of human making insofar as human makers cannot ignore the limits it imposes on their work, form is the *conditio per quam* of human making insofar as it provides the criterion to which human making is answerable. For Philo too, praxis always follows theory, that is, for everyone except God. It seems that praxis and theory function in tandem for God, that is, God acts wisely or God theorizes practically. That is far different from Plato's (and Aristotle's) view of God's non-praxis.

In Philo's biblical creation theology, God alone is uncreated. But whereas philosophical theory is concerned with what is uncreated and uncreative, theological theory is concerned only with God's creativity because it can only know the uncreated God as Creator. That is, theology can only discuss what God *does* in relation to the world He has created rather than what God *is* by Godself apart from the world. As such, humans are to know (theory) what God does (praxis) in order to imitate what God does through our own intelligent and mutually beneficent interactions in the world. And even though Philo is sometimes vague about *how* God created the cosmos, he is clear that God did not make the cosmos like any maker (or "efficient cause") acts in the cosmos. So, we humans are unlike God insofar as our action in the interhuman world presupposes that the world is already there for us to act in it and on it. Our activity in the world at best is done *de novo*: it renews what is already there for us. Only God's acts are done *ex nihilo*, since for God there is nothing already there. But we are like God insofar as we can imitate God by acting intelligently and beneficently with each other like God acts for us. All knowing, then, is ultimately for the sake of doing, even when there is no immediate connection between theory and praxis. Our theorizing is primarily to understand *why* God has commanded us to do what we have been commanded to do in the world. It is much more than a legalistic approach to the law, which is necessary, to be sure, but which only tells us *how* to do what we have been commanded to do. As Philo puts it, "without theoretical knowledge, no activity [*prattomenōn*] is excellent [*kalon*]."[98]

What is important to appreciate is that for Philo, God's creation of the cosmos is a lawful activity, that is, it is done intelligently (hence theoretically significant) and it is done beneficently (hence practically significant). Creation, like law, has a material aspect and a formal aspect, and they function together in tandem. The material aspect of law is *what* the law actually commands to be done. The formal aspect of law is *how* the law is formulated so as to intelligently bring about its aims. God's concerned rule of the cosmos directly impinges on interhuman relations insofar as the law or standard by which God governs the cosmos is the standard by which God governs human society as part of the cosmos. This is what humans are to imitate insofar as they can imitate it. Along these lines Philo writes: "Of all the best powers [*dynameōn aristeōn*] of God, there is one that stands out over all of them: lawmaking [*nomothetikē*]. He himself is the lawgiver [*nomothetēs*], the fount [*pēgē*] of laws. In relation to Him, all lawgivers do so proportionately [*kata meros*]."[99]

The law has two basic purposes: one, to enable humans to interact with each other in a way that is worthy of them as the image of God; two, to enable humans to be related to God. But the question is how the two spheres of human action are related to each other. For Plato (and for Aristotle as well), these two spheres of human action are separate. One interacts with one's fellow humans publicly; one is related to God privately. (Let it be emphasized that the private or individual life of philosophers transcends their public life as citizens of even the best polity, which is because of the transcendent object of their philosophical quest; and that is unlike any privacy in modernity that intends no such transcendence and, therefore, cannot transcend public authority in any cogent way.) Now, as we have seen, Plato, who tries to correlate the two relationalities, does not seem to do so in a satisfactory way. Philo, too, tries to correlate them. For example, he says, "Their father, right reason [*orthou logou*], has taught them to honour the Father [*patera*] of all; but their mother, education [*paideias*], has taught them not to belittle the customs [*thesei*] conventionally recognized [*nomizomenōn*] everywhere."[100] "Mother" here seems to means the earthly nature of humans as essentially political or communal beings, who ordinarily live according to the customary practices of their communities. Moreover, Philo speaks of the two concerns, concern with God and concern with one's fellow humans, as functioning in tandem. "One who is naturally pious [*eusebē*] also [*kai*] loves humans [*philanthrōpōn*] ... piety [*hosiotēs*] is relating to God; justice [*dikaiosunē*] is relating to humans."[101] The question is *how* the two can be seen functioning together. So far we only seem to know *that* they are meant to function together.[102]

Perhaps the answer to this question is that even humanly founded and governed polities are founded and governed by humans whom God has created as rational beings in God's image, and they are created equally. Thus the best human polities (and for Philo the polity the Torah is made for is *the* best human polity possible) are where this ontological equality is most operative in the ordering of human interactions. Commenting on the biblical verse "with Me you are but sojourners and mere residents [*gerim ve-toshavim*]" (Leviticus 25:23), Philo notes that "all are equally privileged [*isotimian*] and equally obligated [*isoteleian*], because to God they are foreigners [*epēlutō*] and resident-aliens [*paroikōn*]."[103] In other words, all the members of the Torah-constituted society are equal, precisely because they are all equally unequal to God in whose earthly community they are all temporarily interned.[104] Philo actually calls equality the "mother of justice," not just earthly justice but essentially cosmic justice, which earthly justice reflects.[105] And when this earthly polity is governed by laws that are truly modelled after "natural right reason" (*physeōs orthou logou*), it reflects the "great [i.e., cosmic] city" (*megalopolis*) that is ruled by God according to His universal law.[106] This pious law and just piety, based as it is on a divine cosmic paradigm, is what has made Jewish law attractive to many gentiles.[107] Philo considers the Essenes, a semi-monastic Jewish sect, to come closest to this cosmic paradigm because of their "love of humanity, benevolence, egalitarianism [*isotēta*], and above all their communitarianism [*koinōnian*]."[108] He is especially impressed that the Essenes do not own slaves, for slavery itself is an unnatural human invention.[109] This community, more than any other, even any other Jewish community, has added the least amount of human-made law to the universal natural law of God.

Now, in the Greek polities some were full citizens and others were foreigners. The ultimate basis of the divide between the two was that citizens and foreigners were the subjects of different gods. In fact, Socrates's crime in Athens was that he was not loyal to the gods of Athens alone, instead acting like a foreigner who is subject to a strange or foreign god.[110] But for Philo, no such political distinction could be made inasmuch as no such polytheistic distinction could be made. All are under the rule of the one Creator God, whether in the cosmos or in a Torah-constituted community. And in both realms, whether cosmic or local, political equality among human creatures prevails.

The Torah teaches what is pleasing to humans who sense that political equality lies at the heart of political justice. This state of affairs is also pleasing to God who rules the cosmos accordingly, that is, fairly. That is how human law participates in divine cosmic justice.[111] What piety does for human justice is to place it in its true cosmic context, by relating it ultimately to God, the lawgiving Creator or creative Lawgiver. Taken by itself, however, human justice at its best seems to be longstanding conventions [*nomima*] that have preserved reasonable political order, saving human societies from anarchy and inequality.[112] Thus it has value in and of itself. But when justice is joined with piety, it shows how God's rule of the cosmos extends all the way down to the level of human polity, albeit through intermediaries, first and foremost Moses.[113] In other words, human justice is sanctified from above when divine justice sanctifies what lies below. Philo speaks of love of humanity, which is the epitome of human justice, as being the "twin" (*didumon*) of piety, thus combining theoretical and practical excellence.[114]

Speaking of what he sees as the superior kind of polity, Philo writes that "its government [*politeia*] is democratic, honouring equality [*isotēta*], whose rulers are law [*nomos*] and justice [*dikē*], which is praise to God." And he immediately contrasts this kind of polity with the inferior kind, which is where "mob rule [*ochlokratia*] admires inequality [*anison*], where injustice and lawlessness [*anomia*] are oppressive."[115] Just lawgiving, then, is the most important imitation of God. It is primarily imitation of divine praxis, which must also be theoretical in the sense that human theorizing imitates the divine wisdom (*sophia*) that informs divine action. Ultimately, justice itself (*to dikaion*) is God's enduring covenant (*diathēkē*) with Abraham and, especially, Moses. It is God's gift to them to instantiate in the world.[116] So, for example, the crime of murder is an affront to created nature of which rational-political human nature is a part, and just as much a sacrilegious affront to God (*hierosylias*) because rational-political human nature is a unique divine possession, which humans can imitate (*mimēma*).[117]

Philo on the Relation of Humans and Nature

When humans become fully aware of their being created in the image of God, they aspire to imitate God. But how do humans imitate God? For Plato, as we have seen earlier, humans imitate the higher gods by separating themselves from the world as much as is possible while they are still embodied beings there. When their souls are released from their bodies at the time of bodily death, humans complete this separation and it becomes permanent. The relation of these gods to earthly nature, that is, what is neither human nor divine, is basically antagonistic: these gods are against earthly nature. So, too, are humans who aspire to be like the gods; they also move against earthly nature, fleeing from it, rather than acting for it by moving towards it. For Aristotle, humans imitate God by thinking about God in the same way God thinks about Godself, which is intransitive or internal action. As such, divine being and divine doing are identical. God *is* what God *does*; there is no difference between the two. Now, when the Septuagint (the Bible of the Hellenistic Jews) translates Exodus 3:14 as "I am Being" (*eimi ho ōn*), it would seem that the God whom Aristotle (and other like-minded philosophers) experienced is the God the Septuagint translators had in mind. For Philo too, God is Being, but not intransitive Being.

Philo teaches that the God revealed in the Torah is beyond our knowledge, hence we cannot say *what God is*. All we can say is *what God does*. But to say what God does is to admit that God engages in transitive activity, that is, God acts in relation to what is not God. This transitive action of God is, to a certain extent, imitable by humans, since humans experience this divine activity in the world as it is directed to them, and as it is directed to the non-human world, that is, "nature." Moreover, humans are often the conduit for this divine care of the non-human world, that is, divine care for the rest of creation is primarily manifest through human efforts to imitate God.

Since God is without need of His creation, anything God does for creation is purely gracious activity. But humans do have need of each other as well as of non-human creation. If so, couldn't it be said that humans are related to non-human creation differently than God is related to it? Thus when explaining the biblical prohibition of destroying fruit trees (Deuteronomy 20:19–20), Philo notes this is because "they benefit [*ōphelei*] you by supplying the necessities [*anagkaiōn*] and luxuries of life."[118] Philo considers this to be motivated by "love of justice," that is, reciprocal justice, where one doesn't harm what has not harmed one, let alone repaying what has actually benefitted one by harming that beneficent thing. Nevertheless, this human relation to non-human creation is not presented as an act done in imitation of God. Not to harm what has not harmed you is like doing good for what has done good for you. Both are examples of ordinary reciprocal decency on the part of humans. No ontology is needed here, at least not at the *prima facie* level.

Philo sees this decency extending to non-human creatures for two reasons. First, those who are considerate of non-rational (*alogōn*), non-human creatures, with whom they have less in common, are more likely to be even more considerate of their fellow rational human creatures, with whom they have more in common (*koinōniais*). That is because they are motivated by more than strict *quid pro quo*–type justice, but rather by *epieikes*, which here means a kind of natural fairness or magnanimity towards all others.[119] Indeed, love of humanity (*philanthrōpia*) extends beyond the circle of those fellow humans with whom, by virtue of our natural commonality, we humans could share a mutual relationship.[120] Philo even compares this attitude, which Moses prescribes in the Torah, to a "gracious spring" (*eumenous*), which benefits all those it can reach without regard for what they can do for it.[121] Second, controlling sub-human, non-rational creation gently and considerately is very much like humans' control of the non-rational nature. Both non-rationalities better serve the truly rational, higher aspect of human nature when they are treated wisely and considerately.[122] It is the choice of the good shepherds, of whom God is the archetype, to do what is advantageous to their flock and not only what is immediately useful to themselves.[123]

Seen in the context of the human relationship with God, the human relationship with the rest of creation gains its ontological significance. We humans are unequal, both to God beyond us and to the rest of creation, especially earthly creation, around us. We are answerable to God; we are responsible for that part of creation of which we have some control through our humanly invented technology. Humans are unequal to God, though, because the Creator is far greater than any of His creatures, even God's most special creatures who are humankind. Humans are also unequal to the rest of earthly creation, over which they have power due to their greater practical intelligence. As for the heavenly bodies, being created souls like humans, they are not divine, even though Philo agrees with Plato, Aristotle, and the entire Greek philosophical tradition that the heavenly bodies are intelligences or souls (*psychai*) who are capable of theoretical reason, as we have already seen. In essence, human souls and heavenly souls are equal. If heavenly souls were, in fact, superior, uncreated entities, there would be no good reason to ban humans from worshipping them. For the same reason, humans are not to worship other humans, even those humans who are superior to them either practically or intellectually. Here the difference is still one of degree, not one of kind.

When humans exercise their control over earthly nature in order to aggrandize themselves, acting as if they are the lord of the estate rather than its caretaker, they inevitably discover that they have more power to destroy the estate than to enhance it; and they often act accordingly. It is only when humans exercise proper care for the part of creation over which they do have some control that they come to understand their power is limited by the very purpose for which this power was given to them by God. That purpose is "to take care [*labōn tēn epimeleian*] of plants and animals, like the prime minister [*hyparchos*] of a great king."[124] This is how humans truly subordinate their authority (*arches*) and power to the authority and power of God.[125] And this is how humans come to recognize their true place in the cosmos, which is in between God above and earthly creation around them. That is the theological significance of commanding humans, minimally, not to harm their earthly environment and what it contains along with them; maximally, to actually benefit it. Any change in this distribution of authority and power results in a radical disordering of the place of humans in the created cosmos.

After Philo

Many of Philo's insights resulting from his engagement of philosophy forecast many of Maimonides's insights resulting from his engagement of Aristotle. Nevertheless, in the over-thousand-year historical hiatus between Philo and Maimonides, a very different climate, both intellectual and political, emerged, making Maimonides's theological relation to philosophy quite different. That is the subject of the next chapter.

Chapter Five

Maimonides and Aristotle

Maimonides's Challenge

The challenge philosophy posed to Jewish theology was, in some ways, the same for Maimonides in the twelfth century as it was for Philo in the first century (examined in the previous chapter); yet in other ways the challenge was quite different for Maimonides. In some ways, Plato's (or Platonism's) challenge to Philo was similar to Aristotle's (or Aristotelianism's) challenge to Maimonides; but, in other ways, the philosophical challenge Maimonides confronted was quite different.

For both Philo and Maimonides, the philosophy they had to confront had both comprehensive content and an accompanying method for its comprehensive explication. The philosophies each of them confronted also had both theoretical and practical comprehensive content. The theoretical content comprised an ontology that thoroughly deals with the relation of God and nature, and the relation of God and humans. The practical content comprised a morality and a politics that deals with interhuman relations more thoroughly, though the relation of humans and nature is dealt with less thoroughly.

Platonism and Aristotelianism (*mutatis mutandis*) comprised complete ways of life, which are deemed to be what is the best way of life for *all* humans. The intent of these philosophies was thus universal, and their adherents were often determined to attract intelligent humans of whatever ethnic origin to them by virtue of their universalism. In the process, the ethnic particularity of these novices would thereby be overcome in one way or another. That is how these respective ways of life, both theoretically and practically, posed a direct challenge to the theologically constituted Jewish tradition, which seemed to be a particular way life only meant for a particular people: the Jews. After all, isn't a whole greater than any of its parts? Isn't what constitutes a way of life for all humankind better than what only constitutes a way of life for a particular people (and a small one at that)? Nevertheless, since biblical theology constantly affirms the God who is Creator of the whole universe, which He has created with a permanent structure or *nature*, Jewish theologians (as well as Christian and Muslim theologians) could not very well ignore the universalistic challenge of philosophy by retreating into an anti-metaphysical, atomistic particularism that denies universal nature altogether. And since biblical theology clearly affirms that all humans qua humankind are capable of a direct relationship with the Creator God, Jewish theologians could not retreat into an ethical relativism that denies universally binding moral norms altogether, because there is no human nature to which they pertain. Therefore, when confronted by philosophies like Platonism and Aristotelianism (and, as we shall see in the next chapter, Kantianism), Jewish theologians have had to argue for Judaism's greater, superior, better universalism than that of any of its philosophical rivals.

Until actually faced by this kind of universalist challenge from philosophy, Jews could regard their own comprehensive way of life as being above any such challenge, because they were only being challenged by some other particular way of life. Moreover, whatever challenge these other particular ways of life posed to the Jews, it was not philosophical. Indeed, such particularistic challenges to the Jewish tradition, made in the name of their "strange gods," were ridiculed in the Bible as being intellectually inferior to Jewish monotheism. Thus the prophet Jeremiah protests in God's name against the people Israel for "exchanging God for no-gods," and thereby "digging for themselves broken wells that hold no water" (Jeremiah 2:11, 13). That kind of retort, however, could hardly be taken seriously if made against Platonism and Aristotelianism.

Now, there is great similarity between Philo and Maimonides in terms of the challenge of philosophy to their theology and the way each of them handled it. The difference between Philo and Maimonides, however, is that the challenge of philosophy in Philo's case was more concrete, while in Maimonides's case it was more abtsract. In Philo's case, Platonism's attraction was the attraction of a way of life actually being lived by real people in that time and place. Thus to become a fully committed Platonist then and there meant there was a real chance that a Jew so attracted would literally become a member of that other community, and thereby be lost to the Jewish people. In Maimonides's time, though, the other communal options for Jews were either Christianity or Islam (in Maimonides's place, Islam was the only other communal option for Jews). Therefore, the problem in Maimonides's time and place was not that philosophically inclined Jews might actually adopt the way of life of another real community to which they were attracted. Instead, the challenge was that philosophically inclined Jews might still practice Judaism as a political pragmatic necessity, yet actually believe that Judaism does not teach universal truth, that is, what is rationally evident to all intelligent humans. Indeed, these Jews might actually believe that what Judaism teaches is metaphysically false and ethically mindless. To live such a lie very much troubled Maimonides, who was convinced that that the Torah must be what Moses said to the people Israel it truly is: "your wisdom [*hokhmatkhem*] and your understanding in the eyes of the peoples" (Deuteronomy 4:6).[1]

Despite this difference between Philo and Maimonides, which was largely determined by different historical circumstances, they were nevertheless similarly concerned with retaining Jews as intelligent adherents of Judaism by showing that Judaism teaches universal truth. As such, Judaism is not only not parochial or particularistic, it is, in fact, a better universalism than that taught by its philosophical competitors. Furthermore, if Judaism is essentially universalistic, its teaching addresses all humans. That explains why both Philo and Maimonides were not only intent on bringing Jews attracted to other universalisms back to Judaism as the best universalism, but also intent on attracting intelligent, philosophically searching gentiles to Judaism.[2] In other words, each of them was very positively disposed to proselytizing gentiles, though the political climate in Philo's first-century Alexandria made explicit proselytizing much easier than the political climate in Maimonides's twelfth-century Cairo, where the Muslim authorities prohibited proselytizing for any religion other than Islam.

Now, to be sure, Islam too seemed to be posing a philosophical challenge to Judaism by claiming to be a purer, less anthropomorphic, monotheistic revelation. Yet, somewhat like Philo, Maimonides painstakingly argued that biblical language was not meant to always be taken literally, for the very consistency and profundity of its message as the revelation of the supremely wise God required that its ostensibly anthropomorphic passages be read figuratively.[3] Only this kind of reading would uncover the Bible's deeper, more philosophically impressive meaning. Nevertheless, Islam and Judaism were both faced with the much bigger common challenge that came with the recovery of the main texts of Aristotle's philosophical corpus by Muslim scholars, who translated them into Arabic and commented on them extensively and insightfully.[4] These texts, which were presented as being rooted in what was at that time an undisputed scientific paradigm, were definitely concerned with God as the Absolute, and with the relation of the absolute God to both the natural world and the human world. Since these two concerns are also central to Islam and Judaism, Muslim and Jewish theologians could not denigrate them or ignore them as they could denigrate or ignore the metaphysically inferior polytheistic texts of earlier antiquity. Nevertheless, these texts had to be treated critically insofar as they seem to implicitly deny the doctrine of absolute divine creation of the universe (*creatio ex nihilo*), which is a doctrine taken to be fundamental by both Muslims and Jews.[5] In fact, almost all Jewish and Muslim theologians were convinced that Jews and Muslims do worship the same Creator God. Moreover, the way Jews and Muslims worship this same God seems to be almost the same. Thus Muslims are definitely not polytheists in theory, nor are they idolaters in practice (*ovdei avodah zarah*).[6]

This philosophic commonality of Judaism with Islam was not the case with Christianity. To be sure, contemporary Christian theologians also faced this same philosophical challenge, yet Maimonides regarded Christianity as inferior to Islam and Judaism on philosophic grounds.[7] So it seems he did not view Christianity as up to the challenge of a metaphysically critical encounter with philosophy. Therefore, he was explicitly in league with contemporary Muslim theologians (whose work and probably some of whom he knew personally) in facing the challenge of Aristotelian philosophy: its ontology primarily, and to a somewhat lesser extent its ethics as well.

Aristotle's Teleology

It can surely be maintained that Aristotle's greatest contribution in the history of human thought is his teleology, which is his idea of a thoroughly purposeful universe.[8] Aristotelian teleology is ubiquitous throughout Maimonides's work, both theoretical and practical. But in order to appreciate Maimonides's critical engagement with Aristotelian teleology, we need to carefully examine Aristotle himself on this idea. This must be done at some length. Too many treatments of Maimonides's relation to Aristotelian teleology simply state that he employed it without, however, analysing both its complexities and Maimonides's own complex employment of it.[9]

In order to understand Aristotle's teleology, we need to examine his theory of causation, since a *telos* or "end" is but one cause out of four. Moreover, as our term "cause" is narrower than Aristotle's *aition*, which is usually translated as "cause," we should think of an *aition* as a necessary principle determining what any entity is, and without which it would be something else.[10] Only when these four causes or principles are seen to be functioning together do they fully explain *what* any kind of entity that shows itself in our world is, and by implication, what it is not. That is, something is what it is, thus being different from other kinds of entities, *because* of these four determining factors. And though they function together in varying ways in variously different entities, nonetheless all four are always found in every entity, *whether* it is natural or artificial.[11] (Anticipating Maimonides's critical reworking of Aristotle's causal theory, however, we should note that Aristotle does not explain causally *why* any natural entity in the universe – or *why* the universe itself – exists rather than not existing.)[12] Thus "the end" (*to telos*), which is the ultimate limit (*peras*) of any entity, must be correlated with the other three causes, even though it seems to be the most important one.[13] The other three causes are: the material cause (*hē hylē*), the formal cause (*to eidos*), and the efficient cause (*to poioun*, literally, "the doer").[14] We shall soon see how each of these causes or determinants actually operates.

In Aristotle, there seem to be five distinct types of causation, yet each of which still employs all four causal factors, though these causal factors function in different constellations in each of these five types of causation. The five types of causation might be termed: (1) technical causation; (2) natural causation; (3) pragmatic causation; (4) ethical causation; and (5) ontological causation.

Technical Causation

In technical causation, the four causes are most evidently distinct from one another and their correlation is most evident. Aristotle's best illustration of this type of causation is the making or crafting (*technē*) of a house. Here the house-builder (*oikodomos*) forms materials like earth and stones according to a preconceived pattern (*paradeigma*). That preconceived pattern functions as the reason (*logos*) for the building process itself. The end result or intended product, the *telos* of that process, is the completed house itself, which is a spatial entity. It is an external object one comes up against.[15] Moreover, in this type of causation, the producer (*causa efficiens* in Latin) is the most prominent factor, as it is his or her choice that determines the existence of the end product, that is, whether it will be or not be *what* it is. Nevertheless, this model of causation, though most evident, is still ultimately incomplete, for the completely built house is not an end in itself. After all, we still need to know just *why* the house was built: what is the activity *for* which either the tenants themselves built the house or somebody else built it for them so that their activities could be conducted within their house? Here form is for the sake of function. That is why technical causation cannot be the model for the type of causation that is of ultimate ontological significance, inasmuch as its *telos* is only penultimate. For one must ask next: *why* are the tenants living in their house; *why* do they want to live there at all? Furthermore, *because* all spatial bodies move, but do not move themselves self-sufficiently, they thus require something external and non-moveable *by* which or *for* which they are moved.[16] Also, in-formed earthly entities are mutable: they come to be and eventually perish, whereas ultimate ends are assumed to be eternal.[17] Therefore, due to their spatial and temporal limitations, technical ends lack the ultimacy that humans seek in their teleological quest.

Natural Causation

For Aristotle, this is the causation one finds in earthly nature, specifically in biological nature's reproductive capacity, and most specifically in zoological reproduction. Though Aristotle occasionally discusses technical causation and natural causation together, there is an important difference between the two. In technical causation, conscious and even willing makers make something different from themselves and also unlike themselves. (Plato used this model to imagine his cosmology, where God's looking to the eternal forms as a model turns chaos into cosmos.)[18] But in natural causation, especially the biological causation that Aristotle as a biologist knew so well, the moving cause (*kinoun*) basically in-forms its product with its own form through a process of reproduction or generation (*genēsis*). So, for example, a human (*anthrōpos*) begets another human as his child, thus making the child in his image.[19] For Aristotle, the child is begotten by the active *in-forming* father, not by the passive *in-formed* mother.

Technical causation and natural-biological-reproductive causation have two essential points in common, however. First, the *telos* in each of them is an *end product*, hence the efficient cause – whether a maker or a progenitor – is superior to what has been made or conceived-then-born. The *telos* here is not ultimate. It is not the determining reason "for which" (*hou heneka*) the causal activity is ultimately being done.[20] Second, the *telos* in each of them is not already there before the efficient cause acts, that is, before he or she makes something or produces somebody. Instead, the *telos* is a future projected product. In fact, it could be said that the *telos* in each of them is actually the formal cause or "idea" (*eidos*) functioning as an *ideal*, which is to be finally realized at some future point in time.[21] Nevertheless, the actual end product in the present inevitably falls short of that ideal, which is an idea projected from the present onto the future. So, for example, the actual house falls short of the plans that informed its building; and the actual child falls short of what the parents hoped he or she would become.

Now in two key ways, natural causation is beneath technical causation in what has been termed "the chain of being."[22] One, whereas a practical maker is a self-conscious, willing person, who chooses to make an artificial entity, that is, create its very existence – and could just as freely choose not to create it at all – those who biologically reproduce offspring need not be willing or even conscious of the end result of their sexual behaviour. Reproduction is basically an animal act. Two, the offspring of the reproductive process are even more perishable than most human-made artifacts.[23] That might well explain why Aristotle (at least in his extant oeuvre) never compares God to a biological father, whereas he does compare God (albeit quite figuratively) to the kind of efficient cause who makes or orders things.[24] (Maimonides, though, will have the problem of explaining how the Creator God of the Bible is even more a Maker than God is the *telos* or final cause.)

Let us now look at practical teleology to perhaps find a different kind of *telos*. Practical teleology is of two kinds: pragmatic and ethical.

Pragmatic Causation

In pragmatic causation, an act is performed now in order that some state of being will come about (i.e., be-come) in the foreseeable future.[25] It is instrumental. So, for example, I eat nourishing food in order to be healthy. The act of eating is the means to this end. But why do I want to be healthy? What is being-healthy for? Aristotle points out that "ends" of this sort are (1) instruments devised for something else, hence lacking teleological ultimacy (for example, money-making), or (2) they are states-of-being that are unworthy of rational humans (for example, bodily pleasure as an end-in-itself), or (3) they are dependent on the whim of others (like fame) that is not a deliberate act, but a contingent experience.[26] That is why the pragmatic ends-means correlation is not the proper mode for truly fulfilling human action; rather, it seems to be a subset of technical causation and its teleology. We have to look at ethical causation as an act done for its own sake, and whose ultimate intent is for a cognitive relation to God. Only this kind of contemplative teleology is worthy of humans as rational beings.[27]

Ethical Causation

Ethical causation is concerned with what makes humans happy in this world. For most of Aristotle's contemporaries (and, in fact, for most people even today), happiness is what happens to one rather than what one does. It is an experience rather than an activity. This comes out in Aristotle's treatment of what is known as "Solon's paradox," where he essentially redefines what had been meant by the term *telos* theretofore.[28] The paradox is as follows: If well-being or "happiness" (*eudaimonia*) is what all rational humans want in their lives and thus strive for it, how does one know if one has *had* a happy life or not? The maxim is "look to the end" (*telos horan*), that is, look at how a person's life *ended* or concluded. Clearly, the "end" here is a temporal limit; it is the exact moment when one's life ends in death.[29] The paradox is: How can a person know whether he or she has been happy during a lifetime *when* that person could only know that *after* he or she had already died? And it seems to be assumed by both Solon and Aristotle that the dead cannot look back on their own lives in this world from some other place in the cosmos to judge whether or not they have enjoyed a happy life on earth. In fact, it seems to be assumed that the dead do not have any posthumous consciousness at all, let alone any rational capacity to judge the quality of the life they have left behind.

The deeper paradox is a person cannot ever know whether he or she actually had happiness in life *altogether* or not. For example, a person may have enjoyed most of his or her life, yet at the end of it suffered terribly from a debilitating disease or some other painful, degrading misfortune. Does whatever that person enjoyed during the rest of their life count in retrospect or not? Also, what if a person enjoyed some sort of epiphany during his or her very last moments in life? Would that person judge his or her life *altogether* to have been happy or not? It seems that for Aristotle, following Solon, it is impossible to stand outside of one's life *after* it has ended so as to be able to judge what transpired before it finally ended.

However, the mistaken assumption in Solon's paradox, Aristotle argues, is that happiness (*eudaimonia*) is a state of well-being; that happiness is something that *happens to* a person at times during their lifespan, that it is good experience. Ultimately, though, it seems to be an accident, a matter of luck or chance (*tychē*). As such, a person has little active control over it, as it comes from without, that is, it is basically contingent on external events. But how can we want happiness when we don't know what it is that we want? How can we devise means to a hidden end? Don't we have to know what an end is before we can choose the means appropriate to it?

In order to resolve this paradox, Aristotle essentially changes the very definition of happiness as the *telos* of human life. Rather than the *telos* being a temporal limit, which is impossible to control or predict, and which a person cannot transcend and thus judge what lies behind it, *telos* is now taken to be a *purpose* rather than an endpoint in either space or time. Knowing that purpose is how a person can intelligently desire it and order one's actions thereto *throughout* one's entire life. And that is done here and now in the present while a person is still within his or her lifespan. It is not, therefore, something that *finally occurs at* some indefinite point in the future. It is not an achievement, but rather a constantly achieving activity. *Eudaimonia* is now seen to be a regularly performed, purposeful activity. It is now *acting-well* or wholesomely (*teleian energounta*) rather than *feeling-good* or having good experiences whether constantly or only intermittently.[30] Some contemporary Aristotelian philosophers like to call this kind of *eudaimonia* "human flourishing." It means living a purposeful life consistently. As Aristotle himself put it:

> Since the future is not shown [*aphanes*] to us, we state that happiness [*eudaimonian*] is an end that is final and totally complete [*telos kai teleion*]. So we say that living persons who possess and continue to possess the qualities already mentioned are supremely happy or blissful [*makarious*, literally "blessed"] – at least as this is humanly possible [*hōs anthrōpous*].[31]

Instead of being a spatial object that is either made artificially or begotten naturally, and instead of being a temporal event, a practical *telos* is no longer named by a noun. Rather, it is named by an adverb: *teleiōs*, meaning living *completely* or harmoniously.[32] Thus the most happy person is one who lives this kind of life "according to standards of excellence" (*kat' aretēn*). This kind of person's life is "ruled (*kyriai*) by his or her activities (*energeiai*)" – not by experiences.[33] And this practical teleology involves a kind of action that is different from that of pragmatic teleology: it is action that is fulfilling in the very present this person is acting in; it is not present action for the sake of some future action or experience.

The question now is whether or not the *telos* of praxis (now so defined) means activities that are self-justifying, that is, that intend nothing but their own continued enactment. The key to answering this question lies in Aristotle's comment above about *human* happiness, which implies that it is inferior to some other kind of happiness. It would seem that other kind of happiness, being superior to human happiness per se, is the happiness of the only other beings who could act intentionally (i.e., rationally), who could only be the gods. And since Aristotle ultimately acknowledges only one supreme God as worthy of a truly rational person's emulation, the difference between divine happiness and human happiness enables Aristotle's teleology to withstand the suggestion that it be rejected by Jewish (and Christian and Muslim) monotheists altogether because it is fundamentally polytheistic. (In fact, Maimonides ignores what was Aristotle's seeming acceptance of the popular polytheism of his time and place, albeit unenthusiastically.) Now the only kind of absolutely complete (*to teleion*) happiness or well-acting is God's happiness, which intends nothing external to itself.[34] Being self-contemplation, its activity is intransitive: "thinking-itself" (*noēsis noēseōs*).[35] This kind of thinking, best termed "contemplation," is what is loved (*agapasthai*) for its own sake.[36] It is what is "most enjoyable" (*hēdiston*) as it is "what is best" (*ariston*).[37] It is what is totally and completely purposeful per se.[38] Therefore, practical teleology, which is a human activity, can only be properly understood when it is compared with ontological teleology, which is a divine activity.[39] In fact, practical teleology is but one step below ontological teleology in Aristotle's hierarchical cosmos.

Ontological Causation

Finally, we can now examine ontological causation, where we find the highest and most perfect teleology.

Even practically excellent or ethically noble human activity must still intend something outside itself. Unlike pragmatic causation, though, this activity does not intend a separate goal to which the intending activity itself is a means or an instrument for it. A means to an end, by definition, cannot be an ultimate end. Moreover, unlike technical causation, this activity is not intended to make anything. And unlike natural causation, this activity is not intended to produce or procreate another body. Nevertheless, ethically active humans still have to intend objects outside of themselves, even though these external objects are not the projected products of human subjects who have made them (*technē*) or reproduced them (*genesis*). So, in the case of ethical action (*praxis*), the external objects of one's action are *other* human persons, *with* whom one interacts: both acting and reacting in regular social interactions. Moreover, acting humans have to consider these other persons as one's equals, who are neither one's instruments nor offspring.[40]

It is only when those rare humans who have metaphysical desire and capability engage in contemplation of the Divine that they become like God, and to such an extent that God is no longer outside them as they are no longer outside God.[41] As Aristotle succinctly puts it: "Divine activity, blissfully surpassing all other activities, could only be contemplative activity; so the human activity most like it is most happy."[42] Nevertheless, whereas God engages in this self-contemplation eternally, without interruption, embodied humans can only do so intermittently. So, when we are not engaging in this exalted contemplation, we humans are involved in our society, where we need the company of our fellow humans and the availability of the things needed by our bodies. In other words, in the practical life (*bios praktikos*) one is always aware of being in time, especially when experiencing events and making choices to act; and one is always aware of being in space because of the other persons and things one has to encounter there. It is only in contemplation of the divine that humans seem to dwell, however briefly, in eternity. But how does one attain the contemplative life (*bios theōretikos*)?

Contemplative action begins in aesthetic experience, when we let external objects act upon us by letting them be seen by our bodily eyes; and we spectators (aesthetes) react by letting ourselves enjoy the visual beauty we have experienced.[43] Then, in the case of contemplation (*theōria*), one lets the heavenly intelligences be known or be seen with the mind's eye – in the act of contemplating God as the Unmoved Mover, who is the *telos* of contemplative desire. This is the God to whom all truly intelligent beings are drawn, whereas this God is drawn to nothing outside of Godself, not even to other beings who seem to be quite close to this God. Truly contemplative humans – who are philosophers of the highest sort, being what we now call "metaphysicians" – imitate the heavenly intelligences by enjoying God as God enjoys Godself. As Aristotle put it: "The activity of God is contemplation; it is transcendently [*diapherousa*] blissful. Hence it is the human activity most happily [*eudaimonikōtatē*] akin [*syngenestatē*] to it."[44]

Note that in both aesthetic action and contemplative action, unlike moral action, the subjects of the action do not affect the object of their action in any way. In fact, the verb we usually translate as "contemplate" (*theōrein*) seems to be originally used to denote aesthetic action and its accompanying pleasure, and subsequently to denote metaphysical action and its accompanying pleasure.[45] But the difference between them rests on the nature of the object before them. In the case of aesthetic action, the object is penultimate, even though this object is the heavens above us, viewed from the perspective of astrophysics, rather than earthly nature beneath us, viewed from the perspective of biology. The heavenly bodies are considered to be greater than humans, whereas unintelligent earthly nature (what we now call the "biosphere") is considered to be less than human. In fact, earthly matter is different from heavenly matter, and in the case of the heavenly bodies form and matter are much more tightly connected than in the case of earthly bodies.[46] (Interestingly, as far as I know, although a biologist himself, Aristotle does not express philosophical *eros* in his biology as he does in his astrophysics – a perspective that Maimonides, though a physician himself, seems to share with him, as we shall see.)

Aristotle: Ethics and Ontology

Practical teleology, in Aristotle's philosophy, is much more like ontological teleology than it is like technical teleology or biological teleology; yet the two are different. However, they are not so different as to be unrelated. So, what is the relation between the two?

Now, it could be said that ethics is applied ontology, that is, ethics is derived from ontology, almost as a conclusion of a proposition is deduced from its premise. That is what Plato tried to do when imagining that in his optimal polity ("the republic") the philosophers whom the polity prepared to rise to the level of metaphysical vision of the eternal Forms (*eidē*) would come down to apply that vision to the ethical/political business of that optimal polity. (We examined this problem in the previous chapter on Philo and Plato.) However, Aristotle was specifically critical of his teacher's ontologically generated ethical-political praxis and, in fact, he did not replicate that model in his own philosophy. Instead, Aristotle emphasized the difference between the divine objects of ontology and the human objects of ethics/politics. And, accordingly, he emphasized the difference between the theoretical reason that deals with the former and the practical reason that deals with the latter.

It would seem that ethical teleology and ontological teleology are essentially unrelated inasmuch as the *telos* of praxis is human, while the *telos* of contemplation (*theōria*) is divine. As such, the means of knowing these respective ends, which is the methodology employed by those seeking them, is essentially different. Aristotle says this explicitly:

> Human reason [*to logon*] is twofold, one with which we contemplate [*theōroumen*] that which has definite first principles [*archai*], and the other that has more variable or indefinite ones [*endechomena*] ... one is scientific [*epistēmonikon*] and the other is discursive [*logistikon*], that is, deliberation [*bouleuesthai*]; for deliberation is never about what is definite.[47]

In other words, ethics as practical reason deals with the possibility of human acts: an act might be done or it might not be done, or it might be done this way or it might be done that way. This is the overall cultivation (or habituation) of an excellent, active way of life called *aretē*.

In fact, *aretē* denotes an active pursuit of what is now called "human flourishing."

That is why these excellent character traits (*aretai*), which are cultivated through reasoned praxis, are different from the excellent character traits to be cultivated through contemplation.[48] There is intellectual excellence (*dianoētikē*) and there is ethical excellence. And whereas the chief intellectual excellence is wisdom (*sophia*), the chief ethical excellence is liberality or generosity (*eleutheriotēs*).[49] The former excellence is best cultivated in private meditation; the latter excellence, though, can only be cultivated in public.[50] That is also why philosophers, dealing as they do with invariable scientific content, make poor political leaders; and that is also why political leaders, dealing as they do with the quite variable moral condition of volitional human persons, make poor philosophers. Truly intelligent persons, for Aristotle, have to choose either the political life or the philosophical life.[51] One cannot combine both ways of life; thus there can be, for Aristotle, no philosopher king as Plato had hoped.[52]

All this notwithstanding, natural science and ethics are both capacities of the same human reason; they are not the respective capacities of two different species. Thus it seems odd to assume there is no relation at all between these two capacities of any one rational human person. Moreover, there is a necessary connection of the practical life and the contemplative life, insofar as ordinary people in society can live virtuous, purposeful lives without engaging in philosophy/metaphysics, but philosophers – no matter how cloistered – cannot avoid at least some political involvement with their fellow citizens in society. For all humans are, as Aristotle insisted, "political beings"; and thus his famous point that anyone not in need of society is either a superhuman god or a subhuman beast.[53]

Nevertheless, the philosopher's general need for society has a specific difference from the political need of ordinary non-philosophers. In the case of ordinary people, their need for society is their deepest need and, as such, their society – if it seems to be fulfilling that need – commands their highest loyalty, it being their ultimate authority. So, for example, suicide – the most private act possible – is considered to be a public offence, because one's society/polity owns all embodied individuals within its domain, hence society has the sole right to determine who shall live and who shall die.[54] Indeed, it might well be said that a rationally ordered polity is the *telos* of the ordinary citizen, and that his or her activities on behalf of the polity therefore require no further justification. Thus the highest excellences are those that habituate a person to be a good citizen, one who gives more to the polity and fellow citizens than he or she takes from it and from them.

For a philosopher, however, being a member of a polity is only a necessity condition (*conditio sine qua non*) of being an embodied person, who is in need of the bodily necessities one can only get by participating in what later came to be called "the body politic." Those necessities are the things his physical body needs to survive and even enjoy, plus there are the other human bodies he needs to be recognized by and to recognize himself in turn because he is a discursive being (*logon ... echei*).[55] But a philosopher's loyalty to the polity and its laws is not the ultimate reason (*conditio per quam*) for his existence. The ultimate *telos* of his existence and activity is God, to whom a philosopher relates himself noetically. Moreover, a philosopher knows quite well that this relationship is not mutual, since God is not interested now or ever in anything or anyone outside Godself. Indeed, for the sake of this higher loyalty, a philosopher must keep his political involvements to a bare minimum, saving as much time and strength as possible to engage in metaphysics, whose activity is primarily directed to God. Nevertheless, total neglect of these political needs will be self-defeating inasmuch as neglected needs are disordered, unlimited drives that inevitably (i.e., necessarily) return to overwhelm the person who has not rationally limited them, but has only irrationally either indulged them or suppressed them. A philosopher is to be neither profligate nor ascetic.

However, ethical/political life is not only a bodily (both physical and political) necessity that stands in contrast to the true desirability of philosophy; it is also necessary preparation for the philosophical life. That is because nobody, no matter how intelligent, who is living a morally disordered life will be in any position emotionally to direct his or her intellectual desire to its true end rationally. That is why Aristotle, like Plato his teacher, sees the moral life, in which the emotions or the passions are rationally controlled, as required for the sake of the cultivation of the intellectual excellences that sustain the true philosophical quest for God.[56] Yet it should be noted that this moral preparation for philosophy is not potential that, when unencumbered, automatically actualizes itself in teleological fulfilment. It is not even the sure means to the end of contemplative happiness (*eudaimonia*). Indeed, we can only say the following: while it is necessary that all philosophers have practical/political excellence, all those who have practical/political excellence will not necessarily become philosophers. Practical excellence makes theoretical excellence possible, but it does not make it inevitable. (As we will see, this is a crucial matter when Maimonides distinguishes prophets from all those of lesser connection to God, even from philosophers.)

The teleological point to be made here is that although the *telos* of the practical/political life is different from that of the philosophical/metaphysical life, they need not be seen as being at loggerheads, at least not in principle. Put differently, although the multiple gods who are invoked in an earthly polity, primarily as lawgivers and benefactors, are different from the one God Aristotle sees as being the object of a philosopher's ultimate concern, these gods are ultimately subordinate to the one God of the heavens. However, the one God of the heavens is in no way subordinate to them.[57] (Maimonides, of course, being a thorough-going monotheist, will not be able to make this kind of metaphysical distinction; hence he will have the much bigger philosophical problem of showing how the God who gives the Law and the God who is the object of philosophical *eros* is still one and the same God of biblical theology.) In other words, penultimate practical teleology looks to ultimate ontological teleology as its cosmological anchor.

Aristotle's Ontology

In Aristotle's teleological ontology, God is the Unmoved Mover who moves the heavenly spheres, not by exercising effective causation, but rather by simply being the attraction to all other, less than perfect, beings beneath him in the cosmic hierarchy. This God neither extends himself towards others nor hides Godself from them. As such, God is *the* Final Cause acting inwardly rather than *the* Efficient Cause acting outwardly. God's action is not transitive but intransitive. However, what kind of motion on the part of the heavenly spheres, which are directly beneath him in the chain of being, does God inspire or attract?

Here is where we have to understand that, for Aristotle (and all his disciples thereafter), the heavens are essentially different from the earth. Earthly motion is linear; it moves between a *terminus a quo* and a *terminus ad quem*. Thus earthly motion has a temporal beginning (*archē*) and a temporal end (*telos*). That is why time thought of as linear progression like a straight line is the measure of motion on earth. Surely, though, that cannot be the motion of the heavenly spheres that is taken to be eternal, and thus without a beginning or an end in time. Obviously, the motion of the heavenly spheres is not linear. Aristotle assumes that it is perfectly circular, hence without a discernible beginning or end.[58] Now, whereas Newton tried to explain heavenly motion, that is, why the heavenly bodies remain moving in orbit and do not collide with one another or fall down to earth, by a rather mysterious force called "gravity" – which one can hardly assume to be conscious or rational or desiring – Aristotle explained heavenly motion as being maintained by the *desire* of the fully *formal* heavenly bodies to forever remain in perpetually cognitive orbit around God as the eternal object of their desire.[59] That perpetual motion is what keeps them from falling down to earth, which wouldn't be the case if their matter (*hylē*) were perishable like all earthly matter.[60] They are thus essentially different from plants and animals that grow upward when alive, but inevitably fall downward when dead; and they are even more different from inert, lifeless objects like stones that do not have the power within them to ever rise up, even briefly, on their own, because they do not have within themselves the capacity for even linear self-movement. That is why the rational desire of humans is to emulate the heavenly spheres, not to emulate the minerals, plants, and animals with which they share the earth.

Now, because heavenly motion is circular rather than linear, there is no total union of the heavenly spheres (nor the humans who attempt to emulate them) *with* God, no final absorption *into* God, which would be the case if God were taken to be a *telos* in the pre-Aristotelian sense, that is, as either a spatial or temporal terminus or destination. As such, no one, whether a heavenly intelligence or an earthly intelligence (*homo sapiens* being the only ones we know), reaches God directly and finally, because God is not a point in either space or time (what we now call, after Einstein, "space-time"). Instead, all intelligences, even heavenly let alone earthly ones, strive to be in continual orbit *around* God. In fact, this is the model or paradigm for the way rational humans can be related to God as their ultimately attractive *telos*. Like the heavenly spheres, humans never reach their end/purpose, because it is not something to be reached, that is, it is not a reachable object or point in either space or time. Truly intelligent humans can only act *towards* God through continual – though quite frequently interrupted – contemplation. By being regularly repeated, this continuity seems like the perpetual orbit around or *about* God of the heavenly spheres, whose efficient cause is their self-moving desire to be in this state of divinely inspired eternal attraction.

The question, though, is whether this view of the heavens with God at their centre is the projection of a human wish on to the cosmos. Is it but an idealized fantasy rather than an actual revelation of a higher reality? In fact, this has long been the critique of Plato's view of the heavenly oriented action of God as the model he imagined for intelligent human praxis on earth. In other words, is philosophy imitating nature, or is nature being made to imitate philosophy?

With his astrophysical-ontological teleology, Aristotle seems to have a metaphysical advantage over Plato. For he is able to use his vision of the heavenly intelligences as divine that he claimed to have received from "ancient tradition" (all such traditions being rooted in revelation) to formulate a metaphysical theory that undergirds astrophysical (and then human) reality better than competing metaphysical theories.[61] In other words, it has greater heuristic value than its competitors. And that enables those who agree with Aristotle's teleological ontology to argue that it is not merely human projection, inasmuch as humans are not the only beings in the cosmos who are so teleologically oriented. Not only are the ends (*telē*) not of human making, but humans also have role models greater than themselves for their teleological striving. Hence human contemplation of the Divine (*to theion*) fits into a larger cosmological reality. Indeed, the heavenly spheres mediate between humans and God. They are gods (*theoi*), whom Aristotle has no problem publicly worshipping, even though they are not *the* one God (*ho theos*), since their difference from the Ultimate God is one of degree rather than one of kind. (As we shall see, this will pose a problem for Maimonides: how can he as a strict monotheist endorse this mediated ontological teleology, teaching as it does that the heavenly beings are gods?!)

Nevertheless, there is a disadvantage to this kind of teleology built on the back of a teleological natural science: it is only as convincing as the scientific paradigm it presupposes.[62] But what if that paradigm is replaced by a better one, just as Aristotle himself replaced earlier scientific paradigms with his own paradigm? And, in fact, this paradigm has been replaced by the new paradigm of Copernicus and Galileo, which did away altogether with final causes in cosmology. In the wake of Copernicus and Galileo, doesn't the whole Aristotelian-Ptolemaic teleological edifice crumble? This will not be a problem for Maimonides, since the veracity of the Aristotelian paradigm was largely undisputed in his day and centuries thereafter (at least scientifically, though not theologically). It only became a problem for Jewish (and Christian) thinkers in the seventeenth century when the Copernican-Galilean cosmological paradigm began to successfully replace the Aristotelian one.[63]

To be sure, Maimonides did not have the problem of contemporary neo-Aristotelians, of formulating an ethic that has to be independent of a long-lost and irretrievable teleological natural science and its metaphysical implications.[64] In his day, the Aristotelian paradigm was undisputed. Nevertheless, he still had the problem that has been the leitmotif of this book: how can any theologian employ any philosophy in a way that neither distorts that philosophy's teachings nor attempts to put their theology into a philosophical Procrustean bed? Thus we need warn any theological attempt that accepts wholesale an ontological/ philosophical paradigm in order to give its theology a more rigorous and more universally acceptable cast that it is playing with fire. That fire can either consume the theology that buys into it, making that theology its fuel, or it can bring that theology down with it when it is replaced by a newer, brighter flame. Theologians might be well advised to be much more selective in their use of any scientific or philosophical theory, only carefully letting the ones they do use critically illuminate rather than consume their traditional theology. In what follows I try to show how Maimonides seems to have mostly heeded that warning.

Let us now look at how Maimonides constitutes the four areas of relationality we have been examining throughout this book: (1) the relation of God and nature; (2) the relation of God and humans; (3) interhuman relations; and (4) the relation of humans and nature.

Maimonides on the Relation of God and Nature

Like Philo, Maimonides believed that God's primary relation to what is not-God is with Nature as the wholly intelligible universe or cosmos. No matter how exalted their status might be in that cosmic order, humans are still parts thereof. The relation with God is subordinate to that order in the way a part is subordinate to its whole; thus the relation of God and humans is mediated by that prior relation of God and nature. And since, for Maimonides, the best insight into the structures and working of cosmic nature is furnished by Aristotelian natural science, his problem is going to be how he can formulate a creationist ontology that is consistent with the Aristotelian cosmology it is meant to undergird. His challenge is how he can affirm – along with the entire Jewish tradition – that God is the Maker of the universe, who is continually concerned with what-has-been-made (*pa'ul* or *ma'aseh* in Hebrew) by Him, yet still honestly engage Aristotelian natural science and the God of which it speaks metaphysically.[65]

Since that cosmology was undisputed in Maimonides's time, and since it is as interested in God as the Absolute as Judaism is, a scientifically interested Jewish theologian like Maimonides could not very well ignore it or the ontology constituted on its back. Nevertheless, the Aristotelians insisted that the universe is not made by God or by anyone else. Furthermore, for the Aristotelians, God couldn't be the maker of anything, much less the universe. Why? To answer this question we need to carefully differentiate Maimonides's ontology from that of Aristotle.

In Aristotle's causal theory, making is one of two kinds of efficient causation. Now, in efficient causation something is moved. In the kind of efficient causation we see in animals, the locomotion is self-movement: animals move themselves. But self-motion cannot be attributed to God since, for Aristotle, all movement is a being's moving from potentiality to actuality. So, to attribute self-movement to God would clearly imply that God *needs* this actualization. But a needy God could hardly be considered to be the Absolute, whether for Aristotle or for Maimonides. The second kind of causation, though, is where someone moves something else. That is what makers or "technicians" do. Makers take materials that are potential for what they make out of them. The seeming advantage of speaking of God as this second kind of efficient cause is that the maker himself, unlike the self-mover, changes something but does not necessarily change himself. That is especially so when the maker is not making something in order to improve himself, that is, change himself for the better. (Aristotle, though, might very well have questioned why any rational maker would make anything without this kind of purpose in mind.) Nevertheless, makers are still dependent on – they are in need of – materials *from* which they make something, plus the plans or the form *by* which they make it. Moreover, they might need to be "creative," and thus in need of their "creations" like parents need to procreate their children.

Aristotle avoids these metaphysical problems by insisting that God is only the *telos* of the cosmos, that is, the cosmos's final cause. As such, God does not relate Godself to the cosmos, neither as a maker who extends himself to his product nor as a less-than-absolute being that moves itself *towards* or (in the case of the heavenly intelligences) *around* the object that attracts it. In that way, God does not relate himself to the cosmos; rather, the cosmos relates itself to God, intelligent beings more directly, others less directly.

Intelligent beings, when exercising the full thrust of their intelligence contemplatively, strive to be related to God by thinking of God like God thinks of Godself, which is their thinking along with God. God, conversely, only relates and is only related to Godself. And even though God is part of nature, God is at the zenith of nature. To use a geometric analogue, the apex of a cone is a point thereof but not a point therein insofar as the apex of the cone is its highest point, the point that the rest of the cone seems to be oriented towards. As such, for God to engage in any external relation, either as a self-mover in relation to its goal or as a maker in relation to his product, would be to compromise God's ultimacy or absoluteness. The comos, then, is a teleological hierarchy, where relationality at the heavenly level is all one way: from the bottom up, not from the top down. But Maimonides will have to figure out how relationality at all levels of the universe, even the highest level, can be from both bottom up *and* top down.

Maimonides's Ontology

Maimonides seems to be very much an Aristotelian, as evidenced by the following statement:

> We designate Him as a maker [*fa'il*] ... Now one of the opinions of the philosophers, an opinion with which I do not disagree, is that God ... is the efficient cause [*fa'il*], that He is the form, and that He is the end. Thus it is for this reason that they say that He ... is a cause [*al'illa*] and a ground [*al-sabab*], in order to comprise these three causes.[66]

Nevertheless, "the philosophers" with whom Maimonides agrees could not be strict Aristotelians since, as we have seen, there is no indication that Aristotle acknowledged or could acknowledge that God is or could be an efficient cause. So, whoever these philosophers were, we still have to see how Maimonides could consistently maintain that God is the Efficient Cause who is the prime or first cause, who could only be the Creator God of the universe (*bor'e olam* in Hebrew). But this is a very difficult task for Maimonides's readers, as he seems to make a number of contradictory statements when dealing with this question.

The task for any serious reader of the *Guide* is to decide what to do with these contradictions. At the outset, one should not presume that Maimonides was a careless writer who didn't bother to be more consistent. Even his most serious critics never considered him to be that careless, that intellectually irresponsible. There are three serious approaches to the problem of what to do with the contradictions in Maimonides's theories, especially those in his theory of divine causation. (1) Some have said that these contradictions are deliberate, and that it is the hard task of serious readers to work out for themselves which statement is Maimonides's true position and which is not, based on the overall thrust of his metaphysical thought.[67] (2) Some others have said that these contradictions are what Aristotle would call *aporia*, which is a question that does not admit of an either/or answer (viz., if A is true, then B is false, or if B is true, then A is false). Questions like whether the universe is made (or created) or unmade (or eternal) do not admit of an either/or answer. The most one can conclude is that A is more plausible than B, or B is more plausible than A.[68] (3) It might be said that Maimonides thinks there is a solution to these contradictions, but that he himself is unable or unwilling to solve them; therefore he left these contradictions so that his readers might work out by themselves the correct answer. (Actually, Maimonides wrote the *Guide* as a private letter to but one reader, his brilliant yet perplexed disciple Joseph ben Judah.)

If this last approach is the one Maimonides wanted readers of the *Guide* to take (like the other two approaches, it at best concludes with a reasoned guess), it is like the "casuistical questions" that Kant, at the end of his discussions of some major moral questions in his *Metaphysics of Morals*, left for his readers to solve for themselves.[69] That is, Kant left the question open so that a reader could come to one of two opposite conclusions, both based on Kant's principles. This last approach is the one I take here, insofar as these contradictions seem to ask the reader to accept one position not only as more plausible than the other, but as more consistent with the overall thrust of Maimonides's theology, even if he himself could not or would not go that far. Furthermore, this approach, in addition to allowing readers to draw a "Maimonidean" conclusion that Maimonides himself did not draw, enables readers to disagree (respectfully, to be sure) with some of Maimonides's principles, not just some of the conclusions that could be drawn by him or by anyone else from those principles.

So, let us now try to put together what might be a consistent theory of divine causation from the disparate statements of Maimonides himself on this question. This involves our thinking through the options he had to entertain before arriving at whatever his reasoned conclusion was, or what he wanted his readers to do before arriving at their own reasoned conclusion. Only thereafter will some of the theological problems even the most consistent reading of Maimonides's theory still faces be pointed out.

It would seem that of the four kinds of Aristotelian causation outlined earlier – technical, natural/biological, pragmatic, and practical – it is technical causation that best bespeaks the biblical doctrine of creation. That is because of the primacy it assigns to the efficient cause or maker. This is already a huge departure from Aristotle, for whom technical causation is the lowest kind of causation, thus the farthest from the ontological causation that is God's totally intransitive activity, which is the activity that is most purely and exclusively teleological.

Nevertheless, there are four problems with Maimonides's adopting this causal model to explain the biblical doctrine of creation philosophically.

First, in technical causation, the maker is not the sole, unconditional creator of the end product. The form or plan by which he or she in-forms the building materials in order to make the end product is usually pre-existent, and even if devised by the maker *de novo*, the plan always shows the influence of other plans; it could not be devised *ex nihilo*. As for the building materials themselves, they are natural entities like clay or wood, so it cannot be said of them necessarily that they were made to be used by the maker or builder for his projects, or by anyone else for anything else. But in biblical theology, there are no such preconditions for God's creation of the universe. Maimonides is quite clear that "the opinion of all who believe in the Law of Moses [is] that the world as a whole ... was brought into existence by God after having been purely and absolutely nonexistent, and that God, may He be exalted, had existed alone, and nothing else ... Afterwards, through His will and His volition, He brought into existence out of nothing all the beings that are, etc."[70]

Second, the traditional Jewish doctrine of creation (*ma'aseh bere'sheet*) seems to teach that God's creation is the result of God's choice to create something, and all choices are made at a certain moment in time; yet Maimonides, following Aristotle, is adamant in his insistence that time (as the measure of change) is itself created. God's activity, though, is atemporal inasmuch as changing is only done by less than perfect beings. God as Being-itself is perfect, hence forever unchanging, that is, eternal.[71]

Third, in technical causation, the efficient cause of the effect, that is, the maker of the product, need only be related to what-has-been-made at the time of its being made. Even if the maker wants to look after what he or she has made, that care does not follow from the act of making itself; instead, that care or looking-after can be delegated to an appointed guardian, or it can be taken up by somebody else who has bought the product from its maker. However, in biblical theology, God Himself is concerned with His creation throughout its entire duration. "The eyes of the Lord, they roam [*meshotetim*] throughout the whole earth" (Zechariah 4:10). "The Lord is good to all; His compassion is over all His works [*al kol ma'asav*]" (Psalms 145:9).

Fourth, in technical causation, the maker and the end product have nothing substantial in common. So, even if one says that from the presence of a made or artificial thing in the world we can infer that someone made it, that inference only tells us *that* this thing was made, and that it did not make itself nor is it simply unmade, that is, having always been there in one way or another. But that doesn't tell us anything about *what* or *who* made it. However, in biblical theology, at least one creature (and for Maimonides, there is more than one such creature) and God do have something substantial in common. Surely, that substantial commonality is expressed when the Bible states (more than once): "God created humankind [*ha'adam*] in His image [*be-tsalmo*]; in the image of God He created him, that is, as male and female He created them" (Genesis 1:26).

Keeping all four problems just mentioned in mind, we might conclude that Maimonides's discussion of the creation of the universe resembles another kind of Aristotelian causation. It would seem that natural/biological (as distinct from natural/astrophysical) causation might afford a biblical theologian like Maimonides a better model to explain divine creation of the universe.

In technical causation, the form is separate from the maker. It does not emanate from the maker. The form with which the maker in-forms matter in order to make the end product is either itself formed out of an earlier form (like one painter adopting and thereby adapting the style of an earlier painter), or it is taken intact to be replicated by the maker for his or her new project/end product as its result (like one painter copying the style of an earlier painter). On the other hand, in biological causation, which is reproduction (*genēsis* in Greek; *piryah ve-rivyah* in Hebrew), the maker or progenitor in-forms his offspring with his own form. That form continues to function within the offspring from the time of its conception until the time of its death. Thus in-formation and generation are continual processes taking place within what has been so generated throughout its lifetime.

This sounds like Maimonides's attempt to describe the process of creating the universe, beginning from the top down, that is, from God to the highest heavenly intellect called the "acting intellect" or the "agent intellect" (*ha-sekhel ha-po'el* in Hebrew), and then further down to the lowest intellects, who are rational humans. Maimonides called this creative process "overflowing" (*hashpa'ah* in Hebrew), which he says is "like a source of water that overflows in all directions ... the world derives from the overflow of God ... And it is His action that is called overflow."[72] What is important to bear in mind here is that this overflowing of a fountain is being employed as a metaphor, since neither God nor God's transitive action is a physical process; they are, rather, mental processes. (Thus the metaphor of the fountain is used similarly to the way Maimonides thinks the Bible uses bodily language to describe God's actions.) And while there are significant differences between divine creative causation and biological creation therefore, their significant point in common, which distinguishes both of them from technical causation, is the virtual identification of the efficient cause and the formal cause. In this causal process, the maker replicates himself in what he has produced, not in the sense of cloning a physical copy of himself (*morphē* in Greek), but rather by transferring his active style (*eidos* in Greek) to his offspring in their formation. Today, we would say, for example, that one's genetic capacity for running has been transferred to one's offspring at the time of their conception, and that it remains with them throughout their life. The form here is an active order, not a passive picture. It is not so much that the one in-formed *looks* or appears like the one who has in-formed him or her (which may or may not be the case with a parent's physical offspring), but rather that the offspring *acts* or functions like the intelligent (i.e., informed or ordered) person who has so in-formed them, and whose form remains with them throughout their lifetime. (Moreover, Maimonides thinks the soul is immortal, insofar as anything so closely created by God through the process of in-formation has to be so perfect so as to be immune to the deprivation of death, hence that form remains with the relatively untarnished soul forever, that is, *a parte post*.)[73] Maimonides puts it this way:

> That He is the ultimate form of the world does not denote that there is an analogy between Him and the form endowed with matter ... so that He, may He be exalted, would be a form to a body ... rather ... every existent thing endowed with a form is what it is in virtue of its form – in fact its being passed away and abolished when its form passes away ... For the universe exists in virtue of the existence of the Creator.[74]

Now, whereas in biological causation in-formation of the effect by the efficient cause can be involuntary, one cannot ascribe involuntary or necessary causation (*anangkē* in Greek) to God and be theologically correct. Thus Maimonides says: "It is absurd to say that the world necessarily proceeds from the being of the deity as an effect proceeds from its cause, and it is further known that the world has come about through an act of the deity."[75] Also, unlike biological causation, in divine creation the *telos* or end result of the act is intended, that is, God has made it for a reason; better (as we shall see presently), God has given every creature a purpose to live for. In this way, divine creation is like technical causation. So, for example, the builder built the house according to a plan so as *to be* a specific kind of dwelling. As such, the *telos* here is the project of the efficient cause operating formally or the formal cause operating efficiently, that is, they operate in tandem; while the final cause in the case of divine creation is separate from it/them as the end product is distinct from its producer. However, unlike practical causation, the creative act is not done for its own sake. Being transitive action, it intends a real other (*l'autre* in French). In other words, *that* the universe exists and *why* the universe exists are both due to God's intentional transitive activity. Nevertheless, biological-reproductive causation, like technical causation, though it need not be volitional, is still a temporal event: *B*'s conception-generation from *A* began at a certain moment in time, and *B's* ending/death will also be at a certain moment in time. That is why Maimonides is quite selective in his use of the various kinds of causation put forth by Aristotle.

From all of this we see that Maimonides's metaphysical use of causal language is metaphorical; indeed, it has to be metaphorical, as God's causation is unique, itself beyond description in ordinary language. As such, it can only be alluded to, which is what metaphors enable us to do.

Maimonides's use of what seems to be the Neoplatonic notion of emanation enables him to surmise that God's creation of what-is-not-God involves the emanation or extension of God's formal intelligibility/intelligence to what is just beneath God in the chain of being: the acting intellect.[76] That extension to the active intellect includes those human intellects who are intelligent enough to rise to this level just beneath God in this ontological hierarchy. Now, this enables Mamonides to speak of a certain formal commonality *between* God and creation that goes both ways. That is, God formally extends Godself *down to* at least the highest levels of the created universe; and at least the most intelligent creatures reciprocate that formal extension by formally (i.e., intelligently) striving to move *up to* being in perpetual orbit around God.

Nevertheless, Maimonides differs from the Neoplatonists on a crucial point, which is that as a Jewish theologian he must regard creation as a willed act, even if it seems to be done via emanation or "overflowing."[77] As such, it is possible that it *could* have been otherwise, that is, it could not be altogether. Moreover, despite the fact that Maimonides can use Neoplatonic ontology to explain some of *how* creation operates, and *what* God's connection to His creation might be, it is still inadequate to explain *that* God has created a material universe altogether, much less *why*. Unlike the Neoplatonists, for whom the material universe is virtual non-being, a Jewish theologian like Maimonides has to admit that "God approved [*va-yar*] all that he made; indeed it is very good [*tov me'od*]!" (Genesis 1:31). In fact, there seems to be no way to adapt Neoplatonic emanation theory to the biblical doctrine that God's concern extends to those with whom God does share some commonality, and even with whom (or with which) God shares no commonality.

Finally, while it is true that Maimonides could adapt the Neoplatonic notion of emanation to his theologically plausible theory of creation, his very use of Neoplatonic ontology put him on a shakier philosophical footing than did his use of Aristotle's ontology. That is due to a crucial difference between Aristotle and the Neoplatonists. Aristotle's ontology draws on and builds upon a demonstrable natural science: astrophysics. The Neoplatonists, on the other hand, do not have any such scientific basis upon which to formulate ontology. Aristotelian ontology, even at its most abstract level, still provides a metaphysical explanation of the observable movements of the heavenly spheres. Neoplatonic ontology – at least as employed by Maimonides and the Islamic philosophers who influenced him – only provides a metaphysical explanation of prophetic experience as a kind of mental telepathy from God to humans. However, despite Maimonides's assertion that prophecy is a universal phenomenon, it is still not demonstrable like the movements of the heavenly spheres in Aristotle's natural science qua astrophysics.[78] Therefore, it might be said that Maimonides's quasi-Neoplatonic emanation theory is not all that adequate to either the classical Jewish doctrine of creation of everything or the Aristotelian natural science so widely accepted in his day. For that reason, its theological employment must be as eclectic as, perhaps even more eclectic than, Maimonides's employment of Aristotle's metaphysical theory of causation. So, perhaps, because Maimonides had no answer to these two challenges posed by Neoplatonic ontology whereas he did propose an answer to the main challenge posed by Aristotle's theology, we should return to looking at how he confronted Aristotle.

Maimonides distinguishes his ontological-cosmological teleology from that of Aristotle. "Aristotle demonstrates regarding all natural things that they do not come about by chance ... if particular things of the world are not due to chance, how can the whole of it be due to chance?"[79] Now, for Aristotle, chance (*tychē*) is an occurrence that does not seem to have either an efficient cause or a final cause, neither a beginning (*archē*) nor an end (*telos*).[80] As such, it is unnatural (i.e., unordered), or at least it is experienced as unnatural. Aristotle would thus say that the cosmos (i.e., the ordered universe) does have a purpose: to be like God, whose intransitive action is an act done by itself for itself alone. (That is why truly teleological human praxis can only be God-like contemplation.) It would thus seem that Aristotle (or Maimonides's contemporary Aristotelians) would regard Maimonides's query above as nonsensical. To ask for the cause of the cosmos itself is to ask for someone who transcends the cosmos as a maker transcends his or her product. However, nothing transcends the cosmos, because the cosmos contains within itself all that exists or could exist. The cosmos must be considered to be not-made at all.

However, Maimonides's query has a barely hidden premise, that the universe itself is made; it is a created entity (*nivr'a* in Hebrew). That means it is possible that the universe *could* not be made, that it could not exist at all.[81] Nevertheless, the universe is not the product of an actual choice made by God in time, for that would presume its possibility to be an ontological possibility, a real option. But the universe need only be thought of as the real, ever-present consequence of God's eternal will. Accordingly, God's willing/being is necessary; it cannot even be thought of not being or imagined not to be. Nevertheless, the universe's willed-existence is possible; the universe could be imagined not to exist. Moreover, nothing is essentially accidental or chancy; it only appears that way due to the limits of human knowledge, which is not omniscient. So, if the existence of the universe is not necessary, but only possible, then its real existence requires the action of an external/transcendent efficient cause or maker who is God.

All that notwithstanding, Maimonides agrees with Aristotle that God is the *telos* of the universe, its supremely attractive *summum bonum*. Note what Maimonides says:

> The order of all ends is ultimately due to His will and wisdom ... He is the ultimate end of everything; and the end of the universe is similarly a seeking to be like unto His perfection as far as it is in its capacity ... He is the end of all ends ... He is an efficient cause, a form, and an end. For this reason the philosophers designated Him as a cause [*sabab*] and not only as a maker [*fa'il*].[82]

But if, for both Maimonides and Aristotle, God is the *telos* of the universe, and all truly intelligent beings knowingly relate to God by wisely desiring to be like God, then what does *also* designating God as the efficient cause of the universe add to our relationship with God as the intelligent beings we humans are? Does it make any real difference whether one regards God as only the *telos*, or as the *telos* plus the Maker/Creator?

The answer to this question might be that, for Maimonides, God is not the universal *telos* because of any immanent, worldly necessity. Thus we do not infer ultimate teleology from the essential behaviour of natural entities, for their ends are made for them by God from above, hence these ends are not essentially *theirs* from within. That is why these natural entities cannot reveal their *raison d'être* to us by themselves.[83] Accordingly, God is the universal *telos* because God *made* Godself to be that *telos*; and God made Godself that *telos* in order to benefit God's created universe. Thus God as the One who has willed Godself to be both efficient and final cause of the universe is greater than Aristotle's God who could not be other than *telos* for Godself alone. The implication of God's wilful creation of the universe, and God's wilful making Godself the ultimately attractive object *for* creation, is that God intends His creatures, especially His intelligent creatures, to be so attracted to Him as their *summum bonum*. In other words, it is God's will that His intelligent creatures desire an intimate, perfecting relationship with God.

Now this creaturely desire is not for something immanent within the created natural world, even at its zenith. Rather, this desire is for God who radically transcends the confines of the created natural world. Thus our prime origin and our ultimate end are both beyond this world. And it would seem we do not know our ultimate end because we desire it; we desire it because that end has revealed Himself *to* us as our end. Moreover, we humans can experience that ultimate teleology at work in our active world, providing us the highest reasons for doing what we have been commanded to do here and now in the world. In fact, only we humans can be sure of this teleology, as only we could know it from our own experience of doing what we have been commanded to do because of it.[84]

I think Maimonides could accept drawing this implication of his creation theory as long as God's desire is seen as pure grace, and that is not due to any lack or privation, which is the usual motivation for creatures *wanting* what they *need*.[85] As such, it is what God *wills for* creation, not what God *wants from* creation. Nevertheless, at this point in our metaphysical speculation along with Maimonides, we might say that not only do naturally intelligent beings (like ourselves) *relate to* God, but that God – even more so – *relates* Godself *to* them (and to us humans therewith). That is an enormous difference.

From Maimonides's metaphysical perspective, God's relation to creation is always initiatory; it is never responsive. That is because a response could only be a temporal event. It could only be God freely choosing to react to something a creature freely chose to do. God's reaction to that creature's act can be either positive or negative, that is, it can either be a reward given for a positive act (*mitsvah*) or a punishment given for a negative act (*aveirah*). Moreover, a reaction is not an automatic consequence of the act, for God could just as easily choose not to react to the negative act punitively and forgive it, or not to react to the positive act favourably by not rewarding it or rewarding it in an altogether unanticipated way. The response too could be God freely replying to a specific request (*baqashah*) a creature freely chose to make by either fulfilling the request, or answering it in an unanticipated way, or denying it. Choices and the acts they cause, and the correlative responses to them, are all done in time.[86]

Whereas humans are uniquely choosing beings (who could only choose *in time*) – a point Maimonides insists is a basic principle of Judaism – being God's direct creation, nature is necessarily determined *ab initio*.[87] This is the metaphysical explanation Maimonides gave to the Talmudic dictum "everything is in God's hands (*bi-ydei shamayim*) except [humans'] awe of God (*yir'at shamayim*)."[88] Nevertheless, the Rabbis thought this truth indicates human superiority over even heavenly nature (over which, unlike earthly nature, humans have no control).[89] But Maimonides (like Aristotle) thought humans as choosing creatures are inferior to nature and its necessity

In Maimonides's ontology, necessity is superior to possibility. Now, the capacity of choice presupposes ontological possibility, that is, there are real options from which a choosing being (*boher*) can elect (as in the Latin *electare*) to actualize one rather than the other or others. But since humans are the only choosing beings, the temporal possibilities their free choice (*behirah hofsheet* in Hebrew) presupposes are the lone exceptions to this otherwise necessarily determined universe. Thus Maimonides (as far as I know) only mentioned the rabbinic doctrine of the election of Israel (*behirat yisra'el*) when he had to codify rabbinically ordained liturgical expressions of this doctrine.[90] It could be said with philosophical integrity that God has free will in the sense of being the Creator who could have created an altogether different universe or no universe at all. But we shouldn't think that God exercises free choice over possible options (*optare* in Latin), for that would insert God into time with its essential changeability. Therefore, miracles, which seem to be God's *de novo* actualization of temporal possibilities, which are experienced *de novo*, and which are accompanied by a *de novo* message to a prophet to predict the actual event in the future, are seen by Maimonides, from his earliest to his latest speculations, to be as follows:

> Miracles too are something that is, in a certain respect, in nature ... [so that] when God created that which exists and stamped upon it the existing natures, He put into those natures that all the miracles that occurred would be produced in them at the time they occurred ... the sign of a prophet consists in God's making known to him the time when he must make his proclamation, and thereupon a certain thing is effected according to what was put into its nature when first it received its particular impress ... it [is] extremely difficult to admit that a nature may change ... or that another volition may supervene after that nature has been established in a definite way.[91]

Thus Maimonides is saying that the *de novo* character of miracles is not ontological, but only epistemological, that is, their novelty is not as events, but only our experience of them and a prophet's prediction of them.[92] For Maimonides, only God is supernatural.[93] Nevertheless, the fact that Maimonides insists that this is sound rabbinic theology did not convince some of his more perceptive critics (especially Nahmanides).[94]

Maimonides on the Relation of God and Humans

Despite the fact that God's relation *to* humans is mediated by God's relation *to* nature of which humans are a part, Maimonides thinks a direct, unmediated relation of humans *to* God is nonetheless possible and desirable. Indeed, that direct relation is not only possible and desirable, it is a necessity if humans are to have a correct relationship with God at all, however rare it is in fact. For if humans are related to God *through* nature as God is related to humans *through* a chain of natural causes, there would be no good reason to prevent humans from acknowledging, that is, worshipping, these intermediaries.[95] One might say that this intermediacy could be acceptable as long as humans acknowledge the Creator God to be the ultimate object of their devotion, just as the Creator God is the original source of the existence of these intermediaries. But that would justify polytheism, which is the theoretical basis of the practice of idolatry (*avodah zarah*), and for which Maimonides thinks humans have an innate propensity.[96] For Maimonides, the true worship of God is designed to sublimate this propensity as much as possible.[97] Surely, he thinks the battle with idolatry is the Torah's second chief concern, expressed as the first negative commandment of the Torah.[98] The Torah's first chief concern is the acknowledgment of God's being, expressed as the first positive commandment of the Torah.[99]

The direct human relation to God can be taken to be the *telos* or purpose of created human existence. That direct human relation to God is most intensely and fruitfully conducted when humans are engaged in worship (*avodah*), especially prayer (*tefillah*) as both individual and communal devotion. This is the activity that intends (*kavvanah*) God and God alone as its direct object.[100]

Maimonides carefully reflects on how and why the Torah mandates, and the attendant Jewish tradition orders, the practice of worship as prayer. Nevertheless, as we shall see, what seems to be a commonality with Aristotle in Maimonides's view of contemplation as the highest type of prayer is actually quite different from Aristotle's view of contemplation as the highest human activity. Surely, fully accepting Aristotle's view of contemplation would ultimately contradict the doctrine of the Creator God. Maimonides's continued acceptance of Aristotle's notion of the immutable timelessness of God's activity involves certain problems with the traditional Jewish doctrine of the interactive, responsive God. In fact, where in Maimonides's theology is the God who responds to the prayers of humans, especially their requests for divine intervention into their existential situation in the world of space-time?

Maimonides divides prayer into three modes, which could be designated as (1) prayer as a psychological exercise, (2) prayer as a political exercise, and (3) prayer as a metaphysical exercise. We shall see that these three modes are cogently interrelated.

Psychological Prayer

Maimonides begins his formulation of the laws of prayer (*hilkhot tefillah*) as follows:

> It is a positive commandment [*mitsvat aseh*] to pray daily as it is said in Scripture: "You shall serve the Lord your God" (Exodus 23:25). From revelation [*mi-pi ha-shemu'ah*] they learned that this service [*she'avodah zo*] is prayer as it is said in Scripture: "to serve Him with all your heart" (Deuteronomy 11:13). The Sages said: "What is this service that is in the heart? This is prayer." ... the obligation [*hiyyuv*] of this commandment is that a person should supplicate and pray [*mitpallel*] daily, declaring God's praise, and afterwards requesting what he needs through entreaty [*be-vaqashah*] and supplication. Afterwards, there is the giving of praise and thanks [*hodayah*] to the Lord for the good bestowed upon him. Each one [is to do this] according to his ability.[101]

Maimonides then goes on to say that until the time of the destruction of the First Temple (586 BCE), daily prayer was an individual matter, whose timing and exact content were left to individual discretion.

However, why is there a need for prayer itself to be commanded? Don't humans from infancy on know that we are dependent on higher powers to whom we need to express our needs and beg these higher powers (beginning with our parents) to fulfil these needs? Surely, Jews like anybody else cry out their needs before being commanded to do so. In fact, did Hannah, who is considered in the Talmud to be *the* model of one who prays, have in mind that her prayer is fulfilling a positive commandment of the Torah? Wasn't her paradigmatic prayer spontaneous, doing what comes naturally, so to speak?[102]

Perhaps, though, the Torah had to make this a positive commandment to ensure those who pray be assured that they are addressing their supplications to *someone*, and that this "someone" could only be God. This kind of supplication, this *cri de coeur*, if addressed to *anyone* other than God, or even to a false image of God, could well be idolatry.

What is expressed by prayer at this elementary level are the bodily needs of individual humans. Prayer is the verbal expression of our bodily appetites as personal desires. Our expression of these desires, which are now directed to God, are themselves the expression of our deeper psychological need to talk to God directly. That deeper need is felt, and one is required to express that need to God, when a person is old enough to know that prayer must be pointedly addressed to its direct object who is God.[103] Humans have a psychological need to express their very neediness, over and above any specific needs. But why couldn't obligatory prayer be left at this level of individual expression?

Maimonides attempts an answer to this question, it seems, soon stating that when the Jewish people had been exiled at the time of the destruction of the First Temple, "they became assimilated [*nit'arvu*] ... and confused [*nitbalbelu*] in their language ... so nobody was able to express all his needs [*tsorkhav*] in any one language." He then goes on to say that "when Ezra and his court saw [the situation] they arose and ordained [*ve-taqnu*] for them the Eighteen Benedictions in order [*al ha-seder*] ... so that these benedictions would be arranged [*arukhot*] in everybody's mouth to be learned; and that the prayer of these stammerers [*ha'ilgim*] be as whole as the prayer of the speakers of the pure language [*ha-lashon ha-tsehah*]."[104] In other words, when the people had the institution of the Temple (*beit ha-miqdash*), their political need for communal affirmation to the divine Sovereign, whose election of them is what constitutes them as the covenanted people, was satisfied by the Temple service. The physical aspect of this service was the offering of the sacrifices (*qorbanot*) by the Aaronide priests (*kohanim*), but the linguistic aspect of this service was the recitation of the psalms by the choir of Levites, with whom the rest of the people assembled there surely joined in. These psalms, certainly expressed in pure Hebrew, provided the model for the prayers of individuals uttered apart from the Temple service, thus assuring linguistic commonality.[105]

This fact would largely prevent individuals from straying too far afield from theologically proper God-talk even in their private devotions, whose primary content is the expression of one's personal needs to God for their satisfaction.[106] What Ezra and his court, known as the "Great Assembly" (*keneset gedolah*), did was to make the "structure of prayer" (*matbe'a shel tefillah*) reflect the communal relation of God and the faithful congregation of Jews (*keneset yisra'el*) constituted by the ordered service of the Temple (*seder ha'avodah*).[107] Here we see the institution of the synagogue (*beit ha-keneset*), which is the place of only verbal worship, and which is different from the institution of the Temple with its multi-sensuous ritual. Thus, when the Second Temple was destroyed in 70 CE, the synagogue, in fact, substituted for the Temple, that is, for the time being, until the Messiah comes and restores the Temple – whenever.[108]

Now, there is proper and improper prayer. Knowing *how* to pray properly requires one to learn enough about to *whom* prayer is to be directed so as to be sure that prayer is directed to its proper divine object. Prayer, then, is a message *from* humans to God, but it is also a message to humans from their communal tradition (beginning with biblical prayer) about *who* is the God they are praying to, and *what* kinds of requests God wants and doesn't want from His people. When Maimonides speaks of "the pure language," he means much more than verbal clarity; he means primarily conceptual clarity.[109] That pertains to both the object and content of our speech, especially our most exalted speech, which is the language of liturgy. That requires the kind of communal coherence and continuity that the Temple as the national sanctuary provided. Moreover, for Aristotelians especially, humans as essentially linguistic beings and humans as essentially political beings are two sides of the same coin.[110] That is, language, being communication *between* persons, requires a plurality of "others" in order to be exercised; and a plurality of "others" are able to come together and live together in a sustained way because they are able to speak to one another and desire to continue to do so.[111] And for Jews, what we desire to speak about to each other most exaltedly is the God whom we all seek, or ought to seek. At the political level, this desire is what we express together in essentially communal prayer. Prayer is the very epitome of language. Thus the most basic theological principles are expressed, perhaps can only be expressed, in liturgy.[112] So, because even individual prayer is expressed in the first-person plural (whether in fact or only in principle), psychological prayer is more a matter of social psychology than of individual psychology, that is, it is never wholly a private matter, no matter how much an individual thinker might abstract from the public religion his or her contemplation is subsequent to rather than prior to.[113]

Political Prayer

Although God is always to be the direct object of prayer, being the only One to whom a person is to pray, both as a psychological exercise and as a political exercise, prayer is nonetheless mediated. In the case of psychological prayer, the experience of bodily neediness and our expression of prayers as desires seeking their satisfaction causes us to direct our desires to God for God to satisfy them. The relation to God, then, is not one's prime concern; it is one's subsequent concern. In the case of political prayer, the experience of the need for a community with which to speak, and the need to speak of the foundations of one's communal life, causes the truly rational members of the Jewish community to direct their attention to God as their community's Founder, Sovereign, and Redeemer. And, just as in psychological prayer individual persons are addressing their own concerns about themselves before addressing God, so in political prayer the members of the community are talking with each other about themselves before addressing God. Here, too, God is the subsequent, not the primary, concern.

Furthermore, Maimonides is quite clear that public prayer is better than private prayer, emphasizing that "one should not pray privately [*be-yahid*] whenever one is able to pray with the community [*im ha-tsibbur*]."[114] On this point, Maimonides has considerable rabbinic, and even biblical, precedent, inasmuch as the most intense and the most primary relation between God and humans is covenantal. It is God's relationship with the community of Israel. Thus, even the prayers said by an individual, even when he or she is alone, are still said in the first-person plural: "we" rather than "I."[115] Therefore, humans' relation to nature via their bodily wants, and humans' relation to their community via their political needs, both mediate the relation of humans and God.

The question, though, is whether there is a kind of prayer that is not mediated by anything prior to the relation of a human person and God.

Metaphysical Prayer

Although there are hints of a higher and unmediated kind of prayer in Maimonides's great legal-theological work *Mishneh Torah*, it is in his philosophical-theological work *Guide of the Perplexed* that he explicitly ranks what we have called "metaphysical" prayer as the most exalted kind of prayer. There he writes:

> This kind of worship ought only to be engaged in after intellectual apprehension ... In my opinion it consists in setting thought to work on

> the first intelligible and in devoting oneself exclusively to this as far as this is within one's capacity ... Mostly this is achieved in solitude and isolation.[116]

Much earlier in this same work, he writes:

> The most apt phrase concerning this subject is the dictum occurring in Psalms (65:2): "Silence [*demiyyah*] is praise to Thee." ... Accordingly, silence and limiting oneself to the apprehensions of the intellects are more appropriate – just as the perfect ones have enjoined when they say: "Commune with your own heart upon your bed, and be still [*ve-dimmu*], Selah" (Psalms 4:5).[117]

Nevertheless, all this seems to contradict what Maimonides has said about both psychological prayer and political prayer in his legal-theological work.[118] First, it seems to contradict his earlier emphasis on prayer as expression in a conceptually articulate language. Now we are told that silence is superior to speech. Second, it seems to contradict his earlier emphasis on prayer as a communal exercise superior to prayer as an individual exercise. Now we are told that the most exalted prayer is conducted by a silent individual in what seems to be splendid isolation. Finally, whereas requests made to God still comprise an essential element in both psychological prayer and political prayer, metaphysical or contemplative prayer seems to be the exercise of an individual person who is oblivious to his or her bodily need for worldly goods, and who is also oblivious to his or her political need to converse with others in a common language. As such, there seems to be no need here to thankfully praise God for what God has done for either an individual person or a community of persons. That is because contemplation seems to be contemplation of what God *is*, or what God does by Himself, but not what God does *for* anybody else – neither for the physical body nor for the body politic.

Of course, one could say (as has been said in the previous section) that this hierarchy of prayer is basically a Jewish version of the Aristotelian hierarchy, moving up from praxis to theory. Hence a person who is able to engage in contemplation and does so is not leading a double, disingenuous life. However theoretical, however contemplatively adept, a philosopher becomes, he or she is still an embodied being and a political being. In rare moments of contemplation, the mind of a philosopher might be in the heavens, but regularly his or her physical body is still connected to the natural world, and his or her political body is still connected to a human community on earth. For a Jewish Aristotelian, that means the God addressed for the satisfaction of bodily needs and of political needs is the same God whom a philosopher desires to apprehend and to love, that is, as this God is by and for Himself rather than because of what He does for anybody else.

The problem, though, is that Maimonides insists no human can possibly know what God is, or what God does by Godself. Even creatures as intelligent as we humans are can only know what God does in relation to creatures outside Godself.[119] But for Aristotle, by means of proper contemplation, which means moving up through astrophysics and then beyond to ontology as ultimate cosmic teleology, even a human can know what God is. God is thought-thinking-itself. In fact, God could be nothing else, for to be anything other than thought-thinking-itself would mean that God is involved in external relations, which Aristotle of course denies. Contemplation, then, seems to be a philosopher silently overhearing God speaking to Godself about Godself.[120] The silence, though, is not on the part of the object being contemplated. As such, not only are contemplating subjects not addressing the object of their contemplation, that object is also not addressing the subjects so contemplating him. For Aristotle, there is no mutual relationship here *between* the subject and the object, not even an asymmetrical relationship. Neither one is a participant in the life of the other, nor do they both participate in a common life together. The subjects are relating themselves *to* God, while God is the sole participant in God's own life, not in the life of anyone outside Godself. This God is not in any way a participant in anyone else's life.

Whereas Aristotle can actually say *what* is being contemplated, Maimonides cannot say so. Without freedom of will, Aristotle's God could not will to be or do anything differently. On the other hand, for Maimonides, God does have freedom of will, and could thus do anything differently because He could so will it. Having free will, God transcends any necessary inclusion in the cosmos, for God wilfully created the cosmos; God is not necessarily found therein. In fact, Maimonides's use of *via negativa* – the view that humans cannot say what God is, only what God is not – has a dialectical function.[121] It basically knocks down any attempt to say what God is, that is, to predicate of God worldly attributes. Since these attempts are constant, the *via negativa* needs to be regularly employed. But without the positive attribution of *what God does*, there would be no answer to David Hume's famous charge that employing negative attribution alone cannot distinguish between God and Nothing.[122] In other words, one can only speak of God using verbs and adverbs that express God's action and qualify it; but one cannot speak of God using nouns and adjectives that express God's being and qualify it.

Nevertheless, how does contemplation of the God of Maimonides differ essentially from contemplation of the God of Aristotle? Perhaps the following text shows what that essential difference is:

> Know that all the practices such as reading the Torah, prayer, and the performance of the other commandments, have only the end of training you to occupy yourself with His commandments ... rather than with matters pertaining to the world ... and not with that which is other than He ... in his heart he is always in His presence ... while outwardly he is with people.[123]

It would seem, though, that Maimonides has set up a tautology, namely, the purpose of practising the commandments is to practise the commandments. However, maybe one could say that a philosophical theologian is to be involved first with practising the commandments in the physical and social world, and then contemplating by himself what are God's reasons (*ta'amei ha-mitsvot*) in commanding what God commands in the Torah. That involves seeing the world from God's perspective, which seems to be the prerogative of a prophet or somebody who could very well become a prophet.

Earlier in the *Guide*, Maimonides asserts that the Torah, like the cosmos itself, is a created entity.[124] And it will be recalled from the discussion in the previous section that God's creation of the cosmos is a teleological act, that is, God creates the cosmos purposefully. However, due to our limited experience of the cosmos, it is difficult for humans to apprehend just what are God's purposes for the cosmos. What we do experience, though, is our own physical and social world, where we live as embodied, political creatures. It is here in our microcosm that we can apprehend, more or less, *why* God commands *what* God commands us humans to do in our world, thus imitating what God does within the entire cosmos. Since Maimonides insists that God did not communicate with Moses in actual words, it would seem that their communication involved Moses's reading God's purposeful creative mind.[125] And that would be Moses's speculating on what are God's creative purposes for humankind, to whom the Torah is given. Moses then translated these purposes into the commandments that intend them. A philosophical theologian, who is at least possibly a prophet, does the same thing Moses did, except that for anybody other than Moses the commandments have already been given.[126] So, whereas Moses's speculation was prospective, the speculation of all his successors is retrospective.[127] They bring no new commandments, only new interpretations and applications of the commandments already given through Moses.[128] In that case, then, this contemplative activity is not moving from the world up to God who transcends even the cosmos. Rather, this activity is our relating *to* the world around us purposefully. But that purposeful perspective is not simply the discovery of mundane, even pragmatic, reasons from within the world for what we have been commanded to do therein. It is now acting in and for the world from the perspective of the purposeful God who created the world and us therein. That is fundamentally different from looking to the world for the purposes we need so as to act with true intelligence, true metaphysical intent in the world.[129]

Maimonides on Interhuman Relations

Looking at Maimonides's discussions of interhuman relations throughout his works, one finds three distinct types of relationality: (1) the relation of persons one to another, which could be termed "moral"; (2) the relation of persons to their community, which could be termed "political"; and (3) the relation of persons to one another and to their community, which could be termed "metaphysical."

In an early work, Maimonides elaborates upon the rabbinic differentiation of commandments that pertain to "what is between humans and God" (*bein adam le-maqom*) from commandments that pertain to "what is between one human and another" (*bein adam le-havero*). About this latter type of interhuman relationality, which is first and foremost interpersonal, he writes:

> They depend upon orderly relations [*be-taqinot yehasei*] of humans, one with another ... it is the commandment to love one another and not to harm one another ... And if a person keeps these commandments ... he will be rewarded in the world-beyond [*l'olam ha-ba*] for his keeping the commandment. He will also attain something beneficial [*to'elet*] in this world because of his good conduct with fellow humans. For if he and somebody else walks in this path, that other person too will enjoy [*ye-heneh*] the same practical benefit ... as Hillel the Elder said ... "What is hateful to you, do not do to your fellow human [*le-haverakh*]."[130]

What characterizes these interpersonal relations is their reciprocity. That reciprocity is both positive and negative. It is positive insofar as I am to love, that is, to benefit, other persons, and I have the right to expect the same dutifully beneficial action from other persons. It is negative insofar as I am not to harm other persons, and I have the right to expect similar dutiful deference from other persons. Nevertheless, negative reciprocity is wider in its scope than positive reciprocity. The very fact that Hillel's maxim is addressed to a gentile (*nokhri*) means that its scope is universal. It prohibits harming *anybody* else, just as nobody wants to be harmed by *anybody* else. The scope of positive reciprocity, however, is not universal but specific. Thus Maimonides paraphrases the biblical commandment "You shall love your neighbor as yourself" (Leviticus 19:18) as follows: "Everything you want others [*aherim*] to do for you, do it for your brother [*l'ahikha*] in the Torah and the commandments."[131] Also, paraphrasing what Rabbi Akivah called "the most inclusive [*klal gadol*] commandment in the Torah," Maimonides writes: "Everybody is commanded to love everybody else from [the people] Israel."[132]

Usually, it is assumed that philosophically formulated morality is more universal in scope than is the morality formulated in a particularistic tradition like Judaism. However, Aristotle too specifies the range of positive justice. "Justice ... is considered to be for the good of another person [*allotrion agathon*], for it is a relation to our fellows, doing what is beneficial to others, whether to a ruler or to a fellow member of the community [*koinōnō*]."[133] Clearly, here "the community" does not mean universal humankind, but rather one's own community, which is governed by its own unique law. Thus he writes: "Political justice [*dikaion*] obtains among those who have a common life [*koinōnōn biou*] ... and who are free and equal [*isōn*] ... whose mutual relationship is according to law [*nomos*]."[134] Usually, "according to law" means according to the positive law of one's particular society. For Aristotle that might be universal justice, but there is no universal law.[135]

Now it could be said that injustice is not merely the absence of justice. So, if justice means benefitting others (for example, by lending them money they need for economic or bodily survival), injustice is not only not benefitting others by doing nothing. Even more than that, injustice is actually harming others. And whereas benefit need only be commanded within a specific community, where one is likely to be benefitted similarly, harm needs to be prohibited everywhere because a person could be harmed anywhere. Moreover, benefit most often means being benefitted in culturally specific ways. Thus something like being honoured takes very different forms in different societies and cultures. Therefore, for Aristotle (and, it would seem, for Maimonides too), positive justice, that is, what is to be done, is primarily determined by "convention" (*to nomikon*). On the other hand, negative justice, that is, injustice or what is not to be done, is primarily determined by "nature" (*to physikon*).[136] Positive justice is what is to be done for my friends, the members of my community I interact with or could interact with.[137] Negative justice or injustice is what is not to be done anywhere. Its prohibition is universal.

Regarding the specific context of positive justice, it is clear that the range of my friends (broadly speaking) is much more limited than the range of my non-friends, who are the rest of humankind. Nevertheless, this does not mean that whoever is not my friend is, *ipso facto*, my enemy whom I may harm with moral impunity.[138] To regard all foreigners as my enemies is to presume there is no universal moral commonality, however minimal. But in most human societies and cultures, violent acts like murder, rape, and robbery are considered unworthy of the rational human nature shared by all humankind.[139] Along these lines, Maimonides asserts that is why a Jewish society can engage a non-Jewish society on moral grounds. Nevertheless, that minimal moral commonality, which involves common, universal prohibitions, does not entail more maximal cultural commonality, which involves specific positive prescriptions. Thus the fact that a Jewish polity can enter into a non-aggression pact with a non-Jewish polity by no means entails any permission of its Jewish members to intermarry or worship with the members of the non-Jewish polity.[140]

The consistent, positive interrelation of individual persons, which we have termed "moral," takes place within a definite society. That leads us to enquire as to what is the function of a particular society in the lives of the individual persons who live and interact there. In modern liberal societies, whose main task is to enforce what Isaiah Berlin famously called "negative liberty," individuals look to society to protect their pursuit of their particular interests from the interference of others, either before or after that interference occurs.[141] Before the occurrence of such interference, society makes laws that stipulate certain harmful consequences of interference. After such interference does occur, society carries out its threat of harmful consequences through the judgment of the courts. But for Aristotle, that is only society's function in what he called "corrective justice [*diorthōtikon*]," namely, redressing the unjustified interference of one party into the affairs of another.[142] This might be society's first business, but it is certainly not its main business.[143] Instead, society is to provide something more positive in order that a more *common* life can be lived *among* its members as well.

Aristotle, however, is rather vague as to what that positive provision actually is in the society he is theorizing about. And whereas Plato envisioned a society whose main function is to nurture philosophers to rise to metaphysical enlightenment and then descend from their philosophical heights to rule the society, Aristotle seems to want as much of a separation of philosophers from politics as is possible. Society is not run for philosophers and, as such, they owe society only the minimal duties of any ordinary citizen. Plato's optimal society (*politeia*) has a *telos*, a transcending purpose, which Aristotle's more realistic view of the Hellenic city (*polis*) seems to lack. In that teleological sense, Maimonides's philosophical-political vision seems to be closer to Plato's. Thus he writes:

> If you find a Law ... directed exclusively toward the ordering of the city [*madinah*] ... and the abolition in it of injustice and oppression ... that Law is a nomos [*sharia'a namusiyya*] ... If, on the other hand, you find a Law all of whose ordinances are due to attention being paid ... to the body and also to the soundness of belief ... you must know that this guidance comes from Him ... and that this Law is divine [*shari'a allahiyya*].[144]

Now, Plato envisions most of the members of his perfect society serving an end in which they themselves (not being philosophers) do not participate.[145] But Maimonides includes all the faithful members of the Jewish people as participants in the end or purpose of their community. That end is the worship of the Creator God as the affirmation of the basic truth of the relation of God and the cosmos. Indeed, this affirmation of basic truth, in both thought and action, is what God originally willed humans to do in the world.[146] Without this overriding purpose, a human society is either a marketplace balancing individual interests or a tribe who can only affirm their common biological lineage as against that of all other tribes. Hence political cohesiveness is not end in itself, nor is it the public means to a private end. Instead, it is what is required if human beings are to be able to engage in the worship of God, which is their ultimate end, as embodied beings in this social world, and not only when they are apart from it in the world-beyond (*olam ha-ba*).[147] The constant pursuit of that end is what alone gives the community its true cosmic status.

Even though these truths can be apprehended through speculation by those few philosophers who are at least would-be prophets, they are accessible to all the members of the community dogmatically. (Dogmas are doctrines whose affirmation is mandated by the law the religious community subscribes to.) That is, the members of the community are all educated to affirm these basic doctrines as true, even before they can be truly apprehended by the gifted few. This is an example of what the mediaeval Christian theologian Anselm of Canterbury termed "belief seeking knowledge" (*fides quaerens intellectum*).[148] Maimonides says: "In regard to the correct opinions through which the ultimate perfection may be attained, the Law has communicated only their end and made a call to believe them in a summary way – that is, to believe in the existence of the deity ... His unity, His knowledge, His power, His will, and His eternity."[149]

Notwithstanding Maimonides's appreciation of the importance of good interpersonal relations on the moral level and on the political level, the highest interpersonal relation is not that which obtains between individual persons. And it is not that which obtains among persons in their community, even when the community together acknowledges its relation to God as its *raison d'être*. Rather, the highest interpersonal relation is what obtains between certain gifted individuals and God. To be sure, as we have just seen, this relation is available to all the individual members of the covenanted community through their participation in the communal liturgy. However, the truth that most of the community's members can affirm can only be affirmed in the first-person plural ("we"). Only those who have attained philosophic enlightenment are actually able to apprehend this truth in the first-person singular ("I").

The question is whether this direct personal relationship with God transcends the moral interrelation of persons and the political (or theological-political) interrelation of persons we have just examined. In fact, one might well conclude that transcendence of the human social world is Maimonides's opinion inasmuch as he seems to regard true worship as what makes one "free from distraction, and not engaged in thinking upon any of the things pertaining to this world."[150] So, it would seem, even when a philosopher has to be in the world, he or she is actually bored with the world and distracted by the world from being alone with God in contemplation. Indeed, it seems that the difference between a philosopher and God is that God is not involved with the world and never has to be involved with it, whereas humans have to be involved with the world, even though philosophers really do not want to be so involved. Philosophers long for the rare moments when, as Maimonides says to them: "you are alone with yourself and no one else is there ... you should take great care during these precious times not to set your thought to work on anything other than that intellectual worship."[151] In fact, Maimonides considers this kind of contemplative activity to be the necessary preparation for would-be prophets.[152] And it is especially appropriate for an individual aspiring to be a prophet "for himself alone."[153]

If one assumes, as a number of modern scholars have, that Maimonides's designation of contemplation of God as the *summum bonum* or the end of all ends is the same as Aristotle's, then there is a disconnect between popular morality and popular theological politics on the one hand, and contemplative or philosophic religion on the other hand. However, as we have already seen, for Maimonides, we can only contemplate what God *does* in relation to us in the world, whereas for Aristotle, we can contemplate what God *is* apart from the world. That means we can contemplate what God does in relation to Godself, that is, with Godself. So, if for Aristotle contemplation is imitation of God thinking of Godself, then for Maimonides philosophers are to contemplate what the Creator God does with the world and thereby imitate that action actively. God's highest purpose for humans in the world is for us to imitate God's purposefully beneficent activity in and for the world. Therefore, rather than moving up to contemplate what is beyond the world, a philosopher is to contemplate what are God's creative purposes from beyond the world for the world – and then simultaneously act accordingly in and for the world.[154] Only in this way does our human relation to God mediate God's relation to the world we occupy, rather than our relation to the world mediating our relation to God. Therefore, Maimonides's conclusion to the *Guide* is most appropriate:

> It is clear that the perfection of man ... is the one acquired by him who has achieved, in a measure corresponding to his capacity, apprehension of Him ... and who knows His providence as manifested in the act of bringing them into being [*be-hamitso*] and in their governance as it is. The way of life of such an individual, after he has achieved this apprehension, will always have in view loving-kindness, righteousness, and judgment, through assimilation [*le-hidamot*] to His actions, may he be exalted.[155]

Maimonides on the Relation of Humans and Nature

When examining Maimonides's views on the relation of humans and nature, we must bear in mind that for him there are two very distinct realms, both of which are called "nature" (*tev'a*). What these two realms share in common is the fact that "nature" denotes a realm that is neither divine nor human. The difference between them, however, is that one realm of nature is considered to be above humans, while the other is considered to be beneath humans.[156] As we have seen earlier, heavenly nature is the realm that is above humans insofar as it is closer to God. Humans must go through this higher nature in order to be able to apprehend God's cosmic ultimacy. That means that the education of a Jewish philosopher-theologian, like that of any normal Jew, begins with learning Bible and Talmud. But those who have philosophical potential then proceed to the study of natural science, especially astrophysics. And then if they desire to know what is the epitome of human knowledge, they are to engage in metaphysical speculation, hoping for apprehension of God's divine ways in dealing with God's own creation.[157]

Conversely, earthly nature is a realm that has potential for humans, and which humans can manipulate to a certain extent for their own worldly, constructive purposes. So, it might be said that one's relation to heavenly nature is purely scientific and non-technological: it is to be known, not used. One's relation to earthly nature, on the other hand, is thoroughly technological. It is to be known only to the extent that it can be used. And like any effective technology, earth-bound technology needs to be based on good science. Since science is to provide useful information for human technology, the subject of its investigation of earthly objects functions as a material cause for human efficiency in the world, but not as a formal cause or a final cause. This is what distinguishes earth-bound technology from the scientific-metaphysical investigation of heavenly objects.

The mistake that too many people make, even too many Jews make, is to miss the essential difference in the way humans are to properly relate to earthly nature as distinct from the way they are to relate to heavenly nature. This comes out in the following assertion of Maimonides, who speaks of the rabbinic prohibition of what are called "Amorite practices" (*darkhei Amori*) as quasi-idolatry:

> For they are branches of magical practices, inasmuch as they are things not required by reasoning concerning nature and lead to magical practices that of necessity seek support in astrological notions. Accordingly, the matter is turned into a glorification and a worship of the stars.[158]

He then differentiates these forbidden practices from what is permitted by the Rabbis for medicinal purposes.[159] (We shall return to the question of the practice of medicine shortly.)

Even though there are a number of medical practices or remedies that seem to be based on "astrological notions," Maimonides is careful to permit employing such practices only if their etiology can be demonstrated scientifically.[160] But he still prohibits medically prescribed remedies whose etiology is only astrologically attributed, for astrology is in his view a pseudo-science,[161] for two reasons. One, it is not demonstrable by either logical or empirical criteria. Two, it is metaphysically false because it attributes causal properties to the stars in relation to life and especially human life on earth, which, if true, would strongly imply that the stars are to be worshipped. Thus Maimonides says that these prohibited practices are not like practices that seem to have been prohibited by the Torah (*huqqim*) for reasons unknown to us humans. Instead, they have been prohibited because they affirm what is demonstrably false.[162] They are false both in terms of their unproven effectiveness and in terms of having been taken to be caused by quasi-divine beings. For Maimonides, there are no such quasi-divine beings. To presume otherwise is to engage in the type of delusion that is the source of idolatry.

Maimonides sees idolatry, and everything related to it, as rooted in a fundamental human error (*ta'ut gedolah*). That error is the presumption that God has created the heavenly bodies "to direct [*le-hanhig*] the cosmos ... and because they serve before God, they deserve [*r'uyyim*] to be praised, glorified, and honour be allotted to them."[163] Humans erroneously think that this is God's will, and that is the root (*iqqar*) of idolatry. Thus the whole human world fell into this error until the patriarch Abraham brought it back to original monotheism, which correctly taught that God alone is the prime cause who "created the universe" (*ve-hu bara ha-kol*).[164] Now, as we have seen, God's creation of the universe is an act of free will, whereas everything else is but an effect of that original, divine free will. It is only the presumption that somehow or other these intermediate astral beings have been allotted some causal freedom by God that would lead humans to worship them as divine or quasi-divine beings, who could be beseeched for supernatural favours. Indeed, whether worship is acknowledgment of God's beneficence in general or beseeching of God to act beneficently towards us humans in particular, it makes no sense to direct worship to anyone who does not have will. For worship is the recognition that someone infinitely greater than ourselves could have done or could do otherwise wilfully in relation to what is other than Himself. That is to attribute will to the object of our worship. Hence by denying that the astral bodies have such will to do otherwise is to make the worship of them practical falsehood. In fact, for Maimonides along with Aristotle, the astral bodies have intelligence, but not will.[165] Hence they do not have freedom of choice.

Humans are unique among all God's creatures in having freedom of choice (*behirah hofsheet*).[166] What is important to bear in mind when looking at the free relation of humans to earthly nature is that, unlike the heavenly bodies, human freedom is an allotment or entitlement from God.[167] That is why humans are responsible for what they have done freely on earth, that is, to one another and, in this case, what they have done to their fellow, non-human, earthly beings (and, indeed, to the earth itself). That is why humans are answerable to God for what they have done to God's creation, that is, to one another and to earthly nature. As such, we humans certainly cannot regard ourselves as being the conduits of false quasi-divine beings and thus blame them or praise them for what we humans ourselves have done freely. Moreover, it is only on earth that humans have enough freedom to effect significant change. When we do that badly, we have no one to blame but ourselves. When humans effect significant change on earth, they may not give credit to any quasi-divine powers, presuming that they are willing efficient causes when they are not. To do so is to engage in superstition.

Many have noted Maimonides's vociferous opposition to all forms of superstition. As he puts it most pointedly: "All of these practices are lies [*sheqer*] and deception ... and it is not fitting that Jews [*yisrael*], who are exceptionally wise, be drawn into these nonsensical matters [*be-havalim*] ... as it is said in Scripture: 'There is no enchantment [*nahash*] in Jacob, no divination [*kesem*] in Israel' (Numbers 23:23)."[168] But fewer have appreciated the ontological basis of that opposition, which we have just examined above. Without that appreciation, though, as we shall soon see, there is no way to distinguish between the revelation of false supernatural, quasi-divine beings and the revelation of the one true Creator God. And without that appreciation there is no way to distinguish between superstition and the proper worship of God. To engage in superstition is, therefore, to seriously flirt with idolatry.

Furthermore, many have noted the difficulty Maimonides had with aspects of the rabbinic tradition that seem to ascribe efficient causality on earth to such superhuman beings, especially to humans who seem to have supernatural powers. Of course, Maimonides has less of a problem with non-legal texts (*Aggadah*) that seem to contradict his metaphysical assumptions; he can simply ignore them. That is because his whole approach to *Aggadah* is eclectic. Occasionally, though, he cannot ignore them, especially if they figure in theological opinions that he finds philosophically unacceptable. But when it comes to legal texts (*Halakhah*) that have normative significance in the present, he cannot be so evasive. Nevertheless, because Maimonides very rarely actually quotes rabbinic texts verbatim in *Mishneh Torah*, his major halakhic work, but usually paraphrases them rather freely, it is harder to see how he radically reinterprets them by being quite selective of which of their points he chooses to paraphrase and which he chooses to ignore. Let us now look at one such problematic halakhic text, which deals with a matter of human interaction with earthly nature, and see what Maimonides does with it halakhically. The *Mishnah* states:

> A sorcerer [*ha-mekhashef*] is one who does something real [*ha'oseh ma'aseh*]; but he is not one who performs an optical illusion [*ha'ohez et ha'einayyim*]. Rabbi Akivah says in the name of Rabbi Joshua that when it comes to two

> different persons who are picking cucumbers: one of them is exempt from punishment [*patur*]; the other is liable for punishment [*hayyav*]. The one who does something is liable; the one who performed an optical illusion is exempt.[169]

The Talmud records the statement of the third-century Babylonian sage Abayye:

> The one who does something real is to be stoned [*seqilah*]; the one who performs an optical illusion [literally, "grasps the eyes"] is innocent, even though what was done is prohibited [*asur*]. It is permitted even initially [*muttar le-khatehilah*] to do what Rav Hanina and Rav Oshiya did every afternoon before the onset of the Sabbath, namely, while engaging in the study of the laws of creating [*be-hilkhot yetsirah*] there was created for them a third-grown calf, which they ate.[170]

The mediaeval commentator Rashi interprets this supernatural power to the fact that "the third-grown calf was created for them automatically because they were combining the letters of the name of God whereby the cosmos was created [*nivra ha'olam*]. It is not because of sorcery [*mekhashfut*], for it is the work [*ma'aseh*] of God by means of His holy name."[171] In this view, then, the only prohibition is if the supernatural act was not performed in the name of God, but rather in the name of someone other than God.

For Maimonides, however, all such acts are prohibited, even if God's name is invoked; and that is so whether the act produces something real or is only an optical illusion. Thus he ignores or cites pejoratively the stories brought in the rabbinic writings of the wondrous deeds performed by various Rabbis and even by biblical heroes.[172] The only difference between acts that produce something real and acts that are optical illusions is the punishment prescribed for somebody who did the act. The former are to receive biblically prescribed corporal punishment that is more severe; the latter are only to receive rabbinically prescribed punishment that is less severe.[173] The reason for this blanket prohibition is that in either case, a falsehood is being perpetrated. In the former case, although the act produced something real, its supernatural etiology is false. It is the act of somebody who knew how to manipulate natural causation on earth, that is, he or she was acting as an ordinary efficient cause using an ordinary material cause in the world. Only those who are unaware of this natural causation will be fooled by those who seemed to have performed a supernatural feat. Maimonides especially castigates Jews who are so fooled.[174] In the latter case, where an optical illusion has been performed, it could be said that even if not done in the name of some quasi-divine being, it is still an act of forbidden deception, even if it is not punishable by any specific humanly administered punishment.[175]

Also, along these lines, since it is impossible to distinguish between a real event and an illusion when there is nothing tangible involved, Maimonides goes so far as to insist that the veracity of the Sinaitic revelation is not due to the physical phenomena that accompanied it, for these phenomena could be humanly effected illusions (*be-l'at ve-kishuf*), which cannot be falsified.[176] Instead, the veracity of the Sinatic revelation resst on the fact that the whole people Israel were able to individually and collectively apprehend, without any worldly intermediacy, the most evidently true principles of the Torah: the existence of God and the uniqueness of God.[177]

Finally, we need to look at why, in Maimonides's view, certain acts done to our fellow earthly creatures are prohibited and others mandated.

When speaking of the prohibition of causing pain to animals (*tsa'ar ba'alei hayyim*) for no legitimate human bodily need (like the need for food), Maimonides writes that this norm "is set down with a view of perfecting us so that we should not acquire moral habits of cruelty and should not inflict pain gratuitously without any utility." He then goes on to say, "we should intend to be kind and merciful even with a chance animal individual, except in a case of need ... for we must not kill out of cruelty or for sport."[178] In other words, the Torah does not teach that animals as God's creatures too have a claim of their own on human consideration.[179] For, if so, God wouldn't have permitted slaughtering animals for our use any more than God would permit one human to take the life of another human for his or her own benefit.[180] God cares for each individual human, whereas God only cares for non-human species, hence God's mercy for humans is far greater than it is for non-human species.[181] And that is because God's relation to physical, earthly nature is that of a distant first cause, whereas with humans the relation is immediate in the case of those humans who have fulfilled the innate human capacity for the direct apprehension of the Creator God. It is the compassion of the Creator God for His creatures, especially for His intelligent human creatures who share intelligence with Him, that is what humans are to imitate in their dealings with each other.

Now, humans do share with animals and can recognize in animals the sensation of pain, as they are both sensate beings able to express their feelings. Humans are therefore able to empathize with animals suffering pain.[182] Were humans unable to recognize animal pain as something akin to their own, how could they know how to alleviate that pain? And if so, humans could not very well be commanded to alleviate something they couldn't recognize in themselves so as to empathize with those suffering from it.[183] Nevertheless, the ultimate reason for commanding this empathetic action is to turn humans away from acting cruelly to one another. Cruelty, being a vice, might begin at the inter-sensate level before moving on to the interpersonal level. Moreover, one can see a more general rational norm (*mitsvah sikhlit*) underlying the prohibitions of practising various forms of cruelty to animals: "What is hateful to you, do not do to somebody else."[184]

Like other moral vices, cruelty is something that impedes the ability of humans to imitate the all-merciful God, which, for Maimonides, is the highest end humans can strive to attain.[185] Since cruelty is directed to humans as sentient beings, cruelty to non-human sentient animals is something that is likely to lead to cruelty to fellow humans. Along these lines, Maimonides sees the reason for the prohibition of cross-breeding different animal species (*kila'im shel behemah*) to be that this practice requires the cross-breeders to directly facilitate intercourse between animals of two different species, when normally they wouldn't do by that themselves. Maimonides thinks that this is an activity that is disgusting, unworthy of rational human nature.[186] In other words, he takes the Torah's concern to be with the moral character of humans who are involved with animals, not with the creaturely integrity of the animals themselves.

In the same way, Maimonides does not see the biblical commandments to let the land lie fallow during the sabbatical year and the Jubilee year to be because of any inherent value in earthly nature that is to be respected therefore. Instead, he emphasizes that their purpose is "to lead to pity and help for all men."[187] That is, the observance of the sabbatical year and the Jubilee year allows agricultural workers to have a holiday as it were. And since stored food is to be shared, and debts are to be cancelled, the differences between rich and poor are very much lessened. This equalization is meant to lead to greater social harmony.

For Maimonides, plants like animals do not have any claim on human consideration because of their being creatures created by God for whom God is concerned. Thus the biblical prohibition of destroying fruit trees, even for military purposes (Deuteronomy 20:19–20), he simply reiterates.[188] He makes no mention of this being an inherent violation of the objects of God's universal providence.[189] In fact, Maimonides only reasons about the general prohibition of "wanton destruction" (*bal tashheet*) that the Rabbis inferred from the more specific biblical prohibition, seeing wanton destruction to be the practical result of uncontrolled anger, which is inherently nihilistic.[190] Along these lines, one cannot assume that the Torah prohibited cross-breeding different plant species (*kila'ei zera'im*) and animal species because of the inherent integrity of created species.[191] This is so despite the fact that many earlier Rabbis taught that such tampering with the "created order" (*sidrei bere'sheet*) is wrong[192] and, indeed, deserving of divine punishment.[193] Instead, Maimonides thinks that the prohibition is because this was some kind of idolatrous practice.[194] And although the ancient idolaters who actually did this are long gone, since the propensity for idolatry in one form or another is, for Maimonides, endemic to human nature, even its manifestations are to be permanently prohibited.[195]

Of course, the greatest human interference with the natural order is the practice of medicine. Thus the Talmud records the view that "permission [*reshut*] is given to the physician to practise the art of healing [*le-rap'ot*]."[196] Now, this has been interpreted to mean that healing is a divine, supernatural prerogative, for which humans require specific dispensation or authorization from God in the Torah in order to engage in it legitimately.[197] However, Maimonides regards the practice of medicine as part of the biblical prescription to restore (whenever possible) something one's fellow has lost, be that their property or their bodily health.[198] This is as natural a practice as any other constructive intrusion into the natural biological order. It is in no way usurpation of God's providence, but only the fulfilment of the general commandment to benefit our fellow humans.[199] And it is not an affront to the integrity of earthly nature inasmuch as earthly nature is to be under total (albeit constructive) human control.

After Aristotelianism

After Maimonides, Jewish rationalist theologians continued to engage Aristotle and the Aristotelian philosophers in an intellectual atmosphere these philosophers still largely dominated. And that engagement was conducted within the mediaeval political realms of Islam and Christendom. However, with the downfall of the Aristotelian cosmic paradigm in the sixteenth and seventeenth centuries, and with the emergence of a more secular political climate, Jewish theologians faced very different intellectual and political challenges from philosophers. Enter Immanuel Kant in the eighteenth century to offer a radically new challenge that continues unabated into the present.

Chapter Six

Kant's Challenge to Theology

The Last Challenge of Philosophy

In the previous chapters, the term "theology" essentially denoted the content of a comprehensive way of being in the world, grounded in a specific verbal revelation of God. Rather than denoting human talk (*logos*) about God (*theos*), which is what the term has been largely taken to mean since Aristotle coined it, "theology" for us now essentially denotes God's word (*dvar adonai*), that is, verbal revelation that has been written down in a book. On the other hand, the term "philosophy" for us now essentially denotes *a* method of understanding such a significant way of being in the world.

One can see philosophy being first employed in antiquity by natural science as *the* method for its explication. And for most of human history until modernity, natural science had a heavy theistic component, namely, its concern with the relation of God and nature. Theology as "natural theology" or ontology became the epitome of philosophy: the "queen of the sciences" (*regina scientiarum*).[1] Yet as a department *of* philosophy, so to speak, there could be no mutual interaction *between* philosophy and theology as there was no true difference between the two. Only in the Hellenistic Age, when Athens met Jerusalem, could philosophy relate to theology insofar as theology now came from a truly independent source: biblical revelation. In modernity, though, the vast majority of philosophers discredit theology from having any noetic content worthy of philosophical analysis, first revealed theology, then natural theology. So, modern philosophy returned to its original home for its content, concerning itself with natural science, but without any need for a theological dimension, whether natural or revealed.

Even though the vast majority of modern philosophers have given up on theology, confining their attention to data with which they are more at home and ignoring data with which they are not at home, that should not inhibit theologians from employing philosophical methods in their concern for the revealed data with which they are very much at home. And this can be done without any real encounter or confrontation with any particular philosophical school. Due to its methodological clarity and rigour, many theologians (Jewish, Christian, and Muslim) have seen philosophy as the best method for explicating the truth theology proclaims, that is, interpreting what that truth means theoretically and how it applies practically.

Now, at the level of methodology alone, philosophy poses no serious challenge to theology, as method per se can be employed for the explication of a variety of ways of being-in-the-world. In fact, the two main philosophical methodologies available today, phenomenology and analytic-linguistic philosophy, have been readily employed by a number of significant theologians with relative ease. One might say that in this case, theology supplies the datum or content *for* a philosophical method to explicate, while a philosophy supplies the method brought *to* theology for such explication. But methodological philosophy cannot, then, dictate where and by whom it may be employed. As a purely contentless method, philosophy cannot have any real independence; hence it must attach itself to or serve something (in fact, almost anything) else. That is because philosophy does not emerge *from* that content itself, nor does philosophy create its own content *out of* itself. Moreover, without that attachment, that is, without a connection to some external referent, philosophy becomes a self-referential "mind game," having no meaning for anything outside itself. Thus phenomenology can interpret a wide variety of experiences it itself neither creates nor is created by, and analytic-linguistic philosophy can interpret a wide variety of what Wittgenstein called "language games," which philosophy itself neither creates nor is created out of.[2] In this contemporary situation, philosophy as a methodological way of knowing (qua epistemology) can, indeed it must, serve some mistress or other in order to be a way of knowing anything already in the world. Philosophy's very coherence, then, seems to require that its origin behind it and its destination ahead of it be supplied for it by something else, but to whom it is still related culturally. So, to be taken seriously, philosophy needs to direct its attention to an object that has already been taken seriously in the culture in which it operates. Surely, theology as content is still taken most seriously in Jewish, Christian, and Islamic cultures (at least by the most serious thinkers there).

Nevertheless, as we have seen in the previous chapters, philosophy does pose a challenge to theology when it is more than just a method. In the preceding chapter, we saw how Aristotle's philosophy challenged Maimonides's theology; in the chapter before that, we saw how Plato's philosophy challenged Philo's theology. The challenge there was that Plato's philosophy and Aristotle's philosophy are more than just methodologies. Each of them has content, both theoretical and practical. Therefore, Jewish theologians like Philo and Maimonides couldn't employ Platonic or Aristotelian epistemological methods without having to confront the content for which these methods were originally devised. And since biblical theology and classical philosophy dealt with many of the same issues both theoretical and practical, inasmuch as these issues are truly universal, a confrontation between these two ways of being in the world was unavoidable. How each of these theologians navigated this confrontation, steering clear of the Scylla of arrogant conquest and the Charybdis of obsequious servitude, has been examined in the two preceding chapters.

The truly mutual confrontation of two such content-laden ways of being in the world requires that neither side subordinate to nor be subordinated by the other. This is done when each side recognizes some points of commonality and some points of difference between them. Surely, without some commonality there could be no encounter as each side, in effect, is living in an altogether different world from the other. But without difference there couldn't be an encounter but only a monologue, in which one side totally subordinates the other side and then claims universal validity for itself because of the disappearance of any alternatives. Locating exactly where there is commonality and where there is difference between theology and philosophy, that calls for considerable judgment.

This dialectic of commonality and difference is what has made these interchanges of theology and philosophy so richly complex. When seen from the side of theology – which is the perspectival locus of this book – this interchange enables theologians to learn from philosophy, albeit critically. Nevertheless, lest the relationship between theology and philosophy turn into a merely comparative enterprise, with its threat of the normative paralysis of relativism, each side needs to affirm that its own tradition provides a more satisfying constitution (both theoretically and practically) on that aspect of human being-in-the-world about which the two sides have both commonality and difference. Therefore, at the ontological level, existential assertions are required. At the epistemological level, assertions of veracity are required. And at the practical level, assertions of rights and duties are required.

In the constellation of being-in-the-world offered here, as we have seen in the previous chapters. those points of commonality and difference are brought out in four spheres of relationality: (1) the relation of God and humans; (2) the relation of God and nature; (3) the interrelation of humans among themselves; and (4) the relation of humans and nature.

The adherents of a tradition need to regularly affirm the superiority of their own tradition's stance on any specific question pertaining to any of these spheres of relationality, especially when some other comprehensive, content-laden, attractive alternative moves into the neighbourhood. When this is not done, they are at a loss to explain, that is, give a positive reason, why they ought to maintain their essential difference from this attractive other. Indeed, when this is not done, they lose the location in the world that gives their lives its essential content, and that they must be willing even to die for rather than abandon. When this is not done, the adherents of a tradition like Judaism are nowhere in the world. (On the side of philosophy, Socrates is the greatest exemplar of this absolute commitment; on the side of Jewish theology, it is Rabbi Akivah.)[3] Nevertheless, this assertion of superiority need only be made to the other side when the other side attempts to subordinate one's own tradition to its own. When that happens, the side so challenged (in our case the challenge to theology coming from a philosophy) should argue to the other side that what it is offering as a replacement is no more creditable, indeed less creditable, than the object of its attempted conquest. Since the burden of proof is on the accuser, in the absence or refutation of such proof, one can fall back on the position of one's own tradition with renewed confidence, a confidence stemming from both positive affirmation and negative rebuttal.[4]

In my view, quite arguable to be sure, the last such sustained interaction was the confrontation/encounter of theology, especially Jewish theology, with the comprehensive, content-laden philosophy of Immanuel Kant. The fact that this relationship is by no means passé (inasmuch as there are real live Kantians today with whom theologians can engage in sustained discussion) is why I have chosen to discuss it here. Hence the subject of this chapter is mostly my own encounter as a Jewish theologian with Kant's philosophy.[5] In fact, this encounter with Kant's philosophy is central to modern Jewish theology in whose enterprise I am actively involved. That is because Kant is to modern Jewish theology what Plato was to ancient Jewish theology and what Aristotle was to mediaeval Jewish theology. Of course, I am talking about the kind of Jewish theology that takes philosophy seriously, as opposed to the kind of Jewish theology that never encountered philosophy or has chosen to forget or suppress any such encounter in its past.[6]

Kant's philosophy became the most significant challenge to modern theology, and especially to modern Jewish theology, because of two interrelated factors. The first factor is that with its universal ethic, Kant's philosophy seemed to be the best formulation of the ethos of the modern nation state that Jews, since the end of the eighteenth century, have aspired to be equal members of. That has been an external political matter. The second factor is a more internal matter. What made and what still makes Kant's philosophy so challenging to Jews is its emphasis on law, especially law as commandment. To Jews who are at home in the Jewish tradition, that sounds very much like the traditional Jewish idea of law as *mitsvah*.[7] As we shall see, that normative dimension, so familiar to Jews, comes when Kant's philosophy deals with the four spheres of relationality with which we have been concerned throughout this book: (1) the relation of humans and nature, where humans prescribe the way natural phenomena are to be ordered, that is, by laws of nature; (2) the relation of humans among themselves, where humans prescribe the way they are to interact with one another as moral beings; (3) the relation of humans and God, where humanly formulated norms need to be looked upon as divine commandments; and (4) the relation of God and nature, where God is thought of as making nature purposeful in an orderly, lawful way.

More than with any other philosopher, Jews can see in Kant someone whose basic philosophical vocabulary and even conceptuality seem to indicate that the Jewish tradition and Kant's philosophy are speaking the same language. So, even today, an important task of Jewish theology is to speak with Kant, but without attempting to either colonize or be colonized by Kant and his contemporary disciples. That means avoiding the formulation of either a Kantian Judaism or a Jewish Kantianism. Neither Judaism nor Kantianism should be reduced to an adjective, modifying or subordinating the other.

The Relation of Humans and Nature

In approaching Kant's philosophy from a theological perspective, both as an encounter and as a confrontation, we should begin by looking at the relation of humans and nature, as that is where Kant himself begins his critical philosophy in the first of his three critiques, his *Critique of Pure Reason*.

For Kant, we humans relate ourselves to the external world (what has been called "nature") by locating it spatially and ordering it temporally. This is how we humans determine (*Bestimmung*) or position the appearances we find or discover in the external world, and which seem to have been placed there (*Darstellung*) for our discovery of them. That is how we give them meaning for us. The content of these appearances are the *data*, that is, what has been given to us (from the Latin *dare*); but the categories such as causality are the means whereby we remake or re-present to ourselves (*Vorstellung*) in our own image the data or "percepts" we perceive in the world. In that way, human knowledge of the external world is both passive and active. It is passive in what it receives *from* the data, which is called "sensibility" (*Sinnlichkeit*). Human knowledge is active in what it imposes on or prescribes *to* the data, which is what we determine the data to be *for* ourselves. This is what is called "understanding" (*Verstand*).[8]

Two questions arise, though. One, *why* do we humans need to engage in this difficult pursuit of knowledge of nature? In other words, why do we humans need to know anything about nature? Surely, it is more than mere curiosity. What is the purpose of our engagement in this ongoing activity? Two, do we humans have to be concerned with the independent existence of the data themselves, or are they simply there for the taking? As we shall see, Kant is very much concerned with these questions, and so is the Jewish tradition. Hence there can be a sustained conversation between the two at this point.

By asking these two questions of Kant, we are dealing with the *Critique of Pure Reason* as an essentially metaphysical enquiry via epistemology rather than as an epistemological enquiry per se. For epistemology only shows us *how* we relate intelligently to the data we experience, while metaphysics enables us to discover *why* we are interested in the existence of the data altogether. Epistemology separated from this metaphysical question (as is so common in Anglo-American philosophy) is not self-justifying, as it does not explain why a rational person should be interested in or concerned with anything. Without this metaphysical justification, the pursuit of knowledge of external nature can be nothing but a trivial pursuit inasmuch as the data or objects it seeks to know could be anything. Surely, Kant's epistemology is the positive means to this metaphysical end. Moreover, Kant skilfully employs his impressive epistemology negatively to critique the pretensions of those who would seek this metaphysical end with a faulty, too hastily conceived epistemology.

There is a ready answer at hand to the first question: Why do we humans need to know anything about nature? The answer is that we need to know enough about nature so as to harness it for our survival therein, for it is what surrounds us. It is the material necessity from which we cannot physically escape. Animals, though, seem to be related to nature automatically, adjusting themselves to their environment (*Umwelt* in German; literally "world around") in order to survive therein. But they don't seem be able to look beyond it, or look at it from a position beyond it. We humans, though, want more than that because we need more than that. We want to make the environment into our home, into our world, by knowing enough of it to have some control of it rather than the environment totally controlling us.[9] In other words, we want to make nature work for us, rather than letting it just work for itself. In fact, when we simply let nature alone by ignoring it, nature often seems to be working against us.

As the most important part of this strategy for the sake of survival and comfort, we humans need enough knowledge of the earthly environment to make it work for rather than against us. Work as *working* or exercising causal power *over* nature (*bewirken*), as in the words of the Bible: "by the sweat of your brow you will eat bread" (Genesis 3:19), is certainly the most basic task of humans on earth. Earthly nature is one we can never become part of without in the end being destroyed by it (a fact that romantic environmentalists today choose to ignore). Instead, our very survival, let alone our more comfortable life here, requires us to increasingly incorporate natural beings into our immanent human world. This is done by human technique, which is also called "instrumental" or "pragmatic" action. As an overall intended approach to the external world, it is called "technology." Technology looks upon everything non-human as grist for the mill of *homo faber* ("the human maker"), whose task it is to domesticate, that is, "to make at home," as much of nature as is needed for human survival and comfort. In fact, as some evolutionary biologists have pointed out, without their technological advantage humans are very poorly equipped with the natural capacity for survival. For example, antelopes can run away from their predators much faster than we humans can; elephants can overpower their predators much more easily than we can.

However, the more we humans learn about the nature that surrounds us, the more we are able to anticipate how we can control it for our own projects. Thus technology becomes less and less of a response to the challenge of nature both positive and negative (i.e., what to come closer to and what to distance ourselves from) and more and more the human attempt to not only control what confronts us here and now, but to control what lies on the horizon there and then. In that case, technology is a celebration of the human power not just to survive and be comfortable in nature, but to dominate nature by treating it as our own creation. Technology becomes its own end.[10] Thus the Bible has the builders of the Tower of Babel saying: "Come, let us build a city for ourselves [*lanu*] and a tower, whose top is in heaven" (Genesis 11:4). One of the ancient Rabbis interpreted this to mean that their intention was idolatrous, that is, by their technology they wanted to displace the Creator God from God's sovereignty over the earth by placing themselves over the earth as its sovereign.[11] Their punishment for their technological audacity, though, was that "the Lord scattered them over the face of all the earth" (Genesis 11:9). In other words, the earth reclaimed them as its temporary residents, not its permanent masters.

So, why can't humans be satisfied to simply "live by bread alone" (Deuteronomy 8:3)? In fact, when we humans only want from nature the means for our bodily survival and comfort, we seem to be no different from other earthly beings, who are more at home in nature than are we. That makes us as much dependant on nature as our fellow earthly beings are, in fact more dependent on nature inasmuch as we have to expend more pragmatic effort in the fulfilment of our needs than do our fellow earthly beings. Moreover, our satisfaction with nature seems to be less than that of our fellow earthly creatures, because our desire seems to be not only to use nature, but to dominate it. However, does that desire to dominate nature enable us to transcend the limits of our bodily needs that tie us to nature, or does it make us more, not less, dependent on nature? (As Hegel famously showed, the slave comes to dominate the master precisely because the master becomes more and more dependent on the slave.)[12] And, as we shall see later in this chapter, this attitude of the domination of nature extends to the domination of less powerful humans by more powerful humans.

Furthermore, doesn't the external world in the end reclaim its human invaders just as much as it reclaims its non-human inhabitants? Indeed, the biblical statement of the necessity of human toil for the sake of survival on earth reminds humans *(adam)* that in the end the earth reclaims us all as if we had never been here at all: "until your return to the earth [*adamah*] from which you have been taken, for you are dust [*afar*] and to dusk you will return" (Genesis 3:19). But if that is the case, our attempts at technological control should be limited to more modest attempts at physical survival and some degree of bodily comfort, since anything more than that is literally a desperate waste of our very ephemeral locus or dwelling on earth. Hence our realistic task on earth, from this pragmatic point of view, is neither to know the world nor to very much change it, but rather to simply endure the world with the least amount of effort and the most amount of leisure possible. Nevertheless, it is clear that this view of human existence, while necessary, is not sufficient. It certainly cannot motivate and sustain the kind of epistemological effort Kant calls for in his great philosophical project, a project with which Jewish theology is in much accord. For the intention of such effort is to enable humans to function *in* nature by cooperating *with* nature, yet not to be *of* nature. It means to *transcend* nature, though not to flee it.

What is the way out of this instrumentalist dead end that, among several other problems, seems to make the pursuit of pure science (contra technology) futile? Long before Kant, Aristotle felt this great problem and began his treatment of what lies-*beyond*-the-physical (though not *away from* it), in what later Aristotelians called his *Metaphysics*, as follows: "Naturally, everyone's desire is to know, a sign of which is [our] love of the senses [*aisthēsis*]. Aside from their usefulness [*chreias*], they are loved for themselves ... and not only for what we do [*prattōmen*] with them."[13] Now, Aristotle does not mean love of all of our senses; instead, he confines his attention to our sense of sight. That seems to be because seeing, more than the other senses, respects the independence of the object it is looking at (*Anschauung*). However much we might locate and order our perceptions of external objects, their very externality seems to remain intact. Nevertheless, that objective independence is destroyed when we look at objects so as to be better able to take hold of them and mould them to our own bodily purposes. Does one look at an apple to better respect its beauty, or does one look at an apple to devise the most efficient way to pick it and eat it? The latter approach removes the desired object from its existence; the former approach lets the admired object remain in its existence.[14] From the perspective of the former approach, the viewed object seems to be saying to the subject viewing it: "Do not touch me!" And in fact, like Aristotle's, Kant's exalted vision of nature is the vision, as he himself put it, "of the starry skies above."[15] Unlike earthly objects, though, they can only be seen, not handled or used.

The desire to know, and to know ultimately, is endemic to human nature. There is no way to permanently supress it. The question is not, therefore, *whether* it is to be pursued or not; the question is *how* knowledge is to be pursued so as to be a pursuit worthy of humans as intelligent beings. That in turn leads to the question of *why* or *for what* it is to be pursued satisfactorily.[16] So far, enjoyable (as distinct from just useful) experience, what we now call "aestheticism," might give us enough transcendence of the ordinary, merely pragmatic use of nature. However, this aesthetic experiencing is by no means the end of the noetic or epistemological pursuit. Instead, it is a launching pad for the move into pure science, that is, what seems to be knowledge qua natural science for its own sake, rather than natural experience for its own sake. Unlike sensory experience, this science, often called "wisdom," is actively concerned with the causes or the indispensable factors that underlie the phenomena that sensory experience more passively receives and enjoys, rather than merely using them. Hence Aristotle says: "That is why theoretical pursuits are better than active ones [*poiētikōn*] ... thus wisdom [*sophia*] is knowledge of certain first principles and causes [*archas kai aitias*]."[17] What moves philosophically inclined persons from enjoying experience to seeking knowledge of what lies behind it and above it is their wondering (*thaumazein*) why what is exists at all, and is what it is.[18]

Yet, is this the final end of the noetic or epistemological pursuit? For "knowledge" is *epistēmē*, literally "what one can stand on." Is this a viewing-place one stands on to look *down* on what these causes effect in nature *beneath* it; or is this a platform upon which one stands to look *up* to the cause that lies *above* it? The answer to this question hinges on what is thought to be the ultimate purpose of knowing, that is, the noetic pursuit. If knowledge qua natural science is meant to give us the power to dominate nature beneath us, then the only real difference between scientific knowledge and pragmatic or technological knowledge is that pragmatic knowledge enables us to makes *things* out of natural materials and thus determine them for our bodily use, while scientific knowledge enables us to dominate natural entities or *beings* by framing natural phenomena by our own categories. This is the way we see phenomena and thus include them in our world, that is, in the way they appear to us. This kind of less useful knowledge gives us the greater and more satisfying power of being able to more and more accurately predict natural events through our knowledge of their causation. That is the case even when our satisfaction comes from how much we can predictably know rather than how much pragmatic use we can get out of what we know. One might say this is the difference between pure and applied science.

For Aristotle, though, this is not the ultimate purpose or *telos* of the noetic pursuit, for it is still *of* nature insofar as it returns to nature with its categories in hand *for* framing nature. It is still dependent *on* nature for its intended object. Thus it is not knowledge for itself alone (*monē*).[19] The knowledge gained in the study of natural phenomena is only penultimate. Its ultimate task is to prepare us for knowledge of what is to be known for its own sake, not for what it enables us to do with natural entities made into useful things, and not even for how it enables us to enjoy the experience of natural phenomena per se. The knowledge or wisdom that is truly ultimate, absolutely teleological, is the science Aristotle calls "divine" (*theiotatē*).[20] (It is "natural" knowledge, but knowledge of a different kind of nature, that is, eternal heavenly nature, which is essentially different from ephemeral earthly nature.) This is like the knowledge that God has of Godself, that is, knowledge for its own sake. It is knowledge that desires nothing outside itself, whether for its physical use or for its theoretical dominance. It is truly and uniquely singular like the object with which it is identical. So, one could say that the only true reason why natural science must intervene between our pragmatic pursuit and our noetic, now truly metaphysical, pursuit is because without this scientific intervention, this ultimate pursuit is not standing on a sure, demonstrable foundation.

At this point we might ask: Why couldn't Kant do something like what Aristotle did in his pursuit of that which is truly an end-in-itself, that is, the *summum bonum*? Like Aristotle, he was surely a metaphysician (despite protests to the contrary), and like Aristotle, he was also a student of natural science (though he seems to have spent far less time in working in natural science than did Aristotle). The answer to this question is that Kant couldn't be a metaphysician like Aristotle because (as we have seen in the previous chapter) the teleological natural science upon whose back Aristotle constructed his metaphysics (with its ontological object) had been displaced (seemingly irretrievably) by the non-teleological natural science, especially physics, of Copernicus, Galileo, and Newton. As such, Kant would have to construct his metaphysics, that is, he would have to constitute his noetic quest, elsewhere. Certainly, that quest is essentially teleological insofar as it seeks the ultimate end which/who intends nothing above itself. Like Aristotle, though, Kant could not dispense with what might be seen as an epistemological/scientific (as distinct from a merely empirical or "naturalist") prelude. For without that scientific intervention, the noetic/metaphysical quest would have no answer to those who argue that useful technology is the only durable approach to our necessarily surrounding environment, that is, to earthly nature. Or, without that scientific intervention, the noetic/metaphysical quest could be seen as a fanciful flight from natural necessity that, instead of reaching for heaven while still keeping our feet on earth, projects us up out of earthly nature, but with no parachute to get us back down to earth safely. Indeed, without that scientific parachute, we inevitably fall back down to earth without a platform there to receive us for a safe landing. (This has been the lot of many Platonists, whose metaphysics has jettisoned or done an end run around natural science.)

What keeps Kant's epistemology from being a ripe target for a technological takeover is his insistence that our knowledge of nature is limited to how we can locate and order the appearances (*Erscheinungen*, literally the "showings") of things we can perceive in our world. But what limits our knowledge is our belief that the source of these appearances is beyond our noetic grasp. These things are more than objects that correlate with the subjects who can perceive them. Rather, these things are what Kant calls "the-thing-by-itself" (*Ding an sich selbst*). Thus Kant says that "there are two stems of human knowledge, namely, *sensibility* and *understanding*, which perhaps spring from a common [*gemeinschaftlichen*], but to us unknown root [*Wurzel*]. Through the former, objects are given [*gegeben*] to us; through the latter, they are thought."[21] Furthermore, Kant says that "the things we intuit are not in themselves [*an sich selbst*] what we intuit them as being, nor their relations [*Verhältnisse*] so constituted [*beschaffen*] in themselves as they appear to us."[22] Earlier, Kant speaks of the-thing-by-itself as what is "unconditioned" (*das Unbedingte*), which is almost like the way theologians speak of God.[23] Knowledge of appearances, however, is certainly conditioned by the categories we must assume *a priori* in order to determine anything at all *about* the data we experience as what has been given (*gegeben*) to us, rather than what has been created by us. As such, we have to assume the existence of a real, extra-mental source of these appearances, "otherwise we should be landed in the absurd conclusion that there can be appearance without anything that appears [*was da erscheint*]."[24] In fact, Kant wonders what "might be" (*mögen*) the source from which "our representations arise (*entspringen*)."[25] In other words, he can only assume *that* such a nexus exists, but not *what* it is, that is, *how* it actually produces the appearances as its effects. Our knowledge, on the other hand "orders, connects, and brings [appearances] into relations [*in Verhältnisse*]."[26]

No matter how much control we have over the noetic ordering of nature, we still have no control over what lies behind what we do know as it actually exists on its own. As we shall discuss later when we examine Kant's notion of rational persons as ends-by-themselves (*Zweck an sich selbst*), being recognized as-is (*an sich*) prevents that person from being *used* as a *means* to someone else's end or project. Although our relation to things-by-themselves is of lesser ontological significance than our relation to persons as end-in-themselves, recognizing persons and even things as what they are rather than only what they are for us is what enables us to respect them. It lets them be apart from us rather than our devouring them so that they lose their ontological independence, having nothing of themselves left for themselves. In the theoretical realm, that metaphysical respect of the object's independence is totally one-sided; it is solely on the part of the knower. In the practical realm, though, that metaphysical respect is mutual; I am to respect the other person's independence of me as that other person is to respect my independence of them. That is why there can only be a truly reciprocal relationship *with* another person in the practical realm. There, any attempt of mine to use the other person for my own ends can be resisted by that other person's assertion of their independence *from* me.

But in the theoretical realm, I cannot have a relationship *with* a thing, because a thing cannot resist my attempt to use it, or even hide itself from my noetic appropriation of its phenomenality. Only my respect for the thing-by-itself inhibits my desire to totally devour it.

The respect for the thing-by-itself that emerges in the theoretical realm, therefore, is what prepares us for the higher respect for otherness that emerges in the practical realm of persons as ends-by-themselves. Without this theoretical interlude that mediates between our instrumental or pragmatic relation to things and our non-instrumental relationship with persons, our pragmatic relation to things would inevitably determine our relations with other persons.

However, why can't science give us knowledge of things-by-themselves as they are in themselves? Isn't science "conceived as a process from description to explanation," that is, when "we begin from things as related to our senses," but "we end with things as related to one another," as the Jesuit philosopher Bernard Lonergan astutely noted?[27] And "what is to be known inasmuch as data are understood is some correlation or function that states universally the relations of things not to our senses but to one another."[28] Now, surely that includes our ability to view the inner relations or workings of natural entities and, moreover, to understand these inner relations as being what they are even if no observer could see them immediately. Nevertheless, whether observing data immediately so as to describe them, or abstracting from our observations so as to explain them, we are still *taking* the data into our own world, whether tactically or only noetically. As such, the data become the means to our own ends. The difference, then, between imaginable things-by-themselves and describable data seems to be one of degree rather than one of kind. The difference is still between what is more or less apparent, more or less available to us. We are still not at the portals of transcendence.

For Kant, though, isn't the difference between percepts and things-by-themselves one of kind? For he says that "representation in itself [*Vorstellung an sich selbst*] does not produce [*vorbringt*] its object in so far as existence [*Dasein*] is concerned, for we are not speaking of its causality by means [*vermittlest*] of the will. None the less the representation is *a priori* determinant [*bestimmend*] of the object ... through [*durch*] the representation is it possible to know anything as object [*Gegenstand*]."[29] Thus Heidegger astutely notes that, for Kant, "our mode of cognition is not ontically creative."[30] Conversely, our representational cognition is only epistemologically creative. As Kant says, "the understanding does not derive [*schöpft*] its laws (a priori) from [*aus*], but prescribes them to [*vorschreibt*] nature."[31] Now that which is "prescribed" is the product of a will. That being the case, our representational categories are the product of our will; not that we devise them willy-nilly, but that we *want* to bring them to the data received sensibly, and in a way that carefully comports with the data. That is the way we determine their desired meaning for ourselves; but that implies that the things-by-themselves do not lend themselves to our meanings. That is because they are the product of a will totally other than our own. As such, they can be thought of as created entities. Since no creature can ever hope to access the creative power of God's will, not even mortal humans (despite our exalted status in creation) can hope to bring anything into existence, or remove anything from existence. (We can only reconfigure other created beings.) Things-by-themselves are to be respected by letting them be, that is, letting them remain out of our totalizing grasp, whether tactical or noetic. Indeed, Kant speaks of "things" (*Sachen*) as "beings whose existence depends [*beruht*], not on our will, but on nature, have nonetheless, if they are non-rational beings [*Wesen*], only a relative value as means."[32] And it would seem that for Kant this is not nature as some kind of blind cause, but rather nature as having will. After all, in this same context Kant speaks of "nature's purposes" (*Zwecke der Natur*).[33] But, surely, anyone who has purposes has a will; hence "nature" (when it is not seen as a mental construct) can certainly be taken to be a euphemism for the Creator God.[34] Furthermore, remembering that truth should help one avoid what the ancient Rabbis called "wanton destruction" (*bal tasheet*) of God's creation, which is our misappropriation of God's property.[35]

At this point, Kant is enough of an heir of biblical theology to still affirm that nothing in the world is uncreated. Everything is either the product of human will or the product of divine will. And because God's will is infinitely more creative than ours, it seems to follow that we do not look for ultimacy in our own will, even our own will to know nature. The products of our will must not, then, be respected above the greater products of God's will. But, for Kant, we cannot access that greater will even through our understanding of nature, let alone through our use of that much of nature we can grab pragmatically. We have to look for that ultimacy or absoluteness elsewhere, since we don't even know how things-by-themselves send their appearances to us, or somehow or other allow them to be received by us through our *a priori* categories that order them for us. So, how could we know how these things-by-themselves came-to-be (like "be-came" in English), that is, what they are altogether, inasmuch as they are much more than the way they appear to us?

As we shall see in the section of this chapter dealing with the relation of God and nature, human appropriation is limited by the theological fact that all of creation belongs to God, and to God alone. "Everything is from You, and from Your hand do we give back to You. For we are transient residents [*gerim*] before you, and mere tenants [*toshavim*] like all of our ancestors; our days on earth are like a shadow, having no immortality [*ein miqveh*]" (I Chronicles 29:14–15).[36] Thus we humans are to respect God's ownership of the universe. We may only appropriate for ourselves what God has permitted us to borrow from Him temporarily.[37] We are to act like respectful guests, not like invading robbers.

All of the preceding that has been noticed in Kant's thought, at least at this level, seems to be in harmony with theological notions of what is the proper relation of humans and nature. We humans are neither nature's masters nor nature's slaves. We are to neither dominate nature nor regard ourselves as being parts of nature. This means that nature is only to be used, but only partially, in order to respect its inherent integrity as a created entity. All of nature, even all of nature within our grasp, is never totally given to us for our use or enjoyment. When this relation of humans and nature is understood philosophically, those who have some understanding of the nature-human relation are now in a position to intelligently seek the source of the integrity of created entities like nature and like ourselves. In Kant's words: "Two things fill the mind with ever new and increasing admiration and reverence [*Ehrfurcht*] ... *the starry sky above me and the moral law within me.*"[38] Nevertheless, Kant is convinced that respect for the moral law so near to me puts me in touch with intelligent creativity to a far greater extent than does my respect for the heavens far away from me. My concern for the moral law within me (*in mir*), though, is not "me" as an idiosyncratic individual, but rather *the* mind (*das Gemüt*) of any rational human person. As such, it is the moral law "within us" (*in uns*), which is the law that governs interhuman relations. It is now to that sphere of relationality where we must go in this enquiry. This is the domain of praxis, that is, that which is done *among* humans living together in society.

Noumena: Intellect and Will

In the preface to the *Critique of Pure Reason,* Kant already asserts that theoretical or scientific thinking is "not sufficient to determine reason's transcendent concept of the unconditioned," and that knowledge is "possible *a priori* ... only from a practical point of view" and "speculative reason has thus made room for such an extension ... indeed we are summoned [*ausgefordert*] to take occupation of it, if we can, by practical data of reason."[39] How, then, do we "occupy" (*auszufüllen*) the domain of the Unconditioned by the exercise of our practical (i.e., moral) reason in a way that we could not do by the exercise of our speculative reason? As we have seen, that requires us to carefully go through speculative reason, distinguishing it from pragmatic or technical reason, in order to see praxis or moral action as metaphysically superior to speculative reason as speculative reason is metaphysically superior to pragmatic or instrumental reason. And while all three forms of reason are interpersonal discursive exercises, only in practical reason are interpersonal relations themselves the subject of the actual discourse. But who are these persons who engage us and with whom we are engaged in these interrelations? And how do we engage in these interpersonal relations differently from the way we relate to nature, either pragmatically or noetically?

Even if we didn't think things-by-themselves are created entities (i.e., that they are the products of a will other than our own), we would still not know whether they are intelligent beings or not. Even though Kant's awe is directed towards "the starry sky above me [and everybody else along with me]," we still have no way of speaking of these things as themselves being conscious let alone intelligent, as did Plato and Aristotle. So, our awe of them doesn't make us humans want to imitate them, as Plato and Aristotle would have us imitate the gods in their eternal contemplation of the Absolute (whether *the* Good for Plato, or *the* God for Aristotle). We cannot very well desire to imitate what we can't speak of truthfully. Therefore, we cannot relate to non-human things-by-themselves personally, neither as formal causes *who* are noetically exemplary nor as efficient causes *who* are practically exemplary. That is why, as Kant would have it, we have to look for this kind of prime causality within ourselves as persons.

Kant does this by connecting his notion of the thing-by-itself with the intelligent being he calls the "noumenon" (from the Greek *nous,* meaning "intelligence").[40] The *noumenon* is a thing-by-itself in a negative sense insofar as "it is not an object of our sensible intuition."[41] As we have seen, this is what we humans cannot employ in any way, whether to use it pragmatically to make artificial things or to use it noetically for the application of our categories. Yet it has an even more important positive meaning insofar as it is apprehended by "a special mode in intuition [*Anschauungsart*], namely, the intellectual."[42] Now this is not so much how we know ourselves as *noumena;* rather, it is much more how we *act* – indeed, how we ought to act – *noumenally* in order *to be* considered things-by-*ourselves*. And, of course, for Kant (unlike Plato, Aristotle, *et alia*), we humans are the only such intelligent beings we have any knowledge of. Kant makes this point by arguing that the moral law(s) within us are "not mere logical rules, but ... also concern our existence – ground for regarding ourselves as legislating [*gesetzgebend*] completely *a priori* in regard to our own existence [*Daseins*], and determining this existence ... a spontaneity through which our reality [*Wirklichkeit*] would be determinable [*bestimmbar*]."[43] And it is "related, in respect of a certain inner faculty [*Vermögens*], to a non-sensible intelligible world."[44]

Now, this "spontaneity" is not the idiosyncratic impulsiveness of various individuals. After all, through psychological introspection it is often discovered that a seemingly spontaneous impulse has, in fact, prior causes that motivated it (even though the emotionally "spontaneous" individual rarely had enough insight at the time of his or her "spontaneous" act to know this, let alone understand it). Thus a seemingly spontaneous act often turns out to be behaviour previously conditioned by sensible factors outside the control of the person so acting – or, in fact, outside the control of the person reactively behaving.

Kant is not advocating, however, anything like the contemplation that imitates the heavenly intelligences by thinking of God as the *summum bonum*, the unsurpassable finality or *telos*.[45] Instead, Kant has human noumena acting as prime efficient causes, who actually effect something in the phenomenal world. So he writes: "When it [reason] considers nature practically, it similarly presupposes its own causality [*Urgrundes*] as unconditioned [*unbedingten*] ... , i.e., its own freedom, since it is conscious of its [own] moral command [*Gebots*]."[46] As such, noumena are not formally intending a higher reality above themselves (which Kant believes is noetically impossible anyway). Noumena are acting for the sake of nothing else; thus their goals are their own subsequent projects or ideals rather than being prior ends already there, discovered by speculative reason, towards which rational beings aspire (as they do for Plato, Aristotle, *et alia*). Noumena make laws for, that is, they govern, events in the phenomenal world. These laws, unlike "laws of nature" or even logical rules, do not state what *must be* if the phenomena experienced as nature or the propositions proposed by logic are to be consistently taken for what they are and not as something else. Instead, these laws are true prescriptions made to intelligent moral subjects by themselves, commanding one another how to *interact* with each other in the world. They concern what-is-to-be-done by us. These acts or interactions to-be-done are what ought to be done by us to each other in the phenomenal world, that is, in the world of plural intelligent bodies who we ourselves are. Noumena qua noumena, then, function autonomously.

Unlike the instrumentalist *homo faber* whom we examined before, *homo noumenon* is not using the natural entities we can see in order to turn them into things for his or her bodily use, for this would make *homo faber* dependent on these natural entities. Qua *homo faber,* a person is hardly functioning as a first cause. Hence, noumenal humans ought not seek to dominate nature. Rather, they should use only a finite amount of natural entities and artificial things (made from natural entities) as means for the sake of the interpersonal world we constitute by our prescription and practise of moral law among ourselves. And since we need only a limited amount of natural resources, this moral approach to nature is quite ready to respect things-by-themselves that are not themselves noumena. Furthermore, our use of nature is not for the sake of enhancing our power over our fellow creatures as much as it is for the sake of supplying our interpersonal community in the world with what is needed (rather than desired) for that public life to be sustainable here. We should always limit our attention to the fulfilment of these needs in order to devote as much time and effort as possible to our vastly more important moral interactions. The natural world is our environment wherein we live; it is not our possession to do with as we please.

Having to devote all our attention to the fulfilment of these bodily needs makes our life on earth subhuman, while turning the fulfilment of these bodily needs into our desire for limitless power over nature often leads to attempts to enslave (literally or figuratively) those of our fellow humans who, if treated as ends-by-themselves, would limit thereby this endless desire for dominance. It is the attempt to make some powerful humans more and more powerful, while many less powerful humans become more and more reduced to virtual subhuman status. Attempts to dominate nature and attempts to dominate fellow humans are two sides of the same coin. That is because our relation to nature is always, whether directly or indirectly, mediated by our interhuman relationships.

By constituting humans as essentially moral beings, Kant has correlated intellect and will in a decidedly new way. We can appreciate this better when we look at the deficiencies of the exercise of intellect without will, and the deficiencies of the exercise of will without intellect.

The exercise of intellect without will is what the contemplative life (*bios theōretikos*) is all about. For efficient causation seems to be the exercise of will in order to bring about something outside of itself, something that has not been in the world before this exercise of will. Now, an efficient cause wilfully *effects* something outside itself, whether that be a new *thing* it has made (*poiēsis*) or a new *act* it has done (*praxis*).[47]

In both cases, there is transitive activity in the world directed to something *other* here. However, this is precisely why those exercising intellect for intellect's sake, that is, doing classical metaphysics, do not want to be efficient causes of that kind. Instead, they desire to escape from the world and to be with what truly transcends the world with all its intellectually disappointing involvements. Thus their intellection, their thinking per se, is not transitive activity; rather, it is intransitive informing oneself by looking to God as the End-of-all-ends, the *summum bonum*, and thereby identifying with God's thinking Godself. Nevertheless, as we have seen, without a foundational launching pad in teleological natural science (which it has long lost), Kant considers this kind of thinking to be an exercise in metaphysical futility, which his *Critique of Pure Reason* is designed to shut down once and for all. Thus the world that pure intellects have sought to escape noetically, this world has had its metaphysical escape hatch meticulously closed by Kant.

Whereas the exercise of intellect without will is essentially ineffective in the natural world, which it cannot escape after all, the exercise of will without intellect is essentially subordinate to the natural world altogether. That is because will without intellect is only desire.[48] Whether desire is for worldly pleasure or for worldly power, in the end desire is utterly dependent on what it needs *from* the very world it takes to be grist for its mill. This might be why when those who have been so dependent on the world for their pleasure or for their power begin to lose their hedonistic or imperial capacity, they desire death, which is the way the natural world reclaims them. "Dust you are and to dust you shall return" (Genesis 3:19), which is what God tells the first humans, Adam and Eve, who have been seduced by promises of worldly pleasure and worldly power by the Serpent in the Garden of Eden. This is pleasure and power for whose exercise they have been deceived by the Serpent into believing they will not be answerable to God for how they have used these capacities. For the Serpent says: "You will be like God ... the tree is good [*tov*] for food, and it is a delight [*ta'avah-hu*] for the eyes, for the tree is desirable [*nehmad*] to make one smart [*le-haskil*]" (Genesis 3:5–6).

Autonomy in Interhuman Relations

Kant's idea of autonomy overcomes these respective deficiencies of either intellect or will when functioning separately.

> When we think of ourselves as free, we transfer ourselves into the intelligible world as members [*Glieder*] and recognize the autonomy of the

> will together with its consequence [*Folge*] – morality ... A rational being counts himself qua intelligence, as belonging to the intelligible world, and solely qua efficient cause [*Wirkender Ursache*] belonging to the intelligible world does he give to his causality the name of "will." On the other side, however, he is conscious of himself as also part of the sensible world, where his actions [*Handlungen*] are encountered as mere appearances [*Erscheinungen*] of this causality.[49]

Here we see how the will commands intelligently and how the intellect operates effectively: both of them being in the world and for the world, but not of the world. One might compare this to the correlation of speech and grammar in language. Ungrammatical speech has no intelligible form. Grammatical rules, on the other hand, have no real subject matter. Or, to paraphrase Kant himself: Just as percepts without concepts are blind, so is speech without grammar, that is, without logical order, unintelligible.[50] And just as concepts without percepts are empty, so is grammar without vocabulary empty. Grammar like morality is prescriptive, that is, it says that when you are to speak intelligently, this is the way you ought to do so. (I say "when" rather than "if" inasmuch as intelligible speech is required of all those who act as persons along with other persons in the world; it is not an option one can take or leave without dire psychic consequences.) Morality says that when you are to act intelligently, this is the way you ought to do so. Moreover, the intelligible criteria that govern intelligent speech and that govern intelligent action are universal: they apply in any and every situation where either speech or action is called for.

At this point in our enquiry, it is important to distinguish Kant's notion of autonomy from modern liberal notions of autonomy, which is what most people (even highly educated intellectuals) today actually mean when they use the term "autonomy."[51] For many liberals, rational persons in a democracy have the right to autonomously determine for themselves (understanding "autonomy" as *nomos autou* in Greek, literally, "his law") whatever individual goods or goals they choose by themselves for themselves. These "goods" could be anything from engaging in metaphysical reflection to playing tennis. In return for society's acceptance of the duty to protect individual citizens' right to pursue their individual goals from being violated by others (given that these individuals do not violate the similar rights of others by their pursuit of their own goals), these citizens are duty bound to obey the laws of the polity. John Stuart Mill stated it most clearly and most influentially: "The only part of the conduct of any one, for which he is answerable to society, is that which concerns others. In the part of which merely concerns himself, his independence is, of right absolute. Over himself ... the individual is sovereign."[52]

Clearly, the exercise of these individual rights is the means to particular ends. Hence, like their ends themselves, they are neither universal nor ultimate. They have no cosmic significance. The benign pursuit of these goals is unlike the exercise of Kantian autonomy in that the liberal notion of autonomy is not ontologically grounded. Thus one can always ask *why* these goods are chosen at all. Lacking ontological grounding, the pursuit of any such good (even if publicly sanctioned) could only be a capricious pursuit of one's own taste. In fact, Kant might well have called such "autonomy" *heteronomy*, since what is done for an end other (*heteros* in Greek) than itself could not be called true autonomy *ipso facto*.[53]

Now liberal notions of autonomy at times do pose a political threat to theology, that is, when its proponents insist (especially when they have political power) that the norms of a liberal democratic society must be self-justifying, and that no metaphysically speculated reasons for their authority may be allowed in public discourse.[54] Indeed, such a political threat (which itself is quite illiberal) would also bar true Kantians from public discourse, having as they do a decidedly metaphysical notion of autonomy. True Kantians would be as much barred from that discourse as have been Jewish, Christian, and Islamic natural law theorists, whose natural law theories are ontologically grounded.

Kant's metaphysical notion of autonomy, however, is philosophically much stronger than the anti-metaphysical (or a-metaphysical) liberal notion of autonomy. For Kant, autonomy is not the capacity of individual selves to choose goals or ends for themselves, thereby becoming a law unto themselves. Instead, Kant has a much more metaphysically exalted notion of autonomy. Autonomy is the idea of moral law itself (*nomos autos* in Greek), which is to govern the will of all rational persons to legislate truly universal norms for themselves and for all those naturally like themselves. Those norms are ultimate insofar as they require no further justification. As such, they cannot be what Aristotle called "instrumental ends."[55] Thus, when Kant speaks of the only absolute good being a "good will," he doesn't mean that a morally legislating will must legislate according to some external criterion (as Plato would have it).[56] Instead, what Kant means is that only a truly moral will would and could legislate what is clearly and finally good for all rational beings. The good is not, therefore, the will's external reason for whose sake it wills what it has willed to be. Rather, what has been willed is the only end product or project (*Absicht*) or ideal that such an absolutely good will could project. And since Kant has substituted the will of the autonomous lawgiver for the will of the Creator God of the Bible (as we shall see very soon), perhaps he had in mind the Bible's first use of the term "good" (*tov*): "And God saw it is good" (Genesis 1:4). One could interpret this to mean that God's intention is beneficial in the creation of both the matter and the form or structure of the universe. Thus God recognizes it to be *well* willed and well made.[57]

The Categorical Imperative: First Formulation

Moral maxims, for Kant, are categorical imperatives. They have universal application because they are what any and every intelligent moral person must will, that is, any person who wants to act according to universal criteria. These criteria are not at all contingent on somebody's particular background or goals. The end or *telos* of any and every such person is to will what is universally valid, and then to choose to do so in any particular situation they might find themselves in. The categorical imperative has three formulations. The first and most famous of them is expressed by Kant as follows:

> The universality [*Allgemeinheit*] of the law governing the production of effects constitutes what is properly called nature in its most general sense (nature as regards its form) – That is, the existence of things [*Dasein der Dinge*] so far as determined [*bestimmt*] by universal laws ... Act as if the maxim of your action were to become through your will a universal law of nature [*Naturgesetz*].[58]

Now, many commentators on Kant forget that he is explicitly engaged in metaphysical speculation in the *Groundwork of the Metaphysic of Morals*; thus they deal with the criterion of the universalizability of moral law as if it were a logical problem alone. So, when Kant takes as an example the universal prohibition of knowingly making false promise to repay a loan, only the logical problem is invoked, namely, if everyone were to do this "no one would believe he was being promised anything," and thus the whole institution of borrowing would "necessarily contradict itself."[59] In other words, if everyone could regard himself or herself as an exception to a moral law, its categorical universality would thereby become meaningless.

However, were this all there is to Kant's first formulation of the categorical imperative, it could be argued that most liars fully recognize that what they are justifying to themselves as an exception to the universal law is rare. If they did this regularly, no one would ever lend them or anyone else anything. Moreover, knowing full well that their own exceptional action is rare, these liars are also convinced that their rare, exceptional action will not destroy the institution of borrowing and lending. In fact, liars of this type are not attacking the law itself, which they know must be generally kept if they are to profit from their exceptional action, and they rationalize this to themselves accordingly. These people are criminals, to be sure, but they are not antinomians. They most often accept the evidently rational prohibition of borrowing without the intention to pay back what they have borrowed, for they look upon this prohibition as being *generally* applicable. Universal lawgiving is not their concern.

Ontological and not just logical universalizability, which is Kant's deeper concern here, is better appreciated when we understand what Kant means by "law of nature." How is a "law of nature" (*lex naturae*) different from what had for a long time earlier been called "natural law" (*lex naturalis*)?[60] It is important to make this differentiation explicit, as many people confuse the two terms and assume that they are conceptually identical.

When Kant speaks of a "universal law of nature" in this first formulation of the categorical imperative, he is not using the term "law" literally. Literally, a "law" is an interpersonal *commandment*: *A* commands *B* to do *C* in relation to *D*. The act so commanded, *C*, constitutes the active interrelation of *B* and *D*. Thus *A* is the source or the authority of the commandment, while *B* is the subject and *D* is the object of the commandment. So, for example, my mother tells me to share my toys with my sister. Moreover, just as *A* is free to either command or not command *B* (or anybody else), so is *B* free to either obey or disobey *A*'s commandment. (If the decision to obey or disobey the command were without any consequences, that is, it could be done with impunity, that would make the "command" into a counsel or advice, but not a *law* in any sense of the term.) A body of law is a publicly enforceable system of morality.[61]

Now, if we consider this type of commandment, which is what *law* literally means, to be what could be expected of any and every human person, that is, to be either its subject or its object, then this body of norms is *universal* moral law. Historically, universal moral law has been called "natural law" (*lex naturalis*). That is because it is endemic to or *natural* for humans to look upon themselves as the subjects and the objects of moral law. Humans *need* to do so, for they cannot conceive of their interactions with other humans except in moral terms. None of us could speak to others with whom we live in the world without invoking the verb "ought" or one of its many synonyms. Even the most immoral persons have to inevitably justify their actions (whether to others publicly or just to themselves privately).

Truly moral norms function universally, that is, they must apply to all those who could be their subjects and their objects, or even only their objects (like infants or those grossly physically or mentally handicapped). Thus moral law is universal because it applies to all humans because of their natural need for it.

Furthermore, for theology, natural law commandments only have ontological validity when their prime source or ultimate authority is the God who specially creates all humans to be rational law-abiding beings. Truly rational, law-abiding humans can only accept in good faith laws they know or at least believe to be norms that protect and enhance their status as intelligent and free beings in the world. This theological affirmation gives natural law not only universal or worldly significance, but also cosmic significance. However, "nature" here is not the same as *Nature* for Plato, Aristotle, and the Stoics, since it does not refer to some all-encompassing whole or cosmic order into which both human action and even divine action are to be included and thus be subordinate.[62] The "nature" in *natural* law only refers to *human nature*, by which humans are related to God and to each other very differently from the way non-humans are related to God and to each other.

A "law of nature" (*lex naturae*), conversely, is not a commandment that constitutes an interpersonal relationship. Here the "law" has neither a personal subject nor a personal object. Rather, a law of nature qua law (however figuratively or connotatively the term is now being used) constitutes a relation of a personal creator (indeed, an impersonal "creator" would be an oxymoron) and impersonal creatures or things. Unlike the subject of a natural law–governed relationship, the subject of a law of nature has nothing to say about how *it* is to be or behave. That is because a created thing, unlike a created person, does not hear a commandment spoken to them by their Creator. This thing has no capacity to decide whether to respond positively/obediently or negatively/disobediently. Instead of being spoken *to*, the created thing is spoken *of* when commanded into existence as, for example, when at the onset of creation (*ma'aseh ber'esheet*, literally "the act of creation") God says: "Let there be light!" (Genesis 1:3). And if nature is universal, then it could only be commanded into existence by the Creator God of the universe. Only the Creator God could command anything *to be*. "By the word [*be-dvar*] of the Lord were the heavens made ... He spoke [*amar*] and it came to be; He commanded [*tsivah*] and it endured" (Psalms 33:6, 9).[63]

Any other "creator," however, like a sculptor or a composer or an author, can only create a particular world, one that draws upon universal matter and that cannot go beyond universal forms or structures. In other words, human creators or artists presuppose (and can thus never transcend) a universe already-there (*da-sein* in German), from which they must originally draw their materials and according to whose forms they must ultimately make their works or products conform. "What [*mah*] was will be ... there is nothing new under the sun ... it has already been there [*kvar*] forever" (Ecclesiastes 1:9–10). Conversely, only the Creator God could create without any such presuppositions, that is, only this God creates, only this God could create, "out of nothing" (*ex nihilo*), which means without anything real presupposed. For this God alone, there is nothing already-there.

The classical philosophers, on the other hand, did not speak of "laws of nature," because they did not affirm the Creator God who, as we have seen, is the only one who could so prescribe anything to be. As such, the natural universe, for them, is already-there and will always be-there. This cosmos is transcended by no one and could not be transcended by anyone, human or even divine .[64] That is because the natural universe or cosmos is not-made. And (as we saw in the previous two chapters) for Plato, Aristotle, and the Stoics, what is not-made is ontologically prior to what-is-made. All that is made, including laws, is made (and, possibly, unmade) therein; and the same is true of all makers, whether human or divine. That is why Aristotle speaks about a "natural order" (*taxis*) rather than a "law of nature."[65] Moreover, this natural order does not require for its full intelligibility an Orderer who transcends the order He has made inasmuch as this order is eternal, hence not-made. Thus all orderers (even like Plato's Demiurge) require a natural order already-there *within* which they act in an orderly and ordering way.

Furthermore, for the classical philosophers, moral law governing interhuman relations is human-made law or *nomos*. To be sure, good law is to be made according to criteria that are natural (*kata physin* in Greek) or according to cosmic justice (*dikē*). All that notwithstanding, even when it was assumed that these laws (*nomoi*) were made by a god, that god was hardly considered to be the unique and absolute Creator of the universe. So, even the difference between human and divine lawgivers was a rather small difference of degree rather than being like the great difference in kind that obtains between the biblical Creator God and His creatures – even God's human creatures created in God's own image.

Furthermore, whereas the Greek philosophers constituted an ontology or natural theology that transcends ethics, Kant thought he had demolished that kind of ontology altogether. That notwithstanding, Kant was not anti-metaphysical or even a-metaphysical, as many Kantians today would have us believe. But instead of constituting his ontology on the back of natural science (as did Aristotle especially), Kant constituted his ontology (which he called "metaphysics") on the back of ethics. (The reason for that move, it seems, is that a truly coherent ontology needs a teleological discipline to be placed upon; and this requirement could still be fulfilled by traditional ethics, but not by the already discredited teleological natural science of Aristotle especially.) That is why, no doubt, Kant called his most important ethical work "*Metaphysics* of Morals." And since ethics now has a stronger, more immediate ontological foundation for Kant than it does for Aristotle, Kant can invest ethics with greater rigour than Aristotle could ever invest it with. So, in this view of the priority of ethics, which is much closer to the Bible than it is to the *Nicomachean Ethics*, Kant comes much closer to Jerusalem than he does to Athens. (Even theorizing about God is theorizing about divine praxis.)[66]

That being the case, why does Kant have to speak of "laws of nature" rather than the "natural order" (*sidrei ber'esheet* in Hebrew) on the one hand and human-made "laws" (*nomoi*) on the other hand?[67] It would seem that Kant did so, despite the problems this connotation of "laws" raises, because his ethics is an ethics of *universal moral law*, where those who issue commandments thereby create truly ethical acts having not only worldly but even cosmic significance. They are universally significant events, by which moral beings reveal to the world their practical rationality. It is at this level of truly wilfully active initiation that moral actors are most God-like. In fact, Kant speaks of moral imperatives as being "divine commandments" (*göttliche Gebote*).[68] Divine commands are what rational beings prescribe for themselves and all others like themselves *as if* they were the Creator God commanding or prescribing the universe into existence. That is, they are willing/acting divinely. Therefore, just as only God could create a universe *ex nihilo*, so rational moral lawgivers must think of themselves as having God-like creative power when making universally valid prescriptions and thus creating and recreating a moral world for themselves and for all other persons like themselves. Nevertheless, these commandments are essentially different from the literal "commandments of God" (*Gebote Gottes*) that the Bible so frequently presents, inasmuch as Kant does not acknowledge divine revelation to be a real event that is directly experienced.

Commandments coming directly from God could only come through God's self-revelation, which Kant denies could be an authentic experience (rather than an illusion). "Divine commandments," though, come through or are discovered by ratiocination; they are not given through revelation.[69]

Now, since humans no longer look upon themselves and their ethically significant actions to be *within* or *of* larger, more intelligent Nature to whose order they are to be subservient, humans can now only look to the natural order by analogy, comparing it to their own moral ordering of their interpersonal world. It is here that humans seem to be most creative. So, when Kant speaks of his awe before "the starry skies above and the moral law within," he is talking about two parallel worlds.[70] Nevertheless, while he (or any other rational being) could not constitute the moral world within the natural cosmos (whose apex is "the starry skies"), he can still think of the natural cosmos by analogy to the moral world that is constituted within himself as a rational being by his willing knowledge of moral law. That is why *law* in this primary interpersonal world is to be understood literally, while "law" in this analogous world is to be understood only figuratively.

One could even say that Kant has better correlated these two parallel worlds in his ethical or practical philosophy than he has correlated them in his speculative philosophy. In his speculative philosophy, he simply leaves as an unresolved antinomy the impasse between natural necessity and practical or moral freedom.[71] But from the perspective of his ethical philosophy, there is an element of freedom in both worlds. Thus the difference between the two worlds, when thought of from this perspective, becomes one of degree rather than one of kind. In the natural world, recognition of a lawgiver (however figuratively) means there is absolute freedom on the side of the creator of the law, whereas the creature-thing has no freedom to react or respond to its being created. But in the practical, human world, the created person does have the freedom to react or respond to the commandment that calls him or her into subjective personhood, which is that person's ethically constituted being. Here there is a personal relationship *between* Creator and creature, whereas in the natural world any connection between creator and creature is only an impersonal relation.

The Categorical Imperative: Second Formulation

Inasmuch as moral law is to govern the relationship of rational persons *with* one another, we now need to look at the second formulation of the categorical imperative that talks about how we are to treat other rational persons. Kant states: "Act in such a way that you always treat [*braucht*] humanity, whether in your own person or in the person of any other [*eines jeden andern*], never simply as a means, but always at the same time [*zugleich*] as an end [*als Zweck*]."[72] And that is because "[r]ational beings [*vernünftige Wesen*] ... are called persons because their nature already marks [*ausgezeichnet*] them as ends in themselves [*Zwecke an sich selbst*] ... whose existence [*Dasein*] is in itself an end."[73]

We now need to ask three questions. (1) What does Kant mean by "humanity" or "humanness" (*Menschheit*)? (2) What does Kant mean by calling humanity an "end-in-itself" (*Zweck an sich selbst*)? (3) Where does a rational person begin this treatment of humanness as end-in-itself: with oneself or with other persons? We shall see that our previous discussion about what law means for Kant leads us to our first question here about what humanness means for him. That in turn leads us to our second question here about Kant's moral teleology; and that in turn leads us to our third question about the original object of our ultimate concern for humanness.

As for the first question, Kant speaks of there being "in humanity capacities [*Anlagen*] for greater perfection [*Vollkommenheit*] which form part of nature's purposes [*Zwecke*] for humanity in our person [*in unserem Subjekt*]."[74] That clearly implies that although we as morally creative beings create a moral world *de novo*, we still do not create our own nature. We intuit that our own being-created as rational or purposeful beings is itself the purposeful act of some will greater than our own. As such, our own purposeful activity in the world is not some cosmic accident. Therefore, it is our task (*Aufgabe* in German) to further develop and continually perfect in ourselves by ourselves our fundamental purpose or *raison d'être*. And like our existence itself, that purpose has been given to us; it is not our invention (as it is in liberal notions of autonomy). Certainly, that essential human purpose is our (not just "my") actively willing the universal idea of moral law into reality (*Wirklichkeit*) in whatever situation we as individual moral actors happen to find ourselves.

As for the second question, our engaging in this never-finished activity is what is done for its own sake. This is truly autonomous activity rather than the type of heteronomous activity that is a means to some other end or purpose. Heteronomy itself is either the law coming *from* an extraneous source, or a lawful act performed *for* an extraneous end. Thus it is the very extraneousness or otherness, whether it be of a source or a purpose, that negates true autonomy according to Kant's notion of autonomy. Whatever good effect an autonomous act has, that effect is a result of the act the law prescribes having been done. It is not, however, the ground or reason of the law.

As for the third question, Kant's very emphasis on autonomy implies moral self-sufficiency. First and foremost, autonomy involves an inner relation within human persons themselves. The autonomous decision to realize the idea of moral law in the world involves a person's intelligent self intelligently commanding his or her sensible self to actually do this in relation to another intelligent self. Moreover, the object of this morally willed act is to enhance my intelligent self and that of the other such selves with whom I interact. So, for example, my decision to study practical philosophy is part of the ongoing development of my moral intelligence. On the other hand, I decide to eat healthful food rather than merely tasty food because a healthy mind requires a healthy body (*mens sana in corpore sano*) to best carry out its decisions. Thus the mind or intelligent self is to use the body or sensible self rather than vice versa. Serving the intelligent self as an end-in-itself involves inner self-sufficiency. All this is surprisingly close to the type of virtue ethic that looks upon self-perfecting action itself as being the true *raison d'être* of human life. It is perfecting what is considered to be the highest in humans, and which then coordinates all lesser human activities in a way that contributes to this end-in-itself.[75]

Nevertheless, whereas for Aristotle that self-perfecting is epitomized by one's engagement in the theoretical life and the ability (albeit intermittently) to think along with God by oneself, for Kant that metaphysical goal is no longer possible (as we have seen). So instead, the inner logic of morality requires that I not look upon my inner relation with myself alone, but look upon those other persons, who are inevitably the objects of my public moral life, as analogues of myself as a moral being. To be sure, I am to begin with myself; but to be satisfied with this self-relationship is to make morality an exclusively private matter. Moral solipsism, though, is an oxymoron. Morality is inherently public. Inevitably, I have to correlate my moral duties with somebody else's rights or claims upon me in order to respond to their claims properly. Thus when I will a moral maxim, I must do so for myself and all others like myself simultaneously. In fact, Kant's notion of interpersonal relations comes quite close to a very common interpretation of the biblical commandment of neighbourly love: "You shall love your neighbour as yourself [*kamokha*]" (Leviticus 19:18). In that common interpretation, the commandment is saying: "As you love yourself, so shall you love your neighbour."[76] However, since Kant seems to regard "love" as being a feeling of pleasure or happiness rather than being properly moral action, his rendition of the biblical commandment would probably be: "As you respect yourself as a rational being, so you shall respect your fellow rational being." This is universalizable interpersonal action, because my duty to myself and to all others like me is what I can rightfully expect from others as their duty to themselves and to all others like themselves.[77]

The Categorical Imperative: Third Formulation

Kant's autonomous rational beings are also political beings. As such, they not only interact with one another on a one-to-one basis, but also interact even more so with one another collectively in a formal societal context. As both the creators and the subjects of moral law, humans need an organized society in which to systematically and consistently pursue that which is an end-in-itself, namely, the actualization of the idea of moral law among themselves. And since their creation of and adherence to moral law must be done autonomously, that is, of their own free will, so too must their creation of and adherence to a morally constituted society be done of their own free will. This kind of society must be the product of their collective autonomy. It is an association of like-minded individuals who create their own society and legislate for themselves from within it. So, whereas Kant's first formulation of the categorical imperative deals with a rational person's relationship with himself or herself, and Kant's second formulation deals with the relationship of individual persons one-to-another, his third and final formulation deals with the political relationship of rational beings. The three formulations follow one from the other. Thus Kant writes:

> For rational beings all stand under the law that each of them should treat [*behandeln*] himself and all others, never merely as a means, but always and at the same time as an end-in-itself. But by so doing there arises a systematic union [*Verbindung*] of rational beings under common [*gemeinschaftlichen*] objective laws – that is, a realm [*ein Reich*]. Since these laws are directed precisely to the relationship [*Beziehung*] of such beings ... this realm can be called a realm of ends [*Reich der Zwecke*] (which is admittedly an ideal).[78]

Although Kant seems to be employing the idea of the social contract in his constitution of the ideal realm of ends, his understanding of it is very different from how liberals (of his time and ours) have understood it. In fact, his difference with liberals on the meaning of the social contract follows from his difference with them on the meaning of autonomy.

For liberals, my autonomy as an individual is to pursue whatever goal or good I have chosen for myself, and for no other reason than that it is what I happen to like. My autonomy gains political significance when I exercise my right against or claim on others not to interfere in whatever pursuit is mine. Indeed, my reason for entering society is so that society through its institutions will collectively take upon itself the public duty to, minimally, protect that individual or private right, and, maximally, to aid me in attaining my own good. That social duty, especially the minimal one of non-interference, is then mandated by the society for all its members. It is assumed that all the freely consenting members of this contractually constituted society accept this political duty of the protection of others in return for the duty of others to protect them. Nevertheless, since my pursuit of my own individual good or "happiness" (*Glückseligkeit*) is my own business – and, at most, that of my small circle of family and friends – my allegiance to the larger society is not my choice of something I consider to be good in and of itself, thus to be chosen for its own sake. As such, I do not desire to be a member of a liberal society – that is, a society primarily dedicated to my "pursuit of happiness" (in the words of Thomas Jefferson in the United States Declaration of Independence); instead, it is what I have to do in order to avoid the kind of political chaos that would seriously jeopardize my liberty, even my life, as well as the pursuit of my own happiness. But this kind of society has no goal, no overriding good of its own. Surely, this is not what Kant would consider to be the *ideal* society, which all rational beings ought to be striving to build and maintain for its own sake. Indeed, liberal efforts to somehow or other move from the pursuit of "individual good" (*bonum sibi*) to the pursuit of public or "common good" (*bonum commune*) are rather unconvincing.[79]

Kant seems to have the liberal state in mind when he distinguishes what he calls a "juridico-civil state" (*Zustand*) from what he calls an "ethical community" (*gemeines Wesen*). Kant speaks of the members of a civil state, or what we today would probably call a "constitutional democracy," as being governed by "coercive laws" (*Zwanggesetze*).[80] Yet how can there be coercion in a society whose members have freely consented to the social contract (whether explicitly as in the case of new citizens, or tacitly as in the case of native born citizens) that both initiated and subsequently sustains this invented society? Freedom is surely the opposite of coercion.

The answer to this question lies in the way Kant characterizes the reason that rational persons would choose to be members of this kind of coercive polity and submit themselves to its legal authority. That is "because legislation proceeds from the principle of limiting [*einzuschränken*] the freedom of each [*jeden*] to the conditions under which it can coexist [*bestehen*] with the freedom of everyone else [*jedes andern*]."[81] In other words, rational persons enter into this kind of polity through a social contract because it both protects and enables or empowers their pursuit of their own good, which is in fact their exercise of their own innate freedom to pursue whatever good they so choose. This individual good is not freely pursued because their society has so entitled them to do so; rather, they are willing to submit to the coercive limitation of their prior freedom in order to protect it from the unlimited aggression of others pursuing their own goods at everyone else's expense, as it were. Of course, that danger could only be real when I and these others are pursuing the same limited goods, that is, when we are competing for them. That is usually the case when we are competing over the same limited economic resources. So, even though the object of our separate pursuits is basically the same, our respective pursuits of it are often at loggerheads. Hence we all freely become members of this essentially coercive society, not because we want to do so, but because we have to do so for the sake of our own long-term interests. In order for rights to have political reality, they must be enforced by a society duty-bound to do so. This society, then, is a necessity, but it is not desirable per se. As Kant himself points out, this kind of polity is only interested in "external right" (*äussern Rechts*).[82] It has no overriding public good. That is why it is in no way the *ideal* realm of ends. It is not the good for which rational persons strive. Furthermore, as a real society, it is "only a particular society," since there is no real (*wirklich* in German) universal society in the world. A universal society, then, could only be ideal, not real.[83]

Conversely, in Kant's realm of ends, the rational pursuit of the good is the projection of an ideal polity in which moral beings by their own efforts deserve the full happiness that could only come from their own efforts to instantiate in the real world the idea of moral law. That instantiating, projecting effort is what turns an idea into an ideal, an ideal that awaits as it were a final realization, as he says, "Since the duties of virtue concern the entire human race, the concept of an ethical community always refers to the ideal of a totality [*Ganzen*] of human beings, and in this it distinguishes itself from the concept of a political community."[84]

At this point, Kant most emphatically differentiates his notion of moral autonomy from the liberal one. For in a liberal state, moral autonomy is the liberty of the citizens, sometimes directly and other times indirectly, exercised through the authority delegated to elected officials, to make their own laws. These laws concern external realities, such as the economy or military matters, and thus govern outward actions and interactions. In fact, here the only concern with inner intent is when a crime has been committed against somebody's person, when we have to discern the exact state of mind of the person who committed the act so as to determine what is to be his or her appropriate punishment.

Nevertheless, despite this judicial concern with *how and why* the person indicted for a crime did what he or she did, there is no concern here with *how and why* those who do obey the law do so. As such, human legislators can only make positive laws for what is externally visible or (in Kant's terms) phenomenal, which is somewhat like the way human perceivers of visible percepts make laws that turn these percepts into intelligible experience.[85] However, human legislators cannot legislate for an ethical community, which persons as noumenal ends-by-themselves make up, because they do not need coercive laws. In this ideal society, there is or there ought to be no conflict of individual interests over visible goods. Everyone here is personally devoted to the common good, which is the constant instantiation of the idea of moral law into morally significant acts done for their own sake and not as the means to some other, ultimately private, goods or ends. Here the concern is with interpersonal acts rather than with impersonal things or possessions. And because of this great difference, Kant states:

> There must therefore be someone other than the people whom we declare the public lawgiver [*öffentlich gesetzgebend*] of an ethical community. But neither can ethical laws be thought of as proceeding originally [*ursprünglich*] merely from the will of this superior ... Hence an ethical community is conceivable only as a people under divine commands [*göttliche Gebote*], i.e., as a people of God, and indeed in accordance with the laws of virtue.[86]

The question now is: If these inwardly intended acts cannot be commanded by political officials who have public coercive power, why can't they be inner or innate commands that simply arise spontaneously from within each and every virtuous person who, at least ideally, is already participating in this realm-of-ends? Wouldn't this be true moral autonomy, subject to no external, heteronomous control? However, for Kant, there has to be more than that, for although that law is internalized, it is not the product of any individual will, nor is it the product of the collective will of the members of a real political society in the world, any more than it is the product of the coercive will of public officials in any real political society. Yet to say that this is literally *God-given* law would be to confuse God with coercive human lawgivers. Wouldn't this be the law *from* the transcendent God of Kant's childhood religion, who is a God who seems to rule coercively with threats of violence to those who disobey His commands? Moreover, this is a God who is bound by no higher idea, so that this God could just as easily will one kind of act or some other kind of act with impunity. Nevertheless, by emphasizing "divine commands" rather than "God's commands" (*Gebote Gottes*), Kant means that these commands are the instantiation of the immanent, higher-than-human (which could only be divine) idea of moral law that is actualized in the world through human practical reason.[87] The actual legislation, then, is done by rational humans acting as it were *in loco Dei.* Yet they are legislating in place of a God who could not do anything other than what the idea of moral law requires. And what the idea of moral law requires cannot be coerced, but only willingly accepted by those who, in effect, worship it. In fact, the only doxology or worshipful praise of what is higher than the merely human that Kant ever seems to have engaged in was not directed to God, but to "duty" (*Pflicht*), that is, to what moral law requires from those who revere and love it by identifying with it.[88]

Indeed, Kant goes so far as to say that humans actually "make their own God" (*sich einen Gott Machen*).[89] But isn't "god-making" idolatry? Kant's answer to this question is that the only god-making that is not idolatry is when humans think of *their* God as the Perfect One who is willing moral law. Humans do that in a variety of ways. Yet whereas religions are many, there is only one moral law. (In fact the multiplicity of religions compared to the univocity of divine/moral law is like the multiplicity of systems of positive law compared to the univocity of natural/moral law.) Idolatry, then, is god-making willy-nilly. It is our imagining a god who is a projection of our wish for a more powerful being to protect us from worldly harm and to fulfil our earthly desires.[90] Conversely, Kant's morally conceived God is the ideal sovereign of this ideal community (and which lies beyond our historical horizon).

Certainly, the kind of purely moral community envisioned by Kant (and many religious Kantians) is as yet an unrealized ideal. It is what Kant calls a "church," which when it is "not the object of a possible experience [*möglicher Erfahrung*] is called the church invisible [*unsichtbare Kirche*] (the idea of the union [*Vereinigung*] of all upright human beings under direct divine [*göttlichen*] world-governance)."[91] So it seems we are left with two disparate societies, one legal-political and the other ethical-religious. Nevertheless, Kant sees a society that stands midpoint as it were between them and, in fact, correlates the two poles. It is "the church visible," which is "the actual union of human beings into a whole that accords [*zusammenstimmt*] with this ideal." As such, it is "one that displays [*dargestellt*] the (moral) Kingdom of God [*Reich Gottes*] inasmuch as [it] can occur [*geschehen*] through human beings."[92] And although it seems that the visible church Kant has in mind would have to be Christian, and although Kant's Prussia had an officially Protestant state church, it is noteworthy that he is quite vague about what exactly is the Christian character of this visible, this-worldly church. (Later we shall deal with why Kant denies Judaism the status of being such an ethical community even in this visible world, and the attempt of liberal Jewish thinkers who are otherwise sympathetic to Kant's philosophy to strongly differ from him on this key point.) That is because the ethical religion that characterizes the visible ethical community is not essentially Christian (nor essentially that of any revealed religion). A Christian church is only a this-worldly manifestation of an essentially non-denominational ethical community. As for the invisible, other-worldly church that is the Kingdom of God, it does not seem to have any historical character at all. It is a pure ideal.

What the visible church does for its members in this world is to give them a foretaste of the invisible church as the ideal Kingdom of God. In that way, the visible church transcends the wholly this-worldly political community. Indeed, its most important difference from a political community is that all its members are there willingly, wanting to be parts of this society for its own sake, whereas the members of a political community (i.e., its citizens) are there because the polity serves their own private interests. For the latter, the public realm is the means to their self-interest, which is a private end or good. Because of that difference, the visible church needs to exercise far less coercion than its political counterpart has to exercise.

Now in terms of the faith the members of the visible church proclaim, they are beyond the control of the secular state (i.e., the state that looks to no particular revelation for its legitimacy). Thus the state oversteps the boundary that separates it from the church when it promises, let alone claims to be able to deliver, salvation. However, when it comes to this-worldly matters such as public policy, the visible church becomes, in effect, a merely private association within the larger public polity. As such, Kant admits that "when human beings command [*gebieten*] something that is evil in itself [*an sich böse*] (directly [*unmittelbar*] opposed to the ethical law), we may not, and ought not obey them. But, conversely, if an alleged divine [*gehaltenes göttliches*] statutory law is opposed to a positive civil law not in itself immoral, there is then cause [*Grund*] to consider the alleged divine law as spurious, for it contradicts a clear duty."[93] But when discussing the role of churches in a civil state or "political community," Kant shows his hand as to where the real moral authority in any civil state lies when he speaks of the state having "a negative right to prevent [*abzuhalten*] ... an influence on the visible political commonwealth [*gemeine Wesen*] that might be prejudicial to public peace [*öffentliche Ruhe*]. Its right [*Recht*] is therefore that of policing [i.e., a religious policy] that endangers civil harmony [*bürgerliche Eintracht*]."[94]

This type of subordination of religious law to moral law, and even to civil law, impacted upon liberal Judaism.[95] This subordination goes back to Kant's Jewish contemporary (and correspondent) Moses Mendelssohn.[96] In fact, it goes even farther back to the seventeenth-century Jewish heretic Baruch Spinoza. Prior to Spinoza, both for Jews and for Christians, even moral law was required to be at least consistent with religious law. This was always the case in those pre-modern societies that looked to institutions constituted according to religious law (like the Jewish *qehillot* and the Christian Church) for their political legitimization. But Spinoza, more than a century before Kant, fundamentally reconfigured what we now call "the church-state relation": Now religions were to become either "civil religions," that is, departments of the secular state that are to reflect official public policy, or they were to be private associations ("churches" or "congregations") that did not claim any original moral authority for themselves.[97] This attitude is still prevalent among many liberal Jews (whether religiously liberal or only politically liberal), who only invoke the Jewish tradition when it provides precedents for the type of liberal regime they identify with.

As we shall soon see, however, a more philosophically cogent constitution of the relation of religion and morality requires a stronger ontological grounding of morality (whether public or private) than Kant provides. Without that stronger ontological grounding, religious people will either uncritically accept the role Kant has envisioned for their religious community (i.e., in his terms, their "visible church") with only minor adjustments, or they will reject Kant's influence altogether and very much underestimate his most powerful thinking on this and many other related issues, and the challenge it presents to theologically perceptive Jews.

Jewish Reactions to the First Formulation of the Categorical Imperative

Because of the enormous influence of Kant's philosophy, especially his ethical philosophy that pertains to interhuman relations, the previous section on his ethical philosophy had to be quite lengthy. Only by such a careful reading of Kant can we appreciate how his powerful philosophy so strongly influenced modern Jewish thinkers (and then those Jews whom they have influenced in turn). Only then can we judge whether that influence needs to be upheld or critiqued (though certainly not ignored). And even though Kant's influence on Christian thinkers was as strong as it was on Jewish thinkers, I shall confine my attention to Kant's influence on the thinkers from the Jewish tradition, the tradition that is theirs and mine. The best way to proceed in this examination is to return to Kant's three formulations of the categorical imperative to see how some Jewish thinkers have reacted to them, and then consider what I think ought to be our reaction to them from a traditional Jewish perspective.

In his first formulation of the categorical imperative, Kant speaks of the type of autonomy that can legislate *universally*. Truly moral norms are universal, and they are *commandments* (i.e., the *nomos* in "auto*nomy*"). However, if legislation as the making of laws is essentially *commanding*, one could well argue that Kantian autonomy does not issue commandments in the strict sense of the term. That is because "command" (*bieten* in German; *metsaveh* in Hebrew) is a transitive verb, requiring a giver of the command and a receiver of the command. One does not command himself or herself, as "command" is not a reflexive verb. If morally valid commandments are those whereby the receivers of the commandments have freely acknowledged the right of the person who has so commanded them, then commandments are by definition *heteronomous*.[98] When persons exercising their right to command are also taken to be benevolent, then the commandment is not only dutifully received, but is also accepted as good for those to whom it has been given. "To keep the commandments of the Lord and His statutes, which I command you this day, for they are good for you [*tov lakh*]" (Deuteronomy 10:13).[99]

For Kant, though, coming as he did from such a biblically charged background (i.e., from the Protestant pietism of his childhood), autonomy is truly normative because it is the exercise of an original, not a delegated, right to command. Moreover, it is not derived either from the will of any individual person or from the collective will of the state (whether the will of the state is considered original or whether its power and authority is delegated to it by its citizens). But to say that "autonomy" means "the commandment commands itself" is absurd, since "commanding" is an act, and acts are the deeds of *actors*; hence commandments are commanded by someone else, and by someone else *willingly*.[100] Commandments do not, indeed they cannot, command themselves. So, perhaps one could say that the *autos* in "*auto*nomy" means "the commandment *itself*" (*autos* in Greek like *an sich* in German). That is, the commandment (the *nomos* here) is not commanded for the sake of something else; it is not a means to some other non-normative end. Instead, the commandment is justified by our recognizing *who* willed/commanded it; and also our recognizing that the lawgiver's intention or reason is to benefit those who have been so commanded.[101]

Furthermore, since God's will is the only will that could will anything absolutely, and it is the only will that could will universal norms as God is the only Creator who could possibly will the universe and all of its categories (i.e., universals) into being, why then does Kant refuse to attribute this original lawgiving power and authority to God? Why does Kant assiduously avoid invoking "God's commandments" (*Gebote Gottes*), yet persist in invoking "divine commandments" (*göttliche Gebote*)? Surely, we need to ask why many modern Jewish thinkers have basically agreed with Kant on this reluctant retention of God-talk. I shall argue that modern Jewish thinkers should be more critical of Kant on this very point.[102]

The primacy of the "commandments of God" (*mitsvot adonai* in Hebrew) seems to be the explicit meaning of the rabbinic dictum "Greater is the one who has been commanded [*metsuveh*] and does [what has been commanded] than the one who has not been commanded, yet does [what others have been commanded anyway]."[103] The difference between the former and the latter is the difference between an actual "duty" (*hovah*) and what is only "good counsel" (*etsah tovah*).[104] The difference here is that the fulfilment of a duty entails serious consequences: positive consequences when it has been fulfilled; negative consequences when it has been violated. A good counsel, on the other hand, entails no such consequences, either positive or negative. Because of this significant difference, a mediaeval glossator notes that the one who is not actually doing something he or she has been commanded to do, that is, who does it voluntarily, might very well have a "take it or leave it" attitude to the act he or she has not been directly commanded to do, while the one directly commanded will approach what he or she has been so commanded with much more anxiety.[105] It would seem that this anxiety is due to their awareness of *who* is directing the commandment to *them*, plus the fact that acts so directly commanded may not be avoided with impunity. Moreover, its fulfilment has both known and unknown consequences.[106]

Let us now look at how the most important, influential, and profound Jewish Kantian, the German-Jewish philosopher Hermann Cohen (1842–1918), reinterprets "God's commandments" along Kantian lines, namely, that they be seen as "divine commandments." About the rabbinic dictum quoted above he queries: "Apparently, through the command the act loses its autonomy and its origin [*Ursprung*] is put in God's command."[107] Now, Cohen seems to be interpreting Kant's insistence that assigning the source of moral law to God's will might only be a kind of negation, that is, moral law is *not* from what Cohen calls "any egotistical reinterpretation of the old rabbinic dictum." But he then gives the rabbinic dictum a clearly positive meaning, stating that "the command comes from God. He is the unique good [*das einzige Gut*]. His command is therefore the command of goodness [*das Gebot der Güte*]." Moreover, "God's command [*das Gebot Gottes*] is the religious expression that ... must be equivalent to the principle [*Grundgesetze*] of autonomy." He then speaks of the change of "the moral law [*Sittengesetz*] into duty [*Pflicht*], which is completed in religion by transforming [*Verwandlung*] moral law into God's command."[108]

What we see here is that Cohen has followed Kant's Platonism, which Kant himself insisted is valid only in the field of praxis, but not in the field of theoretical or speculative knowledge.[109] This practical Platonism comes out as early as the *Euthyphro*, where it is taught that "the holy is loved by the gods because it is holy; it is not holy because it is loved."[110] Moreover, what is holy is part of what is right or just (*tou dikaiou*).[111] Now, for Plato, what is right is the criterion of making laws that apply that criterion to the human world beneath it; and it is the end that human-made laws are enacted to be the means thereto. In other words, what is right is both the formal cause of lawgiving and the end lawgiving ultimately intends to reach. This intelligent lawgiving can only be done by those who are wise enough to understand how what is right both guides and goads them by its inspiring intelligibility. First and foremost for Plato, those who understand this are the gods, and then come the philosophers who in their understanding imitate the gods. (Thus the difference between the gods and the philosophers is one of degree rather than one of kind.) Later, in the *Republic*, in his drive to know what justice (*dikaiosynē*) is, Plato identifies the highest form as "the Good." Thus *the Good per se* or *Goodness itself* is the ultimate reality that determines whether any law is right or good by its participation in this ultimate reality.[112] So, for Cohen, coming as he does from this Platonic tradition, the "command of goodness" is the command of the most excellent being, who looks up to *Goodness* as the ideal criterion for lawgiving.

There is, however, an important difference between a Platonic idea or form (*eidos*) and a Kantian *ideal*. Plato assumes that the idea of Goodness actually exists, and that is the criterion by which the creating god (Demiurge) made primal unintelligible chaos into the intelligible cosmos.[113] As such, philosophers attempting to use this model for the construction of an optimal ethical-political order in this human world are, in fact, attempting to order human nature according to cosmic Nature that is already there. In that sense, the philosophers are imitating the creating god. But Kant had long abandoned this notion of teleological Nature, that is, the Nature or cosmic order according to which teleological human ethical-political nature must conform. Unlike a Platonic idea, a Kantian ideal is not already there; instead, a Kantian ideal lies on the future horizon. Therefore, human lawgiving for the sake of this ideal is not the application of an eternal, prior criterion; instead, it is a future-oriented project in which the will of the lawgiver plays a more important role than that of the philosophical guardians of Plato's optimal "republic" (*politeia*). As such, for Kant, the wise lawgiver does not apply Goodness to the mundane affairs of a human society. What does not yet exist, what is not yet real, cannot be applied to anything; it can only be sought. All action, especially lawgiving, is directed *up towards* it, not *down from* it. Here, Cohen follows Kant's difference from Plato. All lawgiving is ideal projection of what is yet-to-be. But it is not the realization of a supremely intelligible foundation that is eternal.

Cohen reworks Kant's notion of "divine commandments" to mean the commands that religious people are convinced could only come from God, which could very well mean that they are superlative or superhuman, that is, "godly" efforts.[114] Nevertheless, God's commands are not good because God commanded them *ex nihilo* as it were; instead they are good because God has commanded them according to the criterion of ideal Goodness. Humans are to ever strive to attain this Goodness by ordering their lives with norms that become the real means to that ideal end. Thus human lawgivers can very much imitate God, or even assume that they have this "divine" wisdom themselves, to a lesser degree of course.[115] In other words, their aim is for what even God aims at, but that aim is not identical with God. Instead, that ideal aim transcends even Cohen's monotheistic God, just as it transcends the gods affirmed by Plato and Aristotle.

Following Kant who follows Plato, Cohen has taken sides in what has come to be known as the "Euthyphro Problem." For Jewish theologians (as well as for Christian and Muslim theologians), the problem might well be called the "Euthyphro Paradox," which can be stated as follows: If what is just is just because God wills it, then what is to stop God from changing His mind and arbitrarily willing something altogether different? But if so, does this not leave us with a totally capricious God, whom rational humans could hardly be expected to respect and willingly obey, let alone love? On the other hand, if God could only will that which is just already, then isn't God's will subsequent to *what* it has willed *for*? Isn't God's will, then, a means to a higher end? But if so, hasn't God's ultimacy, God's absoluteness that Scripture constantly reiterates, been denied? Isn't God now someone *whom* no one in a biblically based tradition could recognize as the God whose commandments they obey as categorical imperatives, and as the God whom they worship unconditionally?

Conversely, if God is not beholden to a standard other than and greater than Godself, then it seems God could will anything whatsoever, limitlessly as it were. As such, there is no basis for questioning God as to whether God has willed justly or rationally and thus could be imitated by rational persons (created in God's image) who choose to obey God, or whether God has willed unjustly or irrationally and thus could not be imitated by rational persons. In the case of this second option, rational persons could obey God only because they fear God's punishment of their disobedience.

This assumes, however, that all limits on one's will are external to and greater than it. As such, the validity of any choice depends on how that choice *corresponds to* what has limited it from outside and above it. But that is not the only kind of limitation. There is also self-limitation, which is limitation from within. And it is very much connected to the only autonomy that can be entertained by a biblically based theology. I think that understanding this autonomy provides a way out of the "Euthyphro Paradox." In the Jewish tradition, the kind of self-limitation persons can will for themselves is made morally possible (i.e., an option for choice) by the institution of the "oath" or "promise" (*shevu'ah*). Both God and humans make promises, yet there is an essential difference between human promises and God's promises. Let us look at valid human promises first. That will help us better understand the validity of God's promises by contrast.

Humans are able to obligate themselves personally to either do something or not do something by making a promise, that is, by taking an oath.[116] That promise has to have been made both voluntarily and publicly in order to be validly binding.[117] That seems to be "autonomy" in the sense that one is making a law for oneself or "ruling oneself" (like *autarkeia* in Greek).[118] But even this kind of autonomy has four significant, external, superior limits. One, no person may obligate himself or herself to do what the Torah has prohibited anybody from doing.[119] This first limitation is a legal limitation, that is, the oath may not contradict a law already there on the books, so to speak. That assumes one is a member of the law-abiding community, and that one can only exercise one's right to do anything therein when it does not contradict one's prior normative status.[120] Two, a person may be dispended from their oath by a court (*bet din*), if the judges (*dayyanim*) of the court can persuade the oath-taker standing before them that his or her oath was taken without proper recognition of the likely practical, detrimental consequences the promised obligation would entail.[121] The very capriciousness of an oath-taker/promise-maker, who ignores or is ignorant of the likely results of the oath he or she has taken, makes the oath an irrational, impetuous act. Such an oath should be annulled so that it does not cause bad, unintended effects for the oath-taker and for those who will inevitably be affected by this oath. The third limitation is a factual limitation. That is, one may not obligate oneself to do what one, or any normal person, cannot do.[122] And the fourth limitation is that one may not swear about the facticity of something that is too obvious to need affirmation at all.[123]

Unlike the autonomy of the human oath-taker, God's autonomy – here understood to be the capacity to make self-obligating promises – is unlimited. God's autonomy is not limited by a higher law, because to affirm a law higher than God is to contradict the ultimacy or absoluteness of God who is the foundation of all foundations.[124] And unlike humans who stand under the communal authority of a court, God would cease to be God were God to allow Godself to be submitted to a "higher" authority by any creature (i.e., no-God), no matter how exalted that creature happens to be.[125] (That is a direct corollary of the dogma that God is Creator *ex nihilo*, i.e., necessarily beholden to nothing above Him or below Him.) Now, one might easily conclude that the seemingly unrestrained status of God in His relationship with His chosen people makes the relationship a capricious, irrational one and, as such, it is not to be trusted or consistently relied on. Yet that assumes we can only trust those who have subordinated themselves to a criterion or standard not of their own making. But why can't we trust a person who has obligated himself to do something, and who makes that promise to those of us who will be affected by it? Moreover, that promise is not only made *to* us, but just as much *for* us. Indeed, it is not only made for us, but *for* God Himself insofar as God seems to have made this consistent promise to us and for us in order that it be the basis of the ongoing covenant (*ha-berit*) between God and the human community God has elected to have this ongoing covenantal relationship *with*.

Now, such a covenant made *to* us perpetually needs to be evidently rational (minimally, non-contradictory) in order to be intelligible and thus be taken seriously by the rational persons it is addressed *to*. Moreover, a covenant made *for* us needs to be evidently benevolent in order to be freely accepted by anybody but masochists. And a covenant made *with* us needs to have evidence that the One making it has related Himself to us, for us, and with us in our past experience. All this comes out in the very opening words of the Decalogue: "I am the Lord your God, who has taken you out of the land of Egypt, out of the house of bondage. There shall not be for you any other gods in My presence" (Exodus 20:2–3). The question concerns the relation between the first sentence and the second sentence. One could read the first sentence as God's telling the people Israel what He has just done for them so beneficently by freeing them from Egyptian slavery. The implication of this statement is that it is meant to evoke a grateful response from the Israelites. In other words, "This is what I have done *for* you, now this is what you ought to do *for* Me, namely, to obey Me unconditionally. And, first and foremost, you can't very well do that unconditionally if your allegiance to Me is shared with anyone else." So, along these lines, we could say that what God has done for us is to have redeemed us from slavery to some other god (i.e., Pharaoh who considered himself to be a god). It is obvious that the willingness of the Israelites to follow Moses, God's agent, out of Egypt indicates that they believed their lot in the world had been very much improved by God's benevolent redemption of them. In response to what God has done for us, we now actively keep God's commandments given *to* us; yet it would seem these commandments are also to be kept *for* God's sake. Keeping the commandments could be seen as a kind if *quid pro quo*, that is, God did this for Israel so that Israel would obey God in return. Having been willingly redeemed by God, Israel have now willingly obligated themselves to obey God.[126] Nevertheless, doesn't this strongly imply that God somehow or other needs our obedience similarly to the way we need God's redemption of us? And if that is so, then isn't the difference between God and Pharaoh only one of degree rather than one of kind? In other words, both God and Pharaoh seem to have a need to lord it over others and demand their obedience. But, being a more beneficent master, God deserves some measure of voluntary gratitude from His slaves, over and above the usual resentful obedience granted out of fear of punishment by a master. Pharaoh, on the other hand, not being at all beneficent to His slaves, does not deserve any such gratitude. Needless to say, though, giving God and Pharaoh generic commonality and only specific difference is theologically problematic.

However, there is another interpretation of the first two sentences of the Decalogue that is more theologically cogent (in my opinion). What if we interpret these two sentences as follows, by imagining God to be saying: "I have clearly benefitted you Israelites by redeeming you from Egyptian slavery. Yet that is a one-time event, even though you have been commanded to regularly celebrate it forever. But the commandments (*mitsvot*) I am now giving *to* you are also given *for* you, so that you might survive and flourish in the world you have been sent into. Therefore, by keeping these commandments, you are not the passive recipients of my gracious beneficence, you are now the active participants in that beneficence since that active participation can only be done *by* you yourselves. Moreover, in keeping these commandments, I promise to be *with* you insofar as they constitute the active covenantal relationship that is perpetual *between* us."[127]

The upshot of all of this is that God is to be trusted to command us *justly and beneficently* because God has acted for us justly and beneficently in the past. And that is also the reasonable basis for our hope that God will complete our redemption and that of the world with us in the messianic future-yet-to-come. The commandments are what we are to do in order to to keep our faith in God's beneficent justice or just beneficence in the meantime. Finally, this resolves (it seems to me) the "Euthyphro Paradox," at least for a biblically based theology. God's commands are not just because they correspond to some higher standard of justice, as Plato did (and Kant and Cohen accepted, *mutatis mutandis*) by turning the adjective "just" into the noun "justice." The noun "justice" now refers to an ontological reality by which willed actions (that is, commandments) are to be judged as to whether they participate in that reality and are thus deemed "just" by virtue of that participation, or whether these willed actions do not participate in that reality and are thus deemed "unjust." (Kant called that process of turning an adjective into a super-noun "hypostatization.")[128] Instead, from a biblically based theological perspective, God commands *justly*, that is, consistently and benevolently. Here "justice" functions as the adverb "justly" that modifies the verb "command" internally, so that the One who commanded the commandment is only answerable to Himself, and then to those whom He has promised to deal with justly and benevolently.

The key metaphysical point here is that, not being limited or constrained by any external reality, God can do whatever God chooses to do or not do. All that notwithstanding, God does restrain Godself by His promise to deal justly and benevolently with the world. This is God's choice to abide by God's own commitment to be faithful to us. That is because without this rational restraint, a consistent normative relation to the world, especially a consistent sustainable covenant with the people who is capable of being and willing to be in this covenant with God, all that would be practically impossible.[129] Only a rational and benevolent entrance into the world by God could elicit a proportionately rational and willing response from those called into the covenantal relationship with God. Therefore, if God desires this kind of relationship with His people, then God has to rule them (and everybody else) justly with just and righteous commandments.

This comes out when God consults Abraham about God's proposed judgment of the cities of Sodom and Gomorrah as to whether it is evidently just or not. This is because God assumes that Abraham already knows what God's internally imposed standard of justice is.[130] That being the case, Abraham's response to God, which God Himself has invited Abraham to make, is not passive intellectual acceptance, but active imitation. Thus God asserts: "For I know him, that he will command his children and his household after him, that they will keep the way of the Lord to practice righteousness and justice [*tsedaqah u-mishpat*]" (Genesis 18:19). So, when Abraham boldly asks God: "Will the judge of all the earth not do justice [*mishpat*]?!" (Genesis 18:25), he is holding God up to God's own self-imposed standard, not to some higher, eternal justice according to which even God is to be judged.[131] Thus when the people Israel, who are Abraham's children, question God – as they and their prophets do often and with impunity – they do so by virtue of God's self-imposed rational criteria. These internal criteria are made for the sake of God's choice to relate Godself to external creation. However, since God is not totally correlated with creation, but has a totally independent life apart from creation, there is no point in asserting internal restraint except when we are discussing external relations that seem to presuppose God's internal restraint.[132] This is contrary to Hermann Cohen, who assumes God qua "Being" and creation qua "Becoming" are correlated. That is, it cannot even be thought that God has a life of God's own, one that is not correlated with the created world. Yet that compromises God's transcendence inasmuch as God and creation seem to be totally interrelated and interdependent.[133]

This self-restraint is not because God *has* to have this covenantal relationship with anyone else. Rather, it is because this is the only cogent way for the covenantal relationship to be conducted at all. But unlike all of God's creatures (no matter how exalted they might be compared to other creatures of God), God could have just as easily have chosen not to have any such relationship with them, or any relationship at all with anyone or anything that is not-God. God alone has the freedom to enter either into or stay out of the world. God has the choice not only *that* there be this covenantal relationship, but *how* this relationship is to be conducted. The difference between the two choices is that in the first choice, God's options or possibilities are unlimited, since before there is a world these possibilities are all logical possibilities whose range is infinite. In the second, subsequent choice, although God's options are limited inasmuch as there now exists a world, the possibilities are a finite number of real options that actually exist in the finite created world. Thus they have to be workable in the world in order to be accepted there intelligently. Speaking most metaphysically, one could say that the first choice is existential, and the second choice is essential.

Jewish Reactions to the Second Formulation of the Categorical Imperative

In his second formulation of the categorical imperative, Kant implies that our autonomous relationship with ourselves as rational beings is the basis of our discovery of other similar rational beings as analogues of ourselves. (So far in human experience, we have only found other humans to be fellow rational beings with us in the world.) Since rationality is what we discover we have in common with these fellow beings, this rationality cannot be taken to be my individual property as it is taken to be my individual capacity for the projection of my own self-chosen good in liberal notions of autonomy. The question is, how do I connect with my fellow rational/human beings?

Hermann Cohen goes so far as to say "man must create [*erschaffen*] the fellowman [*Mitmensch*] for himself."[134] He seems to mean that in my projection of the idea of moral law outward into the world as an ideal to be approximated, my projection needs to have an object immediately nearby in its idealizing trajectory. Now, this immediate object cannot be somebody who is merely physically proximate (what Cohen calls the *Nebenmensch* or the "next man"), but rather must be someone whom I as a rational being could clone as it were, that is, my alter ego.[135] However, since I did not create myself as a rational being, my ability to "create" another rational being in my image as it were, so as to be the direct object of my moral action, this could only be imitation of God. For it is God who creates me as a rational being by revealing to me – which for Cohen means allowing me to apprehend – Godself as the archetypal moral exemplar to be imitated in my moral dealings with my fellow humans. In other words, as God is related to humans as the imitable Creator of their rational being/moral capacity, so must humans imitate God's moral creativity. As such, humans must do with each other what God does with each of them and all of them. And Cohen is adamant that this does not mean God is the cause (*Ursache*) of morality. To ascribe causality (i.e, efficient causality) to God would surely undercut human moral responsibility. Instead, God is the "precondition" (*Vorbedingung*) who makes morality possible, that is, by revealing or making Godself knowable by humans as the ideal Being, whose rational attractiveness enables humans to devise moral laws as their teleological projection thereto.[136]

Now, if the highest moral action is love of neighbour, then by speculating that God's love of humankind grounds human mutual love, Cohen has given that mutual love a source higher than any finite human will, whether individual or collective. To be sure, in human moral experience, love of neighbour comes before our metaphysical recognition of God's love for humankind. But at the ontological level, God's love for humankind is prior. As Cohen puts it quite succinctly: "This love first [*Zuerst*] teaches man to love men ... Only now, after man has learned to love the fellowman as fellowman is his thought turned back to God, and only now [*Jetzt*] does he understand that God loves man."[137] After all, if God is the exemplar of moral law, whose highest command is to love one's neighbour, then *imitatio Dei* could only be loving one's neighbour by imitating God's love of humans. Nevertheless, God's love of humankind is not directly experienced by humans for, as we shall soon see, that direct experience could only be from historical revelation, that is, God's interaction with humans in history. But that is something Cohen does not regard as an actual event. For Cohen, revelation is the human apprehension of eternal truth.[138] That is why Cohen's notion of God's love for humans is not learned from the experience of a divine-human encounter; instead, it is thought of *a priori* as the presupposition of the interhuman relationship, and what gives it cosmic significance.

In this way, Cohen gives Kant's "metaphysic of morals" an ontologically stronger foundation than Kant himself did. Cohen did this by skilfully drawing upon the sources of Jewish theology, and rethinking them along more cogent philosophical lines. However, did Cohen make his Jewish sources say what either Kant himself said, only using more theological language, or what Kant could have said based on his philosophical principles as further developed by Cohen? In other words, did Cohen force his Jewish sources into a Kantian Procrustean bed, rather than showing that out of the Jewish sources one could develop a better model of the interpersonal relationship than that put forth by Kant and many Kantians? Along these lines, there are two problems regarding this presentation and representation of the second formulation of the categorical imperative. The first problem concerns Cohen's idea of God (which is different from Kant's idea of God, as we shall soon see) as the remote source of ethics. The second problem concerns Kant's and Cohen's characterization of my neighbour being an analogue of myself as a rational-moral being.

The first problem, concerning God's remoteness, will be dealt with more extensively later in this section. However, suffice it to say now that there have been some Jewish thinkers who have also thought of God as the indirect source of ethics.

Maimonides seems to have held this view. Discussing the Noahide commandments (*mitsvot bnei Noah*), which the rabbinic tradition taught are universally applicable to all humankind both before and after the Torah was given to the people Israel (who are not exempt from it thereafter), Maimonides is also convinced that these commandments (such as the prohibitions of murder, robbery, and incest) are universally known to be universally obligatory. That is, any rational human is expected to know that these commandments oblige all humankind. Maimonides says this is a matter of "rational inclination" (*hekhr'e ha-da'at*).[139] Indeed, it would be absurd for anybody to argue that such acts as murder, robbery, and incest may be permitted and are thus matters of moral indifference. Yet Maimonides says that however rational such an attitude might be on mundane grounds, and however we might well designate one taking this attitude to be wise (*me-hakhmeihem*), a person only attains "the-world-beyond" (*olam ha-ba*) when they affirm that these are commandments that all humankind (who are the descendants of Noah) "have been commanded (*nitstavu*) by God."[140] And what Maimonides means by "the-world-beyond" is not an eschatological age yet to come in historical time nor even the end of historical time. Rather, it is an eternal realm, always there, that remains the same while the lesser realm of "this-world" (*ha'olam ha-zeh*) is changeable and ephemeral.[141] In this realm God is both original and ultimate. As such, when intending this realm by the observance of a commandment, one thereby intends God both as the source of the commandment and as its final end. Thus natural law is also divine law.[142]

This notion of commandments coming from God indirectly seems somewhat like Kant's notion of "divine commandments" (*göttliche Gebote*) as distinct from commandments directly received from God (*Gebote Gottes*), which we have examined before. For the Noahide commandments are not seen to have been directly revealed by God in a historical event, an event that is subsequently commemorated like the giving of the Torah to the people Israel at Mount Sinai. Instead, the Noahide commandments are thought of retrospectively as what God has built into normative human nature. Thus these commandments are norms that we can assume the all-wise God would have certainly commanded His human subjects, and these commandments would be known by rational humans even if they hadn't been written down in the Mosaic Torah. Of these norms the ancient Rabbis said that "had they not been written in the Torah, reason [*ba-din hayah*] would require they be written down."[143]

Nevertheless, Maimonides only regards the Noahide commandments, even when they are observed with this truly metaphysical attitude, to be a proto-Torah. The complete relationship with God, on the other hand, only comes through the Mosaic Torah, that is, the law directly given by God at Mount Sinai.[144]

Now, for both Kant and Cohen, the direct interhuman relationship is constituted by the second formulation of the categorical imperative. This is the imperative for us humans to treat each other as ends-by-themselves, rather than using each other as means to some other end, whether that other end be the different good of each of us or a collective good that uses all the members of the society as the disposable and dispensable means thereto. For both Kant and Cohen, there seems to be no higher kind of moral relationship possible for humans. Nevertheless, the first question is whether or not Kant and Cohen have constituted the interhuman ethical relationship in a way that corresponds to general moral experience. The second question is whether or not they have constituted the interhuman ethical relationship in a way that corresponds to the Jewish tradition. This latter question, of course, is especially directed to Cohen, who most definitely saw himself as being part of the Jewish people and the Jewish tradition.

Both for Kant, who sees my discovery of my fellow humans as the discovery of analogues to myself as a morally willing being, and for Cohen, who sees me as actually creating my fellow humans as the objects of my moral will, it would seem that I have a relationship with myself primarily, which then includes other humans subsequently. In this view, my relationship with myself is constituted in my self-reflective thought about myself with myself as a morally creative being. And I can only include my fellow humans in my moral self-projection thereafter by noticing how similar to myself they are, especially when their moral self-projection to me as its object is the same as my moral self-projection to them as its object. This interchangeability is what makes moral projection universal: both the subject of the projection and the object of the projection could be anybody.

Despite the fact that Kant says we are to treat others like we treat ourselves, Kant himself implies and Cohen is explicit that this means we are related to ourselves prior to our being related to other persons *like* (in German, *zugleich*) ourselves, but who are still not quite equal to ourselves.[145] That opens up the possibility, though, for the French-Jewish philosopher Emmanuel Levinas (1906–95) to turn Kantian autonomy on its head. For Levinas, ethics is *heteronomy*, meaning that it is the other (the *heteros* in "heteronomy") person before me who is an end-by-himself. As such, it is *me* who is claimed by this other; it is not *I* who claims him.[146] And when *I* do respond to this other (*l'autre* in French), it is as his or her servant. Now, if the other is an end-by-himself, I may not use him in any way as a means for any end of my own or even for myself as an end-by-itself. He, not I, is the end-by-itself. As Levinas says: "The social relation is experienced pre-eminently, for it takes place before the existent that expresses himself, that is, remains in himself."[147] Nevertheless, just as the autonomy formulated by Kant and Cohen is not the arbitrary exercise of my will acting in my own self-interest and thereby using (even using up or exploiting) the other person, so the heteronomy of Levinas is not the arbitrary exercise of the other person's will for similar exploitation. Like the autonomy of Kant and Cohen, Levinasian heteronomy is for the sake of the object it claims. Thus Levinas's heteronomous other respects my freedom to decide how to respond to him appropriately. As Levinas puts it in his inimitable way: "He joins me to himself for service; he commands me as a Master; consequently this command commands me to command ... a command that commands commanding."[148] But whom am I commanded to command? It seems to me that the commanding presence of the other person is his claim upon me to respond to what he is asking me to do for him in his need. Here Levinas speaks of this as "the destitution of the poor one and the stranger." Perhaps, then, I am commanded to command myself, that is, to decide how exactly I must respond to this commanding presence of this other person (who represents "the whole of humanity") as my own duty. Indeed, one could say that for Kant and Cohen, my duty is to create the right or claim of the other person to have me treat him or her as an end-by-itself. But for Levinas, the right of the other person creates my duty to respond to him. In Levinas's words: "The face summons me to my obligations and judges me."[149]

All this notwithstanding, there is no real ethical mutuality here.[150] That is because the interpersonal relationship is ontologically asymmetrical. In fact, Levinas explicitly distinguishes the heteronomous moral relationship of the other person and myself from the famous "I-Thou" relationship formulated by the Jewish philosopher Martin Buber (1878–1965).[151] Addressing Buber as it were (who was still alive when Levinas published *Totalité et Infini* in 1961), Levinas asserts: "One may, however, ask if the *thou-saying* [*tutoiement*] does not place the other in a reciprocal relation, and if this reciprocity is primordial."[152] However, this asymmetry seems to be at odds with the general view, best expressed by Aristotle, that a true community exists not just in the abstract equality of its members that one finds in rectifying justice, but rather in the more concrete equality of friendship.[153] That is the quality of a truly ethical community, not obviously where everybody is literally the personal friend of everybody else, but rather where one of the main socializing tasks of the community is to continually make opportunities for friendship ever more available by encouraging as much as possible cooperation among its members functioning together as equals.

Interestingly enough, when Levinas critiques Buber's I-Thou relationship as being inadequate to the true, linguistically constituted justice that is to obtain between the other and myself in society, he says: "The Other who welcomes in intimacy is not the *you* [*vous*] of the face that reveals itself in a dimension of height, but precisely the *thou* [*tu*] of familiarity ... The I-Thou in which Buber sees the category of interhuman relationship is not the relation to the interlocutor but with feminine alterity."[154] Now, if Levinas means by "feminine alterity" marriage, then this is precisely where the Jewish tradition sees the original locus of human sociality, which is the founding of the family. And it is here that human mutuality is nurtured and developed.

Let us now look at how the initiation of marriage is treated in the Jewish legal tradition (*Halakhah*) as a mutual relationship, where one partner is not superior to the other as Levinas's other is superior to me. So, a man is commanded to marry and thereby "be fruitful and multiply" (Genesis 1:28). Moreover, in this same verse, the actual commandment (*mitsvah*) is derived from the words "and master [or conquer] it" (*ve-khivshuha*), which the predominant opinion in the Talmud takes to be a masculine act.[155] Nevertheless, a man does not have the right to command any woman to marry him. He must ask her to do so, and she has the right to either accept his offer of marriage or to reject it, and to reject it with impunity.[156] In fact, a woman can choose not to marry at all, since she has no duty to marry and procreate.[157] And even though there are several glaring areas in the law where it seems men have the right to lord it over their wives, it was the tendency in the tradition to correct them as a matter of domestic justice.[158] In Kantian terms, one could say that the trajectory of the tradition was to rectify situations where one partner or the other is not being treated as an end-by-himself or an end-by-herself. Let two specific legal examples suffice.

In the first, a man has the right to divorce his wife (although not without serious financial consequences).[159] But a woman does not have the right to divorce her husband. Nevertheless, if a woman can make a case that her husband is not fulfilling his marital duties to her stipulated by the Torah, she may petition a rabbinical court (*bet din*) to order her undutiful husband to divorce her, and they may use any means at their disposal to have their order accomplished.[160] However, whereas a man has the right to divorce his wife because of incompatibility subsequent to the initiation of the marriage, many authorities did not recognize a woman having a similar right. Maimonides, though, did recognize the right of a woman to say of her husband "he disgusts me" (*ma'is alei*) as being sufficient reason for a court to force him, if need be, to divorce her, "because she is not a captive to be forced into sex [*she-tiba'el*] with somebody she hates."[161] Second, even though a man may marry a woman by proxy (*shelihut*) and a woman may be married to a man likewise, nonetheless the Rabbis prohibit this practice. The reason given is that a man or a woman so married will likely be disappointed in the spouse they have not chosen for themselves. It is therefore likely that they will come to violate the great commandment "You shall love your neighbour as yourself [*kamokha*]" (Leviticus 19:18).[162] Here we see how marital mutuality is the prime locus of all subsequent interpersonal mutuality. It is the basis of all truly symmetrical interpersonal relationships.

Now, the symmetry of the commandment of neighbour-love is not that I first love my neighbour and then infer that my neighbour is to be loved *because* he or she is loved by God. Rather, I first experience the love of God whenever I keep the commandments that constitute my direct relationship with God (*bein adam le-maqom*). But since this experience is through the keeping of commandments that are commanded to my neighbours (plural) as well as to me insofar as we are all together members of the covenanted community elected by God, I cannot narcissistically regard this love from God as my individual possession. So, when reciprocating this love from God back to God, I can only do so along with those of my neighbours who are with me here and now. For example, I cannot very well thank God for the food God has given *us* if my neighbour has not been fed too. And when my neighbour becomes aware of the fact that this food I have given him did not originally come from me but from God, only then can my neighbour join with me in our common thanksgiving to God.[163] Thus my neighbour can be thankful to God for two reasons: one, God has been the prime source of the food he or she has eaten; two, I have become God's partner by keeping the commandment to love my neighbour who is like me. That might mean that if our circumstances are reversed, I could be the object of the commandment and my neighbour could be its subject.

Furthermore, that I am to save the life of my neighbour on the Sabbath, even when that will involve violating the Sabbath with an otherwise prohibited act, is done for their sake of my neighbours as ends-by-themselves. "You are to violate [*challel*] for him one Sabbath so that he will be able to keep many Sabbaths."[164] Thus I save my neighbour's life both for his or her sake and for the sake of the God-human relationship. In both of these cases, commandments pertaining to the interhuman relationship (*bein adam le-havero*) overlap with commandments pertaining to the God-human relationship. But whereas starting from the God-human relationship we can include the direct interhuman relationship therein, starting from the interhuman relationship (as do Cohen and Levinas) we only get an abstract, indirect relationship with God.

Mutual and reciprocal interhuman relationships, with which ethics is concerned, involve proportional equality or symmetry. In the case of marriage, it is not that a man qua husband and a woman qua wife are equals in the sense that their familial roles are the same and therefore interchangeable, as current egalitarian thinking would have it. Such simple or arithmetic equality works in legal disputes, especially in civil disputes involving property that is quantifiable, that is, evaluable by the abstract, mathematically constituted institution of money.[165] But more intangible human interactions do not lend themselves to such quantifiable simplicity. So, in the inner-familial relationship, a husband has certain rights and duties vis-à-vis his wife, and the wife has certain rights and duties vis-à-vis her husband. The respective rights and duties vis-à-vis each other are coordinated by the law, which gives the whole inner-familial relationship an overall balance or symmetry. Most especially, the legal authorities were sensitive to the need for legal rectification when either a husband or a wife would use superiority over the other marital partner to exploit that person's vulnerability. This, of course, disrupts the symmetry or balance that ought to prevail in any human relationship.[166]

The essential symmetry of ethically significant interpersonal relationships is what we do find in the Jewish tradition as well as in Aristotle and the Stoics. However, this is not what Kant or Cohen or Levinas wanted. Each of them (*mutatis mutandis*) looked to ethics as first philosophy, that is, they looked to ethics for what the classical philosophers thought ontology provides: asymmetrical transcendence, which is because of its hierarchal cosmic teleology. But for Kant and those like Cohen and even Levinas who followed in his wake, that kind of ontology is no longer available. It is irretrievable, having lost its anchor in natural science that itself is no longer teleological. And whereas philosophers like Hume and all those who basically followed in his wake regarded ontology (or what they usually called "metaphysics," whose connotation is "other-worldly" or even "occult") to be permanently lost, Kant *et alia* transferred the quest for asymmetrical transcendence over to ethics. Even the God-human relationship is only inferred from the ultimately significant, ethically constituted, interhuman relationship. Thus the divine-human relationship is basically subordinate to the interhuman relationship. In other words, metaphysics is for the sake of ethics, rather than ethics being for the sake of metaphysics. As we shall soon see, there is no direct divine-human relationship for all the Kantians (broadly speaking). Whatever there is between God and humans, in this view anyway, is thoroughly mediated by the ethically constituted interhuman relationship of which it is, in fact, a derivative function.

Levinas states this quite clearly: "God rises to his supreme ultimate presence as correlative to the justice rendered to men ... Ethics is the spiritual optics ... There can be no 'knowledge' of God separated from the relationship with men. The Other is the very locus of metaphysical truth, and is indispensable for my relation with God."[167] The great commonality between Levinas on the one hand and Kant and Cohen on the other hand is that the heteronomous superiority of the Other functions for Levinas very much like the autonomous superiority of the morally willing subject functions for Kant and Cohen. Each side raises what had been a non-ultimate symmetrical relationship up to the level of an asymmetrical ultimate relation that is one-way; it is not mutually reciprocal.

Now it is clear what Levinas means when he says "the Other ... is indispensable for my relation with God," namely, I am first related to the other, and only then do I posit a relation to God who, as it were, is standing behind the other so as to keep the other out of my totalizing grasp. Nevertheless, there is another way of looking at the connection of the interhuman relationship and the divine-human relationship that, contrary to Levinas, takes the divine-human relationship to be prior to the interhuman relationship, which is thus subsequent to it. This will allow the proper, transcendent asymmetry to be restored to the God-human relationship where it rightly belongs; and it will restore the proper, immanent symmetry to the interhuman relationship where it rightly belongs too. Moreover, this view of the connection of the two modes of relationality corresponds to the Jewish tradition better than does Levinas's view. Couldn't it be said that Levinas has postulated the existence of God for the sake of his moral philosophy in the same way Kant did for his moral philosophy? However, one whose existence is only postulated, but not actually confronted, is not directly related to.

The key to the difference between these two views is found in Levinas's emphasis of "*my* relation to God," while the Bible and rabbinic tradition emphasize much more "*our* relation to God." For the covenant between God and humans is not a relationship between God and individual humans: it is not between God and *me*. The relationship is between God and a uniquely elected community. The relationship is between God and *us*. Contra Levinas, it is not that I am related to the superior other, and then I need to think of that relationship intending my relation to God who, as it were, backs up the primary interhuman relationship. Instead, God's covenantal relationship with the community whom God has elected is primary, and the validity of any interhuman relationship within this community depends on how well it serves the primary God-human relationship. So, for example, despite the fact that parents seem to have superiority over their children, in fact, that superiority is relative. Children are obligated to honour their parents by caring for their bodily needs, while parents are obligated to care for their children by supporting their bodily needs.[168] Here there is proportional equality.

There is also more literal equality between parents and children insofar as they are both equally obligated to serve God. Thus, when a parent orders his or her child to violate a commandment like the Sabbath, which is a prime constituent of the direct God-human relationship, the child is obligated to refuse the order. Why? It is as if God says to both parents and their children: "You are all equally [*kulkhem*] obligated to honour Me."[169] Or, as the Talmud asks rhetorically in the case of a similar conflict: "To the words of the pupil or the words of the master; whose words are to be heeded?!"[170] An arrogant attempt on the part of the relatively superior parent to make the parent-child relationship totally asymmetrical so as to trump the ultimately asymmetrical God-human relationship, thereby making the child subordinate to his or her parent rather than being primarily subordinate to God, is thus rejected. It is not only rejected on ethical grounds, but most profoundly on ontological grounds. Even though chronologically in human experience, the interhuman relationship is constituted before the God-human relationship, the God-human relationship has ontological priority.

Finally, getting back to the language of the second formulation of the categorical imperative, from a theological perspective one could say that while in the interhuman relationship the human parties are to be treated as ends-by-themselves, nonetheless that finality (*Endgültigkeit*) is relative in two ways. One, there are times when a person has to subordinate himself or herself to another person, thus not treating themself as an end-by-itself.[171] Two, a person may not act as an end-by-itself if that act, which is often making a claim on somebody usually subordinate to him or her, ignores the truth that God is the only One to be treated (i.e., actively related to) as *the* End-by-Himself totally and unqualifiedly. Yet even when God does waive God's right to be treated absolutely as the sole End-by-Himself, that is because God has chosen to do so, not because there is anyone greater than God who could require God to do so.[172] There is no reality greater than God, according to which a creature could possibly make God answerable. Thus God told Moses after Israel's sin of building the golden calf and worshipping it: "I shall be gracious with whomever [*et-asher*] I shall be gracious; I shall be compassionate with whomever I shall be compassionate" (Exodus 33:19), even though God is not obligated to do so because of anything they have done to deserve it.[173]

Jewish Reactions to the Third Formulation of the Categorical Imperative

Since we have just looked at differing notions of an ethically constituted interhuman community, we need to look back at Kant's first formulation of the categorical imperative: "Act only on that maxim ... that could become a universal [*allgemeines*] law."[174] One could only do that effectively as a member of a society that recognizes all its members as being capable of both making laws and following these universal laws. This involves more than the one-to-one relationship suggested in the second formulation of the categorical imperative. Not only can I not be morally autonomous without another person as the addressee of my moral action, but I also need a society in which these morally significant interactions can be coordinated by public law. This kind of a society is what Kant calls a "realm of ends" (*Reich der Zwecke*); hence Kant's third formulation of the categorical imperative.

As we have seen earlier in this chapter, for Kant, there are three manifestations of the realm of ends: two real and one ideal. The most real and least ideal manifestation of this realm is a secular constitutional democracy, what Kant called a "juridico-civil state."[175] This is a state ruled according to law that is made both by and for its citizens. Yet the fact that coercion is often required in the administration of these laws makes this kind of state still quite removed from the ideal of the full equality of moral beings that ought to pertain in a fully comprehensive realm of ends. For coercion involves hierarchal inequality insofar as some citizens have coercive power over other citizens, even though it is possible that the roles can be reversed under other circumstances. So, closer to that ideal realm of ends, which is an "ethical community" (*gemeines Wesen*), is what Kant calls the "visible church."[176] Here, in this very Protestant version of a church, there is far less hierarchal inequality. To be sure, the visible church comes closest to the ideal realm of ends, what Kant calls the "invisible church."[177] But here and now the visible church is politically and legally subordinate to the secular state, functioning as a private association within its jurisdiction. For matters of public morality inevitably become issues with which the secular state is concerned, and which the state more and more controls with its laws. The visible church, then, is only left alone by the secular state in its strictly "religious" or "ritual" activities.[178] The only advantage the visible church has is that it is closer to the ideal realm of ends than is the secular state. And, as such, its strength is how well it nurtures and promotes what is its eschatological task, for the ideal realm of ends lies in a transcendent future.

Nevertheless, for Kant, religion revealed in history, traditionally transmitted through history, and maintained by its visible institutions (that is, "churches") is only valid when it is the "handmaiden" of morality. As Kant vividly put it: "A human being's moral improvement is likewise a practical affair incumbent upon him, and heavenly influences may indeed always cooperate [*dazu mitwirken*] in this improvement."[179] Religious practises are to be judged at all times according to one criterion alone: are they or are they not done "for the sake of the moral service of God?"[180] Indeed, the ethical community is the only program that can effect positive progress in the real world, for Kant.[181]

Let us now look at how some modern Jewish thinkers appropriated Kant's notion of the realm of ends, and whether their appropriation is consistent or inconsistent with traditional Jewish views of community and society.

Kant's notion of the relation of the secular state and religious communities very much resonated with Jews, especially in the late eighteenth century when Jews were beginning their struggle to be emancipated from the political and cultural isolation of the Ghetto. The foreign status of the Jews in European "Christendom" had precluded any real integration into the "secular" state, for secularity here meant only that the state was not directly governed by the church. Nevertheless, even that secular sphere of society still received its ultimate warrant from the church. As such, secular or civil society was a Christian society by and for Christians, and whose Christianity was defined by the church. Jews, however, were members of a separate nation, who lived in Christian societies by virtue of some sort of social contract between themselves as a community and the reigning monarch of the Christian host society. Now, this situation had its strengths and its weaknesses. Its strength was that Jews had a good deal of communal independence, including the political power to coerce the members of the community (*qahal*) to conform to its law, at least publicly. Its weakness was that Jews were not real participants in the larger society in which they were contained (as *imperium in imperio*) and to which they were politically subordinate, not being citizens of the state. That made them politically and economically vulnerable, often being at the mercy of capricious, untrustworthy monarchs, and their untrustworthy, capricious subjects as well. Moreover, it was often the church who objected to the presence in a Christian society of a community of unbelieving infidels like the Jews, who had rejected Christianity altogether.

All of this, however, began to break down with the growing emancipation of Jews from their external political subordination to a Christians-only, church-warranted polity, plus their emancipation from their internal subordination to a Jewish community ruled by rabbis. In fact, the political emancipation of the Jews, leading towards their attaining full citizenship in secular polities, went hand in hand with the breakdown of the communal authority of traditional Jewish communities. The words of Count Stanislas Clermont de Tonnere at the time of the French Revolution set the tone for this whole process of emancipation throughout Western Europe: "We must refuse the Jews as a nation everything, and accord everything to the Jews as individuals."[182] And while some more traditional Jews (especially the rabbinical establishment whose political power was taken away from them) were wary of being so "emancipated," most Jews were more than happy to accept Clermont de Tonnere's offer. Indeed, they were exhilarated by the promise of becoming equal citizens in the newly emerging, increasingly secular nation states of Europe.

In the *ancien régime*, the relation of church and state was quite similar for both Christians and Jews. In each case, the warrant for civil society came from the legitimating religious authority of *the* religious community. For Christians, it was *the* church ruled by clerics; for Jews it was *the* Jewish community ruled by rabbis. And while there was a certain degree of lay authority in civil society as the locus of human interactions, nevertheless in "Jewry" the same rabbis who adjudicated in strictly "religious" matters like synagogue ritual in a rabbinical court (*bet din*) also adjudicated in civil matters like sales and contracts in these same courts. All areas of both human interaction and divine-human interaction were within the same jurisdiction. (Christians had separated the two spheres of society to a greater extent insofar as the secular jurisdiction was governed according to civil law and the religious or ecclesial jurisdiction was governed according to canon law.)

All of that changed or began to change, however, in the late eighteenth century. Rather than *the* religious community warranting or legitimating the polity, it was now the polity that legitimated religious communities (plural). And whereas only one church could legitimate a plurality of polities (like the Catholic Church legitimating a number of European polities in "Christendom"), one polity could legitimate a plurality of "churches" within its domain. That is because the religious communities had now become (or were becoming) subgroups within the overall polity. They were now taken to be religious parts of an overall secular whole. In fact, the political subordination of the religious communities to the state became more pronounced insofar as the state, being legally constituted, still had the power of coercion, whereas the religious communities, having now become voluntary associations of individual citizens, had lost that coercive power. These voluntary associations were left with only the power of moral persuasion. That is why the religious communities had to justify their very existence to the state, unlike premodern times when the state had to justify its very existence to the church.

While there was no doubt that religious communities needed the state for their very presence in the real world (i.e., the world of *Realpolitik*), there was always the lingering doubt whether the state needed religious communities at all. Nevertheless, "emancipated" Jews were happy to accept this new arrangement, however obsequious it seemed to make them. Thus Kant's older contemporary, the Jewish philosopher Moses Mendelssohn, one of the most prominent advocates of the political emancipation of the Jews, argued for this new status of *all* religious communities within the state, and how the state is benefitted by their new status. "The only aid religion can render to the state consists in teaching and consoling ... imparting to the citizens ... such convictions as are conducive to the public weal."[183] In fact, Mendelssohn's argument had, by anticipation as it were, challenged Kant's later charge that "Judaism is not a religion at all but simply the union of a number of individuals who ... established themselves into a community under purely political laws, hence not into a church ... with no claim on the moral disposition [*Gesinnung*]."[184] And, like a state rather than a church, Judaism in Kant's eyes is a "religion" whose "commands [*Gebote*] are of the kind which even a political constitution [*Verfassung*] can uphold and lay down as coercive laws [*Zwangsgesetze*], since they deal only with external actions ... directed to external observance [*äussere Beobachtung*]."[185] However, the argument that Mendelssohn and others made to the Prussian state was that Judaism is the constitution of a voluntary moral community, not the constitution of a competing, legally coercive polity. And, this argument became the one liberal Jews who came after Mendelssohn (and who looked to him as their "enlightened" inspiration) made to themselves, that is, that Judaism is not a legally or *halakhically* constituted praxis, but rather an ethically constituted faith (*Glaube*).[186] This view is epitomized by the liberal insistence that the classical word for "Judaism," *Torah*, should not be translated as "Law" (following the Septuagint's translation of the Hebrew *torah* into the Greek *nomos*), but rather as the less normative "Teaching" (*Lehre*).[187]

All this notwithstanding, doesn't this suggest that *any* religion could provide this service to the state? So what was there to prevent Jews from assimilating into the majority Christian culture? Why should Jews want to be a small religious minority when they could be more effective citizens of a secular state (both for their own interests and the interests of the state) as members of the majority religion? The answer to this quandary was best provided by Hermann Cohen, who was the most respected and influential philosopher in German Jewry. Cohen argued that the Jews have a unique mission that requires the continued separate existence of the Jewish community from the dominant, majority Christian culture. Indeed, this requires individual Jews to remain within the Jewish community and to thereby resist the great attraction of assimilation into the majority Christian culture. This mission is for Jews and Jewry to be in the vanguard of progress towards the ideal of the Messianic Age.[188] In other words, the Jews are to comprise what Kant would call the real "visible church," which is the religious community that best intends the ideal "invisible church." That Kantian ideal is the true unity of all humankind as a thoroughly moral universal communion.

A religion, and in Cohen's view Judaism is religion superlatively, does much more than morally educate its members for good citizenship in a secular state. Judaism as the best (though not the only) "religion of [practical] reason" (*Religion der Vernunft*) should be seen as the lodestar that inspires the secular state, which is the first real manifestation of the realm of ends in the world. Judaism as practised and advocated by the Jews ought to constantly remind the secular polity not to be satisfied with itself as the final incarnation in history of an ideal that ought never be seen as having been realized or even as realizable in history.[189] Cohen is convinced, however, that Christianity has compromised the great ideal of "the kingdom of God" (*malkhut shamayim*) by settling for less than that universal, messianic ideal.[190] And that turns the usual Christian charge of Jewish "particularism" on its head. Judaism is now the true universalism because of its ideality, while Christianity is more particularistic by comparison. Therefore, any Jew who converts to Christianity, even for what seem to be "idealistic" reasons (although, in fact, many modern Jews converted to Christianity out of far more "realistic" motives), that Jew, in the words of the Talmud, "is descending (*moridin ba-qodesh*) in holiness."[191] Indeed, for Cohen, "the kingdom of God is at hand" is more at hand for Jews than for any other religious community.[192] And Cohen could make this case on decidedly Kantian grounds, even when differing from what are, undoubtedly, Kant's more specific mistakes about Judaism.

Hermann Cohen's messianism, which is his typically brilliant development of Kant's notion of the realm of ends, nonetheless has a major philosophical flaw. For if the realm of ends as the Messianic Age is essentially unrealizable in history, how then does one *progress* towards it? Being unrealizable means it is an infinite goal or *telos*; but as we saw in the previous chapter, where we examined Aristotelian teleology at length, a *telos* by definition is a limit, hence it is finite (*causa finalis*). Indeed, an infinite *telos* is an oxymoron. What difference does it make whether or not one moves closer to an unattainable goal? Isn't striving to reach what is never attainable an exercise in futility?[193]

Now, it seems understandable why Cohen got himself into this difficult position when we understand what other messianisms he was combatting. He was clearly worried about what were, for him, dangerous distortions of the messianic ideal. Most specifically, he was worried about Marxist notions that the end of history can be brought about by materialistic means, for that makes a mockery of any metaphysical, idealistic philosophy. (In fact, many of Cohen's Jewish contemporaries were attracted to Marxism out of seemingly messianic aspirations.) And Cohen was worried about Zionism, which sees its messianic goal as the establishment of a Jewish state in the land of Israel. For Cohen, that is not historical progress but historical regression.[194] For the mission of Judaism and the Jews is to do what a state of their own inhibited them from doing, that is, it distracted them from their true messianic task by burdening them with the local, this-worldly tasks any particular state demands. The loss of political sovereignty brought about by the destruction of the Temple and the exile of Jews into the Diaspora was, in Cohen's eyes, not a cause for mourning, but rather a cause for celebration of historical progress.[195] So, the Jews should leave the business of a this-worldly nation state to their host societies (of which Germany was for him first and foremost) and concentrate their efforts on being in the spiritual vanguard of messianic progress. That alone truly intends an authentic supernational world state, which Cohen thought lies beyond the historical horizon nonetheless. Conversely, both Marxism and Zionism are, for Cohen, pseudo-messianisms. Thus Cohen's idealistic messianism can be seen as functioning as a limitation or containment of the excesses of these two ideologies.

Cohen was correct about the need for authentic Jewish messianism to counter pseudo-messianisms (Jewish or otherwise). Along these lines, I think he was right about Marxism, but wrong about Zionism. Nevertheless, his overall critique is theologically flawed, because he misunderstood the true character of Jewish messianism and how it can function critically to counter pseudo-messianic imitations. Once that is better understood, we can see why Zionism, when theologically conceived, is not the pseudo-messianism Cohen thought it is.

Cohen's theological error was, ironically, the same error of many Zionists, which is their turning Zionism into a messianic idealism. The specific difference between Cohen and many Zionists is that for Cohen the ideal could never be realized in human history, whereas many Zionists believed it could be realized imminently in history. Furthermore, for many Zionists, the goal has been a sovereign Jewish state in the land of Israel, whereas for Cohen the goal is a universal realm encompassing the entire world. Still, for both Cohen and these idealistic Zionists, the ideal is a human project into the future: for Cohen that future is transcendent and can never become present; for these Zionists that future is virtually at hand, thus it can easily become present. For both of them, though, the process's starting point is human. It begins as an idea in the mind of humans that is then projected onto or beyond a foreseeable historical horizon. Perhaps one could say that the Zionists' ideal is too mundane, whereas Cohen's ideal is too utopian.

Now, while both views have some precedents in the Jewish tradition, one could argue that a considerable (perhaps predominant) messianic trend in the Jewish tradition is eschatological and apocalyptic rather than progressive and idealistic. That is, the "days of the Messiah" (*yemot ha-mashiah*) or the "end of days" (*aharit ha-yamim*) is not a perfect future towards which humans will progress from out of an imperfect present and past. Instead, the Messianic Age will be a perfect future that will come *to* humans – not *from* humans – to totally replace our most imperfect present and past. In other words, the radical future (*l'atid la-vo*) will invade the present when God chooses that to be so. It will not be the project of those of us in the present attaining or even attempting to attain the radical future because we humans have chosen to do so. That future will be brought *down to* humans *by* God, rather than being brought *up to* God *by* humans. The fact that this end will be brought into human history is what makes it "eschatological" (*eschaton* in Greek means "last time"). The fact that this end is brought by God Himself is what makes it "apocalyptic" (*apokalyptein* in Greek means "reveal"), that is, that last time is already known to God now; it will be revealed to humans only when it actually happens. As one rabbinic source puts it: "No eye but Yours [*zulatekha*] O' God has seen what He will do for those who wait [*le-mehakeh*] for Him."[196]

From this we can infer that the end time is not infinitely transcendent and thus unknowable per se. Rather, while the end time is only unknown to us humans here and now, God does know it. As such, although we cannot know it and thus be certain of it, we can still hope for God to make it present at a time known to God, but not yet revealed by God to humans.[197] That couldn't be the case if the end time were an infinite, unattainable, ideal goal. Indeed, one could say that both God and humans are waiting for the end time, which will be the final consummation of God's relationship with His people and along with them all humankind.[198] The difference between God and humans is that God knows what He is waiting for, which will come to exist when God judges that His human partners are truly ready to receive it. We humans, on the other hand, do not know *what* we are waiting for, so we can only hope *that*, at a time unbeknownst to us here and now, God will judge us to be ready to receive the "final redemption" (*ge'ulah shlemah*). That hope is most keenly expressed in the ancient Jewish prayer *kaddish*: "May it come speedily [*b'agala*] at a near time!"[199] Perhaps one could say that the end time is a realizable ideal, not by humans at all, but by God alone. In that way, the human hope for the end time here and now becomes the refutation of all the pseudo-messianists, who themselves presume to be able to realize this ideal in human history. But that ideal can only be realized at the end of history when God who transcends history concludes it. To make that end time infinite as does Hermann Cohen, and thus unattainable by anyone, would be to make it greater than God. For even the end time is a creature of God and thus finite, having both a beginning and an end. Only God can say of Godself: "I am the first and I am the last; and other than Me [*u-mibl'adei*] there is no god" (Isaiah 44:6).

Many Zionists, both secular and religious, err in making Zionism an idealistic movement and ideology. A sovereign Jewish state in the land of Israel – which, thank God, has become a political reality in our lifetime – is not a realized ideal, if for no other reason than it is far from being anything like the Kingdom of God as imagined by the prophets. In fact, those who invest it with this messianic quality are often disappointed at how far off is their hope from this-worldly reality.[200] But this certainly does not preclude Jews who are waiting for the Messiah from being Zionists, let alone from enthusiastically living and working in and for the Jewish State of Israel. For, rather than being taken to be the or even a messianic goal, the State of Israel should be seen as the best human political means now available to the Jewish people to settle the land of Israel and build an authentic, thoroughly Jewish society there. This task begins when the Jewish people accepts the divine mandate "You shall possess the land and settle it, for to you have I [God] given the land to possess [*la-reshet*] it" (Numbers 33:53), and then make that commandment a real task in this world here and now.

Now, this seems to mean that commanded Jewish praxis and Jewish waiting for the final redemption are totally separate activities. Nevertheless, they are analogous activities. To wait for the final redemption is to exercise our readiness to accept *whatever* God *will* give us in the future. That will be *whenever* God chooses to do so. It is very much like the readiness of our ancestors to accept God's revelation of the Torah *whenever* God *would* give it to them. Still, the most one can say along messianic lines is that the Jewishly settled land of Israel might well be the site of the Messiah's entrance into the world, though his reign and his influence will certainly not be confined there.[201] "The secret things [*ha-nistartot*] are the Lord our God's, but the revealed things [*ve-haniglot*] are for us and our children to do forever, namely, all the things the Torah [has commanded us] to do" (Deuteronomy 29:28). Surely, the messianic ideal is one of those "secret things" that are our business to accept when they are finally revealed, but as of here and now they are God's business with which we should not interfere. Instead, the Zionist project is the humanly devised political means to the fulfilment of a commandment of God, rather than a humanly initiated program to actually bring about the final redemption of the world. That project is by no means an end-in-itself. In fact, the fulfilment of that commandment is an ongoing human task until the end time.

At present, our theological eschatology functions something like Kant's "limiting concept" (*Grenzbegriff*), which is invoked to curb the metaphysical pretence of speculative reason to "extend its domain [*Gebiet*] over everything which the understanding thinks."[202] Similarly, theological eschatology has been invoked to curb pseudo-messianic pretensions to actually designate the Messiah in the present. The logic here is similar to the logic employed by negative theology (*via negativa*) to curb the metaphysical pretension of actually saying *what* God is, even though we assume that God knows who God is.[203] However, whereas Kant's limiting concept curbs speculative reason from within, Jewish eschatology seems to be teaching that our pseudo-messianic pretensions are curbed (i.e., limited) from without. That is, there is an eschatological reality outside our attempts to access it, which limits our ability to access it by ourselves, yet that reality is known by God. That is why our hoping for the arrival of the end time is not an exercise in futility; it is not just a wish. We do assert that there is something real on the other side, even though we cannot know it ourselves.[204] Therefore, theological eschatology limits theological pretension better than Kant's limiting concept curbs metaphysical pretension, as this theology limits *all* human pretension to project the end time (instead of properly waiting for God to send it to us). Yet, as we have seen, Kant's regulation of the metaphysical pretension to access ultimate reality via speculative reason is sublimated into the metaphysical project of practical reason to attain ultimate reality. Cohen then conflated the end time and ultimate reality, making the access of the Ultimate *the* supreme (i.e., sublime) human project. As such, for Kant, and even more so for Cohen, it is humankind, not God, who becomes "the measure of all things."[205] With Cohen, especially, the ancient Jewish doctrine of the end time or Messianic Age has not curbed his metaphysical pretentions.

Kant's realm of ends, especially in Hermann Cohen's Jewish version of it, is very different from the hoped-for Kingdom of God as taught by the Bible and the rabbinic tradition. And it is also very different from the Zionist project, especially when that project is thought of and acted for idealistically. Nevertheless, Kant's notion of the realm of ends has been very influential in modern Jewish thought, whether directly or indirectly, whether from religious or secular Jewish thinkers, especially in their messianic speculations. Therefore, it has been important for us to distinguish classical Jewish eschatology from Cohen's too idealistic messianism, and from the too mundane, nationalistic messianism of many Zionists (both past and present).

The Relation of God and Humans

It is clear from the several discussions of God throughout his *oeuvre* that Kant did not consider any direct relation between God and humans possible. That is because, in his view, humans have no direct experience of God. On the other hand, Kant was able to constitute a direct relation between humans and nature, and between humans themselves, because of direct human experience in these two areas. Humans do have a direct relation to nature insofar as they are able to directly apprehend the percepts that, in some mysterious way, come from imperceptible things-by-themselves. (That is, we can only say *that* they come from things-in-themselves, but not *how* they come from them, let alone *why* the things-in-themselves have come to exist altogether.) Nature is the conceptual system into which humans order what they have perceived.[206] And even though this abstract conceptualization is logically prior to the percepts it puts into categorizes, it is done retrospectively nonetheless. Only after the percepts or natural data have been directly experienced can the conceptualization be done. Interhuman relations, too, are directly experienced insofar as humans are able to encounter one another as ends-by-themselves and act accordingly by respecting each other and working with each other towards the ideal realm of ends. In neither of these types of experience, though, is God to be encountered. Moreover, God cannot very well be directly encountered or experienced when we speak of God's relation to nature (the subject of the next section in this chapter), for that is certainly not an object of any direct human experience. As God pointed out to Job: "Where were you when I established the earth?!" (Job 38:4).

Now, the only way God could be directly encountered by humans is if God reveals Godself to them. However, Kant doesn't seem to regard revelation to be a type of direct experience at all.[207] So, when he discusses theology as "knowledge of the original being [*Urwesens*] ... based either solely upon reason or upon revelation [*aus Offenbarung*]," he moves right on to consider *theologia rationalis*, never returning to discuss *revelata* at all.[208] Unlike revealed theology, rational theology can be discussed because it connects itself to direct human experience of the external world or to direct human experience of ideas in the human mind. These are universal human experiences, which every human being has, and which thoughtful humans can reflect upon as to what they presuppose and what they entail. But revelation is not universal: it is experienced by a particular group of humans at a particular time. Not being universally accessible to all rational humans, it would seem that *a* revelation needn't be that of the universal God, the God who created the universe. Wouldn't a local tribal deity be sufficient to be the subject of what Kant considers the particular historicity inherent in all revealed religions (plural)?[209] In fact, Kant goes so far as to call a religion grounded on revelation "fetishism," which is essentially different from a revealed religion that looks to rational religion as its ground.[210] Thus, speaking of revealed religion as "superstitious" (*Aberglaube*), Kant says that "this feeling of the immediate presence [*unmittelbaren Gegenwart*] of the highest being ... constitutes the receptivity [*Empfänglichkeit*] of an intuition for which there is no sense [faculty] in human nature."[211] Many liberal Jewish thinkers accepted Kant's denigration of revealed religion per se, only denying that Judaism is such a non-universal, particularistic fetishism.

It was Franz Rosenzweig who most definitely broke with this liberal Jewish trend, especially regarding revelation as a real event in the world, the event in which God addresses a human recipient "where he is at" (Genesis 21:17). This human recipient of revelation does more than merely experience something and then subsume it within ready-made categories. The response to the event of revelation is more than the discovery of an eternal truth always-there, or the projection of an ideal yet to be realized in the future.[212] As such, the event of revelation constitutes a direct relationship between God and a human person.

However, for Rosenzweig, only one direct commandment from God to human emerges from revelation. It is God commanding the human recipient of revelation: "Love me."[213] This involves a two-term relationship of *A* and *B*. All the specific commandments that pertain to the God-human relationship, on the other hand, involve a three-term relationship: *A* commands *B* to do *C*. (No third party, though, can command one to love; love must be elicited from the beloved by the lover.) It is when a commandment (*Gebot*) is commanded by a third party that the commandment thereby becomes a law (*Gesetz*).

The relationship activated by the love-commandment is between the unique God and an individual human person.[214] It is only after this individual self has become a soul awakened by God that he or she is ready to go out into the world to share this awakened love with his or her fellow humans.[215] Here we see a move from the level of the private (between God and a human individual) to the level of the public (among humans themselves).[216] And whereas an ad hoc, individual commandment can be a private matter, a permanent commandment involves the relationship between God and a class of persons to whom the commandment pertains permanently. At this point of specification and perpetuation, the commandment becomes public law.[217]

Whereas spiritually exalted persons (like Franz Rosenzweig himself who, no doubt, experienced a revelation-event/epiphany in his own life) can move from the level of the commandment to the level of law as they are sent out into the world to share God's love with their fellow humans, most people who have not experienced the love-commandment directly first regard themselves as members of the class of persons so directly obligated by communal tradition to obey specific laws. Only thereafter do certain spiritually exalted persons strive to experience the specific obligated acts to be truly commanded by God. However, it would seem that for Rosenzweig, one can best keep the specific law in good faith when one has first accepted the love-commandment that emerges from within God's revelation to oneself beforehand. Yet it is only after the true revelation that humans are now empowered to decide how they are to love God by doing certain specific acts together in a lawful way. Nevertheless, I think Rosenzweig would advise already law-abiding Jews to continue to keep the law, even when they cannot experience it as God's direct commandment to them. As it is put in the Talmud: "One should engage in learning Torah and doing the commandments [*mitsvot*] even not for their own sake [*li-shmah*], for one can move from not doing them for their own sake to doing them for their own sake."[218] Thus Rosenzweig is critical of Buber for his total separation of commandment and law.[219] Instead, he thinks that the law is the human interpretation of the prime love-commandment of God. That interpretation of the prime commandment seems to be the exercise of what some contemporary philosophers call "public reason."[220] Nevertheless, I think the relation of commandment and law is viewed quite differently in classical Jewish theology.

First, as we have seen, the relationship between God and human persons or "man" (*der Mensch*) is between the singular, unique God and a plurality of human creatures. As such, when the norms of the Torah are accepted by the subjects of revelation, addressed to them in the second person ("you" or "ye") and performed by them in the first person ("I" or "we"), these norms are "commandments" (*mitsvot*). When, on the other hand, the norms of the Torah are categorized into a humanly constructed legal system (*Halakhah*), formulated in the third person ("it" or "them"), they are "laws" (*halakhot*).[221] So, it is not that an individual loved by God then goes out into the world to redeem his or her fellow humans with that love in hand. Instead, the individual members of the commanded class or community of persons are required to lovingly interact with each other by actively including themselves and others within that community who together loves God in return. And when others outside the covenanted community want to be included in this shared communal love, whether permanently or even temporarily, and have demonstrated their willingness to accept the authority of the Torah and tradition, they are to be included willingly.[222]

Second, it is not only *that* God commands us to love Him, but God simultaneously commands us just *how* God wants to be actively loved. Moreover, since our love is a response to God's initiatory love for us, we need to be told just how God loves us so that we can know how to imitate God's love for us among ourselves.[223] Rosenzweig, however, seems to consider the specific commandments to be something like Kant's "divine commandments" (*göttliche Gebote*), which, as we have seen, are commandments humans imagine God *would* command, rather than commandments God actually does command (*Gebote Gottes*).[224] And whereas Kant's divine commandments are formulated according to the criterion of the idea of moral law, Rosenzweig's "divine laws" are formulated according to the criterion of the one, single love-commandment from God to individual humans. Nevertheless, while Rosenzweig thinks that there is at least one great commandment coming directly from God to humans, Kant and Cohen do not think there is or there could be any such direct communication from God. So, it would seem that Rosenzweig's notion of the priority of the God-individual relationship – which has much in common with the I-Thou philosophy of his friend and colleague Martin Buber – is the cause of his difference from classical

Jewish theology.[225] Yet this is a difference far less radical than Hermann Cohen's divergence from the Jewish tradition on this essential theological point regarding revelation.

As for God's connection to the relation of humans and nature, what he calls "natural theology" (as distinct from what he called "revealed theology"), Kant is most highly esteemed by subsequent philosophers for his vigorous and thorough attempt to deny any philosophical value whatsoever to natural theology. For Kant argued that constituting the relation of humans and nature has no need (*Bedürfnis*) to posit the existence of a first cause, who could only be God as the Absolute (*ens realissimum*).[226] However, that is only not the need of speculative philosophy, that is, the type of thinking for which metaphysical aspirations lead to a dead end. And whereas many post-Kantian philosophers assume that Kant had killed metaphysics with its inevitable ultimate concern with God, what he actually did was to transfer these metaphysical aspirations from speculative philosophy to practical philosophy, that is, to ethics. In fact, shortly after he published his assault on classical metaphysics in the *Critique of Pure Reason* came his *Groundwork of the Metaphysic of Morals*. Nevertheless, there his treatment of the God question is not substantial.

It is in his second critique, the *Critique of Practical Reason*, that Kant sees a need not to constitute a direct relation between humans and God, but rather for rational persons to acknowledge a function for God within their overall moral life, without which it could be taken to be absurd. Now, that absurdity could be seen at either side of human moral striving: either at the beginning or at the end. At the beginning of the moral life, which is the assertion of autonomy, it is absurd for any individual person or even for humankind collectively to regard themselves as the first cause of morality. Unlike liberal notions of autonomy (as we saw earlier), neither *I* nor *we* can presume that morality itself is the product of *my* will or *our* will. So, in order to avoid that absurdity, Kant wants to attribute will to God. Yet that is not to regard God's will as the source of moral law, but rather to regard God's will as the archetype of all lesser wills who instantiate the idea of moral law into concrete moral action. Thus Kant insists: "I also do not mean by this that it is necessary to assume the existence of God as a basis [*eines Grundes*] of all obligation [*Verbindlichkeit*] as such (for this basis rests ... on the autonomy of reason itself)."[227] So, it is at the end of human moral striving rather than at the beginning where we might see a greater role for God.

Kant states that teleological need of pure practical philosophy as follows:

> Happiness [*Glückseligkeit*] is the state of a rational being in the world for whom in the whole of his existence everything proceeds according to his

> wish and his will; it therefore rests on the harmony [*Übereinstimmung*] of nature with his whole purpose [*Zweck*] as well as with the essential determining basis [*Bestimmungsgrund*] of his will ... but the acting rational being in the world is, after all, the cause [*Ursache*] of the world and of nature itself. Hence there is in the moral law not the slightest basis [*Grund*] for a necessary connection [*Zusammenhang*] between morality and the happiness, proportionate thereto.[228]

Kant then goes on to say:

> Therefore the highest good in the world is possible only insofar as one assumes a supreme cause conforming [*enthalten*] to the moral attitude ... hence is its originator [*Urheber*], i.e., **God**. Consequently [*Foglich*] the postulate of the highest derivative [*abgeleiteten*] good is simultaneously the postulate of the actuality [*Wirklichkeit*] of a highest original [*ursprünglichen*] good ... the existence of God.[229]

By "postulate" (both as noun and as verb) Kant means "an assumption (*Annehmung*) necessary with regard to the subject [of moral law] for complying with ... practical laws, hence merely a necessary hypothesis."[230]

Now, Kant has hardly postulated the existence of a God whom we could consider to be the Absolute, that is, "that than which nothing greater could be thought."[231] Indeed, it would seem that any speaker who uses the name "God" to refer to anyone less than the Absolute is using that name incorrectly. Moreover, even taking God's will to be functioning at the beginning of the process of instantiating the idea of morality still makes God's will subordinate to the idea it is instantiating. Taking God to be the One who coordinates the beginning of the process in the idea of moral law with the end of the process leading to a fundamental transformation of nature *because* of that idea-then-ideal being realized in the world, that seems to make God's will doubly subordinate: both to the beginning idea and to the idealized end result. To retain the name "God" with integrity, "God" has to refer to more, much more than what seems to be some kind of cosmic facilitator. In fact, this might explain why many atheistic Kantians, who want a purely godless Kant, have so little difficulty in excising from their overall Kantian stance in practical philosophy what seem to be Kant's rather feeble theological efforts.[232] And, conversely, many theists (whether Jewish or Christian) avoid Kant because they see no way to connect Kant to their far more robust theism.

Nevertheless, Hermann Cohen, the greatest of the Jewish Kantians (also the leader of the "back to Kant" movement in late-nineteenth-century secular philosophy in Germany), attempted to keep, even strengthen, a theological connection to his overall Kantian position in ethics. We now need to critically examine Cohen's Kantian theism to see if it is consistent with traditional Jewish theology. In other words (to paraphrase Pascal's famous challenge), is the God Cohen as a Kantian philosopher thinks of, is that God still the God of Abraham, Isaac, and Jacob?

Cohen had no problem accepting Kant's subordination of traditional religious praxis (with which Judaism abounds) to morality. Speaking of Jewish law as the system of the commandments (*mitsvot*), he writes: "Of course, there is a distinction among the laws ... But this distinction is not of the sort which introduces a contradiction into the unity of the law. For what is not moral law in itself [*an sich*] is at least thought of and expressly characterized as a means to the promotion of, and education in, moral law."[233] However, at the more theoretical level, Cohen does have a problem not only with Kant's designation of institutional religion as a means to a greater end, but with what seems to be Kant's designation of even God Himself in this less than ultimate role. Moreover, Cohen certainly cannot accept "happiness" (*Glückseligkeit*) – which Cohen called "eudaimonism" – as the "purpose" (*Zweck*) or even the intended final result of rational moral action in the world.[234]

What Cohen did, with remarkable metaphysical ingenuity, was to designate God Himself as the end towards *whom* all moral action is always striving. And since God is infinite, moral striving is forever tending towards that end without ever being able to reach it. Thus any identification with God (what some have called *unio mystica*) is impossible, for an attainable end would have to be finite (a *terminus ad quem*), not infinite (as we have seen). Thus Cohen insists: "God and man do not constitute an identity, but a correlation. God's ideality is fulfilled in his uniqueness [*Einzigkeit*]."[235] We see this in Cohen's ontology, where he constitutes the correlation of Being and Becoming.

At the level of creation, which is the relation of God and the world, God does not act as an efficient cause who makes the world. The world does not derive from God as an effect is derived from its cause. Instead, God is the Unique Being who is only to be thought of when contrasted with the multiplicity of the world, which is always becoming a variety of things. It is not that many come out of one – or emanate from one – but rather the many are many insofar as they are *not* one; and one is one insofar as it is *not* many.[236] That is how Cohen thinks of God as "Origin" (*Ursprung*) *of* the world, rather than functioning as a cause *in* the world.[237] Without this opposition to Becoming, God-as-Being would be unthinkable, just as without this opposition to Being, the world-as-Becoming would be unthinkable. Ontology, therefore, is inherently dialectical.

However, the ontology of creation is negative; it does not involve any positive relation between God-as-Being and the world-as-Becoming. For a positive relation would involve interaction between Being and Becoming as *persons*, and that means the relation involves intentional praxis, that is, moral action. Like Kant, Cohen moves from theoretical reason to practical reason, where interpersonal interaction is its essential subject matter. As Cohen puts it, "only when reason becomes moral reason ... and secures more than the problem of causality ... only the question of wherefrom and whereby [*wohin und wodurch*] is supplemented with the question whereto and wherefore [*wohin und wozu*]; only when ... supplemented by the interest in the purpose [*am Zwecke*]."[238] Moving methodically, Cohen then goes on to say that "with the notion of purpose the concept of correlation moves from the realm of theoretical knowledge into the realm of the ethical."[239]

Unlike the Aristotelians for whom (as we saw in the preceding chapter), ethical teleology functions *within* cosmic or ontological teleology, Cohen follows Kant in assuming that teleology is what ethics as the constitution of the rational world brings to the natural world itself, having a trajectory that goes beyond or transcends the natural world. After the demise of Aristotelian natural science, we do not get teleology from nature any more. Moreover, Cohen has gone farther than Kant insofar as the moral *telos* he envisions is an infinite ideal that, unlike "happiness," cannot be conceived due to its infinity. He has also gone beyond Hegel, whose ideal teleology of history seems to have a realized conclusion at the end of history.[240]

To be sure, the classical Jewish tradition at times seems to give priority to the interhuman relationship governed by moral law over the God-human relationship governed by religious law.[241] Nevertheless, humans are beings who are worthy of being treated as ends-by-themselves because they are the objects of God's direct concern.[242] We humans experience God's direct concern for us in our acceptance of the commandments in order to do what we have specifically been commanded to do.[243] That direct concern of God is what the human objects of that concern most deeply share with other humans; it is what they have in common, especially when they are members of a community covenanted by God.[244] And that direct concern of God for them is what humans reciprocate back to God directly in their common observance of the commandments that pertain to God as the direct object of the commanded act. This is most evident in the commandment to pray to God directly.[245] Moreover, to pray for one's fellow humans, individually and communally, is considered to be both a moral act and a religious act simultaneously.[246] (In fact, with some rare exceptions, even when one is alone, one still prays in the first person plural: *we* not *I*.) But, of course, that assumes the direct relation of humans and God is original, that it cannot be reduced to a relation that is more original and more direct. This relation in no way derives from or functions for anything more original and more direct.

Now, our morality consists of our dutiful response to the rightful or just claims other humans make upon us, and the equally just claims we make on others. Through these symmetrical claims, which are validated by moral law, we learn what others want from us and what we want from them. Our religion consists of our responding to the just claims God makes on us and, asymmetrically, the claims God allows us to make on Him (especially in petitionary prayer).[247] Moreover, we know the just claims of others on us and our just claims on them because they tell us or *reveal to us* what they want from us and what we want from them. So, too, do we know what God wants from us through our learning what has been commanded in the Torah, and God learns what we want from Him by listening to our prayers to Him.[248] However, the difference between the two is that we regularly reveal what we want to each other insofar as we necessarily inhabit the same world. Therefore, this is a matter of ordinary experience, ready at hand. However, unlike our fellow humans, God does not necessarily inhabit a common world with us. God only comes into our world unexpectedly to be with us. As God told Moses when He revealed Himself to Moses at the burning bush: "I shall be wherever and whenever I shall be (*ehyeh asher ehyeh*)" (Exodus 3:14).[249] And as Jeremiah complained to God: "Why are You like a transient [*ger*] in the land, like a guest who only stays for the night?!" (Jeremiah 14:8).

What is similar in both spheres of relationality is that the relationship between the parties, whether between humans themselves or between God and humans, is direct and original. Not only is the God-human relationship not derivative of the interhuman relationship, but even the interhuman relationship is not derivative of the God-human relationship. Rather, the interhuman relationship is included in the God-human relationship insofar as God's relationship is with humans as essentially social beings; yet it is not subsumed by the God-human relationship so that we have to reject our fellow humans in order to have a full relationship with God.[250] We humans cannot enjoy a relationship with God alone, even when our fellow humans are not immediately there with us bodily. Along these lines, the Rabbis interpret God's covenant to be both "with those who are standing here with us today before the Lord our God, but also with those who are not with us here today" (Deuteronomy 29:14). That is, the covenant is also with all those who in the future (*ha-dorot he'atidim*) will be participants in the covenant and included in the covenant's renewal in the Wilderness, even though they are not present there.[251]

Needless to say, all of this is a far cry from what Hermann Cohen (and other liberal Jewish thinkers of lesser mind) did to make the God-human relationship not direct and original, but instead derivative and epiphenomenal. This more than anything else is what Cohen's student Franz Rosenzweig attempted to overcome in his return to the sources of Judaism, as we have seen, even though there are some theological problems with the way Rosenzweig constitutes the God-human relationship.

The Relation of God and Nature

As for the relation of God and nature, Kant is willing to at least admit that the natural world could have been created by God, that is, there is nothing inherently irrational about that assertion. Nevertheless, he insists this admission does not add anything to our understanding of the natural world. Even if, for argument's sake, we assume that God *did* in fact create the natural world, nature itself in no way tells us *how* God did it. As such, our understanding of the internal workings of nature remains the same with or without this theistic assumption.[252] And even more so, nature doesn't tell us *why* God created it. In other words, nature does not indicate to us the way it came to be or any purpose *for which* it came to be. Indeed, to introduce these considerations of original causality or final causality into scientific discourse would be an irrelevant distraction from the interests of modern scientific discourse. Yet without directly indicating how or why God created the world, does nature perhaps suggest what God's connection to its beginning or its end might be? And if so, *to whom* does such a suggestion seem to be addressed?

Now, in the other areas of relationality we have examined with a Kantian lens, there is a connection to us humans: in the relation of *humans and* nature; in the interrelation *between humans themselves*; and in the relation of God *and humans*. Therefore, in order to make the relation of God and nature more than speculation unconnected to any kind of human experience, which is thinking as if we humans were not there, we have to see a connection of the God-nature relation to one of these other spheres of relationality in which we humans are direct participants.

In terms of the relation of humans and nature, we did see an oblique suggestion that because things-by-themselves could not be the products of any human will, they might well be the products of someone else's will; and that other will could only be God's.[253] Only God could bring an entity into existence. As such, we may not totally appropriate an entity's existence, but still appreciate it as a thing-by-itself that is always more than the means to an end of our own that we have willingly projected. (It would seem that such an entity is something like "the starry sky above" that filled Kant with awe, that is, it is an entity that lies beyond our technical grasp.)[254] Nevertheless, this assertion is in fact a negation, that is, this be-coming is *not* what any will other than God's could possibly accomplish. It does not constitute a positive relation with anyone else at all. Furthermore, for Kant and his followers, even the indirect yet positive relation of God and humans is itself epiphenomenal. It only functions for the sake of the direct interhuman relationship. It would seem that the even more indirect relation of God and nature needs to be seen as functioning for that most direct, most original, positive relation too.

There is no doubt Kant deemed the interhuman relationship, constituted by moral law, to be the original foundation for which the other three spheres of relationality function. What humans bring to the world immediately through moral law is purposiveness or teleology per se. The uniquely moral concern of humans is with ends-by-themselves beyond or transcending nature. That is essentially different from our pragmatic concern with things whose ends are immanent within nature, that is, things that are either useful for our worldly work or enjoyable for our worldly play. But how do the relation of humans and nature and the relation of God and nature contribute to the teleology inherent in the morally constituted interhuman relationship? In other words, what are the teleological suggestions or implications of these two subordinate spheres of relationality? (We have already seen in the previous section how the abstract relation of God and humans contributes to concrete interhuman relations and the moral teleology that characterizes them as rational.)

In regard to the cognitive relation of humans and nature, Kant states: "Nature makes its universal laws specific in accordance with the principle of purposiveness [*Zweckmässigkeit*] for our cognitive power – that is, in a way commensurate [*Angemessenheit*] with the human understanding with its necessary task of finding the universal for the particular offered [*darbieten*] by perception."[255] Now Kant seems to be saying the following: To be sure, we do not derive universals, much less purposes, from the perceptual data of nature. Instead, we bring our universal categories to the data of nature so as to order them accordingly. However, we still cannot apply universal categories to the data of nature willy-nilly. Somehow or other, our categories must fit the data to which they are being applied. That seems to imply that the data are *given* to us in a way we can understand them, that is, in a way through which our categories can *receive* them intelligently. Thus one could say, however unscientifically, that the data have been *intended* for our cognition.[256] But, since the things-by-themselves that send the data to us do not have an intending will, who could so intend them except the One who brought the things-by-themselves into existence, namely, God? That is, the data have been intentionally sent forth *by* God *for* us. The data have been intended; their source in the thing-by-itself does not do the intending.

Nevertheless, since we do not know how this intention is actually done, the teleological implications of our cognition of nature get us no further in our attempt to connect this teleology to our own. All it seems to tell us is that teleology is not invented by us; instead, it is intended for us. Thinking of ourselves as the passive objects of a natural teleological intention enables us to then further that intention by ourselves becoming subjects who actively and freely intend ends beyond the confines of the natural world, and who act on their behalf accordingly. But what carries us further? Kant states it quite clearly:

> It is judgment ... this power provides us with the concept that mediates between the concepts of nature and the concepts of freedom. The concept of a purposiveness of nature, which makes possible the transition [*Übergang*] from pure theoretical to pure practical lawfulness [*Gesetzmässigkeit*], from lawfulness in terms of nature to the final purpose [*Endzwecks*] set by the concept of freedom.[257]

How, though, does what nature suggests to us launch us in our willed moral trajectory? Kant answers: "Hence nature is here called sublime [*erhaben*] merely because it elevates [*erhebt*] our imagination [making] it exhibit those cases where the mind can come to feel its own sublimity, which lies in its vocation [*seiner Bestimmung*] and elevates it even above nature."[258] In other words, in our speculating about nature's purposiveness, in our feeling that its data are intended for us, we can thereby think of ourselves as being *like* the God *who* originally intended these data to be received by our cognition. And these data come from the thing-by-itself, which it could be said God created as essentially an end-by-itself rather than as useful material for anyone else. And Kant also speaks of "a remote analogy with our own causality in terms of purposes generally ... for the sake of [assisting] that same practical power in us."[259] In other words, just as God creates natural entities not just to be useful means to some other end but as ends-by-themselves, so do we as morally creative beings ideally project acts that are done for their own sake. Thus God's purposeful creation of nature is the archetype for our purposeful actions done for their own sake. (Acts that we do for worldly purposes are not practical but pragmatic or instrumental insofar as their ends are already within the natural world; they do not go beyond it.) When considered metaphysically, moral praxis is *imitatio Dei*, in the sense that we humans discover our purposive or teleological capacity to be akin to God's. The difference, though, between us and God is that God created that capacity within us, whereas we can only *subsequently* employ it in our moral projection of acts done for their own sake, which is for the sake of the persons who are the objects of these acts. Our moral capacity is not something we invent; it is innate within us before we actually will anything.

In developing his notion of the conjunction of external nature and inner human freedom, Kant speaks of "man ... [as] the ultimate purpose of nature [*als Naturzweck*] here on earth, the purpose by reference to [*in Beziehung*] which all other natural things constitute a system of purposes."[260] Now, the first impression one gets from this statement is that humans may look upon nature as having been put there by God for the sake of our use, as "grist for our mill." In fact, this sounds like the remark attributed to the seventeenth-century Massachusetts Puritan merchant: "How good of God to have made Boston harbour to be so useful for our shipping!" That impression implies that not only is nature made *for* our purposes, but also that our pragmatic purposes are found *in* nature.

Nevertheless, Kant speaks of "nature as harmonizing [*Übereinstimmung*] with our need to find universal principles for them," but that "nature harmonizes with our aim [*Absicht*], though only [*aber nur*] insofar as this is directed to cognition."[261] In other words, Kant's "though only" means there is a fundamental difference between taking nature to be for our noetic purposes and taking nature to be the means for the fulfilment of our bodily or economic needs. Now, taking nature to be useful is our learning how to manipulate nature from within. Yet that means we want to remain therein, only wanting to be in a more dominant active position within the natural order than if we passively waited for the chance to find what we want therein or, even more so, if we waited for nature to actually give us what we need directly (like a mother feeding her infant child). Of course, other animals do that too, but we humans seem to be able to do it with greater technical skill. (Nevertheless, our difference from other animals, in this respect, is a difference of degree, not a difference of kind.) Thus, in this instrumental or pragmatic view of our relation to nature, nature is there for the taking or the finding; whether it has been given to us or not by someone else is irrelevant to our technical purposes.

Let us recall, however, from our discussion of Kant's view of the cognitive relation of humans to nature, especially as regards the thing-by-itself, that nature is basically not to be regarded as simply there for our taking. Rather, as we can now better understand, nature's Creator has *given* to our conceptual *reception* only some of the humanly graspable intelligible aspects of this created entity.[262] Moreover, since the thing-by-itself as an end-by-itself is primarily in the world for purposes that are not ours, our cognition of natural entities is essentially different from our use of natural things. As Kant put it, "if the concept ... is a concept of nature, then the principles will be technically practical ... [they are] not only the means we find in nature for producing them, but even the will (as the power of desire and hence a natural power) as ... determined ... by natural incentives [*Triebfedern*]."[263] On the other hand, "the mere form of purposiveness, insofar as we are conscious of it, is the presentation [*Vorstellung*] by which an object is given [*Annehmlichkeit*] us."[264] Surely, the sense that the natural object is given to us is that it is given to us to appreciate as a spectator, not as a consumer. Our cognitive motivation is aesthetic, not instrumental. The ultimate trajectory of aesthetics is to elevate (*erhebt* in German) us towards what is sublime, whereas the ultimate trajectory of instrumentality is to lower us towards what is mundane, even trivial.

One can tentatively conclude the following from what Kant has written in this regard: God's purpose for creating any natural entity could not be because God has some natural need to do so. For if God had such a need, that would surely imply that God himself is a natural being having needs, and that the means to their fulfilment are available *in* a world already there, *of* which God would be part (however exalted a part God would be). But this does not at all befit the transcendent Creator God. God's purposes are for the world apart from Godself, not for God who is a part of the world. So, too, we humans can imitate God's transcendent purposiveness when we project our morally willed ends that do not refer us back to the natural world, but that enable us to go beyond the purposes already there in the natural world. To be sure, we humans are within a natural world that has already been there before our natal entrance therein and after our mortal exit therefrom; hence we have natural needs that can only be fulfilled in this world. In that way, we are unlike God. God creates *ex nihilo* with nothing before or after Him. Conversely, we humans can only create (i.e., morally) *de novo*; and we can only create acts, whereas God and God alone can create beings.

(And if these acts of ours are to have ontological reality, Kant thinks that requires divine intervention.)[265]

Nevertheless, although we humans are unlike God because of our being *in* the world already there, we are still like God by our not being essentially *of* the natural world. Therefore, to say that we humans are "the ultimate purpose of nature" might mean that we may look upon nature as having a purpose, and that purpose is only thought of when we look at the data coming to us from natural entities as having been given to us by their Creator. But *for what* have they been given? Perhaps they have been given to us by God from nature, not to be given back to nature for our use there. Instead, they are given to us gratuitously as a model for how we are to treat other humans as ends-by-themselves.

Jewish Reactions to Kant's Notion of the Relation of God and Nature

There is no point trying to locate a Jewish Kantian who follows Kant's treatment of the relation of God and nature, for there is none (to my knowledge). That is because Kant took the reality of nature far more seriously than did Hermann Cohen, and Cohen was the greatest of the Jewish Kantians (whom virtually all of the lesser Jewish Kantians have followed). Now, Cohen read Kant in a way that no longer saw any cognitive need to posit the existence of the thing-by-itself lying behind the perceptual data humans cognize; and the thing-by-itself (as we have seen) is what ensures their real externality.[266] As such, the creative relation of God and nature, which Kant himself still thought of seriously, was something that the Jewish Kantians, largely following Cohen, rejected. So, we can now go directly to the sources of the Jewish tradition that offer a more robust view of the relation of God and nature, but that can still be seen as challenged by Kant's view thereof.

As we have seen, in the Jewish tradition the prime sphere of relationality is the relation of God and humans. The other three spheres of relationality are ultimately valid insofar as they contribute to this prime sphere of relationality. The relation of humans and nature is ultimately validated when the first act of a human relating himself to God is when "Cain brought from the fruit of the ground [which he had tilled] an offering [*minhah*] to the Lord" (Genesis 4:3). The relation of humans among themselves is ultimately validated when Eve says, giving birth for the first time due to having been impregnated by Adam, "I have created [*qaniti*] a man with the Lord" (Genesis 4:1).[267] Now, this first birth of a human child is the result of the first interhuman act recorded in Scripture, that is, sexual intercourse between the first man and the first woman. And even though the marital union makes a man and a woman independent of their human parents – "Therefore a man shall leave his father and his mother and cleave to his wife and they shall become one flesh" (Genesis 2:24) – the marital union does not make the human couple independent of God.[268]

Even though the relation of humans and nature and the interhuman relationship are ultimately for the sake of the divine-human relationship, that does not mean that these other two spheres of relationality are simply reducible to the prime sphere of relationality, that is, the relation of God and humans. Each sphere of relationality has its own phenomenological integrity; none is merely epiphenomenal. As such, the other spheres of relationality are not subsumed by the prime relational sphere. The only proviso is that the God-human relationship retain its ultimate priority in cases of doubt.[269] So, even though humans are to regard their relation to nature as ultimately validated by its contribution to the God-human relationship, humans are still entitled to relate to nature for their own mundane purposes as well. For example, once the parts of our produce that the Torah requires we dedicate to God's altar have been so dedicated, we humans are free to do with the rest of what we have acquired from nature whatever we want to do with it, that is, whatever we want to do with it constructively.[270] (To destroy what has been given to us, though, is to act as if we actually *own* nature that is at hand; but that is God's prerogative alone.)[271] Also, we are not to use nature in a way that contradicts divine commandments that pertain to our relation to nature.[272] "And the Lord God commanded humans saying: From all the trees of the garden you may surely eat; but from the tree of the knowledge of good and bad you may not eat" (Genesis 2:16–17). But other than that, there is quite a wide range of foods we may eat.

Furthermore, even though the interhuman relationship is ultimately for the sake of the divine-human relationship, humans are still entitled to relate to each other for their own mundane purposes. So, for example, Maimonides rules that one is not to utter a blessing (*berakhah*), that is, praising God for giving us this commandment, before engaging in an interpersonal act, such as giving charity to a poor person, even though this act has been commanded by God to be done.[273] Perhaps this is because even though all commandments are from God, whoever their object might be, when the object of that act is another human person, one should relate to that other person directly and exclusively.[274] In other words, we are to relate to other human persons as ends-by-themselves, not as the means to our relationship with anyone else, even with God. The only qualification is that this interpersonal act not violate what has been stipulated for the divine-human relationship.[275]

Even though the relation of God and nature is seen to contribute to the prime God-human relationship, it is not reducible to that relationship. It too has its relative independence. As for the contribution of the relation of God and nature to the God-human relationship, there is the rabbinic dictum that has the human person declaring: "For my sake [*bi-shevili*] has the world been created."[276] However, this is not a declaration that the natural world is created to be but a resource for human industry or for human amusement. Instead, humans are to see nature as providing the physical means to the end of serving God, which is for the sake of the covenantal relationship with God.[277] In more ontological terms: "Rabbi Eleazar said that were it not for the Torah, heaven and earth would not endure."[278] Moreover, there is the rabbinic dictum that has the Torah saying, as it were, that "I was God's instrument [*kli umanuto*] ... so did God look into the Torah and created the world."[279] But to dispel any implication that the Torah is prior to God, the late-fifteenth-century exegete Jacob ibn Habib noted that this means that God's purpose (*ha-sibbah ha-takhlitit*) in creating the world was for the Torah to be received therein.[280]

Nevertheless, to presume that the God-human relationship that the Torah constitutes is the sole purpose of the creation of the world could well lead to the most impious human arrogance.[281] The God-human relationship might be the main purpose of creation, but it is not the only purpose. This shows us that the God-human relationship is not a symbiotic correlation. God's interest in all God's creation prevents us from thinking that the God-human relationship totally subsumes God's other relations. Therefore, God's relation to nature is not reducible to God's relationship with humans. In fact, there are numerous passages in the Bible that praise God's creation of nature, irrespective of whether that can be taken as having human benefit as its purpose or not. So, for example, the Psalmist declares that God "causes herbage to grow for human labour, so [that humans] might bring forth bread from the earth" (Psalms 104:14). Yet this exclamation thereafter, "How numerous are Your works O' Lord, all of them You have wisely made; the earth is filled with Your creation!" (Psalms 104:24), is not said at all in connection with God's relationship with humans. In fact, one is supposed to praise God for natural wonders whether their effects on humans are good, bad, or indifferent.[282]

Conclusion

Kant has provided the last major philosophical challenge to Judaism, due to his fulsome constitution of the four spheres of relationality that need to be fully constituted for a complete human life. For that reason,

I do not think Kant's challenge has already run its course. The fruitful interaction of Athens and Jerusalem, especially when it involves Kant's philosophy, is not yet over. Kant has followers who still philosophize with him, and those who still cannot philosophize without him or against him. With both kinds of philosophers, whether "Kantians" or "Neo-Kantians," Jewish and Christian theologians (and perhaps now Muslim too) can engage in fruitful discourse. That is because we both speak the same language. And we can also disagree deeply because each of us conceptualizes that language quite differently.

Notes

1 Philosophy and Theology

1 *De Praescriptione Haereticorum*, 7. Latin text from *Patrologia Latina*, ed. J.-P. Migne (Paris: Migne, 1844), 2:20.

2 Alfred North Whitehead, *Process and Reality* (New York: Free Press, 1969), 53.

3 See II Kings 22:8; II Chron. 34:14–15; *Sifre*: Devarim, no. 356 re Deut. 33:27; *Y.* Taanit 4.2/68a. All translations, unless otherwise noted, are by the author.

4 Though Tertullian is now best known for his anti-Jewish treatise *Adversus Iudaeos*, where he advocates what we now call "supersessionism" (i.e., the Christian church has replaced the Jewish people as God's elected people), he faced a bigger challenge than the persistence of Judaism, Christian supersessionism notwithstanding. His real challenge, even in *Adversus Iudaeos*, was to convince philosophically oriented pagans of the superiority of Christian theology over their pagan philosophies. But by so doing, he had to acknowledge Christianity's Jewish origin, thus affirming what Christian theology still shares in common with Jewish theology. In fact, he also wrote a treatise, *Adversus Marcionem*, arguing against the claims of those Christians who saw Christianity as a total repudiation of Judaism. As such, Tertullian had to make the same type of arguments for the superiority of biblical revelation his otherwise Jewish adversaries had also been making, *mutatis mutandis*. Both Jewish and Christian theologians faced the same challenge from pagan philosophy, and reacted quite similarly. See Marcel Simon, *Verus Israel*, trans. H. McKeating (London: Littman Library, 1996), 70–8, 283; Timothy Barnes, *Tertullian* (Oxford: Clarendon Press, 1971), 92, 106.

5 Origen, *Contra Celsum*, 1.44 and 5.60; see also 1.14, 16, 19, 22; 4.26; 5.43. Greek text from *Patrologiae Graece*, ed. J.-P. Migne (Paris: Migne, 1857), 11:741 and 1276.

6 Origen, *Contra Celsum*, 5.51 (11:1261).
7 *Beresheet Rabbah* 65.20 re Gen. 27:22, ed. Theodor-Albeck, 734–5. For other places in rabbinic literature where this same story is told, see Albeck's note thereon. Oenamaus Gadereus is mentioned in *Shemot Rabbah* 13.1 as someone who posed philosophical questions to Rabbis. He might well have been the second-century Cynic philosopher discussed by Eusebius, *Praeparatio Evangelica*, 5:18–36, who was also a critic of pagan theology for being too mythical.
8 It is unlikely that the ancient Rabbis actually read the written works of Greek philosophers. As my late revered teacher Saul Lieberman asserted in "How Much Greek in Jewish Palestine?" (in *Biblical and Other Studies*, ed. Alexander Altmann [Cambridge, MA: Harvard University Press, 1963], 131): "The Rabbis drew their information from personal conversations with philosophers and other intelligent people." So, in the midrashic text just cited, we do not see *what* philosophy's exact challenge was to Jewish theology, but rather *that* the philosophers were able to challenge, even ridicule, Jewish theology (see, e.g., *T.* Avodah Zarah 6.7; *B.* Avodah Zarah 54b; *Y.* Shabbat 3.3/6a). This informal "philosophy" was part of the "Greek wisdom" (*hokhmah yevanit*) considered to be a distraction from Torah learning (B. Menahot 99b re Ps. 1:2), but knowledge of which was needed by Jews who had to deal with cultured, Greek-speaking Roman officials (B. Sotah 49b). See Saul Lieberman, *Hellenism in Jewish Palestine*, 2nd ed. (New York: Jewish Theological Seminary of America, 1962), 100. However, in at least one place in rabbinic literature, a genuine philosophic dialogue between a *pilosofos* (the Hebrew transliteration of the Greek *philosophos*) and a Rabbi is recorded (*T.* Shevuot 3.6 re Lev. 5:21). In the thirteenth century, Menahem ha-Meiri, *Bet ha-Behirah: Baba Kama* 83a, 3rd ed., ed. Schlesinger (Jerusalem: Mosad ha-Rav Kook, 1967), 239, saw *hokhmah yevanit* to be the kind of philosophical ability needed by those Jews who had to defend Judaism's rationality against philosophically sophisticated Christians. See Gregg Stern, *Philosophy and Rabbinic Culture* (London: Routledge, 2009), 27–95.
9 Now the "chirping" (i.e., chanting) of Scripture by the children took place in the synagogue, which often functioned as an elementary school, while the house-of-learning (*bet midrash*; also called *bet talmud*) was where some of these children graduated to learn the originally oral traditions (*torah she-b`al peh*) rooted in the Scripture (*torah she-bi-khtav*) they had learned in the synagogue-school (*bet sefer*). See *Y.* Megillah 3.1/73d re II Kings 25:9; also *B.* Nazir 23b re Prov. 18:1 and Rashi and *Tosafot*, s.v. "u-ve-khol." By concentrating on what the children learn in the synagogue-school, the text seems to be saying that with this kind of fundamental formation by Scripture, nothing will be able to replace it and the tradition built upon it

thereafter (see *M.* Avot 4.20). Furthermore, "chirping" (*metsaftsafin*) rather than "chanting" (i.e., *zamer*, which is the usual way the Torah is recited; see *T.*: Ohalot 16.8) might have been the gentile philosopher's ridiculing (see Rashi's comment on Isa. 8:19) what we today would call "parroting" rather than truly understanding a profound text. The implication here is that the Torah can only be "chirped" because of its inferiority to the truly intelligent words of the philosophers.

10 For the Rabbis, the epitome of the non-believing ridiculer of Jewish theology (usually gentile, though sometimes a Jewish heretic) is the *apiqoros* or "Epicurean," named after the third-century BCE Greek philosopher Epicurus of Samos, whose influence was widespread in the Roman Empire even centuries later. Unlike Plato, Aristotle, and the Stoics, he taught that since God or the heavenly gods are not interested in earthly humans, therefore humans should not be interested in them; instead humans should find their fulfilment in worldly (usually prudently hedonistic) pursuits. See Epicurus, *Fragments*, trans. Cyril Bailey, in *The Stoic and Epicurean Philosophers*, ed. W.J. Oates (New York: Random House, 1957), 40–4. Although the *apiqorsim* (Epicureans) were seen by some as posing a primarily metaphysical antinomian challenge to biblical theology (Josephus, *Contra Apionem*, 2.180, and *Antiquities*, 10.7.277–80; *M.* Sanhedrin 10.1), for the most part their challenge was more exegetical than strictly philosophical. They are usually portrayed as denigrating the inconsistencies and seeming absurdities in Scripture (e.g., *Y.* Sanhedrin 10.1/27d; also see *Bemidbar Rabbah* 18.2 re Deut. 22:12, etc.). Thus Jewish theologians were advised to "be diligent to learn what [*lilmod mah*] to respond to the *apiqoros*" (M. Avot. 2.14). That usually meant countering the biblical exegesis of the *apiqorsim* with what was seen by the Rabbis to be their own, more profound, exegesis (i.e., by "learning what" in Scripture to use in your counterarguments). In the Middle Ages, when Jewish theologians were confronting the more metaphysically challenging philosophies of Plato and Aristotle, however, *apiqoros* came to designate a metaphysically inclined Jewish heretic (e.g., *MT*: Repentance, 3.8), whose philosophically sophisticated arguments had to be countered accordingly (Maimonides's comment on *M.* Avot 2.14).

11 Furthermore, those Jews who were attracted to Roman political power instead of to Greek philosophy dismissed Judaism on pragmatic grounds, viz., the life of the house-of-learning (*bet midrash* or *bet va`ada*) is economically useless for everybody, both for the individuals themselves and for their society (*Y.* Hagigah 2.1/77a; also *B.* Shabbat 33b).

12 Tertullian and other patristic theologians did employ the methods of the philosophers. See G.D. Dunn, *Tertullian* (London: Routledge, 2004), 65. However, for these theologians, philosophy only supplied them with the

language they needed to proselytize or at least argue against contemporary philosophers. Even Tertullian's famous assertion about Christian doctrine that it is "certain – because it is impossible" (in Tertullian, *De Carne Christi*, 5.25, ed. E. Evans [London: SPCK, 1956], 19), which had been subsequently paraphrased as "I believe because it is absurd" (*credo quia absurdum*), does not mean logical absurdity, i.e., nonsense. Instead, Tertullian means what is "foolish" (*stultus*) or improbable in the eyes of the world (*De Carne Christi*, 5.7, 16–17). "In the world" (*in saeculo*) here means the world of public discourse where philosophers and their language seem to have the upper hand.

13 *B.* Hullin 60b.

14 *B.* Menahot 65b. See *Shemot Rabbah* 13.1, where the queries of Oenamaus Gadereus (see *supra*, n. 7) are called "idle matters" (*devarim betelim*). For the mediaeval continuation of this denigration of philosophy for the sake of theology, see Judah Halevi, *Kuzari*, 1.65, 2.66; and Nahmanides's comment on Lev. 16:8.

15 Those whose discourse is called here "idle chatter" are "Boethusians" (B. Menahot 65a) who were, for the Rabbis, a heretical Jewish sect who, like the Sadducees, denied the Pharisaic doctrine of supernatural other-worldly providence. For their heresy, see *Avot de-Rabbi Nathan*, chap. 5; also Josephus, *Bellum Judaicum*, 2.162–4.

16 *Responsa: ha-Rosh*, no. 55. He also distinguished there between the "decree of reason" (*gezerat ha-sekhel*), i.e., philosophy, and the "decree of divine law" (*gezerat ha-dat*), i.e., the Torah or theology.

17 The ban is found in Joseph Asruc, *Minhat Kenaot*, chap. 38 in *Teshuvot ha-Rashba*, ed. H.Z. Dimitrovsky (Jerusalem: Mosad ha-Rav Kook, 1990), 2:409–14; also Isaac bar Sheshet Parfat, *Responsa: ha-Ribash*, no. 45.

18 *M.* Sanhedrin 10.1. For the appropriateness of using the term "dogma" when doing Jewish theology, see Menachem Kellner, *Dogma in Mediaeval Jewish Thought* (Oxford: Oxford University Press, 1986), 10–65.

19 Joseph Asruc, *Minhat Kenaot*, chaps. 20–1 in *Teshuvot ha-Rashba*, 1:275–310.

20 See Stern, *Philosophy and Rabbinic Culture*, 131–212. For a contemporary defence of Maimonides, see David Hartman, *Maimonides: Torah and Philosophic Quest* (Philadelphia: Jewish Publication Society of America, 1976).

21 For sources, see *Encyclopedia Talmudit*, 7:77–82. The most profound treatment of this rabbinic doctrine is by my late revered teacher Abraham Joshua Heschel, *Heavenly Torah*, trans. G. Tucker and L. Levin (New York: Continuum, 2005), 46–64. For the "in-the-world" nature of the Torah's language, see *Esther Rabbah* 4.13 re Est. 1:22, ed. Tabory-Atzmon, 95; *Pesiqta de-Rav Kahana* 12.24 re Exod. 20:2, ed. Mandelbaum, 223; *Pesiqta Rabbati* 21 re Exod. 20:2, ed. Friedmann, 105b. This notion of the worldly

nature of the Torah's language was continued, *mutatis mutandis*, by many of the philosophical Jewish theologians, especially Maimonides in *Guide of the Perplexed*, 1.26 and 1.46 re *B.* Avodah Zarah and parallels; *MT*: Foundations, 1.9. However, there is another (indeed, the more dominant) rabbinic notion that the language of the Torah is not "human language," but rather it is its own unique language. This notion presupposes the metaphysical notion that the Torah is primordial, that its creation precedes the creation of the world (M. Avot 3.14 re Prov. 4:2; *Beresheet Rabbah* 1.1 re Prov. 8:20, and 64.8 re Gen. 26:20). This rabbinic notion was further developed by the kabbalists, who thought all of the Torah's words are permutations of the names of God. As such, they are not just primordial creations, but rather they are divine themselves, hence they are not creations of any kind at all. Thus the Torah's words are truly an exclusively inner divine monologue. In fact, how could the Torah talk about or to an external world at all since, for the kabbalists, there is nothing real outside of God for God to speak about or to speak to? See Nahmanides's introduction to his *Commentary on the Torah*, ed. C.B. Chavel, vol. 1 (Jerusalem: Mosad ha-Rav Kook, 1963), 6; *Zohar*: Yitro, 3:87a; Gershom Scholem, *On the Kabbalah and Its Symbolism*, trans. R. Manheim (New York: Schocken Books, 1969), 36–45. This is the reason that the Torah is not known by worldly ratiocination, but only by received teaching (*kabbalah*) transmitted via authentic authoritative teachers. See Nahmanides, "Sermon on Kohelet" in *Kitvei Ramban*, ed. C.B. Chavel (Jerusalem: Mosad ha-Rav Kook, 1963), 1:190. That is why, as far as I know, no kabbalistic text invokes the principle *dibrah torah ke-lashon bnei adam*. In this great debate in the history of Jewish theology, I humbly side with the philosophical theologians in their continuation of the less dominant rabbinic notion of the worldly nature of the Torah's language.

22 All Jewish theology does not engage philosophy. The two genres of non-philosophical Jewish theology are rabbinic theology and kabbalistic theology. Rabbinic theology can be said to be "non-philosophical" for, as we have seen, it is quite unlikely that the ancient Rabbis (whether in Palestine or Babylonia) had any real contact with philosophers like Platonists, Aristotelians, or Stoics, i.e., with philosophers of a definite school of thought (see *supra*, n. 8) who proposed an alternative way of life to Judaism. Generally, in the rabbinic writings the term *pilosofos* refers to a non-believer (whether Jewish or gentile) who challenges or ridicules biblical teaching or traditional Jewish practices (see *supra*, n. 10). However, these sceptical, even contemptuous, non-believers seem to have been countering traditional Jewish theology randomly rather than from a definite point of view of their own. So, the ancient Rabbis didn't have to deal with "philosophy" as a comprehensive solid alternative to their

theology as did Jewish theologians like Philo and Maimonides, inasmuch as there was no such alternative in their world. Kabbalistic theology, on the other hand, pretended philosophy wasn't there by itself pretending to be rabbinic theology (thus the foundational kabbalistic work, the *Zohar*, was presented as the work of the second-century CE Rabbi Simeon bar Yohai). But as modern scholarship about Kabbalah has shown, the kabbalists considered their theology itself to be superior to the Jewish philosophical theology in its understanding of the deeper meaning of the Torah. As such, post-Zoharic kabbalah, especially, became explicitly anti-philosophical. See Gershom Scholem, *Major Trends in Jewish Mysticism*, 3rd rev. ed. (New York: Schocken, 1954), 28–32. Nevertheless, modern scholarship about Kabbalah has also uncovered philosophical influences on kabbalistic theology, though not explicitly cited or even acknowledged by the kabbalists. Thus the kabbalists differed sharply from philosophical theologians like Philo and Maimonides, who were explicit in citing the philosophers whom they engaged. See Moshe Idel, *Kabbalah: New Perspectives* (New Haven: Yale University Press, 1988), 42–9, 143–4.

23 For Jewish and Christian proselytizing, often conducted in competition with each other (and with the philosophers), see Salo W. Baron, *A Social and Religious History of the Jews*, 2nd rev. ed. (New York: Columbia University Press, 1952), 2:147–62.

24 Throughout this work, I generally use the term "metaphysics" to designate subjective knowledge of objective ultimate reality or "being," itself designated by the term "ontology."

25 See, e.g., *B.* Shabbat 22a.

26 *M.* Avot 1.17; *B.* Kiddushin 40b, and Baba Kama 17a and Rashi, s.v. "mev'i le-ydei ma`aseh" (cf. *Tosafot*, s.v. "ve-he'amar"). Along these lines, from a Christian perspective, see George Lindbeck, *The Nature of Doctrine* (Philadelphia: Westminster Press, 1984), 33–41.

27 All this was most famously argued by Judah Halevi, *Kuzari*, 1.4.

28 The best such arguments were made by the chief Jewish advocate in the most famous of the mediaeval disputations (where Jews had to defend themselves and Judaism from the arguments of Christian interlocutors), Moses ben Nahman of Gerona or Nahmanides (Ramban). See Robert Chazan, *Barcelona and Beyond: The Disputation of 1263 and Its Aftermath* (Berkeley: University of California Press, 1992), 172–94.

29 See Saadiah Gaon, *The Book of Beliefs and Opinions*, trans. S. Rosenblatt (New Haven: Yale University Press, 1948), 3.7. Living in ninth-century Babylonia (now Iraq), Saadiah was especially aware of the Muslim charges that Mosaic (i.e., biblical) revelation, though having some divinely revealed elements, is nevertheless filled with human interpolations and outright distortions. Thus the Torah deviates from the true Abrahamic

monotheism fully and finally revealed to Muhammed. See *Quran* 2:59, 140; 3:78, 187; 5:13, 43–9, 71; 10:37. Of course, due to his having to live under Islamic rule, Saadiah's critique of Islamic supersessionism had to be implicit, evident only to theologically sophisticated readers.

30 *MT*: Kings, 11.3 (uncensored ed.). Cf. Matthew 12:8. Actually, Christian arguments about the abrogation of the positive commandments of the Torah are less radical than Muslim arguments about the Torah being a seriously flawed, indeed fraudulent, transmission of authentic revelation. That is because Christians accept the Hebrew Bible (their "Old Testament") as unflawed revelation (i.e., as *Torah*). Only on some key points do they offer normatively significant interpretations of canonical Scripture different from those of the Jews. See Maimonides, *Teshuvot ha-Rambam*, no. 149, ed. Blau (Jerusalem: Meqitsei Nirdamim, 1960), 1:284–5. Indeed, one can look upon the rabbinic writings and the New Testament as often differing, yet both being *midrashim* on the same, commonly accepted written revelation, and often making similar theological points.

31 See *MT*: Kings, 11.3 (uncensored ed.); Maimonides, *Guide*, 3.29. This, of course, presupposes that monotheism is required of all humans because it is clearly evident to all rational persons. See *MT*: Kings, 8.10–11 and 9.1. This is based on the rabbinic teaching that idolatry is proscribed even to the gentiles (*T.* Avodah Zarah 8.4; *B.* Sanhedrin 56a). Since idolatry is the practical expression of polytheism, Maimonides sees the rejection of idolatrous praxis as presupposing the theoretical affirmation of the oneness of God (*MT*: Strange Worship, 1.3 and Forbidden Intercourse, 14.2).

32 See esp. Deut. 29:9–14, 28.

33 Cf. Alasdair MacIntyre, *Whose Justice? Which Rationality?* (Notre Dame: University of Notre Dame Press, 1988), 1–11, 389–403.

34 *B.* Makkot 23b–24a re Exod. 20:2–3. *The* historical event in which revelation occurs, i.e., the Sinai theophany, does not lend itself to the type of philosophical generalization in which events are occurrences of a recurring process (like natural events), and are then explained by the theoretical representation of that process. Instead, this event is the core of a master narrative that offers an archetypal explanation of subsequent lesser events that are compared to it as asymmetrical analogues (M. Pesahim 10.5 re Exod. 13:8).

35 Isa. 43:9–12, 44:8; Judah Halevi, *Kuzari*, 1.87; *MT*: Foundations, 7.6.

36 To look upon "history" as having the general intelligibility we see in natural processes had to wait for Hegel, who famously said in *Reason in History* (trans. R.S. Hartman [New York: Liberal Arts Press, 1953], 12) that "only the study of world history itself can show that it has proceeded rationally, that it represents the rationally necessary course of the World

Spirit, the Spirit whose nature is indeed always one and the same." Of course, there are few if any historians today who would make this kind of metaphysical claim for the study of any history as *the* one history of the world (*Weltgeschichte*). In fact, post-Hegelians are closer to ancient pagans who looked upon historical events as being ontologically inferior to nature. That is why more recent historical scholarship has become a social science that tries as much as possible to be like a natural science.

37 See Thomas Aquinas, *Summa Contra Gentiles*, 3.2/139.15. Cf. Hegel, *Phenomenology of Spirit*, trans. A.V. Miller (Oxford: Oxford University Press, 1977), pref., 11: "The True [*Das Wahre*] is the whole. But the whole is nothing other than the essence [*Wesen*] consummating itself [*vollendende*] through its development [*Entwicklung*]. Of the Absolute it must be said that it is essentially [*wesentlich*] a *result*, that only in the end is it what it truly is; and that precisely in this consists its nature, viz., to be actual [*Wirkliches*], subject, the spontaneous becoming of itself [*Sichselbstwerden*]."

38 The Canadian-Jewish philosopher Emil Fackenheim (d. 2003) called these events "root experiences" in his *God's Presence in History* (New York: Harper and Row, 1970), 8–14. In his *To Mend the World* (New York: Schocken Books, 1982), Fackenheim called them "epoch-making events." There on pp. 173–5 he uses the German term *Ereignis*, quoting and accepting Martin Heidegger's formulation and conceptualization of the term in *Zur Sache des Denkens* (Tübingen: Max Niemeyer Verlag, 1969), 53. Heidegger's rethinking *Ereignis* is his secular reconstitution of the theological concept of revelation. Fackenheim restores *Ereignis* to theology.

39 This is the leitmotif of the work of Abraham Joshua Heschel. See his *God in Search of Man* (New York: Farrar, Straus, and Cudahy, 1955).

40 *MT*: Foundations, 7.3.

41 In the *Babylonian Talmud*, this principle is often employed to denote the evident, hence nonmetaphorical, straightforward character of the Torah's prescriptions, i.e., its immediately normative content (e.g., *B.* Kiddushin 17b re Deut. 15:14). In fact, metaphors are considered to be the rare exceptions in the Torah's prescriptions (e.g., *B.* Sanhedrin 72a a là *T.* Sanhedrin 11.9 and *Sifre*: Devarim, no. 237 re Deut. 22:17, ed. Finkelstein, 269). Even midrashic elaboration that seems to ignore the evident meaning (*peshat*) of a scriptural prescription is also considered to be exceptional (e.g., *B.* Yevamot 24a a là *Sifre*: Devarim, no. 289, 307 re Deut. 25:6). For the general rabbinic view that the Torah's descriptive language is metaphorical, see, e.g., *Pesiqta de-Rav Kahana* IV: Parah Adumah re I Kings 8:12, ed. Mandelbaum, 62. That is why norms advocated in the interpretation of descriptive scriptural passages are to be taken as individual opinions having no immediate prescriptive authority. See *Y.* Peah 2.6/17a; B.M. Lewin, *Otsar ha-Geonim*: *B.* Hagigah 14a, nos.

67–9 (Jerusalem: Hebrew University Press Association, 1931), 59–60; Nahmanides, "Disputation," in *Kitvei Ramban*, ed. Chavel (Jerusalem: Mosad ha-Rav Kook, 1963), 1:304–9. And Maimonides employs this principle no fewer than six times in the *Guide* (1.26, 29, 33, 46, 53; 3.13) to explain why most scriptural God-talk is to be taken as metaphor, thus enabling philosophically astute believers to look beyond the metaphor for the metaphysical truth the metaphor is alluding to. Simultaneously, this is meant to prevent those believers who are not philosophically astute from taking the metaphors literally and thus being led into dangerous theological error, or attempting the equally dangerous pursuit of what is beyond their intellectual capability. See Maimonides, *Commentary on the Mishnah*: Hagigah 2.1, ed. Kafih, 250; *MT*: Foundations, 4.13; *Guide*, pt. 1, intro., 5–14; also James A. Diamond, *Converts, Heretics, and Lepers: Maimonides and the Outsider* (Notre Dame: University of Notre Dame Press, 2007), 1–10 et passim. For Maimonides, prevention of metaphysical error requires legal prescription of basic theological principles (see *Commentary on the Mishnah*: Sanhedrin, chap. 10).

42 Y. Peah 1.1/15b re Deut. 32:47.

43 *B.* Sanhedrin 59a re Lev. 18:5. Even though the Rabbis were selective as to the disciples (*talmidim*) to whom they communicated their deepest teaching (e.g., *B.* Berakhot 8a; 28a), nonetheless it seems their more general discourses were open to the public, even including gentile hearers (B. Berakhot 61b; *B.* Baba Metsia 24a; *B.* Avodah Zarah 24a).

44 *B.* Pesahim 64b; *B.* Kiddushin 54a.

45 Plato, *Apology*, 31C–D, 33C, 40B–C. See *Republic*, 493B, 499B.

46 Note *B.* Pesahim 66a: "Even if Israel are not themselves prophets, they are the descendants of prophets [*bnei nevi'im*]."

47 For "faith" (*emunah*) as certain receptivity of revealed truth, see *B.* Berakhot 4a re Ps. 27:13.

48 Plato, *Symposium*, 204C, where love is discussed in terms of what is loved for its own sake (*to eraston*).

49 Aristotle (*Metaphysics*, 12.7/1072b1–5) speaks of what is loved for itself alone (*erōmenon*). Epictetus, in the name of the founder of the Stoics, Zeno of Citium, speaks of desire worthy of a rational human being as what is directed towards his or her true end (*telos*), which is "to follow the gods" (who know truth better than do humans) (*Arrian's Discourse of Epictetus*, 1.20). That is "desire [*orexis*] for the good" (1.4), and what humans "have in common [*koinon*] with the gods" (1.3). See Cicero, *De Legibus*, 1.7.23.

50 This is a profound point I gratefully acknowledge having learned from my late friend the Lutheran theologian Robert Jenson. See my essay "Theology and Philosophy: An Exchange with Robert Jenson" in *Trinity, Time, and*

Church: A Response to the Theology of Robert W. Jenson, ed. C.E. Gunton (Grand Rapids: Eerdmans, 2000), 42–61.

51 Plato, *Apology*, 19A, 30A; *Crito*, 52E–53B.

52 I Kings 21:18–19; *B*. Sanhedrin 20a and *Tosafot*, s.v. "melekh."

53 I Kings 18:17–18; Plato, *Apology*, 29D–31B.

54 Note Spinoza's insistence on "the liberty to philosophize" (*libertas philosophandi*), uncensored by the state, in his *Tractatus Theologico-Politicus* (in *Opera*, vol. 3, ed. C. Gebhardt [Heidelberg: Carl Winter, 1925]), chap. 20, which is something he could not exercise in the rabbinically dominated Amsterdam Jewish community nor in a Netherlands that was still dominated by the Dutch Reformed clergy. And it was something he couldn't have exercised in the Portugal his ancestors fled, which was dominated by the Catholic Inquisition.

55 Plato, *Apology*, 24B; Amos 7:10–17.

56 See Leo Strauss, "The Mutual Influence of Theology and Philosophy," *Independent Journal of Philosophy* (1979), 3: 118.

57 Plato, *Apology*, 23A.

58 Wittgenstein, *Tractatus Logico-Philosophicus*, trans. D.F. Pears and B.F. McGuiness (London: Routledge and Kegan Paul, 1961), 6.54–7.

59 Plato, *Republic*, 337E.

60 Plato, *Euthyphro*, 5D–11E.

61 *B*. Makkot 24a.

62 *B*. Moed Qatan 21b re Ps. 37:31.

63 This follows the reading of the Septuagint (LXX): *synēte*, and the Old Latin: *intelligitis*. The Masoretic text, however, puns *ta'aminu* (you will be faithful) with *te'amenu* (you will not be established). Thus the response *amen* is a confirming expression of certitude, i.e., it is verbal agreement with what has been certainly stated and which is asking for a certain response (see, e.g., *B*. Shevuot 36a re Deut. 27:26 and Nahmanides's comment thereon). Surely, that response is all the more certain when it is based on understanding. See Ps. 119:30.

64 Anselm, *Proslogion*, 1.1. See Karl Barth, *Fides Quaerens Intellectum*, trans. I.W. Robertson (London: SCM Press, 1960).

65 Maimonides, *Sefer ha-Mitsvot*, pos. no. 1, and *MT*: Foundations, 1.6–7 re Exod. 20:2 and Deut. 6:4.

66 Thus when Moses requests a direct vision of God Himself, God only tells him *how* God beneficently interacts with humans (Exod. 33:18–23; 34:5–7). This is *what* humans ought to thereby imitate as exemplary commandments, which pertain to the divine-human relationship as well as well as to the interhuman relationship (B. Shabbat 133b re Exod. 15:2). This also entitles humans to beseech God to act with them in the way (i.e., *how*) God seems to have obligated Himself to act with them and has, in fact,

acted that way and told them just how He so acted (B. Rosh Hashanah 17b re Exod. 34:6).

67 John Rawls, *A Theory of Justice* (Cambridge, MA: Harvard University Press, 1971), sec. 24, 136–42.

68 Thomas Nagel, *The View from Nowhere* (New York: Oxford University Press, 1986); Richard John Neuhaus, *The Naked Public Square* (Grand Rapids: Eerdmans, 1984).

69 John Rawls, *Political Liberalism* (New York: Columbia University Press, 1993), 13–15, 174–6. For a critique of Rawls on this key point, indeed showing how anti-philosophical he truly is, see Lenn E. Goodman, *Religious Pluralism and Values in the Public Square* (Cambridge: Cambridge University Press, 2014), 54–101.

70 *B.* Sanhedrin 24a re Zech. 11:7.

71 For the learned treatment of an early modern disputation in which a Jew had to defend his refusal to convert to Christianity, see Alexander Altmann, *Moses Mendelssohn* (London: Routledge and Kegan Paul, 1973), 194–263.

72 The best modern study of this idea is by Isaak Heinemann, *Taamei ha-Mitsvot be-Sifrut Yisrael*, 4th ed. (Jerusalem: Ha-Mador ha-Dati, 1958/59), esp. 1:9–35.

73 See Aristotle, *Nicomachean Ethics*, 5.6/1134b29–35; Aquinas, *Summa Theologiae*, 2/1, q. 94, a. 2.

74 *B.* Sanhedrin 21b re Deut. 17:17 and I Kings 11:4.

75 Kant, *Critique of Practical Reason*, trans. W.S. Pluhar (Indianapolis: Hackett, 2002), AK5:8 and note thereon.

76 For a critique of John Rawls on this anti-metaphysical stance, see M.J. Sandel, *Liberalism and the Limits of Justice* (New York: Cambridge University Press, 1982), 173. See Jürgen Habermas, *Moral Consciousness and Communicative Action*, trans. C. Lenhardt and S.W. Nicholsen (Cambridge, MA: MIT Press, 1993), 98 and 213 14, n. 15 for a qualified agreement with Rawls over Sandel on the point. For both Rawls and Habermas, there are no valid prior reasons, but only subsequent reasons prospectively agreed upon, why anyone should agree with anyone else. Habermas is more beholden to Hegel in the sense that there is no truth to refer back to, but only truth that emerges into the future. See *supra*, n. 37.

77 Rawls, *Political Liberalism*, 134–49.

78 For the background of this term, see H.A. Wolfson, *Philo* (Cambridge, MA: Harvard University Press, 1947), 1:144–54.

79 See Hegel, *Phenomenology of Spirit*, nos. 178–96, 111–19; also Alexandre Kojève, *Introduction to the Reading of Hegel*, trans. J.H. Nichols (Ithaca: Cornell University Press, 1969), 21–30.

80 Tertullian, e.g., criticizes "Platonic Christianity" in *De Praescriptione Haereticorum*, 7.
81 This point is central in the theology of (for many) the greatest modern Christian theologian, Karl Barth, who has warned theologians about "the injection of metaphysical systems which are secretly in conflict with the Bible," though he affirmed theology's need for "human thinking ... no doubt controlled by the criterion of a philosophy, and with it the work of criticism and systematisation which it has to perform" (*Church Dogmatics*, 1/2, trans. G.T. Thomson and H. Knight [Edinburgh: T. & T. Clark, 1956], sec. 22, 774–5). Barth speaks of one who critically appropriates philosophical *method* (his term is "criterion") as a "theological philosopher" (774–5), where the adjective "theological" does more than modify the noun "philosopher" as adjectives usually do, but actually determines this thinker's essentially exegetical task. See 1/2, sec. 21, 728–9.
82 *B.* Berakhot 19b re Prov. 21:30. Cf. *B.* Yevamot 24a.
83 See *MT*: Kings, 11.3–4 (uncensored ed.), where Maimonides cautiously argues against both Christian and Muslim claims to have superseded the Mosaic Torah. Christians have maintained that parts of the Mosaic Torah, while being authentic divine revelation, were only authoritative until the coming of the Messiah (who for them is Jesus of Nazareth). Muslims have maintained that most of the Mosaic Torah is not authentic divine revelation, but human fabrications; and what is authentic divine revelation therein has been revealed in a fuller, more truthful form, to Muhammed, and then accurately written down in the Quran.
84 However, cf. Hermann Cohen, *Religion of Reason: Out of the Sources of Judaism*, trans. S. Kaplan (New York: Frederick Ungar, 1972), 9: "Therefore it will be our task to investigate in the sources of Judaism the original philosophic motives in which, and by virtue of which, the religion of reason succeeds in making its way [*durchsetzt*]." A fuller discussion of Cohen's interrelation of philosophy and theology is found in chapter 6 ("Kant's Challenge to Theology").
85 Tillich, *Systematic Theology* (Chicago: University of Chicago Press, 1951), 1:18–28.
86 Aristotle, *Metaphysics*, 6.1/1026a20. At 11.7/1064b2, Aristotle speaks of *theologikē* as being "theoretical," which is the "best of the sciences." Hence the earliest Greek philosophers of nature (considered to be "divine," 11.7/1064a34–9) are called "theologians" (*theologoi*),viz., "those who speak of God" (1.3/983b29–984a1, 12.6/1071b27, 14.4/1091a34). But, of course, they speak *of* or *about* God; God does not speak *to* them or *with* them – nor to or with anyone else.
87 Spinoza, *Tractatus Theologico-Politicus*, chaps. 13–15.

88 This modern Jewish discomfort with the term "theology" could well be the subject of a full monograph. Suffice it to say now, some Jews have wrongly seen theology as the preserve of Christian thought, remembering Paul's denigration of "the Law" (i.e., specifically Jewish law) in favour of "faith" (Romans 4:13–16; Galatians 3:7–12), which has been formulated into theological propositions and creedal affirmations in place of the precepts of "the Law." Some Orthodox Jews have been suspicious of the term because its ready use by liberal Jewish thinkers was often part of their delegitimatizing Halakhah's primacy for "modern" Judaism. See Alexander Altmann, "What Is Jewish Theology?" in *The Meaning of Jewish Existence: Theological Essays, 1930–1939*, ed. A.L. Ivry, trans. E. Ehrlich and L.H. Ehrlich (Hanover: University Press of New England, 1991), 41–4. Altmann's insistence on the primacy of Halakhah for any Jewish theology still helps dispel Orthodox Jewish discomfort with calling authentic Jewish religious thought "theology." Earlier, Franz Rosenzweig had sharply criticized the type of liberal Jewish thought that preferred "philosophy of religion" (*Religionsphilosophie*) in place of "theology," insisting that this is part of the modern avoidance of the centrality of revelation, which he considers to be the main concern of theology properly defined. See his *The Star of Redemption*, trans. B.E. Galli (Madison: University of Wisconsin Press, 2005), 151; also "Atheistic Theology," in Rosenzweig, *Philosophical and Theological Writings*, trans. P.W. Franks and M.L. Morgan (Indianapolis: Hackett, 2000), 16–44.

89 See LXX on Jer. 1:2, where *dvar adonai* is translated into Greek as *logos tou theou*, viz., "God's word." Sometimes, though, *dvar adonai* is translated as *logos kyriou* (e.g., LXX on Isa. 38:4), viz., "the word of the Lord," *kyrios* being a more literal translation of *adonai*, which is the circumlocution of the Tetragrammaton (YHWH), already in use by the time of the writing of the Septuagint in the second century BCE.

90 *B.* Berakhot 58a re I Chron. 29:11; *B.* Zevahim 116a. The term *gillui shekhinah*, literally the "revelation of the divine presence" (well translated into German as *Offenbarung*), very rarely appears in rabbinic sources (e.g., *Haggadah shel Pesah*, ed. Kasher, 48). The distinction between *gillui shekhinah* and *mattan torah*, and the preference for the latter, is important. For the content *given* in the Torah is primarily the commandments (*mitsvot*) that apply to *whomever* they apply (and that could be anybody who wants to be included in the normative community: *Y.* Bikkurim 1.7/64a re Gen. 17:5; *B.* Sanhedrin 59a re Lev. 18:5) *whenever* and *wherever* they are to be found. But *gillui shekhinah* is only the experience of those who were *there then*, i.e., at that place and at that time (*Sifre*: Devarim, no. 343 re Exod. 15:2; also Yom Tov ben Abraham Asevilli [Ritba],

Haggadah shel Pesah, ed. Ralbag, 33). That experience itself, of course, is unrepeatable. Cf. *Mekhilta*: Yitro re Exod. 18:1 and Ps. 29:9, ed. Horovitz-Rabin, 188. Therefore, those converting to Judaism are only required to accept the content of God-given law, but like native-born Jews, they are not required to re-experience the revelatory event (B. Yevamot 47a).

91 *B*. Baba Metsia 59b re Deut. 30:12; Maimonides, *Guide*, 1.26.

92 Throughout this book, "Nature" (uppercase *N*) is used when speaking of *physis* in Greek philosophy, whereas "nature" (lowercase *n*) is used when speaking of what God or humans *make* in biblically based theology.

93 Plato, *Republic*, 428E.

94 Plato, *Apology*, 29A.

95 Plato, *Philebus*, 48C–49A, where Socrates takes the Delphic injunction "know yourself" (*gnōthi sauton*) not as calling for knowledge of the wisdom he has, but rather calling for him to know that he lacks wisdom and should, therefore, seek it outside himself with others.

96 Plato, *Symposium*, 201A–C.

97 *B*. Sotah 21b thereto.

98 *B*. Rosh Hashanah 4b; also *M*. Avot 2.15.

99 *B*. Shabbat 31a and Rashi, s.v. "hevantta."

100 *The Assayer*, in *Discoveries and Opinions of Galileo*, trans. S. Drake (Garden City: Doubleday Anchor Books, 1957), 237–8.

101 Leo Strauss, *Natural Right and History* (Chicago: University of Chicago Press, 1953), 81; Strauss, "The Mutual Influence of Theology and Philosophy," 111–18.

102 Strauss, "The Mutual Influence of Theology and Philosophy," 118.

103 For truth (*emet*) as indispensable revelation, see *B*. Shabbat 55a re Ezek. 9:6; *B*. Baba Metsia 60a; *MT*: Rebels, 1.3–4.

104 Plato, *Republic*, 492A–493A. Plato himself seemed to have had such a sublime vision. See *Republic*, 515D.

105 *MT*: Foundations 7.5. It seems that Maimonides himself seemed to have had such prophetic visions. See Abraham Joshua Heschel, "Did Maimonides Believe He Merited Prophecy?" [Heb.] in *Louis Ginzberg Jubilee Volume* (New York: American Academy for Jewish Research, 1945), 2:159–88.

106 Strauss, "The Mutual Influence of Theology and Philosophy," 117.

107 Plato, *Theatetus*, 155D; also Heschel, *God in Search of Man*, 43–53, 106–13.

108 Étienne Gilson, *Reason and Revelation in the Middle Ages* (New York: Chas. Scribners' Sons, 1938), 72.

109 This is a leitmotif in his encyclical *Fides et Ratio*, Vatican translation (Boston: Pauline Books and Media, 1998), passim.

110 See his "On the Essence of Truth," trans. J. Sallis, in *Martin Heidegger: Basic Writings*, ed. D.F. Krell (New York: Harper and Row, 1977), 127.

111 John Paul II, *Fides et Ratio*, 44.
112 Ibid.
113 Ibid., 46.
114 Ps. 119:137–8, 143.
115 That is why one may not utter *amen* to somebody else's prayer until one knows to whom the person praying is directing (*mitkavven*) his or her prayer (M. Berakhot 8.8 and Maimonides's comment; *Y.* Berakhot 8.9/12c; Rabbenu Asher [Rosh]: Berakhot, 8.5; see also *B.* Berakhot 48a). See *supra*, n. 58.
116 Tillich, *Systematic Theology*, 1:110–11.
117 Plato, *Laws*, 716C. Cf. *Theatetus*, 152A; *Cratylus, 386A*.
118 Heidegger, "On the Essence of Truth," 126–41.
119 *Y.* Megillah 1.1/70a re Est. 9:28.
120 Plato, *Apology*, 32C.
121 *M.* Pesahim 10.5.
122 *M.* Avot 2.14. See Obadiah Sforno's comment on Deut. 4:9.
123 Cf. Ernst Cassirer, *The Philosophy of Symbolic Forms: Mythical Thinking*, trans. R. Manheim (New Haven: Yale University Press, 1955), 2:261 et passim, for the view that myths are to be overcome by scientific reasoning, yet this is to be done cautiously, for too hastily overcoming myth makes moderns forget their mythical past and, as such, myths could return to be invoked by those who don't know that they have been overcome and how that has been done. Moreover, Cassirer is explicit (120, 225–6) in recognizing the influence of his teacher, the Neo-Kantian Jewish philosopher Hermann Cohen, who in his posthumous work *Religion of Reason* argued for the greater rejection of myth by Judaism than by Christianity (168–70). One might even see the return of what had been repressed by Cohen and his disciples regarding myth in Judaism in the work of contemporary German-Jewish thinkers of Cassirer's era, especially by Martin Buber, Franz Rosenzweig, and Gershom Scholem (*mutatis mutandis*).
124 Aristotle compares "lovers of wisdom" (i.e., philosophers) to "lovers of myth" (*philomythos*) insofar as myths are composed from the experience of amazing things (*thaumasiōn*). That seems to be experience of a revelation, an experience that could only be extraordinary or wondrous (*Metaphysics*, 1.2/982b20; see Plato, *Theatetus*, 155D).
125 The modern philosopher who dealt with the indispensability of myths for philosophy throughout his extensive oeuvre was Eric Voegelin. See John Bussanich, "Eric Voegelin's Philosophy of Myth," *The European Legacy* 12 (2007): 187–98.
126 In *Tanhuma*: Tetsaveh on Exod. 27:20, ed. Buber, 97, it states that the windows of the Sanctuary (where the master copy of the Torah is located)

are narrow on the inside and wide on the outside, so that "light might go out from the Sanctuary [*bet ha-miqdash*] and enlighten the world." That is, the world needs that light rather than the Sanctuary needing to be enlightened by the world.

127 *Sifre*: Devarim, no. 49 re Deut. 11:22, ed. Finkelstein, 115.

128 Plato, *Timaeus*, 22A–B, 26D.

129 Plato, *Phaedo*, 61B.

130 On this basis, Aristotle was selective in his noetic employment of the myths of his Hellenic culture he had received via tradition: sometimes accepting them for their heuristic accuracy (*Metaphysics*, 12.8/1074a39–1074b4), sometimes rejecting them for their heuristic inaccuracy (3.4/1000a18–20). Plato, too, was selective in his use of *mythoi* in his philosophical enquiry. See *Republic*, 377D–E; *Timaeus*, 26D; *Laws*, 682A, 713A, 865D, 913C, 944A.

131 *B.* Hagigah 3b re Exod. 20:1.

132 *B.* Baba Kama 41b re Deut. 6:13 (the view of Simeon ha-Amsoni); also *B.* Zevahim 115b re Eccl. 3:7.

133 Aristotle, *Prior Analytics*, 1.44/50a16.

134 Karl Popper, *The Logic of Scientific Discovery* (London: Routledge, 1992), 52–3. Nevertheless, Popper denies that scientific hypothetical reasoning can ever reach the type of unsurpassable knowledge that Plato and Aristotle (*et alia*) claim for it (278–81).

135 Both kinds of hypothesis (from Greek *hypotithēmai*, literally, "setting under") are discussed and differentiated by Plato (*Republic*, 510B) as follows: "the soul ... is compelled to investigate from hypotheses ... going down to a conclusion [*epi teleutēn*] ... or moving up towards the first principle [*ep' archēn*] by going through them [*di' autōn*] methodically."

136 The best-known examples of this are Freud's 1913 book *Totem and Taboo* and his 1939 book *Moses and Monotheism.*

137 See Sigmund Freud, *The Future of an Illusion*, trans. W.D. Robson-Scott, rev. J. Strachey (Garden City: Anchor Books, 1964), 6–68.

138 Maimonides's comment on *M.* Avodah Zarah 4.7; *MT*: Strange Worship, 1.2. The Rabbis called lying "stealing someone's opinion" (*genevat da`at*): *B.* Hullin 94a; *MT*: Virtues, 2.6.

139 See Karl Popper, *The Open Society and Its Enemies*, 5th rev. ed. (Princeton: Princeton University Press, 1966), 1:138–44.

140 See Yehezkel Kaufmann, *The Religion of Israel*, trans. M. Greenberg (Chicago: University of Chicago Press, 1960), 13–14, 146–7.

141 See *M.* Berakhot 2.2; *Mekhilta*: Yitro re Exod. 20:2–3, ed. Horovitz-Rabin, 219.

142 See J.B. Schneewind, *The Invention of Autonomy* (Cambridge: Cambridge University Press, 1998), 508–30.

143 Even those who refute the testimony of witnesses of an event by saying that at the time witnesses claim to have witnessed the event in a given place, "you were with us somewhere remote from that place" (M. Makkot 1.4 re Deut. 19:16–19), and the impossibility of two finite persons being together in two different places at the same time proves the witnesses are lying. Nevertheless, those accusing the witnesses of lying are not denying that the event itself couldn't have occurred because it is impossible. They are only claiming that the descriptive testimony is impossible because it denies the logical principle of non-contradiction (see also *M.* Rosh Hashanah 2.6, 8).

144 Wittgenstein, *Tractatus Logico-Philosophicus*, 2.1–222.

145 Exod. 20:15–16; Deut. 5:4–5.

146 *B.* Megillah 28b and Rashi, s.v. "hei tsana."

147 See *M.* Avot 1.1, where "being deliberate [*metunim*] in judgment" causes Obadiah Bertinoro to comment that each new case is to be judged *de novo* and not simply be referred back to an earlier case and be decided accordingly. For the difference between original and subsequent contexts of interpretation and application, see *B.* Rosh Hashanah 30b re Lev. 23:14 and Gittin 36a re Deut. 15:9; *Y.* Berakhot 7.4/11c. For the need to look at biblical sources anew in the light of new cases brought before the Sanhedrin, see *B.* Sanhedrin 34a re Ps. 62:12.

148 *Sifre*: Devarim, no. 33 re Deut. 6:6.

149 *B.* Shabbat 88a re Exod. 24:7. For the distinction between categories that pertain to interhuman relations and the God-human relationship, see *B.* Betsah 38b; *B.* Baba Metsia 20b and *Tosafot*, s.v. "isura." For the notion that interhuman relations involve more ordinary, mundane categories, see Israel Lifshitz, *Tiferet Yisrael*: Baba Batra 10.8, n. 84.

150 For the distinction between categories that come from ordinary reason and categories that come from tradition, see *B.* Pesahim 66a and Rashi, s.v. "ve-khi."

151 Spinoza, *Ethics*, in *Opera*, vol. 2, ed. C. Gebhardt (Heidelberg: Carl Winter, 1925), IV, pref.

152 Spinoza, *Tractatus Theologico-Politicus*, chap. 15.

153 The most original and still the most famous expression of this theological subjectivism is by the early-nineteenth-century German Protestant theologian Friedrich Schleiermacher, especially in his 1821 book *Der christliche Glaube*, where he speaks of religion being rooted in "a feeling of complete dependence" (*ein Gefühl völliger Anhängigkeit*). See *The Christian Faith*, trans. H.R. Mackintosh (Edinburgh: T. & T. Clark, 1999), 12–18 et passim.

154 *M.* Avot 4.1 re Ps. 119:99; also *B.* Pesahim 94b; Maimonides, *Commentary on the Mishnah*: Introduction to Avot, pref.; *MT*: Qiddush ha-Hodesh, 17.24.

2 God, Humans, and Nature

1 Spinoza, *Tractatus Theologico-Politicus*, 17.9.

2 Plato, *Apology*, 29D, 30A. Regarding Socrates's genuine piety, see Gregory Vlastos, *Socrates* (Ithaca: Cornell University Press, 1991), 157–78.

3 Plato, *Apology*, 31D.

4 Ibid., 32A.

5 Ibid., 28E–29A.

6 See ibid., 17C–18C; also *Euthyphro*, 2A–4E.

7 Plato, *Apology*, 31D–32A.

8 Plato, *Phaedo*, 118; Aristotle, *Politics*, 6.5/1322b19–29.

9 *Sifre*: Devarim, no. 313 re Gen. 24:3.

10 *Pesiqta de-Rav Kahana*: ba-hodesh ha-shlishi, ed. Mandelbaum, 212.

11 *B*. Shabbat 133b re Exod. 15:2 (the view of Abba Saul).

12 Maimonides, *Guide*, 1.52.

13 Plato, *Republic*, 506E–507B.

14 Thus *theōrein* (i.e., "theorizing" or "contemplating") is the metaphysical appreciation of truth by the mind, which is analogous to the aesthetic appreciation of physical beauty by the bodily eye (Plato, *Phaedrus*, 247C–E). See Thorleif Boman, *Hebrew Thought Compared with Greek*, trans. J.L. Moreau (New York: W.W. Norton, 1970), 113–18.

15 *B*. Shabbat 31a re Isa.33:6.

16 Plato, *Phaedo*, 62C.

17 Plato, *Laws*, 936E.

18 Plato, *Crito*, 50A–53A.

19 Aristotle, *Metaphysics*, 12.7/1072b10–30; 12.9/1074b15–1075a19.

20 Ibid., 12.9/1075a5–19.

21 Cf., however, Aquinas, *Summa Theologiae*, 2/1, q. 94, a. 2: "Good is what everything desires [*appetunt*], hence the first law is that good is what is to be done [*faciendum est*] and pursued [*prosequendum est*]." For Aquinas, what is good seems to require itself to be done by those who are naturally (i.e., for humans, rationally) inclined or attracted to it. Here Aquinas is most Aristotelian (see Aristotle, *Nicomachean Ethics*, 1.1/1094a1–5; Aquinas, *Commentary on the Nicomachean Ethics of Aristotle*, 1.1.11). This is the influential (though quite arguable) reading of Aquinas by my late revered teacher Germain Grisez in "The First Principle of Practical Reason," *Natural Law Forum* (1965), 10: 168–9, 178–86. Aquinas sees this pursuit of the good as already known by practical reason's inclination to do it. That seems to mean that God's commandment of it as natural law (*Summa Theologiae*, 2/1, q. 90, a. 4, ad obj. 1) is the explicit expression of what God has already created practical reason to pursue (2/1, q. 99, a. 2, ad obj. 2). In the Bible, though, humans are commanded to "turn away from what is

bad [*sur me-r`a*] and do good [*v`aseh tov*]" (Ps. 37:28). In the Vulgate (which, interestingly enough, Aquinas does not quote) the Latin text reads *Declina a malo, et fac bonum.* That is, the commandment is to do good, which is to be done because God has so commanded it (Micah 6:8). As natural law, God's reasons for commanding it are evident (*ratio quoad nos* as Aquinas himself says in *Summa Theologiae*, 2/1, q. 94, a. 2). Therefore, the imperative to do good is due to God's primordial right to command His creatures. Whatever good God commands to be done, however evident are its reasons for being so commanded, is secondary to God's prior right as the Creator who commands all creation to be good, i.e., to act well (Gen. 1:28; Ps. 33:9).

22 For example, the cancellation of debts (*shemittah*) in the sabbatical year, commanded in the Torah, was radically circumvented (but not without criticism; see *B.* Gitin 36b) through a legal fiction called *prosbul*, instituted by Hillel the Elder, whereby the court rather than the individual lender collected the debt, and then turned over the payment to the original lender. Hillel's reason for doing so was to benefit the poor for whose sake he saw the original norm having been commanded, viz., to release them from debts they couldn't repay within the six years between one sabbatical year and the next. However, knowing this would likely happen, rich lenders were refusing to lend to poor borrowers altogether for fear that the debt owed to them would never have to be repaid. See *M.* Gittin 4.3; *M.* Sheviit 2.3; *B.* Gittin 36a.

23 Ps. 133:1, 135:3, 147:1; Song of Songs 1:16.

24 *T.* Berakhot 4.1 re Ps. 24:1; *Y.* Berakhot 6.1/9d re Deut. 22:9; *B.* Berakhot 35a re Lev. 19:24.

25 *B.* Yoma 67b re Lev. 18:4.

26 *B.* Nedarim 10a re Num. 6:11.

27 See Maimonides, *Guide*, 1.2.

28 *M.* Nedarim 4.2, 4; *MT*: Nedarim 6.8; 7.1.

29 *M.* Berakhot 9.5 re Deut. 6:5. Many have wrongly translated *ra* ("bad") as "evil" or "wicked." However, the word for "evil" or "wickedness" is *resha* (e.g., Ps. 84:11), meaning "wrong-doing" or "injustice" (e.g., Gen. 18:23–5; Exod. 23:7). God creates what is experienced by us as bad as well as what is experienced by us as good (Isa. 45:7). Only humans, though, can be evil or wicked, as the ultimate wickedness is rebellion against God (e.g., Exod. 9:27).

30 *B.* Berakhot 60b.

31 Thus punishment, whether coming from God through nature or mandated by God to be done by humans to other humans, is to be taken as ultimately beneficial, reconciling the victim of punishment with God as atonement (*kapparah*) as in *M.* Sanhedrin 6.2 re Josh. 7:25; also *B.* Sanhedrin 6b re II Sam. 8:15.

32 Note *Y.* Berakhot 9.5/74b: "One who loves [God] does not hate [God]."

33 Blasphemy (*qilelat ha-shem*) is considered to be universally proscribed (*T.* Avodah Zarah 8.4; *B.* Sanhedrin 56a re Lev. 24:15). That is consistent with a rabbinic view that Job and his family were not Jews, but gentiles (B. Baba Batra 15b).

34 *M.* Sanhedrin 7.5 on *B.* Sanhedrin 56a, where it would seem the ultimate blasphemy is telling God to kill Himself at human behest. *MT*: Strange Worship, 2.8. Nobody understood better than Nietzsche in *Also Sprach Zarathustra*, prologue, 3: "One of the greatest crimes [*Frevel*] was the crime against God, but God died [*starb*] and also these criminals [*Frevelhaften*] died with it." Here Nietzsche clearly means blasphemy, which is the only crime committed against God directly. Also, when he says the blasphemers "died" (*starben*), this is not bodily death, but means that their crime has "died" inasmuch as there is no longer God to be the real object of their verbal assault. Hence their criminal status has now died in a world where God has already been killed.

35 Those who regularly, arrogantly, and publicly sin are considered to be doing so to "anger" (*le-hakh`is*) the object of their anger, who is God (B. Sanhedrin 27a re Exod. 23:1; also Jer. 32:30).

36 *B.* Niddah 73a; Maimonides, *Commentary on the Mishnah*: Sanhedrin, chap. 10, intro., no. 8.

37 Thus God can be challenged by humans to keep His promises when it appears He is not doing so (B. Berakhot 32a re Exod. 32:13).

38 *M.* Ketubot 9.2.

39 *B.* Sanhedrin 6b re Deut. 1:17. Cf. 6b–7a re Zech. 8:15 for the opposite view, that compromise (*pesharah*), at least in civil disputes, is to be officially encouraged.

40 *B.* Sanhedrin 90a re II Kings 7:1.

41 *B.* Baba Metsia 83a re Prov. 2:20; *B.* Shabbat 10a re Exod. 18:13.

42 *B.* Yoma 86b re Ezek. 33:19.

43 *B.* Berakhot 7a.

44 *B.* Sanhedrin 110b re Ps. 95:11 and 50:5. Cf. Jer. 4:27, 5:18, 30:11, 46:28.

45 *B.* Berakhot 32a re Exod. 33:1.

46 Isa. 54:9–10 and the comment of David Kimhi (Radaq) thereon; Jer. 33:25 and *B.* Pesahim 68b thereto.

47 Conversely, the human oath/promise of the people Israel to be bound to God's covenant with them is not voluntary (B. Shevuot 39a re Deut. 29:13), hence its validity *de jure* is questioned, but explained *de facto* (B. Shabbat 88a–b re Exod. 19:17 and Est. 9:27).

48 *B.* Berakhot 7a re Isa. 56:7; *B.* Yoma 86b re Ezek. 33:18.

49 Aristotle, *Metaphysics*, 11.7/1064a35.

50 See Alexandre Koyré, *From the Closed World to the Infinite Universe* (Baltimore: Johns Hopkins University Press, 1957), 5–27.
51 Aristotle, *Nicomachean Ethics*, 1.10/1100a10–1100b9; *Physics*, 194a30; *Metaphysics*, 5.17/1022a5–14. Cf. Sophocles, *Oedipus Rex*, 1527–30.
52 Aristotle, *Metaphysics*, 5.17/1022a5–10.
53 Ibid., 6.2/1027a15–29.
54 See W.D. Ross, *Aristotle* (New York: Meridian Books, 1959), 122–7. Aristotelian teleology is more thoroughly examined in chapter 5 ("Maimonides and Aristotle").
55 Aristotle, *Nicomachean Ethics*, 10.7/1177a12–1177b30.
56 Epictetus, *Discourses*, chap. 15; *Encheridion*, no. 4.
57 Plato, *Timaeus*, 46D.
58 Ibid., 28A–30D, 69A.
59 Maimonides, *Guide*, 2.13.
60 See Rosenzweig, *The Star of Redemption*, 31–48.
61 See T.F. Torrance, *Divine and Contingent Order* (Oxford: Oxford University Press, 1981), 26–37, 71–2.
62 Hume, *A Treatise of Human Nature*, ed. L.A. Selby-Bigge (Oxford: Clarendon Press, 1978), 1.3.14. Cf. *B.* Avodah Zarah 54b; *B.* Shabbat 53b.
63 See Bernard Lonergan, *Insight* (New York: Harper and Row, 1978), 4.2–3, 54–62; 6.67, 99–100.
64 See Maimonides, *Guide*, 2.15, 22–9 for theological acceptance of the sufficiently demonstrated findings of natural science, but the theological rejection of metaphysical implications drawn from natural science, i.e., when these insufficiently demonstrated metaphysical implications contradict theological dogmas. One could indeed say that Maimonides as a theologian was rejecting the metaphysical excesses of the "scientism" of his day as theologians today ought to reject the metaphysical excesses of current scientism. However, when the metaphysical implications drawn from natural science or from modern "social science" do not contradict theological dogmas, theologians may justifiably employ them, albeit selectively and critically.
65 See Strauss, *Natural Right and History*, 81–82.
66 See, e.g., *M.* Baba Batra 4.1. The verb *tove`a* often denotes imposing an invariable structure on something (B. Gittin 5b; *T.* Berakhot 4.5 and *B.* Berakhot 40b). In *M.* Sanhedrin 4.5, God's unique ability to mint radically different human individuals with one stamp (*hotam*), which was used to create the first humans and their nature, is contrasted with the far lesser ability of humans to only mint identical coins from one stamp. That is because God endows His human creatures (who are radically different from all other creatures, being created in God's

"likeness" [*demut* – Gen. 1:26]) with freedom of choice. That is why humans are held responsible for all their acts, and are answerable to God for when they have acted badly (Gen. 3:9; 4:9). Human freedom of choice is analogous to God's freedom of choice (B. Hullin 7a; *Y.* Rosh Hashanah 1.3/57b re Ps. 33:15 and Moses Margolis, *Pnei Mosheh*, s.v. "amar Rabbi Berakhyah" thereon). Neither divine freedom nor even human freedom is determined by any natural order. In the case of humans, their freedom is only conditioned (*bedingt* in German) by that prior order, whereas there is no order prior to God by which God could be conditioned. Nevertheless, God does choose to respect the natural limits within His voluntary creation so as to be able to coherently relate to the human creatures created in God's image in the world.

67 Plato, *Gorgias*, 508A.

68 This conception of nature as what is *usual* (hence generally predictable) rather than what is universally necessary comes out in a talmudic discussion (B. Baba Kama 91a) of a person who was injured by another person, the latter being responsible for the former's medical expenses. The physicians estimated (*amdudhu*) that his recuperation would take a certain amount of time, and that it would cost a certain amount of money. But if he recuperated sooner than the estimated time, Rava ruled he should receive the full amount of money originally estimated to cover his medical expenses, because "God [*min shamaya*, literally "from Heaven"] had mercy on him." Now, God's unpredictable intervention in a *usual* process doesn't mean that this person's sooner-than-predicted recovery wasn't a possibility in nature as it is known by God. In fact, "from Heaven" (*me-shamaya*) can refer to "nature" (*tiv`o shel olam*) according to Maimonides (*MT*: Murderers, 1.9 re *B.* Sanhedrin 72b). For the less than mathematical precision of "estimation," see, e.g., *M.* Sanhedrin 4.5 and 9.1; *M.* Avot 1.16; *B.* Menahot 54b–55a re Num. 18:27. For the difference between what is only possibly and therefore doubtfully caused and what is more certainly caused, see *B.* Baba Kama 118a; Maimonides's comment on *M.* Nazir 9.4; *MT*: Murderers, 4.5.

69 Saadiah Gaon, *The Book of Beliefs and Opinions*, 1.3, 63–4.

70 Note Boman, *Hebrew Thought Compared with Greek*, 151: "The commonest word for boundless time is *`ôlam* ... derived from *`alam* meaning 'hide, conceal' ... a boundless time." On 153–4, Boman continues: "For the Greeks the content of the world was eminently spatial, for the Israelites it was principally temporal ... in all the Old Testament writings, however, *`ôlam* has only a temporal meaning."

71 Cordevero, *Pardes ha-Rimonim*, 12.2 re Exod. 8:15 (Jerusalem: n.p., 1962). Thus the numerical values of *Elohim* and *ha-tev`a* are the same (i.e., 86). Cf. the comments of Rashi, Ibn Ezra, and Nahmanides on Exod. 8:15.

72 *Tanhuma*: Va'era, 1 re Exod. 6:2.

73 *Beresheet Rabbah*, 12.15 re Gen. 2:4.
74 *Zohar*, 1:181a–b re Job 34:10.
75 Judah Loewe, *Gevurot Hashem*, intro. 2, chaps. 41 and 61; Loewe, *Netsah Yisrael*, chap. 27. See also the early-twentieth-century Hasidic theologian Judah Leib Alter (Gerrer Rebbe), *Sfas Emes* (Brooklyn: n.p., 1989/90): ha-Hodesh, 2:18; Pesah, 2:43, for an elaboration of Maharal's view of miracles.
76 See *B.* Avodah Zarah 4a–b re Ps. 7:12; *B.* Sanhedrin 15b re Exod. 19:13.
77 *M.* Kelim 9.8; *Y.* Sukkah 4.6/54d and *B.* Sukkah 49a re Cant. 7:2; *B.* Shabbat 108a; Maimonides's comment on *M.* Betsah 1.1.
78 See *Y.* Shabbat 14.3/14c and *Vayiqra Rabbah*, 16.8 re Deut. 7:15; also *B.* Ketubot 30a and *Tosafot*, s.v. "ha-kol"; *B.* Niddah 16b and *Tosafot*, s.v. "ha-kol"; *B.* Baba Metsia 107b and *Tosafot*, s.v. "tish`im," where diseases of which God is the first cause (as of all natural processes) are contrasted with diseases caused by human carelessness or actual sin. Also, there is a difference between death as the inevitable result of the natural mortality inherited because of the sin of the first humans, and death as the result of one's own freely chosen sin (B. Shabbat 55a–b re Ezek. 18:4, etc.). In the case of the latter, God promises to intervene in the world to directly rectify the evil that humans themselves have caused (B. Yoma 85b re Ezek. 33:19). Nevertheless, it is considered to be a "vain prayer" (*tefillat sh'av*) to request God to supernaturally change an event that has already occurred naturally (M. Berakhot 9.3 and Maimonides's comment thereon).
79 Sometimes *be-ydei shamayim* does not refer to God's natural handiwork, but rather to God's directly commanding humans supernaturally (B. Yoma 74b re Lev. 23:7 and Rashi, s.v. "innuy be-ydei shamayim"). This is contrasted with the commandment of a human ruler (*be-ydei adam*; see *Haggadah shel Pesah* re Deut. 26:7). Usually, though, direct divine commandments are deemed as coming *min ha-shamayim* (from Heaven). See *M.* Sanhedrin 10.1; *Y.* Shabbat 1.1/2d re Exod. 20:19. Rarely, *be-ydei shamayim* refers to direct divine supernatural intervention in the world (B. Ketubot 30a and Rashi, sv. "be-yedei shamayim," and *Tosafot*, s.v. "ha-kol"; B. Niddah 16b and *Tosafot*, s.v."ha-kol").
80 For example, there is a difference between wine considered to be a natural product (i.e., the fermentation of grapes, even without humans acting on them) and bread considered to be the product of human effort (B. Pesahim 110b and Isaiah di Trani, *Tosfot Rid* thereon; *B.* Bekhorot 17a re Lev. 23:37). This also seems to be why calling God the One "who brings forth [*mots'i*] bread from the earth" is referring to God's supernatural intervention in the eschatological future (*atidah le-hiyot*) rather than being an ordinary matter of God's natural causation *be-ydei shamayim* (*Y.* Berakhot 6.1/10a re Ps. 72:16; *B.* Ketubot 111b re Ps. 72:16; *Midrash Tehillim* 104.11 re Ps. 72:16). Normally, bringing bread forth (i.e., grinding the grain, kneading the dough, and baking) is done by human hands, i.e., *be-ydei adam*.

81 *B*. Berakhot 33b re Deut. 10:12; *B*. Hullin 7b re Ps. 37:23.
82 *B*. Megillah 10b re Exod. 14:20.
83 Exod. 14:30.
84 *T*. Avodah Zarah 7.7; *B*. Avodah Zarah 54b.
85 *B*. Pesahim 64b. See also *B*. Shabbat 32a.
86 *M*. Gittin 4.5 re Isa. 45:18; *B*. Kiddushin 54a.
87 *B*. Sanhedrin 67b–68a.
88 *B*. Yevamot 90b and *Tosafot*, s.v. "u-li-gmor"; *Y*. Megillah 1.7/70d re Lev. 27:34; *MT*: Foundations, 8.1–2.
89 *B*. Baba Batra 12a re Ps. 90:12.
90 Judah Loewe, *Gevurot Hashem*, intro.
91 *B*. Baba Batra 12b.
92 *Y*. Peah 2.6/17a re Eccl. 1:9.
93 Loewe, *Gevurot Hashem*, chap. 61 re *B*. Shabbat 118b.
94 *B*. Berakhot 31a re Kings 8:28 and 32a re Deut. 3:24; also *B*. Avodah Zarah 7b–8a.
95 One etymology for the noun *nes* has it coming from the verb *nassoh*, meaning to "conspicuously display." Hence a *nes* is a "banner" or "ensign." See, e.g., Num. 21:8; Ps. 60:6.
96 *B*. Yevamot 90b re Deut. 18:15, and see Rashi, comment on Deut. 18:22.
97 *B*. Shabbat 156a re Gen. 15:5.
98 Ibn Ezra's comment on Exod. 8:15.
99 *Beresheet Rabbah*, 10.6 re Job 38:33. For *mazal* as designating a natural condition, see *B*. Baba Kama 2b.
100 LXX on Deut. 32:8; *Devarim Rabbah*, 2.34 re Lam. 3:24; *Pirqei de-Rabbi Eliezer*, chap. 24. See Louis Ginzberg, *Legends of the Jews* (Philadelphia: Jewish Publication Society of America, 1955–61), 1:181, 5:204–5, n. 91.
101 *B*. Moed Qatan 28a; *B*. Shabbat 156a and *Tosafot*, s.v. "ein mazal le-yisrael."
102 See David Novak, *The Theology of Nahmanides Systematically Presented* (Atlanta: Scholars Press, 1992), 77–87.
103 Hume, *A Treatise of Human Nature*, 3.2.
104 Cf. Kant, *Critique of Pure Reason*, trans. N. Kemp Smith (New York: Macmillan, 1929), B473–9.
105 Heidegger argued quite insightfully that the correspondence theory of truth (*veritas est adaequatio rei et intellectus*) presupposes the biblical doctrine (which he calls "the Christian theological belief") of verbal creation. For without this as the ontological presupposition of this doctrine, he asks, "Wherein are the thing and the statement supposed to be in accordance [*übereinstimmt*], considering that the relata are manifestly different ... The coin is made of metal. The statement is not material at all?" ("On the Essence of Truth," 122). His answer is that "truth is the

accordance (*homoiōsis*) of a statement (*logos*) corresponds to the essence of a thing (*pragma*) because the essence of the thing corresponds to the divine *logos* [what Heidegger, here too beholden to Augustine, calls *intellectus divinus*; 120]. For it is the divine word (*dvar adonai* or *verbum Dei*) that speaks creatures into being." I might add here that just as Spinoza as a former Jewish believer understood quite well the biblical ontology he was rejecting in favour of his own ontology, so too does Heidegger as a former Christian believer (*mutatis mutandis*) do something quite similar for his ontology.

106 Much of what is said here about miracles is influenced by Franz Rosenzweig's *The Star of Redemption*, 103–21.

107 Thus angels (*mal'akhim*), who are considered to be personifications of natural forces, do not have free choice. That is why the Torah's commandments were not given to them, because the subjects of these commandments could only be creatures who have this capacity of moral beings. *B.* Shabbat 88b–89a re Ps. 8;2, 5–10; Maimonides, *Guide*, 2.6; *MT*: Repentance, 5.1–4.

108 See Nancy Cartwright, *How the Laws of Physics Lie* (Oxford: Clarendon Press, 1983), 101–2.

109 The most frequently used Hebrew word for "miracle" is *nes*. One etymology has it coming from the verb *nassoh*, which means "to experience." Thus David says to King Saul about the armour the king wants him to wear when confronting Goliath: "I have no such experience [*lo nissiti*]" (I Sam. 17:39), i.e., "I am untested in its use." Hence "miracles" (*nissim*) are events that are experienced because they are experienceable (cf. Job 38:4–5). However, such unusual or extraordinary events do not lend themselves to being explained according to the categories devised to explain ordinary events.

110 This will be more fully discussed in chapter 6, when Kant's notion of the laws of nature is considered.

111 *M.* Sanhedrin 10.1.

112 Ps. 104:14–15.

113 *B.* Pesahim 116b re Exod. 13:8.

114 *MT*: Sanctification of the New Moon, 1.1, 6.

115 *Shemot Rabbah* 3.3. Cf. *MT*: Foundations, 8.1–3, though, for the notion that the acceptance of the Torah by Israel at Sinai was not due to the miracles Moses performed, but rather to their direct collective apprehension of the revelation of the two most fundamental principles of God's law (Maimonides, *Guide*, 2.33; *MT*: Foundations, 8.1–2), which is something any intelligent, metaphysically interested person could (but hardly ever does) apprehend anywhere anytime.

116 *B.* Pesahim 116b.

117 Nahmanides's comment on Exod. 13:16. Maimonides distinguished between public prophecy, for which a miracle is required to ascertain the prophet's authenticity, and private prophecy, for which no such public authentication is required, as it is a matter between God and the prophet alone (*MT*: Foundations, 8.7).

118 Nahmanides's comment on Gen. 2:17. See Novak, *The Theology of Nahmanides*, 61–75.

119 *B.* Shabbat 123b re Exod. 15:2; *B.* Rosh Hashanah 17b re Exod. 34:6.

120 Nahmanides's comment on Num. 21:9 re *Mekhilta*: Be-shalah on Exod. 15:25, ed. Horovitz-Rabin, 156; *B.* Shabbat 97a re Exod. 7:12.

121 *Mekhilta*: Yitro on Exod. 19:16, 214.

122 Note Ibn Ezra's comment on Num. 12:8: "without an intermediary" (*emtsa`i*). Even though this verse refers to Moses, as distinct from all other prophets, it should be remembered that the Rabbis taught that all Israel heard the first two utterances of the Decalogue directly from "God's mouth" (*mi-pi ha-gevurah*; *B.* Makkot 24a). Moreover, Scripture teaches that the people responded verbally: "All that the Lord has spoken, we shall do" (Exod. 19:8), and their response was brought directly back to God (19:9). It was only after the people heard God's speech directly that they felt they couldn't hear any more, and they appointed Moses to be their *intermediary* (*Shir ha-Shirim Rabbah* 1.14 re Exod. 20:16).

123 *B.* Shabbat 88a.

124 *Beresheet Rabbah*, 39.1.

125 *M.* Shabbat 2.1; 16.1.

126 Josephus, *Antiquities*, 1.155.

127 Isa. 2:2 and LXX thereon; Dan. 8:19 and LXX thereon.

128 *B.* Berakhot 34b.

129 Aristotle, *Metaphysics*, 12.6/1071b5; 12.7/1072a25–1072b5. Though a Hebraic thinker, Maimonides nevertheless seems to accept this Hellenic-Aristotelian doctrine. See *Guide*, 2, intro., premise 4. See also David Kimhi's (Radaq) comment on Mal. 3:6.

130 Aristotle, *Metaphysics*, 12.9/1074b35.

131 Deut. 30:19; *B.* Berakhot 33b re Deut. 10:12; *MT*: Repentance, 5.1 re Lam. 3:39–40.

132 See *B.* Berakhot 32a re Exod. 32:13 and Rashi, s.v. "asher nishb`ata" re Gen. 22:16, where Moses is portrayed as demanding that God keep His promise sworn by an oath (*shevu`ah*) taken in His own immutable name. See also *T.* Maaser Sheni 5.29 re Deut. 26:15, and *Eikhah Rabbah* 1 re Ps. 77:9 (the view of Rabbi Seemon), ed. Buber, 30a and n. 185 thereon. As for reminding God to keep His promises, see Isa. 62:6–7.

133 *Die Fünf Bücher der Weisung*, trans. Martin Buber and Franz Rosenzweig (Cologne: Jakob Hegner, 1954), 158. See *Shemot Rabbah* 3.6.
134 Cf., however, *B.* Taanit 23a re Job 22:28; Judah Halevi, *Kuzari*, 4.3 re Exod. 3:14.
135 *Beresheet Rabbah* 68.9 re Gen. 28:11.
136 Gen. 15:6 and Nahmanides's comment thereon. Translating *ehyeh* as "I shall" rather than the more literal "I will" better conveys this meaning.
137 See also Isa. 54:9–10; Ezek. 20:22–33; *B.* Shabbat 88a re Exod. 19:17.
138 Isa. 54:9–10.
139 The ontological difference between authentic divine autonomy and the pseudo-autonomy of humans is more fully discussed in chapter 6 ("Kant's Challenge to Theology").
140 *B.* Pesahim 68b re Jer. 33:25.
141 Aristotle, *Physics*, 2.5/196a10–197a35.
142 *B.* Shabbat 119b re Gen. 2:1.
143 *Sifre*: Devarim, no. 229, ed. Finkelstein, 262 re Deut. 22:8; *B.* Shabbat 32a re Deut. 22:8.
144 *Beresheet Rabbah* 17.4 re Gen. 2:7; *B.* Shabbat 88b–89a re Ps. 8:2.
145 *M.* Avot 3.15.
146 Plato, *Laws*, 899D.
147 Aristotle, *Metaphysics*, 12.8/1074b1–14. See Plato, *Apology*, 26D; *Republic*, 508A; *Laws*, 899B.
148 Aristotle, *Metaphysics*, 12.6/1072a20–35.

3 Humans and Nature

1 Strauss, "The Mutual Influence of Theology and Philosophy," 111.
2 *M.* Yoma 8.9.
3 *Y.* Berakhot 9.1/12d re Gen. 1:26.
4 *B.* Yevamot 63a.
5 *B.* Taanit 23a.
6 In some rabbinic sources (B. Avodah Zarah 8a re Ps. 69:32; *Beresheet Rabbah* 34.9 re Gen. 8:20), the initiation of worshipful sacrifice is attributed to the first human (*adam ha-rish'on*). Maimonides (*MT*: Temple, 2.2) attributes this to the time of Adam's creation (*ke-she-nivr'a*), which might be his way of emphasizing that the desire for a worshipful relationship with God is endemic to human nature.
7 *Sifra*: Vayiqra, ed. Weiss, 4c re Lev. 1:2; *B.* Betsah 20a re Lev. 9:16 and Rashi, s.v. "ve-ye`aseh ke-mishpat"; *B.* Menahot 110a re Lev. 19:5. See Exod. 25:2 and Rashi's comment thereon.
8 *T.* Avodah Zarah 8.4–6; *B.* Sanhedrin 56a–b.

9 *Y.* Hallah 1.5/58a re Ps. 10:3 and Lev. 27:34; *B.* Baba Kama 94a re Ps. 10:3; *B.* Sukkah 30a re Isa. 61:8.
10 Maimonides, *Guide*, 3.32. Cf. Nahmanides's vociferous criticism of Maimonides on this whole point in his lengthy comment on Lev. 1:9.
11 *MT*: Kings, 9.1 re *B.* Sanhedrin 56b a là Gen. 2:16 (the view of Rabbi Isaac); also Maimonides, *Sefer ha-Mitsvot*, neg. no. The Rabbis consider idolatry to be the ultimate outcome of following the "bad" or base inclination (*yester ha-r`a*) (*Y.* Nedarim 9.1/41b re Ps. 81:10; *B.* Shabbat 105b; also *T.* Baba Kama 9.31).
12 *MT*: Kings, 11.1; 12.1–3.
13 *Y.* Hagigah 3.6/79b re Ps. 122:3.
14 *B.* Baba Metsia 59b re Deut. 30:12; *B.* Kiddushin 66a.
15 *M.* Yoma 8.9 re Lev. 16:30.
16 *Sifra*: Vayiqra, ed. Weiss, 27d re Lev. 5:21; *T.* Shevuot 3.6.
17 *Sifra*: Emor, re Lev. 23:27, ed. Weiss, 102a.
18 *M.* Menahot 13.11; *B.* Zevahim 46b re Lev. 1:9.
19 *Beresheet Rabbah* 22.8 re Gen. 4:8.
20 See *B.* Megillah 3b re Num. 6:7; *B.* Shabbat 127a re Gen. 18:3. Cf. *B.* Berakhot 19b re Prov. 21:30; *B.* Sanhedrin 74a.
21 Hence "I-Thou" prayers are considered private prayers uttered by particular individuals. Originally, these prayers were only by individuals for themselves, and were only subsequently included in the public ritual (*matbe`a shel tefillah*). Yet they do not have the same liturgical status as what had originally been ordained collectively by and for the community (*Y.* Berakhot 6.2/10b; *B.* Berakhot 17a, 33a; *Tur*: Orah Hayyim, 123 and Joseph Karo, *Bet Yosef* thereon, s.v. "teshuvah").
22 *M.* Yadayim 3.5; *Shir ha-Shirim Rabbah* 1.11.
23 *B.* Berakhot 34b re Isa. 64:3.
24 *B.* Sanhedrin 97b re Isa. 30:18; *MT*: Kings, 12.2.
25 *B.* Berakhot 28a and parallels.
26 *Tanhuma*: Korah, 5 re Num. 16:5 and Gen. 1:5.
27 *B.* Sanhedrin 59a
28 *B.* Berakhot 20b re Deut. 8:10. Cf. *Beresheet Rabbah* 43.7 re Gen. 14:19.
29 Hermann Cohen, "Spinoza über Staat und Religion, Judentum und Christentum," in *Jüdische Schriften*, ed. B. Strauss (Berlin: C.A. Schwetschke, 1924), 3:302.
30 See my late revered teacher Abraham Joshua Heschel's *God in Search of Man*, 336–42.
31 *B.* Shabbat 119b re Gen. 2:1–3.
32 See *Encyclopedia Talmudit*, 20:568–96, s.v. "ta`ama di-qra."
33 Note *Sifre*: Devarim, no. 49 re Deut. 11:22, ed. Finkelstein, 115: "If you want to recognize He-who-spoke-and-the-world-came-to-be, learn

haggadah, out of which you will recognize God and cleave to His ways." Now, there are two types of *haggadah* or *aggadah*. One, there are *aggadot* considered to be fanciful, imaginative (even idiosyncratic) interpretations of Scripture (e.g., *Y.* Maasarot 3.4/51a), which are clearly individual opinions having no normative force (*Y.* Horayot 3.8/ 48c re Eccl. 6:2; *Y.* Peah 2.6/17a; *Otsar ha-Geonim*: Hagigah, nos. 67–9, ed. Lewin, 59–60; Nahmanides, *Vikuah ha-Ramban*, no. 14 in *Kitvei Ramban*, ed. Chavel, 1:304–5). Two, there are deep theological speculations on the foundations (*yesodot*) of the Torah, and which ultimately explain Jewish praxis, thus having meta-normative force (Maimonides's comments on *M.* Berakhot, end, and *M.* Sanhedrin 10.1, beg.; Nahmanides's comment on Gen. 1:1 contra Rashi; Joseph Albo, *Sefer ha-Iqqarim*, 1.3), even though specific norms may not be directly derived from them (*Y.* Peah 2.6/17a; also *B.* Baba Batra 130b). These speculations are most often based on narrative statements in Scripture, or they are derived from *aggadic* interpretations (*midrashim*) of these narrative statements, no matter how philosophical their method of expression might be. Clearly, the *Sifre* text quoted above is of this second, meta-normative type.

34 *B.* Sotah 14a re Deut. 13:5.
35 *M.* Avot 2.4.
36 Maimonides, *Guide*, 3.26.
37 Plato, *Theatetus*, 176A–B.
38 Plato, *Laws*, 631B–D; Cicero, *De Legibus*, 1.15.42–43.
39 Aristotle, *Nicomachean Ethics*, 5.7/1134b18–1135a5. There is only a hint that Aristotle saw humanly administered justice as being godlike in *Politics*, 3.11/1287a29–34.
40 Aristotle, *Politics*, 1.1/1253a29; *Nicomachean Ethics*, 10.7/1177b25–35.
41 Aristotle, *Nicomachean Ethics*, 1.4/1095b15–30.
42 *Digest*, 1.1.10.1. See Plato, *Republic*, 331E.
43 Plato, *Apology*, 41C.
44 Plato, *Crito*, 50A–51C; also *Apology*, 19A.
45 Plato, *Phaedo*, 63B..
46 *B.* Berakhot 5b. See also *B.* Avodah Zarah 18a.
47 Plato, *Crito*, 54E.
48 Plato, *Phaedo*, 67B.
49 Aristotle, *Metaphysics*, 6.1/1026a20–5.
50 Plato, *Republic*, 413C.
51 Plato, *Symposium*, 212D–222D.
52 Plato, *Seventh Letter*, 345C–350B. Cf. *Apology*, 32B–E.
53 See, e.g., John Finnis, *Natural Law and Natural Rights* (Oxford: Clarendon Press, 1980), 52–3; Alasdair MacIntyre, *After Virtue* (Notre Dame: University of Notre Dame Press, 1981), 152. Cf. Strauss, *Natural Right and*

History, 7–8; Jürgen Habermas, *Communication and the Evolution of Society*, trans. T. McCarthy (Boston: Beacon Press, 1979), 201–2.

54 Aristotle, *Politics*, 2.1/1261a5–30.

55 Ps. 111:7–8; *B*. Shabbat 53b. Cf. Strauss, *Natural Right and History*, 81.

56 *M*. Sanhedrin 4.5.

57 This is what differentiates humans from animals, viz., their respective relations to nature (B. Pesahim 118a re Gen. 3:18–19).

58 *B*. Baba Metsia 85a re Ps. 145:9.

59 *B*. Berakhot 7a and 32a re Exod. 32:13.

60 Nahmanides's comment on Deut. 6:16; also *B*. Taanit 9a re Deut. 6:16.

61 *B*. Shabbat 119b re Gen. 2:1.

62 *Commentary on the Writings*: Ps. 115:16.

63 Purposeful work is called *mel'ekhet mahshevet* (B. Betsah 13b and parallels). It is essentially different from ordinary *avodah* ("labour") or "exertion" (*tirha*) (Y. Pesahim 10.4/ 37d re Exod. 12:26). For the distinction between labour and work, see Hannah Arendt, *The Human Condition* (Garden City: Doubleday, 1959), 72–88, 119–39.

64 *B*. Berakhot 43b; *MT*: Blessings, 10.13.

65 Hume, *A Treatise of Human Nature*, 3.1.1; G.E. Moore, *Principia Ethica* (Cambridge: Cambridge University Press, 1903), 4.67, 113–15.

66 Ludwig Wittgenstein, *Philosophical Investigations*, 2nd ed., ed. and trans. G.E.M. Anscombe (New York: Macmillan, 1958), 1.7–10.

67 The prescription of a norm requires descriptive knowledge of *what* the prescribed act necessarily involves for its proper enactment (B. Baba Kama 2b re I Kings 22:11 and Deut. 33:17). This prescriptive enunciation is prior, both chronologically and logically, to the required description enunciated for it. Moreover, when the act of a sage is reported or described, plus assumed to be a normative precedent to be emulated by others, that is because it is assumed that this sage had a normative warrant for his action (e.g., *B*. Hullin 105a and *Tosafot*, s.v. "le-se`udata"; also *B*. Baba Batra 130b).

68 See Y. Peah 1.1/15d re Prov. 3:15.

69 Wittgenstein, *Philosophical Investigations*, 1.256–71.

70 See Aristotle, *Politics*, 3.5/1280a31–6; Jürgen Habermas, *The Philosophical Discourse of Modernity*, trans. F. Lawrence (Cambridge, MA: MIT Press, 1987), 309–26.

71 See Jonathan Lear, *Love and Its Place in Nature* (New Haven: Yale University Press, 1990), 141–2.

72 Even though this is not considered to be a virtue (*Beresheet Rabbah* 22.3 re Gen. 4:2), nonetheless, this verse comes to explain just why King Uzziah was such a successful developer.

73 Martin Heidegger, *Being and Time*, trans. J. Stambaugh (Albany: SUNY Press, 1996), 1.2.12–13, 49–58.

74 https://en.wikiquote.org/wiki/Archimedes.
75 *B*. Sanhedrin 38a re Prov. 8:1–2.
76 *B*. Taanit 2a re Deut. 11:13.
77 Ibid., 6b.
78 *B*. Shabbat 75a; Maimonides, *Teshuvot ha-Rambam*, no.150, ed. Y. Blau (Jerusalem: Miqitsei Nirdamim, 1960), 285–6.
79 *Y*. Berakhot 6.1/9d re Ps. 24:1; *Beresheet Rabbah* 43.7 re Gen. 14:19.
80 *B*. Berakhot 35a re Lev. 19:24.
81 *B*. Avodah Zarah 7b re Ps. 142:3; *B*. Berakhot 32a re Deut. 3:23; *MT*: Prayer, 1.2.
82 *B*. Berakhot 9a re Exod. 11:2.
83 *M*. Berakhot 9.5 re Deut. 6:5; also *B*. Berakhot 33b and *Y*. Berakhot 5.3/9d re *M*. Berakhot 5.3.
84 *M*. Avot 2.1; *B*. Berakhot 34b re Isa. 64:3; *B*. Kiddushin 39b re Deut. 5:16 and 22:7.
85 *Y*. Berakhot 7.4/11c re Deut. 10:17.
86 *M*. Berakhot 9.2.
87 *B*. Avodah Zarah 7b re Ps. 102:1.
88 *B*. Yoma 53b; also *B*. Taanit 22b.
89 *M*. Avot 5.10; *B*. Baba Batra 12b.
90 See, e.g., Gordon D. Kaufman, *Theology for a Nuclear Age* (Philadelphia: Westminster, 1985), 31.
91 I Chron. 29:14–15; *Sifra*: Behar re Lev. 25:23, ed. Weiss, 108a–b.
92 See *B*. Berakhot 60b; *MT*: Blessings, 10.3.
93 *MT*: Repentance, 5.1–4; Maimonides, *Guide*, 3.17.
94 *B*. Berakhot 40a re Deut. 11:15; also *B*. Shabbat 155b; *B*. Baba Metsia 85a re Ps. 145:9.
95 Plato, *Republic*, 431A, 444B, 490B.
96 Guardianship, which is the assignment by a higher authority to their agent to care for their property, requires the explicit appointment of a guardian (*shomer*) to exercise this responsibility, and for which the guardian is answerable to the person who so appointed him or her (Isa. 62:6; *M*. Baba Metsia 3.1). So, when Cain answers God's indictment of him for the murder of his brother Abel by saying, "Am I my brother's keeper [*ha-shomer*]?!" (Gen. 4:9), he seems to be saying, "since You didn't appoint me to be my brother's guardian, I am not therefore responsible for what happened to him nor am I answerable to you for it! Indeed, the responsibility for him is Yours as Creator!" (See *Tanhuma*: Beresheet, 9.) Of course, Cain's fallacy is that he assumes not harming others presupposes one has been appointed to care for them. However, the prohibition of not doing to someone else what you would hate being done to yourself (B. Shabbat 31a) is not entailed by the positive commandment to "love

[i.e., care for] your neighbor as yourself" (Lev. 19:18; see *MT*: Mourning, 14.1). Moreover, in rabbinic exegesis a positive commandment (*aseh*) only entails a prohibition or negative commandment (*l'av*) when the latter can be clearly inferred from the actual wording of the positive commandment in the Torah (B. Pesahim 41b re Exod. 12:8).

97 See William Wallace's "Earth Day Anthem" (https://en.wikipedia.org/wiki/Earth_Day). This anthem is sung in praise of nature, not in praise of God for creating nature.

98 https://en.wikipedia.org/wiki/Ecofeminism.

99 See Naomi Klein, *This Changes Everything: Capitalism vs. the Environment* (New York: Simon & Schuster, 2014).

100 Some mundane things become "sacred" and are thus removed from ordinary, private use because they have been dedicated to some higher public use like the service of the Temple (M. Meilah 5.1; *T.* Meilah 2.1; *M.* Kiddushin 1.6; *Y.* Kiddushin 1.6 re Ps. 24:1), or because they have been made into sacred objects *ab initio*, thus designated for the higher relationship with God (B. Megillah 26b). Other mundane objects become "sacred" insofar as their use is prohibited because they have been degraded by some illicit private use (*Y.* Kelaim 8.1/31b and *B.* Kiddushin 56b re Deut. 22:9). Thus the term "sacred things" (*qodashim*) came to designate anything forbidden for private use irrespective of whether it became sacred due to elevation or degradation by a person (B. Kiddushin 57a and Rashi, s.v. "ke-qodashim").

101 See Karl Marx, *Capital*, 7.1, trans. B. Fowkes (New York: Vintage Books, 1977), 283–92.

102 As such, *avodah zarah* as nature worship is an innovation that alienates or estranges humans from their historic relationship with God. See *Y.* Berakhot 9.1/13a re Isa. 46:7.

103 *B.* Baba Metsia 32b. Cf. Maimonides, *Guide*, 3.17 re Deut. 12:20, who argues that this is prohibited because causing unnecessary pain to an animal inculcates the vice of cruelty in humans. See also his comments on *M.* Berakhot 5.3 re *B.* Berakhot 33b and *Y.* Berakhot 5.3/9c, where he argues that if cruelty to animals were absolutely prohibited, how could the Torah permit the slaughter of animals for food (*shehitah*)? Nevertheless, the thirteenth-century theologian Levi ben Abraham argues in his book *Leviyat Hen*, chap. 15, ed. Kreisel, 373, that even an animal deserves a "a quick and pleasant death" (*mitah yafah*), which seems to imply he thought this is for the animal's sake, not just for the sake of the virtue of the person slaughtering the animal for food. See *B.* Sanhedrin 45a re Lev. 19:18 and Rashi, s.v. "mitah yafah," where *mitah yafah* refers to the quick, painless execution of a criminal. All of this implies that torture, whether of humans or of animals, is forbidden, both because of the harm to the body and soul of anybody tortured and the harm to the soul of the torturer.

104 Ezekiel Landau, *Responsa: Noda bi-Yehudah*, 2, Yoreh Deah, no. 10.
105 See Num. 27:16–17; also Isaac Abravanel's comment on Gen. 4:2 (answer to q. 4).
106 *B.* Avodah Zarah 36a.
107 *B.* Kiddushin 21b–22a re Deut. 21:10.
108 Maimonides, *Guide*, 3.17 re Deut. 12:20.
109 This is like voluntarily vowing (*neder*) to avoid partaking of certain things ordinarily permitted to be partaken of (*Sifre*: Bemidbar, no. 153 re Num. 30:3; *B.* Nedarim 12a). This kind of voluntary abstention is frowned upon by some (B. Nedarim 10a re Num. 6:11; *B.* Nedarim 77b re Deut. 23:23; *MT*: Vows, 13.25) but encouraged by others (B. Yevamot 20a; Nahmanides's comment on Lev. 19:2).
110 *Sifre*: Devarim, no. 203; *B.* Makkot 22a; Maimonides, *Sefer ha-Mitsvot*, neg. no. 57.
111 *M.* Kelim 9.8; *M.* Negaim 11.3; *M.* Betsah 1.1 and Maimonides's comment thereon.
112 *B.* Shabbat 129a.
113 *B.* Baba Kama 91b.
114 *B.* Shabbat 105b.
115 *B.* Sotah 14a.
116 This was more fully discussed in the previous chapter in connection with God's relation to nature. That is why there is much overlapping of the discussion of the human relation to nature here and that of God's relation to nature there. For each relation can only be understood when either compared to or contrasted with the other relation. So, in some ways the human relation to nature is comparable to God's relation to nature, and in other ways it is different.
117 In fact, the same question arose in the Jewish tradition as to whether medical intervention is also human intrusion into a realm that should be seen as God's alone. Thus Nahmanides is of the opinion that the human practice of medicine requires special divine dispensation (*reshut*). See his comment on Lev. 26:11 re the interpretation of Exod. 21:19 on *B.* Baba Kama 85a. Conversely, in the view of Maimonides, for whom God's beneficence is experienced within the natural order rather than from anything miraculous, no such dispensation is needed. Thus humans are supposed to imitate God's beneficence as they discover it in nature (*Guide*, 3.54). There is nothing supernatural about it. That is why, I think, Maimonides interprets what seems to be a "dispensation" in a strictly legal rather than a deeper theological sense, viz., it is an exemption (*reshut*) of physicians from *lex talionis* in the event of unintended injury to a patient during medical treatment (*MT*: Personal Injury, 1.5).
118 For the prohibition of *kel'ayim* to Jews, see Lev. 19:19 and Deut. 22:9–11.
119 *B.* Sanhedrin 56a.

120 *Sifra*: Aaharei-Mot, ed. Weiss, 86a and *B.* Yoma 67b re Lev. 18:5. See *Bemidbar Rabbah* 19.1 re Num. 19:2.
121 *B.* Sanhedrin 56b.
122 *B.* Sanhedrin 60a and *Tosafot*, s.v. "huqqim."
123 *B.* Baba Kama 55a.
124 Ibid., and *Tosafot*, s.v. "le-minehu" and s.v. "ha-manhig."
125 *Y.* Kelayim 1.7/27d.
126 Comment on Lev. 19:19.
127 Aristotle, *Metaphysics*, 12.8/1074b1–5.
128 W.D. Ross, *Aristotle* (New York: Meridian Books, 1959), 69–71. For the fuller discussion of Aristotelian teleology, see chapter 5 ("Maimonides and Aristotle").
129 Plato, *Symposium*, 202E–203A.
130 Aristotle, *Metaphysics*, 12.6/1071b10.
131 A.O. Lovejoy, *The Great Chain of Being* (Cambridge, MA: Harvard University Press, 1936).
132 E.g., Aristotle, *Topica*, 1.15/107b6–10; *Metaphysics*, 11.3/1060b36–1061a7.
133 Aristotle, *Nicomachean Ethics*, 3.5/1113b5–20. See G.E.M. Anscombe, "Modern Moral Philosophy," *Philosophy* (1958) 33: 1–5.
134 Throughout this book, "Nature" (upper case "N") is used when speaking of physis in Greek philosophy, whereas "nature" (lower case "n") is used when speaking of what God or humans make in biblically based theology.

4 Philo and Plato

1 See *B.* Sanhedrin 106a and *Bemidbar Rabbah* 20.23 re Num. 25:1–2.
2 I Maccabees 1:41–49; Josephus, *Antiquities*, 12.253–56. Jewish religious practices, especially circumcision, were outlawed. Frequently, the justification for this prohibition was that they were unnatural.
3 The term *Ioudaismos* is found in Hellenistic Jewish texts (II Maccabees 14:39; see also Galatians 1:13–14) and denotes the ancestral religion of the Jews. Thus, anybody who renounced polytheism was considered to be a Jew (B. Megillah 13a re Dan. 3:12; *Esther Rabbah* 6.4 re Est. 2:5) or, at least, a potential Jew (Y. Yevamot 8.1/8d).
4 It is important to note that for the Greek philosophers, whose nomenclature Philo so skilfully employed, *theōria* comes from the verb *theōrein*, meaning "to gaze." In its philosophical usage, it does not mean to look at the objects of ordinary experience or even to categorize them. *Theōria* is apprehension of the highest truth, not comprehension or conceptualization of sense experience (cf. Kant, *Critique of Pure Reason*, B105, 126–7). It means to contemplate or ponder the highest beings, and

since they are in the heavens, *theōrein* means "to gaze upwards." That is why I use "theory" and "contemplation" interchangeably. See Aristotle, *Nicomachean Ethics*, 6.7/1141a15–22; *Metaphysics*, 4.2/1003b15–20. *Theōria* is unlike *phronēsis*, practical reason, which deals with possible human actions rather than necessary, ultimate reality. As such, only *theōria* is true science, providing the only adequate foundation or platform (*epistēmē*) for true knowledge, and the most satisfying and enduring way of life. See Aristotle, *Nicomachean Ethics*, 6.7/1140b1–7; 10.7–8/1177a15–1179a32.

5 Philo, *De Migratione*, 16.88–93.

6 Plato, *Theatetus*, 172D; *Laws*, 781E. Aristotle, *Nicomachean Ethics*, 10.7/1177b5; *Politics*, 2.8/1273a34–5 and 7.2/1324a25–33.

7 Philo, *De Decalogo*, 20.101.

8 Philo, *De Confusione*, 2.2.

9 Philo, *De Vita Mosis*, 2.7.43–4.

10 Philo, *De Confusione*, 5.14, 38.190.

11 Philo, *De Vita Contemplativa*, 10.78.

12 Philo, *De Congressu*, 26.146–7; *De Abrahamo*, 31.164; *De Specialibus Legibus*, 3.1.1.

13 Philo, *Ad Gaium*, 23.156.

14 These potentially Jewish gentiles were called "fearers of the Lord" (*phoubomenoi tou theou*). See LXX on Ps. 118:4; Wolfson, *Philo*, 2:373–4. These de-paganized gentiles were the objects of both Jewish and Christian proselytizing efforts in the first three centuries CE (see Acts 13:16, 26).

15 This is precisely how the great Christian theologian Karl Barth, in his Gifford Lectures of 1937–8 at the University of Aberdeen, dealt with Lord Gifford's charge in his will of 1887 that the lectures in his memory deal with "natural theology" as distinct from "revealed theology." Barth presented a "theology of nature," grounded in revealed theology, from which he saw "natural theology" as proposed by Christian theologians to be a major deviation. See his *The Knowledge of God*, trans. J.L.M. Haire and I. Robertson (New York: Chas. Scribner's Sons, 1939), 3–12.

16 Since Philo's writings were lost to the Jews until the sixteenth century, when they were rediscovered by the Italian-Jewish theologian Azariah di Rossi, it is hard to situate Philo in and appropriate him for rabbinically formulated Jewish theology. See David Winston, "Philo and Rabbinic Literature," in *Cambridge Companion to Philo*, ed. A. Kamesar (Cambridge: Cambridge University Press, 2009), 231–53. Nevertheless, there have been some highly speculative attempts to show similarities, if not real mutual influence, between Philo and the Rabbis. See, e.g., B. Ritter, *Philo und die Halacha* (Leipzig: J.C. Hinrich, 1879); S. Belkin, *Philo and the Oral Law* (Cambridge, MA: Harvard University Press, 1940).

17 Philo, *Quis Rerum*, 62.316.

18 Philo, *Legum Allegoria*, 1.13.38. Note also 3.33.102: "One receives the vision [*emphasin*] of the Prime Cause directly from Himself [*ap' autou*]." Moreover, Philo asserts (1.13.37) that this allowance is a purposeful (*tinos heneka*) act of God for humans. See Philo, *Quod Deterius*, 24.86–7.
19 Philo, *De Opficio Mundi*, 2.7.
20 Ibid., 61.171.
21 Ibid., 2.16.
22 *Phaedrus*, 247B. See Richard Bodéüs, *Aristotle and the Theology of the Living Immortals*, trans. J. Garrett (Albany: SUNY Press, 2000), 54–71.
23 Plato, *Apology*, 26D; also *Republic*, 508A; *Laws*, 899B.
24 Plato, *Phaedo*, 98C; *Apology*, 26D.
25 Plato, *Phaedrus*, 252D–E.
26 Plato, *Phaedo*, 63B; *Apology*, 40C–42A.
27 Plato, *Phaedo*, 62C–D.
28 Plato, *Theatetus*, 176A–B; *Phaedrus*, 250C. See Philo, *Legum Allegoria*, 3.27.84; *De Fuga*, 12.63.
29 Plato, *Republic*, 341E–342D.
30 Though Plato speaks of a god who willingly made the cosmos (*Timaeus*, 28A–29B), this god is called "sort of a worker" (*dēmiourgos*) or "technician," which is hardly an exalted status in the aristocratic culture of his time. Moreover, this god does not seem to be interested in any relation with his "creation" once it has been made. Following Aristotle's critique of Plato for suggesting a temporal beginning of the cosmos (*Physics*, 8.1/251b14–26 contra *Timaeus*, 38B–C), many subsequent commentators have assumed that Plato's cosmology on this point is highly metaphorical. See, e.g., A.E. Taylor, *Plato*, 6th ed. (New York: Humanities Press, 1952), 442–3; cf. Sarah Broadie, *Nature and Divinity in Plato's Timaeus* (Cambridge: Cambridge University Press, 2011), 243–77.
31 Aristotle, *Metaphysics*, 12.8/1074b1.
32 Plato, *Laws*, 716B–C. Cf. *Cratylus*, 386A; *Theatetus*, 152A.
33 Plato, *Apology*, 28E.
34 Plato, *Republic*, 534D.
35 Plato, *Euthyphro*, 14E. Moreover, Socrates calls it *technē*, which means "making something tangible." Even if made by a god, such making is too mundane to be considered truly divine.
36 Plato, *Crito*, 50C–51C.
37 Ibid., 51B.
38 Plato, *Apology*, 29D.
39 Ibid., 24B.
40 Plato, *Crito*, 54E.
41 This is the famous definition of the name "God" given in the eleventh-century Christian theologian Anselm of Canterbury's *Proslogion*, chap. 3,

all of which is based on his probing the deeper meaning of Ps. 14:1 and 53:2, viz., "the fool says in his heart that there is no God [*ein elohim*]." In the Vulgate's Latin translation (Anselm's biblical text), it reads *dicit insipiens in corde suo non est Deus.*

42 Philo, *De Opficio Mundi*, 3.23.

43 II Maccabees 7:28. Note David Winston, *Logos and Mystical Theology in Philo of Alexandria* (Cincinnati: Hebrew Union College Press, 1985), 45: "The conception of absolute transcendence must be seen as a product of the theological formula of creation *ex nihilo*, which introduces an unbridgeable gap between God and the cosmos ... Since ancient Greek philosophy was free of the *ex nihilo* formulation, it could yield only concepts of relative transcendence."

44 The Rabbis seem to have been aware that *creatio ex nihilo* is a Jewish doctrine that is taken by Greek philosophers to be absurd, primarily because they could not conceive of even the supreme God transcending Nature. Thus in one important rabbinic text (*Beresheet Rabbah* 1.9), a "philosopher" argues with Rabban Gamliel the Younger that God created the cosmos out of pre-existent materials (Plato's position in *Timaeus*, 28A–29B). But Rabban Gamliel insists that even the "chaos" (*tohu va-vohu*), which is "unformed" (LXX: *akataskeuastos*), mentioned in Gen. 1:2, was itself created by God and was not already there to be formed by God subsequently. See also *Beresheet Rabbah* 1.5 (ed. Theodor-Albeck, 3 and n. 7 thereon); cf. *Y.* Hagigah 2.1/77c. Moreover, whereas Plato asserts that God made the cosmos by in-forming pre-existent chaos (i.e., formless matter) below according to the pre-existent forms above, it is asserted in *Beresheet* Rabbah, 1.4 re Prov. 8:22, that the Torah, which was used as the "device" (*kli umanato*; *Beresheet Rabbah*, 1.1) by which God created the universe, is itself created by God, hence it is not divine (i.e., uncreated). Instead, the Torah is God's first creation. See *Sifre*: Devarim, no. 37 re Prov. 8:22–3; *B.* Pesahim 54a and *B.* Nedarim 39b re Prov. 8:22. Accordingly, God's creation of the universe is uniquely presuppositionless.

45 Philo, *Quod Deus*, 10.46–8.

46 Cf. Kant, *Critique of Pure Reason*, 655B.

47 Ibid., 630B.

48 Philo, *Legum Allegoria*, 3.3.7.

49 Philo, *De Opficio Mundi*, 61.171.

50 Philo, *Quod Deus*, 30.143.

51 Philo, *De Confusione*, 20.97.

52 Philo, *De Migratione*, 8.39.

53 Philo, *De Opficio Mundi*, 17.54.

54 Ibid., 25.77.

55 Philo, *Quod Deus*, 14.69.

56 Philo, *De Opficio Mundi*, 24.73.

57 Philo, *De Confusione*, 36.180. As for God creating what is "bad" (*kakos*), albeit indirectly, Philo seems to follow the Septuagint (LXX on Isa. 45:7), which distinguished between *kakos* (*ra* in Hebrew) and *ponēron* or "evil" (*resha* in Hebrew). God is the creator (however indirectly) of what humans experience as bad or uncanny and, therefore, God can be considered responsible for it (see Lam. 3:37–8). But "evil" is what humans chose to do, which, for Philo, is their choice to submit themselves to their appetites that are bad or uncanny.

58 Philo, *De Vita Mosis*, 1. 31.174, 2.47.261.

59 Philo, *De Cherubim*, 9.27–9.

60 See Plato, *Timaeus*, 29E–30A.

61 Cf. Philo, *De Opficio Mundi*, 61.172.

62 Philo, *De Opficio Mundi*, 24.75; *De Fuga*, 14.71–2.

63 Philo, *De Cherubim*, 2.74.

64 Thus in his three discussions of Gen. 1:31 ("God saw all that He made, and indeed it is very good") – *De Migratione*, 8.42 and 24.135 and *Quis Rerum*, 159–60 – Philo takes this to be Moses's praise of God's wise creativity, not God's designation of material existence as itself being "very good" (LXX: *kala lian*), i.e., being pleasing to God because of any inherent goodness of its own.

65 Plato, *Republic*, 505E, 508A.

66 Aristotle, *Metaphysics*, 12.9–10/1074b35–1075a20; *Nicomachean Ethics*, 10.7/1177b25–9.

67 Philo, *De Abrahamo*, 17.78, 80.

68 Philo, *De Gigantibus*, 13.60–1. See *Quis Rerum*, 55.274; *De Congressu*, 2.11.

69 Philo, *De Fuga*, 29.163–4.

70 Philo, *Quis Rerum*, 9.45, 16.84, 53.264–5; *De Somniis* 2.34.232–3.

71 See Carlos Lévy, "Philo's Ethics" in *Cambridge Companion to Philo*, 146–9.

72 Aristotle, *Politics*, 1.1/1253a29.

73 Philo, *Legum Allegoria*, 3.88.246–7.

74 Plato, *Republic*, 439D–E.

75 Ibid., 440B–441A.

76 Philo, *Legum Allegoria*, 3.87.245.

77 Ibid., 3.39.116.

78 See *B.* Berakhot 5a re Ps. 4:5 and Rashi thereon, s.v. "yargiz." However, like Philo's *aretē*, the *yetser ha-tov* is not good autonomously, but is good because it is the internalization of God's Torah in the soul of the righteous person. That is what enables the *yetser ha-tov* to rule over the "bad [i.e., uncanny] impulse" (*yetser ha-ra*) rather than serving it and thus being ruled by it. See also *B.* Kiddushin 30b re Gen. 4:7; *B.* Yevamot 103b; *B.* Baba Batra 16a re Job 15:4.

79 Philo, *Legum Allegoria*, 3.88.245.

80 Émile Durkheim, *Suicide*, trans. J.A. Spaulding and G. Simpson (Glencoe: Free Press, 1951), 254–7.

81 Plato, *Republic*, 412C–427C.

82 Even though Plato speaks of "the form of the Good" (*tou agathou*) as "cause" (*aitia*) of all that is correct and beautiful, and that it "rules" (*kyria*) truth and what is intelligible (*Republic*, 517B–C), this "causality" is not conscious or willed because it has any interest in its "effects." Rather, it is what automatically follows from its exposure to certain lesser beings who have been able to apprehend it.

83 Plato, *Apology*, 30A.

84 Plato, *Crito*, 53A.

85 This discussion of the *Republic* is adapted from my *Suicide and Morality* (New York: Scholars Studies Press, 1975), 21–4.

86 Plato, *Republic*, 516C.

87 Plato, *Timaeus*, 29E.

88 Plato, *Republic*, 508A–E, 516A–C.

89 This is the key point of Karl Popper's famous and controversial argument against Plato's political philosophy in *The Open Society and Its Enemies*, 1:120–56. Needless to say, Philo agrees with Plato much more than did Popper; hence his differences with Plato are much milder.

90 Plato, *Crito*, 51D.

91 Plato, *Republic*, 473D; also *Epistle* VII, 326B–350E.

92 *Republic*, 520B–C.

93 Plato, *Crito*, 50A–53A. Note Plato, *Republic*, 519E, where it is said that the polity has the right to unify its citizens by getting each of them to benefit each other and the polity as a whole by doing their civic duty. This political harmonization is done either by "persuasion" (*peithoi*) or by "compulsion" (*anangkē*), i.e., coercion. Clearly, irrational citizens frequently need to be coerced to do what the polity requires be done for the common good. But, just as clearly, philosophers will be more easily persuaded to do their civic duty willingly because they have been intellectually persuaded to accept the fact that the common good of their society is simultaneously their personal good, even if it is not their primary personal good. For Philo, too, only those who are intellectually imperfect need a "prohibition" (*apagoreusis*), which is accompanied by a threat of punishment, itself a form of psychological coercion. But those who are intellectually perfect do not need to be either coerced or even "counselled" (*parainesis*) to do what is right, since they have been persuaded naturally by "right reason" (*orthos logos*) to act on behalf of their society (*De Cherubim*, 29–30.90–3). Even in the Talmud, it had to be admitted that God's imposition of His law on the people Israel at Mount Sinai only became effective when the people freely accepted that law, and that was long after it had actually been imposed on them (B. Shabbat 88a–b re Exod. 19:17 and Prov. 11:3).

94 Plato, *Republic*, 521B.

95 To be sure, Philo at times seems to echo what might be called Platonic political boredom (e.g., *De Somnis*, 2.33.225). Nevertheless, it is a far less serious factor in his political theology than it is in Plato's political philosophy, because, it seems to me, Philo's God is not bored with His creation. How, then, could those who imitate God be consistently bored with the mundane world? Moreover, Philo's admiration for the ascetic Jewish sect called the "Therapeutae" includes his admiration for the way they were still concerned with those they left behind in the mundane world, despite their pursuit of a purely contemplative way of life apart from the world. He contrasts this with some theoretically oriented Greek philosophers who showed no such concern, who not only left the mundane world, but actually abandoned it (*De Vita Contemplativa*, 2.13–14).

96 See E.R. Goodenough, *The Jurisprudence of the Jewish Courts in Egypt* (New Haven: Yale University Press, 1929).

97 Aristotle, *Physics*, 2.7/198a21–9.

98 Philo, *De Praemiis*, 8.51.

99 Philo, *De Sacrificiis*, 39.131.

100 Philo, *De Ebrietate*, 20.81.

101 Philo, *De Abrahamo*, 37.208.

102 Philo, *De Vita Mosis*, 1.9.48; Philo, *De Decalogo*, 22.110.

103 Philo, *De Cherubim*, 34.120. *Paroikos* was the term used in the Hellenistic Age to designate resident-aliens as distinct from full citizens (who, in the Roman Empire, could say *civis Romanus sum*, and claim full civil rights therefore). See M. Rostovtzeff, *The Social and Economic History of the Hellenistic World* (Oxford: Oxford University Press, 1941), 2:1103–4. LXX translates the Hebrew *toshavim* as *paroikoi*, and *gerim* as *prosēlytoi*, viz., those who have converted to Judaism. The latter term designates a uniquely Jewish status. Both *paroikoi* and *proselytoi*, minimally, have come to be part of the Jewish people, the former partially and the latter fully, because of their explicit rejection of any other gods and their at least implicit acceptance of the kingship of the one Creator God. For a similar rabbinic view, see Ibn Ezra's comment on Lev. 24:22.

104 Philo, *De Decalogo*, 10.42; also *De Specialibus Legibus*, 3.33.182, 4.62.237.

105 Philo, *De Specialibus Legibus*, 4.42.230–2, 4.52.237; also *De Plantatione*, 28.122; *Quis Rerum*, 33.163–4; *De Vita Contemplativa*, 2.17.

106 Philo, *De Josepho*, 6.29–31.

107 Philo, *De Vita Mosis*, 2.4.17, 2.7.43–8, 2.9.51. See Helmut Koester, "NOMOS PHUSEŌS: The Concept of Natural Law in Greek Thought," in *Religions in Antiquity*, ed. J. Neusner (Leiden: Brill, 1968), 538–40; Hindy Najman, "The Law of Nature and the Authority of Mosaic Law," *Studia Philonica Annual* (1999), 11: 55–73.

108 *Quod Omnis*, 12.79–84.
109 Ibid., 12.79; *De Specialibus Legibus*, 2.16.69, 3.25.137.
110 Plato, *Apology*, 24B. Cf. I Sam. 26:19; Ezek. 20:32.
111 Philo, *De Vita Mosis*, 2.7.43–4.
112 Philo, *Quod Deterius*, 20.84; *De Confusione*, 23.112; *De Somnis*, 2.22.154; *De Ebrietate*, 20.81; *De Specialibus Legibus*, 1.15.63.
113 Philo, *De Specialibus Legibus*, 2.2.9, 2.3.12–14.
114 Philo, *De Virtutibus*, 9.51; *De Praemiis*, 2.11.
115 Philo, *De Confusione*, 23.108.
116 Philo, *De Somnis*, 2.33.223–7.
117 Philo, *De Decalogo*, 25.132; also *De Specialibus Legibus*, 3.15.83.
118 Philo, *De Specialibus Legibus*, 4.41.228.
119 Philo, *De Virtutibus*, 13.81.
120 Ibid., 26.140.
121 Ibid., 25.125.
122 Philo, *De Agricultura*, 9.41.
123 Ibid., 10.48, 12.50.
124 Philo, *De Opficio Mundi*, 29.88; also *Quod Omnis*, 3.20.
125 Philo, *De Opficio Mundi*, 52.148.

5 Maimonides and Aristotle

1 Maimonides, *Commentary on the Mishnah*: Avodah Zarah 4.7; *MT*: Strange Worship, 1.1–3 and 11.16; *Guide*, 3.31.
2 *Teshuvot ha-Rambam*, no. 293, ed. Y. Blau (Jerusalem: Meqitsei Nirdamim, 1960), 1:548–50.
3 Maimonides, *Guide*, 1.26, 33, 46. See J.A. Diamond, *Maimonides and the Hermeneutics of Suspicion* (Albany: SUNY Press, 2002).
4 Scholars debate how much of the corpus of Aristotle's work, translated into Arabic, was actually available to Maimonides. In what follows I quote only from those works of Aristotle that Maimonides himself quoted (though I cite other works of Aristotle that deal with issues that Maimonides dealt with). Even though Maimonides knew no Greek, it is a further sign of his brilliance how well he understood Aristotle's philosophy. The same could be said of Thomas Aquinas, who understood Aristotle and Maimonides quite well, but didn't know Greek, Hebrew, or Arabic. (Nevertheless, for the sake of those who do read Greek, I have cited some of the key Greek terms Aristotle uses.) For a good discussion of Maimonides as an Aristotelian, see H.A. Davidson, *Moses Maimonides* (Oxford: Oxford University Press, 2005), 98–121.
5 Maimonides, *Guide*, 2.13.
6 *MT*: Forbidden Foods, 11.7.

7 Maimonides, *Guide*, 1.50. See also *Commentary on the Mishnah*: Avodah Zarah 1.3; *MT*: Strange Worship, 9.4. Cf. *Teshuvot ha-Rambam*, ed. Blau, no. 149, 284–5, where Maimonides explicitly asserts that Judaism has more theological affinity with Christianity than with Islam, because of the Christian acceptance of the Hebrew Bible in its totality as the word of God. The theological difference between Judaism and Christianity, for Maimonides, is due to their differing interpretations of some key biblical doctrines. Christianity, however, posed much less of a philosophical challenge to Judaism than did Islam, since its core metaphysical-theological doctrines of the Incarnation and the Trinity were considered by both Jewish and Muslim theologians to be philosophically flawed. The most famous of these Jewish refutations is Hasdai Crescas's *The Refutation of the Christian Principles*, trans. D.J. Lasker (Albany: SUNY Press, 1992). Christianity, though, has posed more of a historical-theological challenge to Judaism insofar as its theologians have claimed their newer religion to be based on biblical revelation, first given to the Jewish people but subsequently superseded by Christianity. Countering these supersessionist claims, the twelfth-century Jewish theologian Judah Halevi argued that biblical theology and the prime revelatory event it is based on (i.e., the Sinai theophany) are superior to anything the two derivative religions, Christianity and Islam, have added to it. In fact, their additions are dilutions of the original revelation rather than higher developments of it (*Kuzari*, 1.4–26, esp. 1.25 re Exod. 20:2). Maimonides too argued against both Christian and Muslim supersessionist claims, asserting that instead of going beyond Judaism, the two have in fact lessened or diluted the full authority of the most perfect revelation: the Mosaic Torah (*MT*: Kings, 11.4 re Zeph. 3:9, uncensored ed.).

8 Aristotle, *Physics*, 2.7/198b4.

9 This is even true of what many consider the best treatment of Maimonides as a philosopher who revered Aristotle (*Guide*, 1.5, 2:23), H.A. Davidson's *Maimonides the Rationalist* (Oxford: Littman Library of Jewish Civilization, 2011), 115–16, 138.

10 Aristotle, *Posterior Analytics*, 1.24/85b34–7, 2.11/94a20–5. Hence nothing that exists is not caused (*Rhetoric*, 2.23/1400a25). Even chance occurrences (*tychē*) are events whose full causality is not known by us, but that still are part of the whole, causal cosmic order, an order that is ultimately teleological (*Physics*, 2.5/197a8–2.6/198a9). "Nature" (*physis*) is the overall name for this orderly (*taxeōs*) cosmos (*Physics*, 8.1/152a11–13).

11 Aristotle, *Posterior Analytics*, 2.11/94b37–95a9.

12 Aristotle cannot answer the question "Why does the universe exist rather than not exist?" because it could only be answered by positing an external first cause of the universe, that is, who transcends it and could be the only

one to determine its existence or non-existence. Note how Aristotle rules out this question altogether: "The universe [*to pan*] is nowhere ... for to say 'where' [*pou*] about something is to say what it is, and also requires that there be something else that contains it [*periechei*]; but there is nothing besides [*para*] the whole universe, nothing outside [*exō*] the All" (*Physics*, 4.5/212b15–17).

13 Thus *telos* is a *peras*, but not every *peras* is a *telos* (Aristotle, *Metaphysics*, 5.17/1022a5–13). As such, only finite, delimited reality is knowable (*Posterior Analytics*, 1.24/86a5–7; *De Generatione Animalium*, 1.1/715b15).
14 Aristotle, *Physics*, 2.1/94b37–95a9.
15 Aristotle, *Metaphysics*, 3.2/996b6–8.
16 Aristotle, *Physics*, 8.4/255b34–256a5.
17 Ibid., 8.6/259a15.
18 Plato, *Timaeus*, 29E–32B.
19 Aristotle, *De Partibus Animalium*, 2.1/646a30–5.
20 *Magna Moralia*, 2.12/1211b27–39.
21 *De Partibus Animalium*, 1.1/640a1–7.
22 See Lovejoy, *The Great Chain of Being*.
23 Aristotle, *De Anima*, 2.4/415a26–415b8.
24 Aristotle, *Metaphysics*, 12.9/1075a10–14.
25 Aristotle, *Nicomachean Ethics*, 1.1/1094a1–4.
26 Ibid., 1.5/1095b15–1096a10.
27 Ibid., 10.6/1176b30–5, 10.7/1177b1–4, 10.8/1178b22–4.
28 Ibid., 1.10/1100a10–1101a18.
29 Cf. *Qohelet Rabbah* 7.4 re Eccl. 7:1.
30 Aristotle, *Nicomachean Ethics*, 1.10/1101a15.
31 Ibid., 1.10/1101a18–21.
32 Ibid., 1.10/1101a19.
33 Ibid., 1.10/1100b13.
34 Aristotle, *Metaphysics*, 12.7/1072a20–1072b14.
35 Ibid., 12.9/1074b35.
36 Aristotle, *Nicomachean Ethics*, 10.7/1177b1–5.
37 Aristotle, *Metaphysics*, 12.7/1072b30; also *De Motu Animalium*, 6/700b24–8.
38 Aristotle, *De Caelo*, 1.4/271a35.
39 Aristotle, *Nicomachean Ethics*, 1.2/983a5–10.
40 Ibid., 10.7/1178a10–14.
41 Ibid., 10.7/1177b26–9.
42 Ibid., 10.8/1178b22–4.
43 Aristotle, *Metaphysics*, 1.1/980a22–30; *De Caelo*, 3.2/301a6.
44 Aristotle, *Nicomachean Ethics*, 10.8/1178b22–4.
45 See Plato, *Gorgias*, 474D.
46 Aristotle, *De Caelo*, 1.3/270b21–2.

47 Aristotle, *Nicomachean Ethics*, 6.1/1139a6–13. Although Aristotle tried to determine what are the first principles of ethics, they are still unlike scientific (or ontological) first principles whose derivative principles are quite precise and follow in strict logical sequence. For practical/ethical reason works *towards* or *up to* first principles, while scientific/philosophical reason works *down from* them to its derivatives (1.3/1095a30–1095b4). That is why scientific precision cannot be expected when dealing with morally variable humans (1.3/1094b24–7).
48 Nevertheless, note *Nicomachean Ethics*, 6.8/1144b25–6: "Virtue [*arête*] is not only what conforms to right reason [*kata ton orthon logon*], but which habitually [*hexis*] functions with it." Hence, even in true praxis there is thought, and even in true thought there is praxis.
49 Aristotle, *Nicomachean Ethics*, 1.13/1103a5–10; 6.7/1141a20.
50 Ibid., 10.7/1177a12–36.
51 Aristotle, *Politics*, 7.2/1324a25–37.
52 Cf. Plato, *Republic*, 473D.
53 Aristotle, *Politics*, 1.1/1253a1–7.
54 Aristotle, *Nicomachean Ethics*, 5.11/1133a5–18. Cf. Plato, *Phaedo*, 62C.
55 Aristotle, *Politics*, 1.1/1253a9–15.
56 Plato, *Republic*, 389D–392C.
57 See Bodéüs, *Aristotle and the Theology of the Living Immortals*, 95–104.
58 Aristotle, *Physics*, 8.6/259b25–7 et passim; *De Caelo*, 1.2/268b15–269a20.
59 Aristotle, *Metaphysics*, 12.7/1072a16–35.
60 For Aristotle's distinction between sensible [*aisthētai*] and intelligible [*noētē*] matter, see *Metaphysics*, 7.10/1036a10–11; *De Caelo*, 1.2/270b22–7. Even though form is never without matter (contra Plato), except in God's case, one can at least imagine sensible matter apart from its form insofar as sensible matter (i.e., earthly matter), unlike its form, is perishable. But intelligible matter, being imperishable like mathematical objects, cannot even be imagined apart from its form. See Maimonides, *Guide*, 1.76, beg., for much the same point.
61 Aristotle, *Metaphysics*, 12.8/1074b1–14. Maimonides follows Aristotle, and Plato before him, assuming that the heavenly bodies are living, cognizing beings. *MT*: Foundations, 3.9; *Guide*, 2.5 re Ps. 19:2.
62 See Thomas S. Kuhn, *The Structure of Scientific Revolutions* (Chicago: University of Chicago Press, 1962), 91–108.
63 This became most explicit in the work of the seventeenth-century Jewish scientist-philosopher Joseph Delmedigo. See J. Brown, *New Heavens and a New Earth: The Jewish Reception of Copernican Thought* (New Haven: Yale University Press, 2013), esp., 66–78. Earlier, the fourteenth-century Jewish theologian Don Hasdai Crescas had criticized the Aristotelian theory of cosmic causation, yet he didn't provide or know of any new paradigm to

replace it. See H.A. Wolfson, *Crescas' Critique of Aristotle* (Cambridge, MA: Harvard University Press, 1929), esp., 114–27.

64 For two attempts by contemporary Aristotelians to do that, see Alasdair MacIntyre, *After Virtue*, 56, 152, 183 (referring to Aristotle's "metaphysical biology"); and John Finnis, *Natural Law and Natural Rights*, 51–2. Both argue (Finnis explicitly) against Leo Strauss (*inter alia*) who, in his influential book *Natural Right and History* (Chicago: University of Chicago Press, 1953), 8, speaks of "the fundamental dilemma" of trying to formulate a "teleological science of man" (which is needed to provide a subject for a teleological ethics) without a teleological natural science (presumably physics and, in fact, his sole reference on this page is to Aristotle's *Physics*) so as to put it into an ultimate, universal, cosmological context. But I think Strauss begs the question in his *What Is Political Philosophy?* (Glencoe: Free Press, 1959), 38–40. There he seems to assume that merely positing *that* there is an ultimate, pre-existent object of rational human desire, i.e. "the whole" (39), thereby escapes the charge that this *telos* is but the projection of human rational desire on to the cosmos. See also Strauss, *The City and Man* (Charlottesville: University Press of Virginia, 1964), 21. However, assuming *that* something exists (especially the cosmic *telos* qua *summum bonum*), without being able to say *what it is* (a là Aristotle) or *what it does* (a là Maimonides, as we shall see), is only a hope; it is not the assertion of a metaphysical truth. As Kant pointed out, the fact we desire something and hope it must therefore be doesn't necessitate the reality of what we desire (*Critique of Pure Reason*, B625–31). Nevertheless, we do need some kind of cogent ontology/cosmology for our ethics if it is to satisfy the irrepressible metaphysical longing of truly intelligent humans for the ultimate significance of what we do. That is what Aristotle tried to do by constituting his teleological ontology on the back of the natural science of his day, and then connecting his ethics to it. The question is, however, whether that kind of ontology needs to be constituted on the back of natural science, Aristotelian or not. So, if the currently accepted paradigm in natural science is not as "metaphysically friendly" as was the Aristotelian paradigm, can a teleological anthropology be constituted on the back of some other science (in the broader sense of the German term *Wissenschaft*), which deals with the world we experience and interact with before we speculate about its foundation?

65 For Spinoza's argument against Maimonides's attempted integration of creationist ontology and Aristotelian cosmology, see his *Tractatus Theologico-Politicus*, chap. 7 re *Guide*, 2.25, 112–15.

66 Maimonides, *Guide*, 1.69, 167.

67 See Leo Strauss, *Persecution and the Art of Writing* (Chicago: University of Chicago Press, 1988), 67–78.

68 See Kenneth Seeskin, "Maimonides' Conception of Philosophy," in *Leo Strauss and Judaism*, ed. D. Novak (Lanham: Rowman and Littlefield, 1996), 87–110.

69 Immanuel Kant, *The Metaphysics of Morals*, trans. M. Gregor (Cambridge: Cambridge University Press, 1996), 176–7 et passim.

70 Maimonides, *Guide*, 2.13, 281.

71 Ibid., 2.12–13, 17–18. Cf. 2.25.

72 Ibid., 2.12, 279.

73 *MT*: Repentance, 8.2–3; Maimonides, *Guide*, 2.27, 29.

74 Maimonides, *Guide*, 1.69, 169.

75 Ibid., 2.21, 315.

76 In *Guide*, 2.6, Maimonides ascribes the notion of *emanation from God* to Plato. In his "Translator's Introduction: The Philosophic Sources of *The Guide of the Perplexed*," Shlomo Pines writes: "This is in all probability, a reference to some perhaps (though not necessarily) Neo-Platonic interpretation of the doctrine of the *Timaeus* (28Aff.) concerning the eternal model imitated by the Demiurge" (lxxxv–lxxvi).

77 Ibid., 2.6–7, 21. Cf. 2.intro., 2.1.

78 *MT*: Foundations of the Torah, 7.1; Maimonides, *Guide*, 2.36–7.

79 Maimonides, *Guide*, 2.20, 312.

80 Aristotle, *Physics*, 2.5/196b10–197a35.

81 Maimonides, *Guide*, 2.17.

82 Ibid., 1.69, 170.

83 Kant noted the difference between a teleology inherent in natural entities and a teleology "imposed [*aufdringt*] upon nature" by a transcendent Creator (*Critique of Pure Reason*, B720–1). Since Aristotelian immanent cosmic teleology had long been rejected by post-Galilean natural science, Kant could only recognize a teleology made for the cosmos externally by an "Author of all things." However, this he takes to be an "anthropomorphic illusion" (724B, note a).

84 Zvi Diesendruck designated this as "commanding teleology" (*das Gebiet der Teleologie*) in his essay "Die Teleologie bei Maimonides," *Hebrew Union College Annual* (1928), 5: 513.

85 Maimonides, *Guide*, 2.7.

86 In rabbinic theology, the ultimate reward is to be given in "the-world-beyond" (*olam ha-ba*) or "the-coming-future" (*l'atid la-vo*), which clearly designates epochs yet to come. See *Encyclopedia Judaica*, 6:860–83, s.v. "eschatology." Yet Maimonides denies the temporality of the world-beyond and considers it to be eternal (*matsui v'omed*), as contrasted with the worldly messianic era (*MT*: Repentance, 8.8; also *MT*: Kings, 12.1–5). For this he is criticized by his most persistent (though not the most systematic) critic, Abraham ben David of Posquières (Rabad) in his note on *MT*: Repentance, 8.8, citing *B*. Sanhedrin 97a re Isa. 2:11. See also *Y*. Yevamot 15.2/14d.

87 Maimonides, *Commentary on the Mishnah*: Avot, intro., chap. 8, ed. Kafih, 262–3; Avot 5.5, 298.

88 *B.* Berakhot 33b re Deut. 10:12. See Maimonides, *Commentary on the Mishnah*: Avot 3.18, 284; *MT*: Repentance, 5.1–5. It is surprising, though, that Maimonides does not include the doctrine of free choice among the thirteen dogmas he considers to be foundational for Judaism in his *Commentary on the Mishnah*: Sanhedrin, chap. 10, intro.

89 E.g., *B.* Shabbat 88b–89a.

90 *MT*: Prayer, 7.1.

91 Maimonides, *Guide*, 2.29, 345. His prooftexts are Eccl. 1:9; *B.* Avodah Zarah 54b; *Beresheet Rabbah* 5.5.

92 That is why the seemingly most miraculous event in Scripture, the theophany at Sinai (*ma`amad har sinai*), is for Maimonides a mass apprehension of an eternal truth, viz., God's absolute Being, and the unreality of any other god or gods. *MT*: Foundations of the Torah, 1.1–6 and 8.1; *Guide*, 2.33 re *B.* Makkot 23b–24a citing Exod. 20:2–3. Hence the novelty (*hiddush*) here is all subjective, and not at all objective.

93 Furthermore, the miracles do not involve legendary beings of which no one present has had any experience. Miraculous events are unusual, not fantastic (comments on *M.* Kilayim 8.5 and *M.* Hullin 9.6). Note also *MT*: Murder, 11.5, where Maimonides reiterates the rabbinic prohibition of involvement with things or situations that are dangerous to human life (B. Pesahim 8b and *B.* Kiddushin 39b). But he then exempts certain things from this prohibition since they are not all that dangerous (12.3), and what is unusual is not made the subject of a prohibition (see *B.* Eruvin 63b; *Guide*, 3.34). However, this seems to go against the sense of two parallel rabbinic texts (B. Avodah Zarah 30b; *Y.* Terumot 8.3/46a) where one is exempt from this prohibition because, in some cases, God miraculously "watches the simple" (see, esp., *B.* Yevamot 12b re Ps. 116:6).

94 Nevertheless, Maimonides is quite selective in his use of rabbinic sources, and is quite critical of "preachers and commentators" (*Guide*, 2.29, 347) whose theological inadequacies lead them to interpret many seemingly fantastic rabbinic texts about God imaginatively rather than scientifically (i.e., with metaphysical insight). For Nahmanides's considerably different view of miracles being supernatural, see, e.g., *Commentary on the Torah*: Gen. 17:1.

95 For the permission granted to gentiles, but not to Jews, to pray to God through semi-divine intermediaries, see *B.* Sanhedrin 63a re Exod. 22:19 and 63b and Tos., s.v. "asur." Nevertheless, this view, most famously put forth by the eleventh-century Ashkenazic jurist-theologian-exegete Rabbenu Jacob Tam would not have been accepted by Maimonides, who saw the prohibition of idolatry to be for all humankind, with few if any differences between Jewish and gentile idolatry acknowledged (*MT*: Oathes, 11.2).

96 *MT*: Strange Worship, 1.1–2.

97 Ibid., 3.7; Maimonides, *Guide*, 3.37, 49. To my knowledge, Maimonides never invokes the opinion in the Talmud (B. Yoma 69b re Zech. 5:8) that by the time of the Second Temple, Jews had lost the propensity for idolatry. That is because, so it seems, Maimonides thought the propensity for idolatry is endemic in human nature, thus it cannot be permanently eradicated but only sublimated into more acceptable praxis. Perhaps that is why Maimonides asserts (*MT*: Kings, 11.1) that the Messiah will rebuild the Temple and restore its sacrificial cult. This cult was not only meant to sublimate the idolatrous inclinations of the generation of Jews to whom the Torah was given at Sinai (see *Guide*, 3.33) inasmuch as this natural human propensity for idolatry cannot ever be overcome in history or by history.

98 Maimonides, *Sefer ha-Mitsvot*, neg. no. 1.

99 Ibid., pos. no. 1; *Guide*, 2.33. Cf. *B*. Makkot 23b–24a re Exod. 20:2–3.

100 *MT*: Prayer, 4.15–16.

101 *MT*: Prayer, 1.1–2.

102 *B*. Berakhot 20b and 31a–b re I Sam. 1:13.

103 *B*. Berakhot 48a.

104 *MT*: Prayer, 1.4. By "stammers," he means those who are theologically inarticulate and confused.

105 See *B*. Baba Kama 82b–83a and Tos., s.v. "lashon sursi."

106 Indeed, individual prayer is theologically purified by being expressed in the language stipulated for common prayer. As such, individual prayer is subordinate to common prayer (*MT*: Prayer, 8.1 and 10.16). See also *B*. Yoma 53b.

107 *MT*; Prayer, 1.5 re Berakhot 33a and *B*. Megillah 17b. See *Y*. Berakhot 6.2/10b. In fact, the synagogue service probably originated in the Temple as preparation for the sacrificial service (M. Tamid 5.1).

108 *B*. Megillah 29a re Ezek. 11:16.

109 *MT*: Prayer, 1.4 and 6.3.

110 Aristotle, *Politics*, 1.1/1253a9–19; also Maimonides, *Guide*, 2.40.

111 Thus a "private language" is, as mentioned earlier, an oxymoron, since it couldn't be publicly communicated, being a monologue rather than a dialogue, and dialogue is essentially linguistic. This point was most famously made by Ludwig Wittgenstein, *Philosophical Investigations*, 1.243–71.

112 This is comparable to the principle *lex orandi, lex credendi* (the rule of prayer is the rule of belief) in early Christian theology. See Paul de Clerck, "Lex orandi, lex credendi," *Studia Liturgica* (1994), 24: 178–200.

113 Cf. William James, who famously wrote (in his Gifford Lectures in 1901–2): "Religion ... shall mean for us *the feelings, acts, and experiences of*

individual men in their solitude, so far as they apprehend themselves to stand in relation to whatever they may consider the divine ... In these lectures ... the immediate personal experiences will amply fill our time" (*The Varieties of Religious Experience* [New York: Mentor Books, 1958], 42).

114 *MT*: Prayer, 8.1.

115 For some exceptional private prayers, see *M*. Berakhot 4.2; *B*. Berakhot 17a. One of them eventually became part of the official communal liturgy, though still retaining the first-person singular form (*Tur*: Orah Hayyim, 122 and Joseph Karo, *Bet Yosef*, s.v. "v'omer").

116 Maimonides, *Guide*, 3.51, 620–1.

117 Ibid., 1.59, 139–40. Here one is reminded of Wittgenstein's famous maxim (*Tractatus Logico-Philosophicus*, 7): "What one cannot speak of, one must be silent about" (*Wovon man nicht sprechen kann, darüber muss man schweigen*). Cf. *B*. Megillah 18a re Ps. 65:2, where even though silence is considered to be greater than speech, speech is still not disqualified.

118 For the views of Julius Guttmann, Alvin Reines, Marvin Fox, and Oliver Leaman (and Yeshayahu Leibowitz somewhat differently), all of whom see some sort of contradiction here, see Ehud Benor, *Worship of the Heart: A Study in Maimonides' Philosophy of Religion* (Albany: SUNY Press, 1995), 63–74. I am indebted to Benor's insightful arguments against these scholars. His own argument (58–61 et passim) is that contemplative prayer inspires true *imitatio Dei* as praxis in the world, and that unlike Aristotelian contemplation it is not meant to take us away from the world.

119 Maimonides, *Guide*, 1.52, 58.

120 Cf. Rashi's comment on Num. 7:89 (and on Exod. 33:9), stating that Moses overheard an inner-divine conversation. Also, cf. Obadiah Sforno's comment on Num. 7:89, which was no doubt influenced by Maimonides, and asserts that Moses's overhearing God's dialogue with Godself emanated from God (*hashpa`ah*) rather than Moses actually being addressed by God directly (see Maimonides, *Guide*, 1.65).

121 Maimonides, *Guide*, 1.58.

122 See Hume, *Dialogues Concerning Natural Religion*, pt. 4. See also Aquinas, *Summa Theologiae*, 1, q. 13, a. 5 and a. 12.

123 Maimonides, *Guide*, 3.51, 622–3.

124 Ibid., 1.65.

125 Ibid.

126 Ibid., 2.39. See *MT*: Foundations, 8.1–2; *Y*. Megillah 1.7/70d re Lev. 27:34. For what makes one a possible prophet, see *MT*: Foundations, 7.1–5.

127 See *Y*. Peah 2.4/17a re Eccl. 1:10.

128 They are not additions to the Mosaic commandments, which Maimonides limits to 613 (*Sefer ha-Mitsvot*, intro. re *B*. Makkot 23b) and, as such, they

do not share the irrepealable status of the commandments of the Mosaic Torah, nor the benefit of the doubt given to them (M. Eduyot 1.5; *MT*: Rebels, 2.1–2; *B.* Betsah 3b and parallels).

129 See *MT*: Kings, 8.11 (uncensored ed.)

130 *Commentary on the Mishnah*: Peah 1.1 re *B.* Shabbat 31a. See *M.* Yoma 8.9.

131 *MT*: Mourning, 14.1. For similar reciprocity, see *MT*: Robbery, 11.13 re *B.* Baba Metsia 30b. Also, in his *Sefer ha-Mitsvot*, pos. no. 206, Maimonides speaks of "my compassion and my love for my brother [*l'ahi*]" being commanded. "My brother" there seems to correspond to "your brother in the Torah and commandments" here. See *B.* Baba Metsia 59a re Lev. 25:17; *B.* Sanhedrin 86a re Deut. 25:11.

132 *MT*: Moral Characteristics, 6.3 a là *Y.* Nedarim 9.3/41c.

133 Aristotle, *Nicomachean Ethics*, 5.1/1130a3–4.

134 Ibid., 5.6/1134a25–30.

135 Ibid., 5.7/1134b19–35.

136 Ibid., 5.7/1134b 19–30.

137 Ibid., 8.1/1155a1–30 re *philia*, which means those with whom one could be what we now call "friendly," even if our relationship with them is not intimate. The more intimate the relationship, the less need there is for the precise criteria of formal justice (8.1/1155a26–7). Cf. *B.* Sanhedrin 6b–7a; *MT*: Sanhedrin, 22.4 re Zech. 8:16.

138 See Plato, *Republic*, 332A–335C. In his *The Concept of the Political*, trans. G. Schwab (Chicago: University of Chicago Press, 1996), 25–37, Carl Schmitt insisted that the friend-enemy dichotomy is insurmountable politically. This rejection of any common or universal humanity might well explain why Schmitt was such an important political and legal theorist in the Nazi regime. Cf. Jacques Maritain, *The Rights of Man and Natural Law* (London: Geoffrey Bles, 1958), 24–5, who speaks of "the racial type of community" and "the Germanic notion of community" that is only able "to define itself by its opposition to other human groups," thus having "essential need of an *enemy against whom* it will build itself; it is by recognizing and hating its enemies that the political body will find its own common consciousness." Perhaps Maritain had Schmitt's well-known work *Der Begriff der Politischen* in mind when he wrote these memorable words (which still move me as much as they did when I first read them as an undergraduate at the University of Chicago in 1960).

139 Cf. *Sifre*: Devarim, no. 343.

140 *MT*: Kings, 6.1–5 re *Y.* Sheviit 6.1/36c; *MT*: Forbidden Intercourse, 12.1–2 a là *B.* Avodah Zarah 36b.

141 Isaiah Berlin, "Two Concepts of Liberty," in *Four Essays on Liberty* (Oxford: Oxford University Press, 1969), 121–31.

142 Aristotle, *Nicomachean Ethics*, 5.4/1131b25–1132a19.

143 In rabbinic tradition, this enforcement of negative justice is only a society's minimal function, its necessary but not sufficient condition to be a real community. Thus six of the seven Noahide commandments are prohibitions (*T*.: Avodah Zarah 8.4–6; *B*. Sanhedrin 56a–b). Even the first commandment (according to most rabbinic sources) that mandates "establishing courts of law" (*dinim*), though a positive commandment, commands the correction or rectification of the injustice caused by the violation of the other six prohibitions. That is why, it seems, Maimonides (*MT*: Kings, 9.1) regards the full Mosaic Torah as "completing" (*ve-nishlamah*) what might be termed the Noahide "proto-Torah," i.e., its potential.

144 Maimonides, *Guide*, 2.40, 383–4.

145 Plato, *Republic*, 503B.

146 Maimonides, *Guide*, 1.2, 3.27.

147 *MT*: Repentance, 8.2–3, 7–8.

148 See Anselm, *Proslogion*, chap. 2. See LXX on Isa. 7:9 and the note in *Biblia Hebraica*, 11th ed., ed. R. Kittel (Stuttgart: Privilegierte Württenburgische Bibelantstalt, 1959), 618.

149 Maimonides, *Guide*, 3.28, 512. In his *Commentary on the Mishnah*: Sanhedrin, chap. 10 (Heleq), intro., Maimonides presents thirteen such dogmas. See Kellner, *Dogma in Medieval Jewish Thought*, 10–65.

150 Maimonides, *Guide*, 3.51, 622–3.

151 Ibid.

152 *MT*; Foundations, 7.1–5.

153 Ibid., 7.7. This could be called "private" prophecy as distinct from what could be called "public" prophecy, which is when a prophet's task is to morally admonish others.

154 See Hartman, *Maimonides: Torah and Philosophic Quest*, 193–209.

155 Maimonides, *Guide*, 3.54, 638.

156 Ibid., 2.10, 1.72. Cf. 3.43.

157 *MT*; Foundations, 4.13 and Torah Learning, 1.11–12; Maimonides, *Guide*, intro.

158 Maimonides, *Guide*, 3.37, 543.

159 *B*. Shabbat 67a.

160 Maimonides, *Commentary on the Mishnah*: Pesahim 4.10; *MT*: Strange Worship, 11.4 re Hullin 95b, and Joseph Karo, *Kesef Mishneh* thereon.

161 In his letter to the rabbis of Montpelier, Maimonides distinguishes astrology (*gezerat ha-kokhavim*) from astronomy (*hokhmat ha-kokhavim*), which is a "certain science" (*hokhmah vada'it*). Astronomy is the science that attempts to know the heavenly bodies for what they are, not what they do to or for us humans. The latter is what astrology attempts to know and thus appropriate technologically. See *Igrot ha-Rambam*, ed. and trans. I. Shailat (Maaleh Adumim, Israel: Maaliyot Press, 1988), 2:282.

162 *MT*: Strange Worship, 11.16; also *Commentary on the Mishnah*: Avodah Zarah 4.7.

163 *MT*: Strange Worship, 1.1.

164 Ibid., 1.3.

165 See Maimonides, *Guide*, 2.4.

166 *MT*: Repentance, 5.1 re Gen. 3:22 à la *B*. Berakhot 33b re Deut. 10:12. Cf. Maimonides, *Guide*, 1.2, 3.17.

167 *MT*: Repentance, 5.4.

168 *MT*: Strange Worship, 11.16.

169 *M*. Sanhedrin 7.11; also *T*.: Sanhedrin 10.11. The biblical commandment is "The sorceress [*mekhashefah*] is not to live" (Exod. 22:17), which, although stated about a female "sorceress," applies to both women and men who perform sorcery (*kishuf*). *B*. Sanhedrin 67a; *Y*. Sanhedrin 7.13; *Mekhilta*: Mishpatim, ed. Horovitz-Rabin, 309.

170 *B*. Sanhedrin 67b.

171 Ibid., s.v. "asqei be-hilkhot yetsirah."

172 For a critique of Maimonides, see Abraham ben David of Posqières, *Hasagat ha-Ra'avad* on *MT*: Strange Worship, 11.4 re *B*. Hullin 95b. See also *Hasagat ha-Ra'avad* on *MT*; Repentance, 3.7.

173 Maimonides, *Commentary on the Mishnah*: Avodah Zarah 7.11. Cf. *Hagahot Maimoniyot* on *MT*: Strange Worship, 11.9.

174 *MT*: Strange Worship, 11.16 re Num. 23:23.

175 For the actual prohibition, see *B*. Sanhedrin 65b re Lev. 19:26. See Joseph Karo, *Kesef Mishneh* on *MT*: Strange Worship, 11.15; David ibn Abi Zimra, *Teshuvot ha-Radbaz*, no. 1695, where he attempts to explain Maimonides's overall position. For the rabbinic prohibition of deceiving anybody (*genevat da`at*), see *B*. Hullin 94a; *MT*: Human Characteristics, 2.6.

176 *MT*: Foundations, 8.1 re Deut. 5:4.

177 Maimonides, *Guide*, 2.33 re *B*. Makkot 24a a là Deut. 4:35; *Shir ha-Shirim Rabbah* 1.13 re Song of Songs 1:2.

178 Maimonides, *Guide*, 3.17, 473–4. See also 3.26. The talmudic source of this norm is *B*. Baba Metsia 32a–b (also see Jacob ben Asher, *Tur*: Hoshen Mishpat, 272). Furthermore, there is the positive prescription of alleviating the pain of an animal (M. Shabbat 18.2; *Shiltei ha-Gibborim* and Rabbenu Nissim [Ran] on *Alfasi*: Shabbat 18.2/51b). See also *Y*. Ketubot 5.5/30a re Job 31:15; *MT*: Slaves, 9.8 re Ps. 145:9 re Ps. 145:9 and Deut. 13:18 for biblical texts invoked to mandate the proper treatment of human slaves, yet these biblical texts deal with the ontological status of fellow creatures, not just fellow human creatures. See *B*. Baba Metsia 85a re Ps. 145:9 ("The Lord is good to all; His mercies are over all His works").

179 Maimonides, *Commentary on the Mishnah*: Berakhot 5.2 re *Y*. Berakhot 5.2/9c and *B*. Berakhot 33b; *MT*: Prayer, 9.7.

180 *M.* Ohalot 7.6; *B.* Pesahim 25b.

181 Maimonides, *Guide,* 3.17.

182 Ibid., 3.48. There Maimonides includes in the rationality of the prohibition of causing an animal pain the Noahide prohibition (*T.*: Avodah Zarah 8.6 and *B.* Sanhedrin 56a-b re Gen. 2:16) of eating a limb torn from a living animal (*ever min he-hai*), a prohibition that in *MT*: Kings, 9.1 he saw as being an addition to the six rational commandments all rational humans are expected to know. One could say that part of created human rationality is to recognize the often painful lot we humans share with the rest of creation and act to alleviate it as much as possible. See *Guide,* 3.17 re *Beresheet Rabbah* 44.1; Deut. 32:47 and Isa. 45:19.

183 Interestingly enough, one could say that humans are commanded to aid a birthing animal to be affectionate to her child because humans can recognize this affectionate instinct in themselves. See *T.*: Shabbat 15.2; *B.* Shabbat 128b and Rashi, s.v. "merahamin." See also *B.* Ketubot 49b.

184 *B.* Shabbat 31a. The rationality of this norm can be seen in the way Maimonides bases it on the biblical verse that reports an angel castigating the gentile prophet Balaam: "Why have you beaten your donkey?!" (Num. 22:32) in *Guide,* 3.17. Yet this is not the biblical basis of this norm proposed in the Talmud (B. Baba Metsia 32a). It is found in the later *Midrash ha-Gadol*: Bemidbar, ed. Rabinowitz, 408, which itself is a later mediaeval Yeminite text influenced by rather than influencing Maimonides (see Z.M. Rabinowitz's introduction to this *midrash,* 12–13). In other words, nobody has the right to harm somebody who has not harmed them, let alone somebody who has actually benefitted them. Thus Balaam's donkey is reported to have said to him: "I am your donkey upon whom you have ridden up until this day; have I ever been wont to do this to you?!" (Num. 22:30). That is, not only didn't Balaam's donkey harm him, the donkey actually served his needs.

185 Maimonides, *Guide,* 3.54 re Jer. 9:23.

186 Ibid., 3.49.

187 Ibid., 3.39, 553.

188 Maimonides, *Sefer ha-Mitsvot,* neg. no. 57; *MT*: Kings, 6.8.

189 Cf. the comment of Gersonides (Ralbag) on Deut. 20:19–20 (no. 5) about the reason for this commandment being to affirm that God's providence extends even to plants, which implies that earthly creation is not totally made for human use.

190 *MT*: Moral Characteristics, 2.3 re *B.* Shabbat 105b.

191 *B.* Sanhedrin 60a and *Tosafot,* s.v. "huqqim"; *B.* Hullin 60a–b and *Tosafot,* s.v. "hirkhiv"; *B.* Hullin 60a–b and *Tosafot,* s.v. "hirkhiv."

192 *B.* Shabbat 53b (the view of Abayye).

193 *T.* Berakhot 5.31; *Y.* Berakhot 8.5/12b, *Beresheet Rabbah* 82.14, ed. Theodor-Albeck, 993–5 re Gen. 36:24; *Midrash ha-Gadol*: Beresheet, ed. Margulies, 611, 613 re Gen. 36:24; also *B.* Yoma 49a and *B.* Hullin 7b.
194 Maimonides, *Guide*, 3.37.
195 Ibid., 542.
196 *B.* Baba Kama 85a re Exod. 21:19.
197 This view was most consistently advocated by Nahmanides (Ramban). See, e.g., his comment on Lev. 26:11.
198 Maimonides, *Commentary on the Mishnah*: Nedarim 4.4 re Deut. 22:2, and *B.* Sanhedrin 73a.
199 *MT*: Mourning, 14.1 re Lev. 19:18.

6 Kant's Challenge to Theology

1 As earlier noted, throughout this book I have used the term "metaphysics" to denote the subjective method that applies itself to the objective content denoted by the term "ontology." In fact, one might say that ontology is "bespoken-being" (*logos tōn ontōn* in Greek) enunciated through human metaphysical discourse (*lashon bnei adam* in Hebrew).
2 Wittgenstein, *Philosophical Investigations*, 1.21.
3 Each one was a "martyr" in the sense that each of them was willing to die rather than betray what he believed is God's unconditional requirement of them; thus each "witnessed" (the original meaning of *martyrein* in Greek) that truth, even though each of them could have avoided death by compromising with those who would have them deny the truth. For Socrates's martyrdom, see Plato, *Apology*, 38A. For Rabbi Akivah's martyrdom, see *B.* Berakhot 61b re Deut. 6:5. For Christians, it is the martyrdom of Jesus; see John 18:11. All three martyrs, each in his own way, said about himself what Martin Luther supposedly said about himself: "I cannot do otherwise" (*Ich kann nichts anders tun*).
4 In Jewish law, an accuser is required to bring valid proof that the one being accused of illegally appropriating his or her property has in fact stolen it, even if heretofore it had been presumed that the now-disputed property rightfully belonged to the accused (*hazaqah*) (*Sifre*: Devarim, no. 16 re Deut. 1:16; *B.* Baba Kama 46a).
5 However, one might very well ask: What about the encounter with G.W.F. Hegel's philosophy or with Karl Marx's philosophy? My answer is that neither Hegel nor Marx poses the challenge to theology that is presented by the philosophy of Plato, or Aristotle, or Kant, all of whom constituted the four separate spheres of relationality, the acknowledgment of which, if not the direct involvement in which, seems to be indispensable for full human being-in-the-world. In Hegel's case, the God he affirms is

not revealed until the final completion of history. As such, Hegel's God does not at all resemble the God of the philosophers or the Creator God affirmed by Judaism, Christianity, and Islam. There is no relation of Hegel's God and humans in this world as is the case with the God of the classical philosophers and the Creator God of the Bible and the Quran. See Cyril O'Regan, *The Heterodox Hegel* (Albany: SUNY Press, 1995), 44–8, 95–6. Moreover, for Hegel, there seems to be no relation of God and nature; his God is fully immanent within human history, albeit at its apex. See Emil L. Fackenheim, *The Religious Dimension in Hegel's Thought* (Bloomington: Indiana University Press, 1967), 90–106. As for Marx, there is no God; God's existence is vigorously denied, and the belief in God's existence, let alone God's relation to anything outside Godself, is taken to be the illusionary product of false consciousness (following Ludwig Feuerbach) and thus to be reductively explained away. That is why Marx can only deal with two of our four spheres of relationality: interhuman relations and the relation of humans to nature. And, in fact, since interhuman relations are in Marx's view essentially material, i.e., *homo faber*, nature is simply fodder for humans' conquest; it has no integrity to be respected. See Louis Dupré, *The Philosophical Foundations of Marxism* (New York: Harcourt, Brace and World, 1966), 221–2; also Shlomo Avineri, *The Social and Political Thought of Karl Marx* (Cambridge: Cambridge University Press, 1968), 70–7.

6 See chap. 1, passim.

7 For "lawfulness" (*Gesetzmässigkeit*) as a key feature of Kant's philosophy, see *Critique of Judgment*, trans. W.S. Pluhar (Indianapolis: Hackett, 1987), AK5:196.

8 Kant, *Critique of Pure Reason*, B29.

9 Cf. Lev. 25:23; Ps. 119:19; I Chron. 29:15.

10 See Martin Heidegger, "The Question Concerning Technology," trans. W. Lovitt, in *Martin Heidegger: Basic Writings*, ed. D.F. Krell (New York: Harper and Row, 1977), 296–305; also Jacques Ellul, *The Technological System*, trans. J. Neugroschel (New York: Continuum, 1980), 125–55.

11 *Mekhilta*: Mishpatim re Gen. 11:4, ed. Horovitz-Rabin, 332; *B.* Sanhedrin 109a.

12 Hegel, *Phenomenology of Spirit*, B.IV.A.

13 Aristotle, *Metaphysics*, 1.1/980a22–4.

14 Nevertheless, in the Jewish tradition, even when one eats (i.e., devours) fruit or vegetables, he or she is still required to recognize that what is about to be eaten, and then has been eaten, has been created by God and, therefore, God is to be acknowledged as its Creator (M. Berakhot 6.1). That is why Scripture teaches that not only are farmers not allowed to keep all their land's produce for themselves, that some of it is to be redistributed to others less fortunate (Lev. 19:9–10; Num. 18:8–11), but their land is to

be left fallow periodically (Lev. 25:1–12), i.e., it is not to be redistributed to anybody else. Indeed, the first act of human worship of God is when Cain and Abel return to God as an offering some of their produce, thereby relinquishing their total control over it (Gen. 4:4–5).

15 Kant, *Critique of Practical Reason*, AK5:162.
16 See Plato, *Parmenides*, 130C.
17 Aristotle, *Metaphysics*, 1.1/982a1–3.
18 Ibid., 1.2/982b11–20.
19 Ibid., 1.2/982b28.
20 Ibid., 1.2/982b29–983a10.
21 Kant, *Critique of Pure Reason*, B29, 61–2.
22 Ibid., B59, 82. The phrase *so an sich beschaffen sind* could also be translated as "so they themselves have been created."
23 Ibid., Bxx, 24. There Kant calls it "things-by-themselves" (*die Sache an sich selbst*).
24 Ibid., Bxxvii, 27.
25 Ibid., A99, 131.
26 Ibid.
27 Bernard Lonergan, *Insight* (New York: Harper and Row, 1978), 4.2, 164.
28 Ibid., 2.6, 44. Note Lonergan's criticism of phenomenology for not leading from direct observation to more abstract explanation: "Husserl begins from relatedness-to-us, not to advance to the relatedness of terms one to another… the whole enterprise is under the shadow of the principle of immanence ... phenomenology is a highly purified empiricism" (4.3, 415).
29 Kant, *Critique of Pure Reason*, B125, 125–6.
30 Martin Heidegger, *Kant and the Problem of Metaphysics*, trans. J.S. Churchill (Bloomington, IN: Indiana University Press, 1962), sec. 16, 76.
31 Immanuel Kant, *Prolegomena to Any Future Metaphysics*, trans. L.W. Beck (Indianapolis: Bobbs-Merrill, 1950), sec. 36, 67.
32 Immanuel Kant, *Groundwork of the Metaphysic of Morals*, trans. H.J. Paton (New York: Harper and Row, 1964), AK4:428, 96.
33 Ibid., AK4:430, 97.
34 This is not the same as Spinoza's *Deus sive Natura*, since Spinoza's natural God or Godly nature has no purposes and thus God has no purpose-projecting will; hence Spinoza's God is most definitely not the Creator God. See *Ethics*, I, Appendix.
35 *MT*: Kings, 6.10 and Karo, *Kesef Mishneh* thereon.
36 The translation of the last, enigmatic, phrase (*ein miqveh*) follows Rashi and David Kimhi (Radaq).
37 *B.* Berakhot 35a–b; *Y.* Berakhot 6.1/9d re Deut. 22:9.
38 Kant, *Critique of Practical Reason*, AK5:162, 203.
39 Kant, *Critique of Pure Reason*, Bxxi–xxii, 24–25.

40 Ibid., B312, 273, where he calls it "an unknown something" (*unbekannten Etwas*), i.e., unknown by speculative reason about nature, but not unknown by practical understanding of what we are to do or not do in relation to the other rational persons we engage in the world.
41 Ibid., B307, 268.
42 Ibid.
43 Ibid., B430, 382.
44 Ibid., B431, 383.
45 See chaps. 4 and 5, passim.
46 Immanuel Kant, *Critique of Judgment*, AK5:403, sec. 76, 286; also *Critique of Practical Reason*, AK5:48.
47 Aristotle, *Nicomachean Ethics*, 6.4/1140a1–1140b5.
48 Note *Critique of Judgment*, AK5:172, 10: "For the will, as the power of desire [*Begehrungsvermögen*], is one of the many natural causes in the world, namely, the one that acts in accordance with concepts [*nach Begriffen*] ... as distinguished from the physical possibility or necessity of an effect whose cause is not determined to [exercise] its causality through concepts (but through mechanism, as in the case of lifeless matter, or through instinct, as is the case of animals)."
49 Kant, *Groundwork of the Metaphysic of Morals*, AK4:453, 121.
50 Kant, *Critique of Pure Reason*, B75.
51 For background, see Schneewind, *The Invention of Autonomy*, 515–18. For an accurate yet critical view of this notion of autonomy, see Joseph Raz, *The Morality of Freedom* (Oxford: Clarendon Press, 1986), 369–95.
52 John Stuart Mill, *On Liberty*, ed. G. Williams (London: Everyman's Library, 1972), chap. 1, 78.
53 Kant, *Groundwork of the Metaphysic of Morals*, AK4:441.
54 The most influential proponent of this view was John Rawls, *Political Liberalism*, 216–26. For an incisive critique of Rawls, see Goodman, *Religious Pluralism and Values in the Public Square*, 54–101.
55 See Aristotle, *Nicomachean Ethics*, 1.1/1094a1–10.
56 Kant, *Groundwork*, AK4:393. Cf. Plato, *Timaeus*, 28A–29A. For Kant's attempt to internalize in human reason what Plato designated as external and above it, see *Critique of Pure Reason*, B313–19.
57 Moreover, the plan according to which God created the universe is not prior to God, but rather, it is God's first creation (*Beresheet Rabbah*, 1.1 re Prov. 8:22, 30; also *B*. Pesahim 68b re Jer. 33:25).
58 Kant, *Groundwork*, AK4:421, 89.
59 Ibid., AK4:422, 90. See *B*. Kiddushin 13b and *Tosafot*, s.v. "milveh."
60 For Kant's use of *natürliche Gesetze* rather than *Naturgesetze*, see *The Metaphysics of Morals*, AK6:224, 17. There he contrasts "natural law" with "positive law," both of which are "obligatory" (*verbindenden*). Natural law

here is practical or moral law, i.e., the moral law that addresses its human subjects as essentially or "naturally" rational, normative beings. However, unlike laws of nature, "these practical (moral) laws first make known a property of choice [*Eigenschaft der Willkür*], namely, its freedom" (AK6:225, 17). What Kant called *natürliche Gesetze*, his follower Hermann Cohen called *Naturrecht* in his *Ethik des reinen Willens*, 5th ed. (Hildesheim: Georg Olms Verlag, 1981), 68–70.

61 Aristotle, *Nicomachean Ethics*, 10.9/1180a23–4.

62 Cicero, *De Legibus*, 1.6; also Strauss, *Natural Right and History*, 7–8, 120–30.

63 Although having moved far away from biblical theology in his political philosophy, Thomas Hobbes still had a very biblical notion of law. Thus he writes in *Leviathan*, pt. 1, chap. 15, ed. C. B. Macpherson (London: Penguin, 1968), 217, that "law ... properly is the word of him that by right hath command over others." That is how Hobbes speaks of God who "by right commandeth all things; then are they properly called lawes" (217). See Hobbes, *The Elements of Law: Human Nature*, ed. J.C.A. Gaskin (Oxford: Oxford University Press, 1994), 1.14.6, 76; also *The Elements of Law: De Corpore Politico*, 2.29.5, 179.

64 See Aristotle, *Physics*, 4.5/212b15–20.

65 Ibid., 8.1/252a10–15.

66 Maimonides, *Guide*, 1.52.

67 *B*. Shabbat 53b.

68 Kant, *Critique of Pure Reason*, B846–47; *Critique of Practical Reason*, AK4:129; *Critique of Judgment*, AK6:460; *Religion within the Boundaries of Mere Reason*, trans. A. Wood and G. di Giovanni (Cambridge: Cambridge University Press, 1998), AK6:110. See also Cohen, *Ethik des reinen Willens*, 69.

69 Note *Religion within the Boundaries of Mere Reason*, AK6:108, 117: "Now whenever ... a church passes itself off as the only universal one (even though it is based on faith in a particular revelation [*besondern Offenbarungsglaube*] which, since it is historical, can never be demanded of everyone ..." Commandments based on *particular*, historical revelation, not being universalizable, cannot be truly moral obligations.

70 Kant, *Critique of Practical Reason*, AK4:161.

71 Kant, *Critique of Pure Reason*, B473–80.

72 Kant, *Groundwork*, AK4:429, 96. The German *jederzeit zugleich als Zweck* could also be translated as "at whatever time *equally* as an end."

73 Ibid., AK4:428, 96.

74 Ibid., AK4:430, 97–8.

75 Aristotle, *Nicomachean Ethics*, 1.13/1102a5–1103a10.

76 Comment of Joseph Bekhor Shor on Lev. 19:18. Also see Aristotle, *Nicomachean Ethics*, 8.1/1155a33–5.

77 Kant, *Critique of Practical Reason*, AK4:83–5.

78 Kant, *Groundwork*, AK4:433, 101. I have changed Paton's translation of *Reich* as "kingdom" to "realm." Although *Reich* can mean a "kingdom," as when Kant throughout his *Religion within the Boundaries of Mere Reason* writings on religion speaks of "the Kingdom of God" (*das Reich Gottes*) as the equivalent of the Hebrew *malkhut shamayim*, here Kant seemed to mean more of a democratic republic as when he speaks of moral duty (*Pflicht*) as applying to "every member and all members (of this realm) equally" (101). A kingdom, on the other hand, is ruled by a monarch, who is unequal to his or her subjects. Now Kant himself was no fan of monarchy as evidenced by his support of the French Revolution that destroyed *l'ancien régime*, which was the epitome of an autocratic polity, one that discouraged any autonomy, and which Jean-Jacques Rousseau (a major influence on Kant) had so eloquently defined in his 1762 book *Le Contrat Social*.
79 Cf. Rawls, *A Theory of Justice*, 233–46.
80 Kant, *Religion within the Boundaries of Mere Reason*, AK6:95, 106.
81 Ibid., AK6:98, 109.
82 Ibid., AK6:98 (note), 109.
83 Ibid., AK6:96, 107.
84 Ibid.
85 Kant, *Critique of Pure Reason*, Bxiii, B93, A126, B163–64.
86 Kant, *Religion within the Boundaries of Mere Reason*, AK6:98–99, 109–110.
87 Note Kant, *Critique of Judgment*, AK5:447, 339: "Moral teleology does not require an intelligent cause outside us [to account for that inner lawfulness]."
88 Kant, *Critique of Practical Reason*, AK5:86, 111: "Duty! – you sublime [*erhabener*] grand name ... which demands submission [*Unterwerfung*] ... , yet also does not move the will by threatening anything ... yet gains grudging veneration [*Verehrung*]... what origin [*Ursprung*] is worthy of you ... the root [*Wurzel*] from which to be descended is the irremissible condition of that worth which human beings alone can give themselves."
89 *Religion within the Boundaries of Mere Reason*, AK6:169, note.
90 See Sigmund Freud, *The Future of an Illusion*, who reduces all religion to what Kant would call "idolatry."
91 *Religion within the Boundaries of Mere Reason*, AK6:101, 111.
92 Ibid. Here *Reich* does mean "kingdom" and not just "realm."
93 *Religion within the Boundaries of Mere Reason*, AK6:99, 110.
94 Kant, *The Metaphysics of Morals*, AK6:327, 102.
95 See Cohen, *Ethik des reinen Willens*, 240–54, who privileges the clearly secular *Genossenschaft* or *Gesellschaft*, which has been translated as "society," over the more traditional and inevitably religious *Gemeinschaft*, which has been translated as "community." This distinction had already been made by the German sociologist Ferdinand Tönnies in his influential 1887 book, *Gemeinschaft und Gesellschaft*.

96 Moses Mendelssohn, *Jerusalem*, trans. A. Arkush (Hanover: University Press of New England, 1983), 45.

97 Spinoza, *Tractatus Theologico-Politicus*, chap. 19; *Tractatus Politicus*, ed. and trans. S. Zac (Paris: J. Vrin, 1968), 8.46.

98 Aristotle, *Nicomachean Ethics*, 6.8/1141b24–30.

99 *B.* Shabbat 88a–b.

100 See Karl Barth, *Church Dogmatics*, 2/2, ed. G.W. Bromiley and T.F. Torrance, trans. G.W. Bromiley, J.C. Campbell, I. Wilson, J.S. McNab, H. Knight, and R.A. Stewart (Edinburgh: T. & T. Clark, 1957), sec. 38, 650–66.

101 Thus Aristotle, who like Kant would have rejected the liberal notion of individual autonomy, by anticipation as it were, criticizes the notion that the polity and its law are only there by contract (*synthēkē*) to protect the rights or claims of individuals on each other, rather than "to make its citizens good and just" (*Politics*, 3.5/1280a10–13). In other words, Kant is like Aristotle, who holds that the *telos* of a truly rational human society is to promote the common good (3.4/1278b20–5), and that the protection of individuals' rights is secondary thereto. The former is what Aristotle calls "distributive justice"; the latter is what he calls "rectifying justice" (*Nicomachean Ethics*, 5.2/1130b30–1131a3). Clearly, the former takes precedence over the latter. This similarity, though, should not obscure the fact that Aristotle and Kant have very different views about what is the source and purpose of law.

102 On the other hand, there is almost an allergy among many contemporary philosophers who call themselves "Kantians" to even take Kant's retention of God-talk into consideration. We see this in Christine Korsgaard's *Creating the Kingdom of Ends* (Cambridge: Cambridge University Press, 1996). There she argues, quite correctly, that for Kant, if a person did an act "because God so commands," then "conformity to divine law can only make a maxim extrinsically not intrinsically legal" (62). However, by equating what "God so commands" with "divine Law," she ignores the crucial distinction Kant himself made between *göttliche Gebote* and *Gebote Gottes*. When I obey a law as a *göttliche Gebot*, I am obeying it for the same *intrinsic* reason that God *would* make such a law. That is what makes my autonomous decision to obey the law "godlike" (i.e., *göttlich*). In this case, I am imitating God's conformity to the idea of moral law rather than simply obeying God per se.

103 *B.* Kiddushin 31a; *B.* Baba Kama 38a and 87a; *B.* Avodah Zarah 3a.

104 See, e.g., *B.* Baba Batra 120a re Num. 36:6. I call this a *hovah*, even though the Talmud uses the verbal form of *mitsvah* because, as Maimonides taught (*MT*: Blessings, 11.2), a *hovah* is a stronger obligation than a *mitsvah*, inasmuch as one can choose to avoid the type of situation that calls for the doing of a *mitsvah*, while no such avoidance is permitted

when a *hovah* is called for. Usually, a *hovah* is a bodily obligation (see, e.g., *B*. Menahot 41a), and obviously one cannot avoid his or her own body. It would seem that this stronger sense of obligation is what is being emphasized in this rabbinic dictum.

105 *B*. Kiddushin 31a, *Tosafot*, s.v. "gadol." In that same place (*Tosafot*, s.v. "de-la") it is taught that somebody who has not been commanded to do a certain *mitsvah*, yet does it voluntarily anyway (e.g., a woman doing what has only been explicitly commanded to men), that person may do the act so commanded. But it is important to note that these volunteers are not creating new commandments for themselves, but rather are including themselves in a specific class of obligated persons, a class from which they had heretofore been excluded. Moreover, that volunteer may also recite the appropriate blessing (*berakhah*) that expresses her intention (*kavvanah*) to be included among those so explicitly commanded. It also seems that this voluntary duty becomes a true obligation when this becomes a regular activity and not just an ephemeral deed. See *Rashi: Responsa*, ed. Elfenbein, no. 68; Nahmanides, *Hiddushei ha-Ramban*: Kiddushin 31a. This consistent voluntarism is like the self-imposed obligation a person can assume by making a "vow" (*neder*) or by taking an "oath" (*shevu`ah*) upon themselves (*B*. Nedarim 2b). However, for what might be called "anti-volunteerism" in ritual matters, see *B*. Nedarim 10a re Num. 6:11;Y; Berakhot 2.9/5d; *Y*. Hallah 4.5/60b; *Y*. Eruvin 10.1/26a. See *Y*. Terumot 8.4/46b; Solomon Luria, *Yam shel Shlomoh*: Baba Kama, chap. 8, s.v. "din sh'asur le-hovel" for approval of what might be called "moral volunteerism," especially volunteering to save another life. Cf. David ibn Abi Zimra, *Teshuvot ha-Radbaz*, 5, no. 1582.

106 *M*. Avot 2.1; *Y*. Peah 1.1/ 15d re Prov. 5:22.

107 Cohen, *Religion of Reason*, 324. The original German text is *Religion der Vernunft aus den Quellen des Judentums*, 2nd ed. (Darmstadt: Joseph Melzer Verlag, 1966), 377.

108 Cohen, *Religion of Reason*.

109 Kant, *Critique of Pure Reason*, B371–2.

110 Plato, *Euthyphro*, 10A–E.

111 Ibid., 12D.

112 Plato, *Republic*, 505A.

113 Plato, *Timaeus*, 28A–29A.

114 Plato, *Republic*, 379A. See Aristotle, *Nicomachean Ethics*, 7.1/1145a30.

115 Cf. Plato, *Laws*, 716A–B.

116 *MT*: Nedarim, 1.4 re Num. 30:3.

117 *B*. Shevuot 26a re Lev. 5:4.

118 See Plato, *Republic*, 431A.

119 *M*. Shevuot 3.8; also *M*. Baba Metsia 7.11; *B*. Kiddushin 19b.

120 An oath may be taken by an individual to perform a positive *mitzvah*, even though that person (and all others like him or her) has already been commanded to do so by the Torah (B. Nedarim 7b–8a re Ps. 119:106). This is permitted if this kind of subjective motivation will better inspire the performance of the *mitsvah* by this individual. Nevertheless, the very heteronomous character of the *mitsvah*, i.e., its being commanded by God, is what obliges all those so commanded, whether or not they subjectively motivate themselves to perform it.

121 *B.* Hagigah 10a re Num. 30:3; *M.* Nedarim 9.1–5; *MT*: Oaths, 6.1. Moreover, a single sage (*hakham*) may dispense somebody from their oath or vow (*neder*) upon request (B. Nedarim 77b–78a re Num. 30:2).

122 *M.* Shevuot 3.8 and Maimonides's comment thereon.

123 *Y.* Shevuot 3.8/34d; *MT*: Oaths, 1.5.

124 *MT*: Foundations, 1.1; also Maimonides, *Commentary on the Mishnah*: Sanhedrin, chap. 10 (Heleq), intro., foundation no. 1.

125 *B.* Berakhot 32a re Exod. 32:13; also *Beresheet Rabbah* 56.8 re Ps. 89:35.

126 *Mekhilta:* Yitro re Exod. 20:2, ed. Horovitz-Rabin, 222–3. In this text, God tells the people to accept His "decrees" (*gezerotai*). "Decrees" connotes prohibitions whose beneficence is not at all evident (B. Berakhot 33b; Y. Berakhot 5.3/9c; *Bemidbar Rabbah* 19.1 re Num. 19:2).

127 Jews are commanded to accept God's kingship (*ol malkhut shamayim*) in general regularly (twice daily in fact) and freely, and then accept God's specific commandments (*ol mitsvot*) regularly and freely (M. Berakhot 2.2). The first commandment is from Deut. 6:4 ("Listen Israel: the Lord is our only God"), followed by Deut. 6:5 ("You shall love the Lord your God ..."). But does anyone really love the person to whom they owe a debt, even only a debt of gratitude, for a past favour? Rather, doesn't one love the person who continues benefitting them in the present into the future? Thus Israel desires more of God's commandments (M. Makkot 3.16 re Isa. 42:21; also *Midrash Leqah Tov*: Mishpatim, ed. Buber, 174, and Rashbam's comment on Exod. 24:7), whereas debtors only want to pay back their creditors and thus to be relieved of their obligation to them once and for all (Prov. 22:7).

128 Kant, *Critique of Pure Reason*, B643.

129 This idea is similar to (though not identical with) the kabbalistic idea of *tsimtsum*, i.e., the self-limitation of God to "make room" as it were for what is not-God. See Gershom Scholem, "Schöpfung aus Nichts und Selbstverschränkung Gottes," *Eranos Jahrbuch* 25 (1956), esp. 90–100; also David Novak, "Self-Contraction of the Godhead in Kabbalistic Theology," in *Neoplatonism and Jewish Thought*, ed. L.E. Goodman (Albany: SUNY Press, 1992), 299–318. I have not directly employed kabbalistic ideas in this work because in kabbalistic ontology, there is little or no concern

with external relations. All relations, for almost all the kabbalists, are ultimately internal to the Godhead (*elohut* in Hebrew; *die Gottheit* in German). What is not-God is a finite emanation (*atsilut* in Hebrew) from the infinite God (*ein sof*). As such, all external relations *between* God and creation are apparent, not real. The only real relations are relations *within* the Godhead itself. Seemingly external relations are only symbolic of these truly real internal relations.

130 Conversely, in *Beresheet Rabbah* 49.9 re Gen. 18:25, and *Tanhuma*: Tazria 9, ed. Buber re Eccl. 8:4, 37, Abraham is imagined to have said to God that human rulers always have superiors (or at least equals) to restrain them from acting unjustly, whereas God seems to have no such external restraints on His acting unjustly. In these texts, though, the notion that God has His own internal restraints does not seem to be considered here. For the notion of God's autonomous observance of the *mitsvot* as a way God relates Godself to His human creatures, see *Y.* Rosh Hashanah 1.3/57a re Lev. 22:9.

131 God obligates, but God Himself is not obligated by some higher external standard of eternal justice like Kant's notion of even God being answerable to "the idea of moral law" or "divine laws" (*göttliche Gebote*), i.e., laws expressed as God's will, but not essentially caused by God's will. So, when the Psalmist speaks of God having "established Your testimonies forever (*l`olam*)" (Ps. 119:152), "forever" does not mean "eternity," which no one could transcend, but rather *Weltzeit* or "world-time," which God surely transcends. "Forever" refers to creatures in relation to God, not to God in relation to Godself. Note the translation by Martin Buber and Franz Rosenzweig, *Die Fünf Bücher der Weisung*, 193, of Exod. 15:18: *König sein wird ER in Weltzeit und Ewigkeit*. Here the Hebrew *va`ed* becomes in German *Ewigkeit*. It seems that Buber and Rosenzweig were, in effect, punctuating the Hebrew *va`ed* as *ve`ad* (literally, "and beyond" like LXX: *kai eti*) to express God's transcendence of *Weltzeit* (see *Die Fünf Bücher der Weisung*: Deut. 29:28, 555). (In my opinion, they should have rendered the phrase *in Weltzeit und jenseits*.) In fact, even when the Septuagint translates *l`olam* into Greek as *ep' aiōna*, it doesn't seem to be using *aiōna* in the metaphysical sense of "eternity" (see Baruch 4:1, where *eis ton aiōna* is, no doubt, a translation of the Hebrew *l`olam*). Conversely, for the metaphysical sense of "eternity" (*aidios*) as being beyond time and its inherent changeability, thus prior to what God does in time, and which is the ultimate standard God is answerable to, see Plato, *Timaeus*, 37E; Aristotle, *Metaphysics*, 1069a30–4; also Sophocles, *Antigone*, 450–7. In his last essay before his death in 1929, "Der Ewige," in *Kleinere Schriften* (Berlin: Schocken Verlag, 1937), Rosenzweig rejected *Ewigkeit* (and its metaphysical synonym *notwendige*

Existenz) for theological reasons, viz., as being inadequate to the Bible and biblically based theology. His critique is specifically directed against the Enlightenment Jewish philosopher Moses Mendelssohn (1729–86), who translated the Tetragrammaton (YHWH) as *das ewige Wesen*, and whom Rosenzweig virtually dismissed as being "pre-Kantian" (187) and thus still beholden to "rational theology" (which Kant had demolished in the *Critique of Pure Reason*, and which Rosenzweig obviously accepted). However, in his 1921 magnum opus *Der Stern der Erlösung*, Rosenzweig still spoke of *Ewigkeit* frequently, but very differently from the way "eternity" is spoken of in pre-Kantian metaphysics. See Karl Löwith, "M. Heidegger and F. Rosenzweig or Temporality and Eternity," *Philosophy and Phenomenological Research* (1942) 3: 53–77.

132 Thus when Thomas Aquinas speaks of God's wisdom as *lex aeterna* in *Summa Theologiae*, 2/1, q. 91, a. 1, it seems to me he got himself into philosophical trouble. For how can a law of God, which means a commandment commanded by God to what is not-God, i.e., to mortal creatures, how can it be "eternal" when the very subjects of the commandments are themselves mortal, temporally conditioned creatures? Even if God's internal self-restraint be called "law" (Aquinas himself, *Summa Theologiae*, q. 90, a. 1, opines that the noun *lex* is derived from the noun *ligare* meaning to "bind," i.e., to "obligate"), that internal self-restraint is for the sake of God's external relationship with created humankind who, being created in God's image, have been given or entitled with enough independence to be able to freely respond to God's law, thus making the God-human relationship a truly moral/legal reality. This law is still *made* in order that God be able to relate Godself to these mortal creatures in a way that is intelligible to their finite, creaturely minds. It doesn't refer to an internal divine relation per se. Aquinas's answer to this objection raised against his notion of *lex aeterna*, i.e., that created beings are "foreknown by Him" (91, a. 1, ad 1) is still problematic. For if that "foreknowledge" is an eternal anticipation of what God will do in time, how could God's decision to realize that anticipation be considered a free, creative choice, since all choices are made in time? It seems, then, Aquinas has begged the question in his response to it. Furthermore, Aquinas cites Prov. 8:23 and Augustine (*De Libero Arbitrio*, 1.15) as his authorities. However, a careful reading of these texts shows that both the proverbist and Augustine were talking about law "forever" (Hebrew *me`olam*), i.e., a law for mortal humans in the created world that may not be changed by them *throughout* their temporal sojourn in this world. Augustine in *De Libero Arbitrio* paraphrased the Vulgate's *ab aeterno ordinata* by designating *lex aeterna* as *qua justum est ut omnia ordinatissima*. It seems that for the proverbist and for Augustine, the law

is not absolutely primordial, but only relatively primordial insofar as it has been *ordered* by God. Similarly, the ancient Rabbis saw the Torah's creation as preceding the creation of the cosmos. This is like an architect who draws up a blueprint before building the house that the drawing of the blueprint anticipated (*Beresheet Rabbah* 1.1 re Prov. 8:22). The blueprint is still *ens creatum*, only created earlier than the cosmos made according to its form.

133 Cohen, *Religion of Reason*, 59–70.

134 Ibid.,, 147.

135 Ibid., 114–15.

136 Ibid., 71–2. Cf. Kant, *Critique of Pure Reason*, B597.

137 Cohen, *Religion of Reason*, 147.

138 Ibid., 72.

139 *MT*: Kings, 8.11, ed. Frankel.

140 Ibid.

141 *MT*: Repentance, 8.2. Cf. critique of Abraham ben David of Posquières (Rabad) thereon, who invokes a more temporal eschatology, based on rabbinic sources.

142 Maimonides, *Guide*, 2.40.

143 *Sifra*: Aharei-Mot, 13.10, ed. Weiss, 86a re Lev. 18:4; *B.* Yoma 67b. The examples given of such "rational commandments" (*mitsvot sikhliyot* is the term put forth by Saadiah Gaon, *Book of Beliefs and Opinions*, 3.1–3) are also Noahide commandments, which themselves are not explicitly prescribed in the Mosaic Torah (*T.*: Avodah Zarah 8.4–7; *B.* Sanhedrin 56a–b). Nevertheless, it is also implied that the prohibitions in Lev. 18:6–23 apply to gentiles (i.e., Noahides) as well as to Jews (B. Sanhedrin 57b re Lev. 18:6). But if so, why did these commandments have to be written down in the Mosaic Torah at all? Isn't the Torah only supposed to tell us (either to do or to know) what we couldn't know independently, employing our reason (*sevara*; e.g., *B.* Baba Kama 46b re Exod. 24:14)? The fifteenth-century Spanish-Jewish theologian Joseph Albo answers that including rational commandments (including what he calls both *dat tiv`it*, or "natural law," and *dat nimusit*, or "human law") in the written *dat elohit* or "divine law" gives them a gravity and indisputable character they wouldn't have otherwise (*Book of Principles*, 1.8–9). Cf. Thomas Aquinas, *Summa Theologiae*, 2/1, q. 91, a. 4. It would seem that due to his role as the Jewish spokesman in disputations with Dominican friars (Aquinas's order), Albo was well acquainted with Aquinas's work and was (selectively, to be sure) influenced by it.

144 *MT*: Kings, 9.1.

145 Cf. *Sifra*: Behar, 5.3 re Lev. 25:36, ed. Weiss, 109c; *B.* Baba Metsia 62a.

146 Emmanuel Levinas, *Totality and Infinity*, trans. A. Lingis (Pittsburgh: Duquesne University Press, 1969), 88.

147 Ibid., 109.

148 Ibid., 213.

149 Ibid., 215.

150 For a trenchant critique of Levinas on this key point of his, see Paul Riceour, *Oneself as Other*, trans. K. Blamey (Chicago: University of Chicago Press, 1992), 330–41.

151 Martin Buber, *Ich und Du* (Heidelberg: Verlag Lambert Schneider, 1962) = *I and Thou*, trans. Walter Kaufmann (New York: Chas. Scribner's Sons, 1970).

152 Levinas, *Totality and Infinity*, 68.

153 Aristotle, *Nicomachean Ethics*, 8.1/1155a25–9.

154 Levinas, *Totality and Infinity*, 155.

155 *M.* Yevamot 6.6; *B.* Yevamot 65b; *Y.* Yevamot 6.6/7d.

156 *B.* Kiddushin 2b; *MT*: Marriage, 4.1. The fact that the offer must be made verbally (B. Kiddushin 5b) might reflect the opinion that the first man (Adam) was able to have a true relationship with the first woman (Eve) because he was able to converse with her, unlike the other creatures over which he had control, but no true relationship with (B. Yevamot 63a re Gen. 2:23; see *B.* Bekhorot 8a).

157 *MT*: Forbidden Intercourse, 21.26. Nevertheless, it is suggested that a woman should choose to be married, if for no other reason, so as to avoid extramarital sexual relations: *T.*: Yevamot 8.6; *MT*: Marriage, 15.16; Rabbenu Nissim (Ran) on Alfasi: *B.* Kiddushin, chap. 2, ed. Vilna, 16b; *Teshuvot ha-Ran*, no. 32, ed. Feldman, 129–30.

158 E.g., *B.* Ketubot 2b–3a.

159 *B.* Shabbat 16b; *B.* Ketubot 82b.

160 *M.* Arakhin 5.5; *M.* Gittin 9.8, 10; *B.* Gittin 88b.

161 *MT*: Marriage, 14.8 re *B.* Ketubot 63b. Cf. *Tosafot*, s.v. "aval"; *Tur*: Even ha`Ezer, 77.

162 *B.* Kiddushin 41a; *MT*: Marriage, 3.19. The term for "neighbour" is *re`a*, one of whose meanings is "spouse" (B. Ketubot 8a and Rashi, s.v. "re`im ha'ahuvim").

163 *Beresheet Rabbah*, 43.7 re Gen. 14:19; *B.* Berakhot 46a.

164 *B.* Yoma 85b re Exod. 31:16.

165 *B.* Baba Kama 84a re Lev. 24:22.

166 *B.* Baba Batra 48b.

167 Levinas, *Totality and Infinity*, 78.

168 *B.* Ketubot 49b re Ps. 147:9; *B.* Kiddushin 32a.

169 *Sifra*: Qedoshim, beg., ed. Weiss, 87a; *B.* Yevamot 5b re Lev. 19:3.

170 *B.* Kiddushin 42b and parallels.

171 *M.* Rosh Hahanah 2.9; *B.* Kiddushin 32a.

172 Note *Tanhuma*: Vay'era, no. 8 re Gen. 18:33, where it is taught that contrary to what is normally expected – that the lesser person asks leave of the greater person (e.g., *B.* Shabbat 127a re Gen. 18:3) – God chose to ask leave of Abraham nonetheless.
173 *B.* Berakhot 7a.
174 Kant, *Groundwork of the Metaphysic of Morals*, AK4:421, 106.
175 Kant, *Religion within the Boundaries of Mere Reason*, AK6:95.
176 Ibid., AK6:101.
177 Ibid.
178 Ibid., AK6:100.
179 Ibid., AK6:88, 101.
180 Ibid., AK6:177, 172.
181 Ibid., AK6:93–4.
182 Quoted in L. Hunt, *The French Revolution and Human Rights* (Boston: St. Martin's Press, 1996), 88. See Arthur Hertzberg, *The French Enlightenment and the Jews* (New York: Columbia University Press, 1968), 359–68.
183 Mendelssohn, *Jerusalem*, 45.
184 Kant, *Religion within the Boundaries of Mere Reason*, AK125–6, 130–1.
185 Ibid.
186 See Leora Batnitzky, *How Judaism Became a Religion* (Princeton: Princeton University Press, 2011), 13–31.
187 Cohen, *Religion of Reason*, 338–40.
188 Ibid., 267–8.
189 Ibid., 307–8.
190 Ibid., 309.
191 *B.* Berakhot 28a and parallels.
192 See Matthew 3:2.
193 Aristotle, *Nicomachean Ethics*, 3.3/1112a19–35.
194 Cohen, *Religion of Reason*, 360–2; also "Religion und Zionismus," *Jüdische Schriften* (Berlin: C.A. Schwetschke und Sohn, 1924), 2:319–27.
195 Cf. the 1893 essay of the Zionist theoretician Ahad Ha`Am (1856–1927), "Priest and Prophet" in *Selected Essays*, trans. L. Simon (Philadelphia: Jewish Publication Society of America, 1912), 137: "We do, indeed, occasionally hear some such exclamation from the lips of Jewish scholars and preachers in Western Europe, who uphold the doctrine of the 'mission of Israel.' ... [However,] this influence, being practical and not theoretical, demands, as a necessary condition of its possibility, not the complete dispersion of Israel among the nations, but, on the contrary, a union and concentration, at least partial, of all its forces, in the place where it will be possible for the nation to direct its life in accordance with its own character."

196 *B.* Berakhot 34b and parallels re Isa. 64:3. This rendition of the verse from Isaiah is itself a *midrash*. The literal (*peshat*) meaning of the whole verse (of which only the second clause is quoted in the Talmud) is: "It has never been heard of or learned of, no eye has seen a god other than You [*elohim zulatekha*] who will do for those who wait for Him." This is how Rashi and David Kimhi (Radaq) interpret the literal meaning of this verse; and they both explicitly contrast this with the rabbinic *midrash* quoted in the text above. Nevertheless, the *midrash* above, when cited by the Talmud in the name of the third-century Palestinian Rabbi Yohanan bar Nappaha, is said to be about "the world-to-come" (*olam ha-ba*) as distinct from the "days of the Messiah" (*yemot ha-mashiah*). This distinction comes later in rabbinic theology, when eschatology was sharply distinguished from politics. Thus the view of the third-century Babylonian Rabbi Samuel of Nehardea is juxtaposed with the view of Yohanan bar Nappaha, for Samuel sees the messianic era being the time when the Jewish people will only no longer be politically subservient to the rule of the gentile nations (*sh`ibud malkhiyot*). In earlier rabbinic theology, however, the "radical future" (*atid la-vo*) includes the coming-of-the-Messiah (*bi'at ha-mashiah* in the transcendent, supernatural event, e.g., *Shir ha-Shirim Rabbah* 6.1 re Zech. 9:1). Interestingly, in the New Testament (I Corinthians 2:9), Paul states the same *midrash* of Isa. 64:3 that appears later in the Talmud. In fact, he calls it the "hidden wisdom" (*apokekrymmenēn*) known to God alone heretofore. Even though the New Testament is an earlier text than that of the Babylonian (or Palestinian) Talmud, one should not conclude from this fact that the Talmud actually drew upon the New Testament. Rather, it is more accurate to say that *both* the New Testament and the Talmud drew upon earlier Pharisaic theology's decidedly supernatural, transcendent eschatology. See, e.g., II Maccabees 7:1–3 (which is an apocryphal book, written in pre-rabbinic and pre-Christian times).

197 *B.* Berakhot 4a re Ps. 27:13–14.

198 *B.* Sanhedrin 97b re Hab. 2:3 and Isa. 30:18. These biblical texts are invoked here to warn against those who would actually "calculate the end times" (*mehashvei qitsin*) rather than waiting for God to act according to His own schedule.

199 *Sofrim*, 14.12.

200 *B.* Sanhedrin 97b.

201 All of this is extensively and intensively dealt with in my book *Zionism and Judaism: A New Theory* (Cambridge: Cambridge University Press, 2015).

202 Kant, *Critique of Pure Reason*, A255, B311, 272. This is one of Kant's "regulative principles," whose purpose is to limit the excesses of human speculation. Thus eschatological/apocalyptic messianism functions as a

regulative principle, limiting human messianic pretension in this world. See *Critique of Pure Reason*, B223.

203 Maimonides, *Guide*, 1.52, 68.

204 Cf. Wittgenstein, *Tractatus Logico-Philosophicus*, pref., 3: "[I]n order to be able to set a limit [*Grenze*] to thought, we should have to find both sides of the limit thinkable." And even though Wittgenstein there claims to be indifferent to the thoughts of other philosophers, it seems that this remark is directed against Kant's notion of the *Grenzbegriff*.

205 Plato, *Theatetus*, 152A. Cf. *Laws*, 716C.

206 Kant, *Critique of Pure Reason*, B263.

207 For a critique of Kant's too narrow notion of experience, see Karl Jaspers, *Kant*, trans. R. Manheim (New York: Harcourt, Brace and World, 1962), 141.

208 Kant, *Critique of Pure Reason*, B659.

209 Cohen, *Religion of Reason;* Kant, *Religion within the Boundaries of Mere Reason*, AK6:12.

210 Ibid., AK6:179, 173–4.

211 Ibid., AK6:174–5, 169–70.

212 Rosenzweig, *The Star of Redemption*, 173.

213 Ibid., 190–2.

214 Rosenzweig uses the first-person singular *Ich* and the second person *du*, which was later made famous by his colleague and friend Martin Buber in his 1923 book *Ich und Du* (twice translated into English as *I and Thou*). However, Buber differs from Rosenzweig in that for him, the human person is the I addressing God as the "eternal Thou." See *I and Thou*, 150. Closer to Rosenzweig's view than to Buber's, see my late revered teacher Abraham Joshua Heschel's *Man Is Not Alone* (Philadelphia: The Jewish Publication Society of America, 1951), 125–9.

215 Rosenzweig, *The Star of Redemption*, 221. This page begins the section of *The Star* on "Redemption" (*Erlösung*).

216 Rosenzweig compares the relation of commandment and law to the relation of marriage as a private relationship *between* husband and wife and marriage as a publicly identifiable union. The latter becomes meaningless without constantly being regenerated by the former. See "Letter of November 1924 to the faculty of *Freies Jüdisches Lehrhaus* in Frankfurt am-Main," in *On Jewish Learning*, trans. N.N. Glatzer and W. Wolf (New York: Schocken, 1955), 120.

217 Rosenzweig sees the prime commandment (*Gebot* or *mitsvah*) as constantly enriching law (*Gesetz* or *halakhah*) and thus preventing Jewish law from becoming law for its own sake. See "The Builders: Concerning the Law," in *On Jewish Learning*, 85–6.

218 *B.* Nazir 23b.

219 Rosenzweig's letter to Buber of 6 June 1925, in *On Jewish Learning*, 118.
220 See Rawls, *Political Liberalism*, intro., l–lvii.
221 For *Halakhah* denoting a system, see *B.* Horayot 14a and Rashi, s.v. "Rav Yosef." For *halakhah* denoting a specific norm, see, e.g., *B.* Kiddushin 38b; see also my late revered teacher Saul Lieberman's *Hellenism in Jewish Palestine*, 83–4, n. 3.
222 *B.* Yevamot 47a–b.
223 *B.* Sotah 14a re Deut. 13:5 etc.
224 Thus one is to thank God for commanding positive commandments that, in fact, have been legislated by the Rabbis (B. Shabbat 23a re Deut. 17:11; Y. Sukkah 3.4/53d; *MT*: Blessings, 11.3). The reason for this formulation seems to be that the Rabbis, at times, are legislating *in loco Dei.*
225 It would seem that the differences between Rosenzweig and Buber over the relation of commandment and law can be traced back to their metaphysical differences regarding the I-Thou relationship. For Rosenzweig, that relationship begins with God-as-I reaching out towards the human individual-as-thou; then this awakened individual soul begins to reach out to other human souls in a social trajectory. That trajectory necessarily involves law. But for Buber, the I-thou relationship begins with the human-individual-as-I first moving away from the I-it relationship, where persons are treated as members of predetermined classes. By the time the human I reaches God-as-the-eternal-Thou, law as the structure of society has been doubly transcended.
226 Kant, *Critique of Pure Reason*, B670–2.
227 Kant, *Critique of Practical Reason*, AK5:125, 159.
228 Ibid., AK5:124, 158.
229 Ibid., AK5:125, 159.
230 Ibid., AK5:12 (note).
231 This is the minimal definition of the name "God." See Anselm, *Proslogion*, chaps. 3, 4; Barth, *Fides Quaerens Intellectum*, 73–89. The name of God that both Anselm and Barth are discussing is *elohim* (*Deus* in Latin) as in Ps. 53:2. This is the most general name of God used in the Bible. See A. Marmorstein, *The Old Rabbinic Doctrine of God* (London: Oxford University Press, 1927), 50.
232 See, e.g., Gordon Michalson, Jr., *Kant and the Problem of God* (Oxford: Blackwell, 1999).
233 Cohen, *Religion of Reason*, 345. Also see Leo Baeck, *The Essence of Judaism*, trans. V. Grubenwieser and L. Pearl (New York: Schocken, 1948), 263–5.
234 Cohen, *Religion of Reason*, 46, 259.
235 Ibid., 255.
236 Cohen, *Religion of Reason*, 43–6.

237 Ibid., 66–9. See *Logik der reinen Erkenntnis*, 4th ed. (Hildesheim: Georg Olms Verlag, 1977), 79, where Cohen sees *Ursprung* as being what the Greek philosophers called *archē*, viz., an ontological ground rather than a "beginning" (*Anfang*) in time. *Ursprung* is more than any natural cause (*Ursache*). It is also not a *datum*, i.e., a "given" (*nichts gegeben sein*), but it would seem it is a "giver" (*dator* in Latin; *Gebener* in German) (*Logik der reinen Erkenntnis*, 36).
238 Cohen, *Religion of Reason*, 92.
239 Ibid., 93; also 106.
240 Cohen, *Ethik des reinen Willens*, 331.
241 *B.* Shabbat 127a re Gen. 18:3; *Y.* Kilayim 9.1/32a. Cf. *B.* Berakhot 19b re Prov. 21:30.
242 *M.* Avot 3.14 re Gen. 9:6.
243 Nahmanides's comment on Deut. 27:26.
244 *M.* Avot 3.14 re Deut. 14:1.
245 *B.* Taanit 2a re Deut. 11:13.
246 *B.* Nedarim 40a; *B.* Hullin 78a re Lev. 13:45.
247 E.g., *B.* Berakhot 19a re Prov. 23:25.
248 *B.* Yevamot 64a.
249 This English translation of Exod. 3:14 follows the German translation of Martin Buber and Franz Rosenzweig in *Fünf Bücher der Weisung*, 158: "Ich werde dasein, als der ich dasein werde." See Ezek. 35:10; 48:35. For the background of this translation, see Buber, *Zu einer neuen Verdeutschung der Schrift* (Olten: Verlag Jakob Hegner, 1954), sec. 9, 28–31.
250 Cf. *B.* Yevamot 63b re Gen. 9:6–7 (viz., Ben Azzai's response to his fellow scholars about his celibacy). It seems only Maimonides (whose ascetic tendencies are evident, see, e.g., *MT*: Forbidden Intercourse, 22.21) spoke of Ben Azzai's approach approvingly (*MT*: Marriage, 15.3).
251 *Tanhuma*: Nitsavim 3.
252 Kant, *Critique of Pure Reason*, B655.
253 Kant, *Groundwork of the Metaphysic of Morals*, AK4:428.
254 Kant, *Critique of Practical Reason*, AK5:162.
255 Kant, *Critique of Judgment*, AK5:186, 25.
256 The scholastic formula "truth is the mind matching the thing" (*veritas est adaequatio intellectus et re*) means both "mind matching thing" (*intellectus ad rem*) and "thing matching mind" (*re ad intellectum*). This is the correspondence theory of truth. In his essay *Vom Wesen der Wahrheit*, Heidegger points out that this epistemological correspondence presupposes a creationist ontology, viz., both mind qua subject and thing qua object have the ontological status of "creature" (*ens creatum*), because both are created by God's word (*verbum Dei*). That is what they

both have essentially in common: both are be-spoken into existence and, therefore, they can "speak" to each other. See "On the Essence of Truth," 118–22. Heidegger's rejection of creationist ontology is presupposed by his epistemological rejection of the correspondence theory of truth, but Kant is still beholden enough to Judaeo-Christian creationist theology (probably more than he could admit) to retain the correspondence theory of truth in his epistemology.

257 Kant, *Critique of Judgment*, AK5:196, 36–7. Note: "Perhaps nothing more sublime [*Erhabeneres*] has been said, or thought ever expressed more sublimely, than that inscription above the temple of *Isis* (Mother Nature): 'I am all this is, that was, and that will be, and no mortal has lifted my veil'" (AK5:316, 185, n. 51).

258 Ibid., AK5:262, 121.

259 Ibid., AK5:375, 255.

260 Ibid., AK5:429–30, 317.

261 Ibid., AK5:187, 26.

262 This is what my late revered teacher Germain Grisez called "an intellect-sized bite of reality" in his by now classic article "The First Principle of Practical Reason," 174.

263 Kant, *Critique of Judgment*, AK5:172, 10–11.

264 Ibid., AK5:221, 66. *Annehmlichketi* literally means "acceptability."

265 Kant, *Critique of Practical Reason*, AK5:124–31.

266 See Andrea Poma, *The Critical Philosophy of Hermann Cohen*, trans. J. Denton (Albany: SUNY Press, 1997), 44–8.

267 This translation follows Rashi's comment thereon: "When He created [*ke-she-bar'a*] me and my man, he alone created us, but in this matter we are partners [*shuttafim*] with Him (a là *B*. Niddah 31a)." In other words, Rashi seems to have Eve saying: "I have been a co-creator with my man [*ishi*] and the Lord." See also *B*. Baba Kama 25a and *Tosafot*, s.v. "qal ve-homer." For the Hebrew *qanoh* as "create," see Rashi's comment on Gen. 14:19 re Ps. 134:3. For the notion that God is the ultimate cause and parents are the immediate cause of their child's existence, see Nahmanides's comment on Exod. 20:12.

268 *Y*. Berakhot 9.1/ 12d re Gen. 1:26.

269 *B*. Gittin 63b.

270 *B*. Berakhot 35a–b.

271 *MT*: Kings, 6.10 and Joseph Karo, *Kesef Mishneh* thereon re *B*. Shabbat 105b.

272 *B*. Sanhedrin 6b re Ps. 10:3; *MT*: Blessings, 1.9 and Karo, *Kesef Mishneh* thereon.

273 *MT*: Blessings, 11.2 and Karo, *Kesef Mishneh* thereon.

274 *B*. Taanit 21a; also *B*. Eruvin 100b; *MT*: Character Traits, 5.4.

275 *B.* Avodah Zarah 27b and *Tosafot*, s.v. "sh'ani."
276 *M.* Sanhedrin 4.5.
277 *M.* Kiddushin 4.14; *B.* Shabbat 30b re Eccl. 12:13; also *Pesiqta Rabbati*, chap. 25, ed. Friedmann, 126b re Deut. 14:22; *MT*: Repentance, 9.1.
278 *B.* Pesahim 68b re Jer. 33:25.
279 *Beresheet Rabbah* 1.1 re Prov. 8:30.
280 Jacob ibn Habib, *Ein Yaakov*, intro. (This text was first called to my attention by my late revered teacher Abraham Joshua Heschel.)
281 *B.* Sanhedrin 38a.
282 *B.* Berakhot 54a; *MT*: Blessings, 10.14–15.

Bibliography

Abbreviations

B. = *Babylonian Talmud (Bavli)*
M. = *Mishnah*
MT = Maimonides, *Mishneh Torah*
T. = *Tosefta*
Y. = *Palestinian Talmud (Yerushalmi)*

Classical Judaic Texts

Abraham ben David of Posquières. *Commentary on Sifra in Sifra.*
– Notes on *Mishneh Torah.*
Abraham ibn Ezra. *Comentary on the Torah.* Edited by A. Weiser. 3 vols. Jerusalem: Mosad ha-Rav Kook, 1977.
Abravanel, Isaac. *Commentary on the Former Prophets.* Jerusalem: Torah ve-Daat, 1956.
Albo, Joseph, *Book of Principles.* Edited and translated by I. Husik. 5 vols. Philadelphia: Jewish Publication Society of America, 1946.
Alfasi (Rif). In *Babylonian Talmud.*
Asher ben Yehiel. *Teshuvot ha-Rosh.* Venice, 1607.
Avot de-Rabbi Nathan. Edited by S. Schechter. New York: Feldheim, 1967.
Babylonian Talmud (Bavli). 20 vols. Vilna: Romm, 1898.
Biblia Hebraica. 7th ed, edited by R. Kittel. Stuttgart: Priveligierte Württembergische Bibelanstalt, 1951.
Bemidbar Rabbah. In *Midrash Rabbah.*
Beresheet Rabbah. Edited by J. Theodor and C. Albeck. 4 vols. Berlin: Akademie Verlag, 1912–29.
Cordevero, Moses. *Pardes ha-Rimonim.* Jerusalem: n.p., 1962.
David ibn Abi Zimra. Notes on *Mishneh Torah.*

– *Teshuvot ha-Radbaz*. 2 vols. Bnei Brak: Hekhal ha-Sefer, 1971.
David Kimhi (Radaq). *Commentary on the Latter Prophets*. In *Miqraot Gedolot*: Prophets and Writings.
Devarim Rabbah. In *Midrash Rabbah*.
Eikhah Rabbah. Edited by S. Buber. Vilna: Romm, 1899.
Esther Rabbah. Edited by J. Tabory and A. Atzmon. Jerusalem: Schechter Institute, 2014.
Die Fünf Bücher der Weisung. Translated by M. Buber and F. Rosenzweig. Cologne: Jakob Hegner, 1954.
Gersonides. Commentary on the Former Prophets. In *Miqraot Gedolot*.
Ginzberg, Louis. *Legends of the Jews*. 7 vols. Philadelphia: Jewish Publication Society of America, 1909–38.
Haggadah Shelemah. Edited by M.M. Kasher. Jerusalem: Torah Shelemah Institute, 1967.
Hasdai Crescas. *The Refutation of the Christian Principles*. Translated by D.J. Lasker. Albany: SUNY Press, 1992.
Holy Scriptures According to the Masoretic Text. English translation. Philadelphia: Jewish Publication Society, 1955.
Isaac ben Jacob Alfasi. *Rif*. In *Babylonian Talmud*.
Isaac bar Sheshet Parfat. *Teshuvot ha-Ribash*. Jerusalem: Makhon Or ha-Mizrah, 1992.
Isaiah di Trani. *Tosafot Rid*. In *Babylonian Talmud*.
Isserles, Moses. *Darkehei Mosheh*. In *Tur:* Even ha`Ezer.
Jacob ben Asher. *Tur* [*Arba`ah Turim*]. 7 vols. Jerusalem: Feldheim, 1969.
Jacob ibn Habib. *Ein Yaakov*. Jerusalim: Mif`al Ein Ya`akov, 1997.
Jonah Gerondi (Rabbenu Yonah). Commentary on Alfasi. In Babylonian Talmud.
Joseph Astruc. *Minhat Kenaot*. In *Teshuvot ha-Rashba*, edited by H.Z. Dimotrovsky. Jerusalem: Mosad ha-Rav Kook, 1990.
Joseph Bekhor Shor. *Commentary on the Torah*. Edited by Y. Nevo. Jerusalem: Mosad ha-Rav Kook, 1994.
Josephus. *Bellum Judaicum*. Edited and translated by H. St. John Thackeray. 2 vols. Cambridge, MA: Harvard University Press, 1927.
– *Contra Apionem*. Edited and translated by H. St. John Thackeray. Cambridge, MA: Harvard University Press, 1926.
– *Jewish Antiquities*. Edited and translated by H. St. John Thackeray, R. Marcus, A. Wikgren, and L.H. Feldman. 6 vols. Cambridge, MA: Harvard University Press. 1930–65.
Judah Halevi. *Kitab al-khazari*. Edited by H. Hirschfeld. London: Calingold, 1931.
– *Kuzari*. Translated by J. ibn Tibbon. Vilna: Romm, 1905.
– *Kuzari: An Argument for the Faith of Israel*. Translated by H. Hirschfeld. New York: Schocken, 1964.

Judah Leib Alter. *Sfas Emes.* 3 vols. Brooklyn: n.p. 1989–90.
Judah Loewe (Maharal). *Gevurot Hashem.* Krakow, 1582.
– *Netsah Yisrael.* Prague, 1599.
Karo, Joseph. *Kesef Mishneh.* In Maimonides, *Mishneh Torah.*
Maimonides. *Commentary on the Mishnah.* Edited and translated by Y. Kafih. 3 vols. Jerusalem: Mosad ha-Rav Kook, 1964–7.
– *Dalalat al-ha'irin.* Edited by S. Munk and I. Joel. Jerusalem: J. Junovitch, 1931.
– *Guide of the Perplexed.* Translated by S. Pines. Chicago: University of Chicago Press, 1963.
– *Igrot ha-Rambam.* Edited and translated by I. Shailat. 2 vols. Maaleh Adumim: Maaliyot Press, 1988.
– *Mishneh Torah.* Edited by S. Frankel. 12 vols. Bnai Brak: Shabse Frankel, 2001.
– *Moreh Nevukhim.* Translated by S. Ibn Tibbon. New York: Om, 1946.
– *Sefer ha-Mitsvot.* Edited by C. Heller. Jerusalem: Mosad ha-Rav Kook, 1946.
Margolis, Moses. *Pnei Mosheh.* In *Palestinian Talmud,* edited by Pietrkov.
Meir Abulafiah, Yad Ramah. New York: Sifrei Qodesh, 1961.
Mekhilta. Edited by S.H. Horovitz and I.A. Rabin. Jerusalem: Wahrmann, 1960.
Menahem Meiri. *Bet ha-Behirah*: Avodah Zarah. Edited by A Sofer. Jerusalem: Qedem, 1964.
– *Bet ha-Behirah: Baba Kama.* 3rd ed., edited by K. Schlesinger. Jerusalem: Mosad ha-Rav Kook, 1967.
– *Bet ha-Behirah*: Kiddushin. Edited by A. Sofer. Jerusalem: Qedem, 1964.
Midrash Aggadah. Edited by S. Buber. Vienna: A. Fanto, 1894.
Midrash ha-Gadol: Bemidbar. Edited by Z.M. Rabinowitz. Jerusalem: Mosad ha-Rav Kook, 1967.
Midrash ha-Gadol: Beresheet. Edited by M. Margulies. Jerusalem: Mosad ha-Rav Kook, 1966.
Midrash Leqah Tov. Edited by S. Buber. 2 vols. Vilna: Romm, 1884.
Midrash Tehillim. Edited by S. Buber. Vilna: Romm, 1891.
Midrash Rabbah. 2 vols. New York: Anafim, 1957.
Miqraot Gedolot: Pentateuch. 5 vols. New York: Otsar ha-Sefarim, 1953.
Miqraot Gedolot: Prophets and Writings. 3 vols. New York: Pardes, 1951.
Mishnah. Edited by C. Albeck. 6 vols. Tel Aviv: Mosad Bialik and Dvir, 1957.
Nahmanides (Ramban). *Commentary on the Torah.* Edited by C.B. Chavel. 2 vols. Jerusalem: Mosad ha-Rav Kook, 1959–63.
– *Hiddushei ha-Ramban.* 2 vols. Bnei Brak: n.p., 1959.
– *Kitvei Ramban.* Edited by C.B. Chavel. 2 vols. Jerusalem: Mosad ha-Rav Kook, 1963.
Nissim Gerondi (Ran). Notes on Alfasi. In *Babylonian Talmud.*
– *Teshuvot ha-Ran.* Edited by L.A. Feldman. Jerusalem: Institute Schalem, 1984.

Obadiah Sforno. *Commentary on the Torah*. Edited by Z. Gottlieb. Jerusalem: Mosad ha-Rav Kook, 1980.

Otsar ha-Geonim: Gittin. Edited by B.M. Lewin. Jerusalem: Mosad ha-Rav Kook, 1941.

Otsar ha-Geonim: Hagigah. Edited by B.M. Lewin. Jerusalem: Hebrew University, 1931.

Otsar ha-Geonim: Baba Kama. Edited by B.M. Lewin. Jerusalem: Mosad ha-Rav Kook, 1943.

Palestinian Talmud (Yerushalmi). Edited by Pietrkov. 7 vols. Jerusalem: n.p., 1959.

– Edited by Y. Sussmann. Jerusalem: Academy of the Hebrew Language, 2001.

Pesiqta de-Rav Kahana. Edited by B. Mandelbaum. 2 vols. New York: Jewish Theological Seminary of America, 1962.

Pesiqta Rabbati. Edited by M. Friedmann. Vienna: n.p., 1880.

Pirqei de-Rabbi Eliezer. Edited by H.M. Horovitz. Jerusalem: Makor, 1972.

Philo. Edited and translated by F.H. Colson and G.H. Whitaker. 10 vols. Cambridge, MA: Harvard University Press, 1939–62.

Philo. *Ad Gaium*. In *Philo*, vol. 10.

– *De Abrahamo*. In *Philo*, vol. 6.

– *De Agricultura*. In *Philo*, vol. 3.

– *De Cherubim*. In *Philo*, vol. 2.

– *De Confusione*. In *Philo*, vol. 4.

– *De Congressu*. In *Philo*, vol. 4.

– *De Decalogo*. In *Philo*, vol. 7.

– *De Ebrietate*. In *Philo*, vol. 3.

– *De Fuga*. In *Philo*, vol. 5.

– *De Josepho*. In *Philo*, vol. 6.

– *Legum Allegoria*. In *Philo*, vol. 1.

– *De Migratione*. In *Philo*, vol. 4.

– *De Opficio Mundi*. In *Philo*, vol. 1.

– *De Platatione*, vol. 3.

– *De Praemiis*. In *Philo*, vol. 8.

– *Quis Rerum*. In *Philo*, vol. 4.

– *Quod Deterius*. In *Philo*, vol. 2.

– *Quod Deus*. In *Philo*, vol. 2.

– *Quod Omnis*. In *Philo*, vol. 9.

– *De Sacrificiis*. In *Philo*, vol. 2.

– *De Somniis*. In *Philo*, vol. 5.

– *De Specialibus Legibus*. In *Philo*, vols. 7 and 8.

– *De Virtutibus*. In *Philo*, vol. 8.

– *De Vita Contemplativa*. In Philo, vol. 9.

– *De Vita Mosis*. In *Philo*, vol. 6.
Qohelet Rabbah. In *Midrash Rabbah*.
Rashi. *Commentary on the Torah*. Edited by C.B. Chavel. Jerusalem: Mosad ha-Rav Kook, 1982.
– *Commentary on the Talmud*. In *Babylonian Talmud*.
Ruth Rabbah. In *Midrash Rabbah*.
Saadiah Gaon. *The Book of Beliefs and Opinions*. Translated by S. Rosenblatt. New Haven: Yale University Press, 1948.
– *Commentary on the Torah*. Edited by Y. Kafih. Jerusalem: Mosad ha-Rav Kook, 1963.
– *Kitab al-amanat wal-Itikadat*. Edited and translated by J. Kafih. Jerusalem: n.p., 1960.
Septuaginta. 6th ed., edited by A. Rahlfs. 2 vols. Stuttgart: Privilegierte Württembergische Bibelanstalt, 1952.
Shiltei ha-Gibborim. Notes on Alfasi. In *Babylonian Talmud*.
Shir ha-Shirim Rabbah. In *Midrash Rabbah*.
Sifra. Edited by I.H. Weiss. New York: Om, 1947.
Sifre: Devarim. Edited by L. Finkelstein. New York: Jewish Theological Seminary of America, 1969.
Shemot Rabbah. In *Midrash Rabbah*.
Shir ha-Shirim Rabbah. In *Midrash Rabbah*.
Sofrim. In *Babylonian Talmud*.
Solomon ibn Adret (Rashba). *Teshuvot ha-Rashba*. Edited by H.Z. Dimitrovsky. Jerusalem: Mosad ha-Rav Kook, 2011.
Tanhuma. Jerusalem: Lewin-Epstein, 1962.
Tanhuma. Edited by S. Buber. 2 vols. Vilna: Romm, 1885.
Targum Jonathan ben Uziel. In *Miqraot Gedolot*.
The Torah. 2nd ed. Philadelphia: Jewish Publication Society of America, 1962.
Tosefta. Edited by Saul Lieberman. 5 vols. New York: Jewish Theological Seminary of America, 1955–88.
Tosefta. Edited by S. Zuckermandl. Jerusalem: Wahrmann, 1937.
Tosafot. In *Babylonian Talmud*.
Tosafot Ri. In *Babylonian Talmud*.
Tosafor Rid. In *Babylonian Talmud*.
The Traditional Prayer Book for Sabbath and Festivals. Translated by D. de Sola Pool. New York: Behrman House, 1960.
Vayiqra Rabbah. Edited by M. Margulies. 4 vols. Jerusalem: American Academy for Jewish Research, 1953–6.
Vidal of Tolosa. *Magid Mishneh*. In Maimonides, *Mishneh Torah*.
Yom Tov ben Abraham Asevilli (Ritba). Commentary on *Haggadah shel Pesah*. In *Hiddushei ha-Ritba*: Pesahim. Jerusalem: Mosad ha-Rav Kook, 1983.
Zohar. Edited by R. Margaliot. 3 vols. Jerusalem: Mosad ha-Rav Kook, 1970.

Classical Texts

Anselm. *Proslogion*. In *St. Anselm: Basic Writings*, translated by S.N. Deane. LaSalle: Open Court, 1962.

Aristotle. *De Anima*. Edited and translated by W.S. Hett. Cambridge, MA: Harvard University Press, 1936.

– *De Caelo*. Edited and translated by W.K.C. Guthrie. Cambridge, MA: Harvard University Press, 1939.

– *De Generatione Animalium*. Edited and translated by A.L. Peck. Cambridge, MA: Harvard University Press, 1943.

– *Magna Moralia*. Edited and translated by G.C. Armstrong. Cambridge, MA: Harvard University Press, 1935.

– *Metaphysics*. Edited and translated by H. Tredennick. 2 vols. Cambridge, MA: Harvard University Press, 1933.

– *De Motu Animalium*. Edited and translated by M.C. Nussbaum. Princeton: Princeton University Press, 1985.

– *Nicomachean Ethics*. Edited and translated by H. Rackham. Cambridge, MA: Harvard University Press, 1926.

– *De Partibus Animalium*. Edited and translated by A.L. Peck. Cambridge, MA: Harvard University Press, 1937.

– *Physics*. Edited and translated by P. Wickstead and F.M. Cornford. 2 vols. Cambridge, MA: Harvard University Press, 1957.

– *Politics*. Edited and translated by H. Rackham. Cambridge, MA: Harvard University Press, 1932.

– *Posterior Analytics*. Edited and translated by H. Tredennick. Cambridge, MA: Harvard University Press, 1960.

– *Prior Analytics*. Edited and translated by H. Tredennick. Cambridge, MA: Harvard University Press, 1960.

– *Rhetoric*. Edited and translated by J.H. Freese. Cambridge, MA: Harvard University Press, 1926.

– *Topica*. Edited and translated by E.S. Forster. Cambridge, MA: Harvard University Press, 1960.

Augustine. *De Libero Arbitrio*. Edited by G.M. Green. Vindobonae: Hoelder-Pichler-Tempsky, 1956.

– *On Free Choice of the Will*. Translated by A.S. Benjamin and L.H. Hackstaff. Indianapolis: Bobbs-Merrill, 1964.

Cicero. *De Legibus*. Edited and translated by C.W. Keyes. Cambridge, MA: Harvard University Press, 1928.

Digest of Justinian. Edited by T. Mommen and P. Krueger. Translated by A. Watson. Philadelphia: University of Pennsylvania Press, 1985.

Epictetus. *Discourses, Enchiridion*. Edited and translated by W.A. Oldfather. 2 vols. Cambridge, MA: Harvard University Press, 1925.

Epicurus. *Fragments*. Translated by Cyril Bailey. In *The Stoic and Epicurean Philosophers*, edited by W.J. Oates. New York: Random House, 1957.
Eusebius. *Praeparatio Evangelica*. In *Werke*, vol. 8, edited by R. Helm. Berlin: Akademie Verlag, 1956.
Galileo, Galilei. *The Assayer*. In *Discoveries and Opinions of Galileo*, translated by S. Drake. Garden City: Doubelday, 1957.
Novum Testamentum Graece. 24th ed., edited by E. Nestle. Stuttgart: Privilegierte Württembergische Bibelanstalt, 1960.
Origen. *Contra Celsum*. In *Patrologia Graece*, vol. 11, edited by J.-P. Migne. Paris: Migne, 1857.
Plato. *Apology*. Edited and translated by H.N. Fowler. Cambridge, MA: Harvard University Press, 1914.
– *Cratylus*. Edited and translated by H.N. Fowler. Cambridge, MA: Harvard University Press, 1926.
– *Crito*. Edited and translated by H.N. Fowler. Cambridge, MA: Harvard University Press, 1914.
– *Epistles*. Edited by and translated by R.G. Bury. Cambridge, MA: Harvard University Press, 1929.
– *Euthphro*. Edited and translated by H.N. Fowler. Cambridge, MA: Harvard University Press, 1914.
– *Gorgias*. Edited and translated by W.R.M. Lamb. Cambridge, MA: Harvard University Press, 1925.
– *Laws*. Edited and translated by R.G. Bury. 2 vols. Cambridge, MA: Harvard University Press, 1926.
– *Parmenides*. Edited and translated by H.N. Fowler. Cambridge, MA: Harvard University Press, 1926.
– *Phaedo*. Edited and translated by H.N. Fowler. Cambridge, MA: Harvard University Press, 1914.
– *Phaedrus*. Edited and translated by H.N. Fowler. Cambridge: Cambridge University Press, 1914.
– *Philebus*. Edited and translated by H.N. Fowler. Cambridge, MA: Harvard University Press, 1925.
– *Republic*. Edited and translated by P. Shorey. 2 vols. Cambridge, MA: Harvard University Press, 1953.
– *Seventh Letter*. In *Epistles*, edited and translated by R.G. Bury. Cambridge, MA: Harvard University Press, 1929.
– *Symposium*. Edited and translated by W.R.M. Lamb. Cambridge, MA: Harvard University Press, 1925.
– *Theatetus*. Edited and translated by H.N. Fowler. Cambridge, MA: Harvard University Press, 1925.
– *Timaeus*. Edited and translated by R.G. Bury. Cambridge, MA: Harvard University Press, 1929.

Quran. Translated by H.M.N. Ahmad. London: The London Mosque, 1981.
Sophocles. *Oedipus Tyrannus*. Edited by and translated by H. Lloyd-Jones. Cambridge, MA: Harvard University Press, 1994.
Tertullian. *Adversus Ioudaeos*. Edited by and translated by R. Hauses. Turnhout: Brepols, 2007.
– *De Carne Christi*. Edited by E. Evans. London: SPCK, 1956.
– *De Praescriptione Haereticorum* in *Patrologia Latina*. Vol. 2, edited by J.-P. Migne. Paris: Migne, 1844.
Thomas Aquinas. *Commentary on the Nicomachean Ethics of Aristotle*. Translated by C.I. Litzinger. Notre Dame: Dumb Ox Books, 1993.
– *Summa Contra Gentiles*. Translated by V.J. Bourke. Notre Dame: University of Notre Dame Press, 1975.
– *Summa Theologiae*. Edited by P. Caramello. 3 vols. Rome: Marietti, 1962.
– *Summa Theologiae*. [English translation]. In *Basic Writings of Saint Thomas Aquinas*, edited by A. Pegis, 2 vols. New York: Random House, 1945.
Vulgate. Paris: Garnier, 1922.

Modern Judaic Texts

Ahad Ha`Am. "Priest and Prophets." In *Selected Essays*, translated by L. Simon, 125–38. Philadelphia: Jewish Publication Society of America, 1912.
Altmann, Alexander. *Moses Mendelssohn*. London: Routledge and Kegan Paul, 1973.
– "What Is Jewish Theology?" In *The Meaning of Jewish Existence: Theological Essays*, edited by A. Ivry, translated by E. Ehrlich and L.H. Ehrlich, 40–56. Hanover: University Press of New England, 1991.
Baeck, Leo. *The Essence of Judaism*. Translated by V. Grubenwieser and L. Pearl. New York: Schocken, 1948.
Baron, Salo W. *A Social and Religious History of the Jews*. Vol. 2. New York: Columbia University Press, 1952.
Batnitzky, Leora. *How Judaism Became a Religion*. Princeton: Princeton University Press, 2011.
Belkin, S. *Philo and the Oral Law*. Cambridge, MA: Harvard University Press, 1940.
Benor, Ehud. *Worship of the Heart: A Study in Maimonides' Philosophy of Religion*. Albany: SUNY Press, 1996.
Boman, Thorleif. *Hebrew Thought Compared with Greek*. Translated by J.L. Moreau. New York: W.W. Norton, 1970.
Brown, J. *New Heavens and a New Earth: The Jewish Reception of Copernican Thought*. New Haven: Yale University Press, 2013.
Buber, Martin. *Zu einer neuen Verdeutschung der Schrift*. Olten: Jakob Hegner, 1954.

Chazan, Robert. *Barcelona and Beyond: The Disputation of 1263 and Its Aftermath.* Berkeley: University of California Press, 1992.

Cohen, Hermann. *Religion der Vernunft aus den Quellen des Judentums.* 2nd ed. Darmstadt: Joseph Melzer Verlag, 1966.

– *Religion of Reason: Out of the Sources of Judaism.* Translated by S. Kaplan. New York: Frederick Ungar, 1972.

– "Religion und Zionismus." In *Jüdische Schriften,* vol. 2, 319–27. Berlin: C. Schwetschke und Sohn, 1924.

– "Spinoza über Staat und Religion, Judentum und Christentum." In *Jüdische Schriften,* vol. 3, 290–372. Berlin: C. Schwetschke und Sohn, 1924.

Davidson, H.A. *Maimonides the Rationalist.* Oxford: Littman Library, 2011.

– *Moses Maimonides.* Oxford: Oxford University Press, 2005.

Diamond, James A. *Converts, Heretics and Lepers: Maimonides and the Outsider.* Notre Dame: University of Notre Dame Press, 2007.

– *Maimonides and the Hermeneutics of Suspicion.* Albany: SUNY Press, 2002.

Diesendruck, Zvi. "Die Teleologie bei Maimonides." *Hebrew Union College Annual* (1928), 5: 415–534.

Fackenheim, Emil. *God's Presence in History.* New York: Harper and Row, 1970.

– *To Mend the World.* New York: Schocken, 1982.

Goodenough, E.R. *The Jurisprudence of the Jewish Courts in Egypt.* New Haven: Yale University Press, 1929.

Hartman, David. *Maimonides: Torah and Philosophic Quest.* Philadelphia: Jewish Publication Society of America, 1976.

Heinemann, Isaak. *Taamei ha-Mitsvot be-Sifrut Yisrael.* 4th ed. Jerusalem: Ha-Mador ha-Dati, 1958.

Hertzberg, Arthur. *The French Enlightenment and the Jews.* New York: Columbia University Press, 1968.

Heschel, Abraham Joshua. "Did Maimonides Believe He Merited Prophecy?" [in Hebrew]. In *Louis Ginzberg Jubilee Volume,* 159–88. New York: American Academy for Jewish Research, 1945.

– *God in Search of Man.* New York: Farrar, Straus and Cudahy, 1955.

– *Heavenly Torah.* Translated by G. Tucker and L. Levin. New York: Continuum, 2005.

– *Man Is Not Alone.* Philadelphia: Jewish Publication Society of America, 1951.

Idel, Moshe. *Kabbalah: New Perspectives.* New Haven: Yale University Press, 1988.

Kaufmann, Yehezkel. *The Religion of Israel.* Translated by M. Greenberg. Chicago: University of Chicago Press, 1960.

Kellner, Menachem. *Dogma in Mediaeval Jewish Thought.* Oxford: Oxford University Press, 1986.

Lévy, Carlos. "Philo's Ethics." In *Cambridge Companion to Philo,* edited by A. Kamesar, 146–71. Cambridge: Cambridge University Press, 2009.

Lieberman, Saul. *Hellenism in Jewish Palestine.* 2nd ed. New York: Jewish Theological Seminary of America, 1962.

– "How Much Greek in Jewish Palestine?" In *Biblical and Other Studies,* edited by A. Atmann, 123–41. Cambridge, MA: Harvard University Press, 1963.

– *Tosefta ki-fshuta.* 11 vols. New York: Jewish Theological Seminary of America. 1955–88.

Marmorstein, A. *The Old Rabbinic Doctrine of God.* London: Oxford University Press, 1927.

Mendelssohn, Moses. *Jerusalem.* Translated by A. Arkush. Hanover: University Press of New England, 1983.

Najman, Hindy. "The Law of Nature and the Authority of Mosaic Law." *Studia Philonica Annual* (1999), 11: 55–73.

Novak, David. "Self-Contraction of the Godhead in Kabbalistic Theology." In *Neoplatonism and Jewish Thought,* edited by L.E. Goodman, 299–318. Albany: SUNY Press, 1992.

– "Theology and Philosophy: An Exchange with Robert Jenson." In *Trinity, Time, and Church: A Response to the Theology of Robert W. Jenson,* edited by C.E. Gunton, 42–61. Grand Rapids: Eeerdmans, 2000.

– *The Theology of Nahmanides Systematically Presented.* Atlanta: Scholars Press, 1992.

– *Zionism and Judaism: A New Theory.* Cambridge: Cambridge University Press, 2015.

Ritter, B. *Philo und die Halacha.* Leipzig: J.C. Hinrich, 1879.

Rosenzweig, Franz. "Atheistic Theology." in *Philosophical and Theological Writings,* translated and edited by P.W. Franks and M.L. Morgan, 10–24. Indianapolis: Hackett, 2000.

– "Der Ewige." In *Kleinere Schriften,* edited by E. Rosenzweig. Berlin: Schocken Verlag, 1937.

– *The Star of Redemption.* Translated by B. Galli. Madison: University of Wisconsin Press, 2005.

– *Der Stern der Erlösung.* Frankfurt am-Main: Kaufmann Verlag, 1921.

– *On Jewish Learning.* Translated by N.N. Galtzer and W. Wolf. New York: Schocken, 1955.

– *Philosophical and Theological Writings.* Translated by P.W. Franks and M.L. Morgan. Indianapolis: Hackett, 2000.

Scholem, Gershom. *Major Trends in Jewish Mysticism.* 3rd rev. ed. New York: Schocken, 1954.

– *On the Kabbalah and Its Symbolism.* Translated by R. Manheim. New York: Schocken, 1969.

– "Schöpfung aus Nichts und die Selbstverschränkung Gottes." *Eranos Jahrbuch* (1956), vol. 25.

Seeskin, Kenneth. "Maimonides' Conception of Philosophy." In *Leo Strauss and Judaism*, edited by D. Novak, 87–110. Lanham: Rowman and Littlefield, 1996.

Simon, Marcel. *Verus Israel*. Translated by H. McKeating. London: Littman Library, 1996.

Stern, Gregg. *Philosophy and Rabbinic Culture*. London: Routledge, 2009.

Winston, David. *Logos and Mystical Theology in Philo of Alexandria*. Cincinnati: Hebrew Union College Press, 1985.

– "Philo and Rabbinic Literature." In *Cambridge Companion to Philo*, edited by Adam Kamesar, 231–53. Cambridge: Cambridge University Press, 2009.

Wolfson, H.A. *Crescas' Critique of Aristotle*. Cambridge, MA: Harvard University Press, 1929.

– *Philo*. 2 vols. Cambridge, MA: Harvard University Press, 1947.

– *The Philosophy of Spinoza*. 2 vols. Cambridge, MA: Harvard University Press, 1934.

Modern Texts (General)

Anscombe, G.E.M. "Modern Moral Philosophy." *Philosophy* (1958), 33, no. 124: 1–19.

Arendt, Hannah. *The Human Condition*. Garden City: Doubleday, 1959.

Avineri, Shlomo. *The Social and Political Thought of Karl Marx*. Cambridge: Cambridge University Press. 1968.

Barnes, Timothy. *Tertullian*. Oxford: Clarendon Press, 1971.

Barth, Karl. *Church Dogmatics*. Vol. 1, part 2, translated by G.T. Thomson and H. Knight. Edinburgh: T. & T. Clark, 1956.

– *Church Dogmatics*. Vol. 2, part 2, edited by G.W. Bromiley and T.F. Torrance, translated by G.W. Bromiley, J.C. Campbell, I. Wilson, J.S. McNab, H. Knight, and R.A. Stewart. Edinburgh: T. & T. Clark, 1957.

– *Fides Quaerens Intellectum*. Translated by I.W. Robertson. London: SCM Press, 1960.

– *The Knowledge of God*. Translated by J.L.M. Haire and I. Robertson. New York: Chas. Scribner's Sons, 1939.

Berlin, Isaiah. "Two Concepts of Liberty." In *Four Essays on Liberty*, 118–72. Oxford: Oxford University Press, 1969.

Bodéüs, Richard. *Aristotle and the Theology of the Living Immortals*. Translated by J. Garrett. Albany: SUNY Press, 2000.

Broadie, Sarah. *Nature and Divinity in Plato's Timaeus*. Cambridge: Cambridge University Press, 2011.

Buber, Martin. *I and Thou*. Translated by W. Kaufmann. New York: Chas. Scribner's Sons, 1970.

– *Ich und Du*. Heidelberg: Verlag Lambert Schneider, 1962.

Bussanich, John. "Eric Voegelin's Philosophy of Myth." *The European Legacy* 12, no. 2 (2007): 187–98.

Cartwright, Nancy. *How the Laws of Physics Lie*. Oxford: Clarendon Press, 1983.

Cassirer, Ernst. *The Philosophy of Symbolic Forms*. Translated by R. Manheim. 2 vols. New Haven: Yale University Press, 1955.

Cohen, Hermann. *Ethik des reinen Willens*. 5th ed. Hildesheim: Georg Olms Verlag, 1981.

– *Logik der reinen Erkenntnis*. 4th ed. Hildesheim: Georg Olms Verlag, 1977.

de Clerck, Paul. "Lex orandi, lex credendi." *Studia Liturgica* (1994), 24: 178–200.

Dunn, G.D. *Tertullian*. London: Routledge, 2004.

Dupre, Louis. *The Philosophical Foundations of Marxism*. New York: Harcourt, Brace and World, 1966.

Durkheim, Émile. *Suicide*. Translated by J.A. Spaulding and G. Simpson. Glencoe: Free Press, 1951.

Ellul, Jacques. *The Technological System*. Translated by Joahim Neugroschel. New York: Continuum, 1980.

Fackenheim, Emil. *The Religious Dimension in Hegel's Thought*. Bloomington: Indiana University Press, 1967.

Finnis, John. *Natural Law and Natural Rights*. Oxford: Clarendon Press, 1980.

Freud, Sigmund. *The Future of an Illusion*. Translated by W.D. Robson-Scott, revised and edited by J. Strachey. Garden City: Anchor Books, 1964.

– *Moses and Monotheism*. Translated by K. Jones. London: Hogarth, 1939.

– *Totem and Taboo*. Translated by J. Strachey. London: Routledge and Kegan Paul, 1950.

Gilson, Étienne. *Reason and Revelation in the Middle Ages*. New York: Chas. Scribner's Sons, 1938.

Goodman, Lenn E. *Religious Pluralism and Values in the Public Square*. Cambridge: Cambridge University Press, 2014.

Grisez, Germain. "The First Principle of Practical Reason." *Natural Law Forum* (1965), 10, no. 1: 168–201.

Habermas, Jürgen. *Communication and the Evolution of Society*. Translated by T. McCarthy. Boston: Beacon Press, 1979.

– *Moral Consciousness and Communicative Action*. Translated by C. Lenhardt and S.W. Nicholsen. Cambridge, MA: MIT Press, 1993.

– *The Philosophical Discourse of Modernity*. Translated by F. Lawrence. Cambridge, MA: MIT Press, 1987.

Hegel, G.W.F. *Phaenomenologie des Geistes*. Edited by J. Hoffmeister. Hamburg: Felix Meiner Verlag, 1952.

– *Phenomenology of Spirit*. Translated by A.V. Miller. Oxford: Oxford University Press, 1977.

– *Reason in History.* Translated by R.S. Hartman. New York: Liberal Arts Press, 1953.

Heidegger, Martin. *Being and Time.* Translated by J. Stambaugh. Albany: SUNY Press, 1996.

– *Kant and the Problem of Metaphysics.* Translated by J.S. Churchill. Bloomington: Indiana University Press, 1962.

– "On the Essence of Truth." Translated by J. Sallis. In *Basic Writings,* edited by D.F. Krell, 113–41. New York: Harper and Row, 1977.

– "The Question Concerning Technology." Translated by W. Lovitt. In *Basic Writings,* edited by D.F. Krell, 283–317. New York: Harper and Row, 1977.

– *Sein und Zeit.* 15th ed. Tübingen: Max Niemeyer Verlag, 1979.

– "Vom Wesen der Wahrheit." 4th ed. In *Wegmarken,* 177–202. Frankfurt am-Main: Vittorio Klostermann Verlag, 1967.

– *Zur Sache des Denkens.* Tübingen: Max Niemeyer, 1969.

Hobbes, Thomas. *Leviathan.* Edited by M. Oakshott. New York: Collier. 1962.

Hume, David. *Dialogues Concerning Natural Religion.* Edited by H.D. Aiken. New York: Hafner, 1959.

– *A Treatise of Human Nature.* Edited by L.A. Selby-Bigge. Oxford: Clarendon Press, 1978.

Hunt, L. *The French Revolution and Human Rights.* Boston: St. Martin's Press, 1996.

James, William. *The Varieties of Religious Experience.* New York: Mentor Books, 1958.

Jaspers, Karl. *Kant.* Translated by R. Manheim. New York: Harcourt, Brace and World, 1962.

John Paul II. *Fides et Ratio* (On the Relationship between Faith and Reason). Vatican translation. Boston: Pauline Books and Media, 1998.

Kant, Immanuel. *Critique of Judgment.* Translated by W.S. Pluhar. Indianapolis: Hackett, 1987.

– *Critique of Practical Reason.* Translated by W.S. Pluhar. Indianapolis: Hackett, 2002.

– *Critique of Pure Reason.* Translated by N. Kemp Smith. New York: Macmillan, 1929.

– *Groundwork of the Metaphysic of Morals.* Translated by H.J. Paton. New York: Harper and Row, 1964.

– *Grundlegung zur Metaphysik der Sitten.* Prussian Academy of Sciences ed. (AK). In *Kants Werke,* vol. 4. Berlin: Walter de Gruyter, 1968.

– *Kritik der praktischen Vernunft.* Prussian Academy of Sciences ed. (AK). In *Kants Werke,* vol. 5. Berlin: Walter de Gruyter, 1968.

– *Kritik der reinen Vernunft.* Edited by R. Schmidt. Hamburg: Felix Meiner Verlag, 1956.

– *Kritik der Urteilskraft*. Prussian Academy of Sciences ed. (AK). In *Kants Werke*, vol. 5. Berlin: Walter de Gruyter, 1968.

– *Die Metaphysik der Sitten*. Prussian Academy of Sciences ed. (AK). In *Kants Werke*, vol. 6. Berlin: Walter de Gruyter, 1968.

– *The Metaphysics of Morals*. Translated by M. Gregor. Cambridge: Cambridge University Press, 1996.

– *Prolegomena to Any Future Metaphysics*. Translated by L.W. Beck. Indianapolis: Bobbs-Merrill, 1950.

– *Prologomena zu einer jeden künftigen Metaphysik*. Prussian Academy of Sciences ed. (AK). In *Kants Werke*, vol. 4. Berlin: Walter de Gruyter, 1968.

– *Die Religion innerhalb der Grenzen der blossen Vernunft*. Prussian Academy of Sciences ed. (AK). In *Kants Werke*, vol. 6. Berlin: Walter de Gruyter, 1968.

– *Religion within the Boundaries of Mere Reason*. Translated by A. Wood and G. di Giovanni. Cambridge: Cambridge University Press, 1998.

Kaufman, Gordon D. *Theology for a Nuclear Age*. Philadelphia: Westminster, 1985.

Klein, Naomi. *This Changes Everything: Capitalism vs. the Environment*. New York: Simon and Shuster, 2014.

Koester, Helmut. "NOMOS PHUSEŌS: The Concept of Natural Law in Greek Thought." In *Religions in Antiquity*, edited by J. Neusner, 521–41. Leiden: Brill, 1968.

Kojève, Alexandre. *Introduction to the Reading of Hegel*. Translated by J.H. Nichols. Ithaca: Cornell University Press, 1969.

Korsgaard, Christine. *Creating the Kingdom of Ends*. Cambridge: Cambridge University Press, 1996.

Koyré, Alexandre. *From the Closed World to the Infinite Universe*. Baltimore: Johns Hopkins University Press, 1957.

Kuhn, Thomas S. *The Structure of Scientific Revolutions*. Chicago: University of Chicago Press, 1962.

Lear, Jonathan. *Love and Its Place in Nature*. New Haven: Yale University Press, 1990.

Levinas, Emmanuel. *Totality and Infinity*. Translated by A. Lingis. Pittsburgh: Duquesne University Press, 1969.

Lindbeck, George. *The Nature of Doctrine*. Philadelphia: Westminster, 1984

Lonergan, Bernard. *Insight*. New York: Harper and Row, 1978.

Lovejoy, A.O. *The Great Chain of Being*. Cambridge, MA: Harvard University Press, 1936.

Löwith, Karl. "M. Heidegger and F. Rosenzweig or Temporality and Eternity." *Philosophy and Phenomenological Research* (1942), 3, no. 1: 53–77.

MacIntyre, Alasdair. *After Virtue*. Notre Dame: University of Notre Dame Press, 1980.

– *Whose Justice? Which Rationality?* Notre Dame: University of Notre Dame Press, 1988.

Maritain, Jacques. *The Rights of Man and Natural Law.* London: Geoffrey Bles, 1958.
Marx, Karl. *Capital.* Translated by B. Fowkes. New York: Vintage Books, 1977.
Michalson, Gordon. *Kant and the Problem of God.* Oxford: Blackwell, 1999.
Mill, John Stuart. *On Liberty.* Edited by G. Williams. London: J.M. Dent, 1993.
Moore, G.E. *Principia Ethica.* Cambridge: Cambridge University Press, 1903.
Nagel, Thomas. *The View from Nowhere.* New York: Oxford University Press, 1986.
Neuhaus, Richard John. *The Naked Public Square.* Grand Rapids: Eerdmans, 1984.
Nietzsche, Friedrich. *Also Sprach Zarathustra.* In *Werke,* edited by K. Schlechta, 2 vols. Munich: Carl Hanser Verlag, 1967.
Novak, David. *Suicide and Morality.* New York: Scholars Studies Press, 1975.
O'Regan, Cyril. *The Heterodox Hegel.* Albany: SUNY Press, 1994.
Poma, Andrea. *The Critical Philosophy of Hermann Cohen.* Translated by J. Denton. Albany: SUNY Press, 1997.
Popper, Karl. *The Logic of Scientific Discovery.* London: Routledge, 1992.
– *The Open Society and Its Enemies.* 5th rev. ed. 2 vols. Princeton: Princeton University Press, 1966.
Rawls, John. *Political Liberalism.* New York: Columbia University Press, 1993.
– *A Theory of Justice.* Cambridge, MA: Harvard University Press, 1971.
Raz, Joseph. *The Morality of Freedom.* Oxford: Clarendon Press, 1986.
Riceour, Paul. *Oneself as Other.* Translated by K. Blamey. Chicago: University of Chicago Press, 1992.
Ross, W.D. *Aristotle.* New York: Meridian Books, 1959.
Rostovtzeff, M. *The Social and Economic History of the Hellenistic World.* 2 vols. Oxford: Oxford University Press, 1941.
Rousseau, Jean-Jacques. *The Social Contract.* Translated by M. Cranston. London: Penguin, 1968.
Sandel, M.J. *Liberalism and the Limits of Justice.* New York: Cambridge University Press, 1982.
Schleiermacher, Friedrich. *Der christliche Glaube.* Edited by M. Redeker. Berlin: de Gruyter, 1999.
– *The Christian Faith.* Translated by H.R. Mackintosh. Edinburgh: T. & T. Clark, 1999.
Schmitt, Carl. *Der Begriff der Politischen.* Munich: Duncker and Humblot, 1932.
– *The Concept of the Political.* Translated by G. Schwab. Chicago: University of Chicago Press, 1996.
Schneewind, J.B. *The Invention of Autonomy.* Cambridge: Cambridge University Press, 1998.
Spinoza, Baruch. *Ethics.* In *Opera,* vol. 2, edited by C. Gebhardt. Heidelberg: Carl Winter, 1925.

– *Ethics*. In *A Spinoza Reader*, edited and translated by E. Curley. Princeton: Princeton University Press, 1994.

– *Theological-Political Treatise*. Translated by M. Silverthorne and J. Israel. Cambridge: Cambridge University Press, 2007.

– *Tractatus Politicus*. Edited and translated by S. Zac. Paris: J. Vrin, 1968.

– *Tractatus Theologico-Politicus*. In *Opera*, vol. 3, edited by C. Gebhardt. Heidelberg: Carl Winter, 1925.

Strauss, Leo. *The City and Man*. Charlottesville: University Press of Virginia, 1964.

– "The Mutual Influence of Theology and Philosophy." *Independent Journal of Philosophy* (1979), vol. 3: 111–18.

– *Persecution and the Art of Writing*. Chicago: University of Chicago Press, 1988.

– *Natural Right and History*. Chicago: University of Chicago Press, 1953.

– *What Is Political Philosophy?* Glencoe: Free Press, 1959.

Taylor, A.E. *Plato*. 6th ed. New York: Humanities Press, 1952.

Tillich, Paul. *Systematic Theology*. Vol. 1. Chicago: University of Chicago Press, 1951.

Tönnies, Ferdinand. *Community and Society*. Translated by C.W. Loomis. East Lansing: Michigan State University Press, 1957

– *Gemeinschaft und Gesellschaft*. Darmstadt: Wissenschaftliche Buchgesellschaft, 1963.

Torrance, T.F. *Divine and Contingent Order*. Oxford: Oxford University Press, 1981.

Vlastos, Gregory. *Socrates*. Ithaca: Cornell University Press, 1991.

Whitehead, Alfred North. *Process and Reality*. New York: Free Press, 1969.

Wittgenstein, Ludwig. *Philosophical Investigations*. 2nd ed, edited and translated by G.E.M. Anscombe. New York: Macmillan, 1958.

– *Tractatus Logico-Philosophicus*. Translated by D.F. Pears and B.F. McGuiness. London: Routledge and Kegan Paul, 1961.

Index

The Kenneth Michael Tanenbaum Series in Jewish Studies

Michael L. Morgan, *Fackenheim's Jewish Philosophy: An Introduction*
Daniel R. Schwartz, *Judeans and Jews: Four Faces of Dichotomy in Ancient Jewish History*
Michael Marmur, *Abraham Joshua Heschel and the Sources of Wonder*
David Novak, *Athens and Jerusalem: God, Humans, and Nature*

Other Books by David Novak

Law and Theology in Judaism I
Suicide and Morality
Law and Theology in Judaism II
The Image of the Non-Jew in Judaism, 1st edition
Halakhah in a Theological Dimension
Jewish-Christian Dialogue: A Jewish Justification
Jewish Social Ethics
The Theology of Nahmanides Systematically Presented
The Election of Israel: The Idea of the Chosen People
Natural Law in Judaism
Covenantal Rights: A Study in Jewish Political Theory
The Jewish Social Contract: An Essay in Political Theology
Talking with Christians: Musings of a Jewish Theologian
The Sanctity of Human Life
In Defense of Religious Liberty
Tradition in the Public Square: A David Novak Reader
The Image of the Non-Jew in Judaism, 2nd revised edition
Natural Law: A Jewish, Christian, and Islamic Trialogue (with Anver Emon and Matthew Levering)
Zionism and Judaism: A New Theory
Jewish Justice

www.ingramcontent.com/pod-product-compliance
Lightning Source LLC
LaVergne TN
LVHW090803070826
844660LV00022B/1060

* 9 7 8 1 4 8 7 5 2 4 1 5 9 *